D1709377

An Eponymous Dictionary of Economics

An Eponymous Dictionary of Economics

A Guide to Laws and Theorems Named after Economists

Edited by

Julio Segura

Professor of Economic Theory, Universidad Complutense, Madrid, Spain,

and

Carlos Rodríguez Braun

Professor of History of Economic Thought, Universidad Complutense, Madrid, Spain

Edward Elgar

Cheltenham, UK • Northampton, MA, USA

Published by
Edward Elgar Publishing Limited
Glensanda House
Montpellier Parade
Cheltenham
Glos GL50 1UA
UK

Edward Elgar Publishing, Inc.
136 West Street
Suite 202
Northampton
Massachusetts 01060
USA

A catalogue record for this book
is available from the British Library

ISBN 1 84376 029 0 (cased)

Typeset by Cambrian Typesetters, Frimley, Surrey
Printed and bound in Great Britain by MPG Books Ltd, Bodmin, Cornwall

Contents

Contributors and their entries

Albarrán, Pedro, Universidad Carlos III, Madrid, Spain
Pigou tax

Albert López-Ibor, Rocío, Universidad Complutense, Madrid, Spain
Learned Hand formula

Albi, Emilio, Universidad Complutense, Madrid, Spain
Simons's income tax base

Almenar, Salvador, Universidad de Valencia, Valencia, Spain
Engel's law

Almodovar, António, Universidade do Porto, Porto, Portugal
Weber–Fechner law

Alonso, Aurora, Universidad del País Vasco-EHU, Bilbao, Spain
Lucas critique

Alonso Neira, Miguel Ángel, Universidad Rey Juan Carlos, Madrid, Spain
Hayekian triangle

Andrés, Javier, Universidad de Valencia, Valencia, Spain
Pigou effect

Aparicio-Acosta, Felipe M., Universidad Carlos III, Madrid, Spain
Fourier transform

Aragonés, Enriqueta, Universitat Autònoma de Barcelona, Barcelona, Spain
Rawls justice criterion

Arellano, Manuel, CEMFI, Madrid, Spain
Lagrange multiplier test

Argemí, Lluís, Universitat de Barcelona, Barcelona, Spain
Gossen's laws

Arruñada, Benito, Universitat Pompeu Fabra, Barcelona, Spain
Baumol's disease

Artés Caselles, Joaquín, Universidad Complutense, Madrid, Spain
Leontief paradox

Astigarraga, Jesús, Universidad de Deusto, Bilbao, Spain
Palgrave's dictionaries

Avedillo, Milagros, Comisión Nacional de Energía, Madrid, Spain
Divisia index

Ayala, Luis, Universidad Rey Juan Carlos, Madrid, Spain
Atkinson index

Ayuso, Juan, Banco de España, Madrid, Spain
Allais paradox; Ellsberg paradox

Aznar, Antonio, Universidad de Zaragoza, Zaragoza, Spain
Durbin–Wu–Hausman test

Bacaria, Jordi, Universitat Autònoma de Barcelona, Barcelona, Spain
Buchanan's clubs theory

Badenes Plá, Nuria, Universidad Complutense, Madrid, Spain
Kaldor–Meade expenditure tax; *Tiebout's voting with the feet process*; *Tullock's trapezoid*

Barberá, Salvador, Universitat Autònoma de Barcelona, Barcelona, Spain
Arrow's impossibility theorem

Bel, Germà, Universitat de Barcelona, Barcelona, Spain
Clark problem; *Clark–Knight paradigm*

Bentolila, Samuel, CEMFI, Madrid, Spain
Hicks–Hansen model

Bergantiños, Gustavo, Universidad de Vigo, Vigo, Pontevedra, Spain
Brouwer fixed point theorem; *Kakutani's fixed point theorem*

Berganza, Juan Carlos, Banco de España, Madrid, Spain
Lerner index

Berrendero, José R., Universidad Autónoma, Madrid, Spain
Kolmogorov–Smirnov test

Blanco González, María, Universidad San Pablo CEU, Madrid, Spain
Cowles Commission

Bobadilla, Gabriel F., Omega-Capital, Madrid, Spain
Markowitz portfolio selection model; *Fisher–Shiller expectations hypothesis*

Bolado, Elsa, Universitat de Barcelona, Barcelona, Spain
Keynes effect

Borrell, Joan-Ramon, Universitat de Barcelona, Barcelona, Spain
Berry–Levinsohn–Pakes algorithm

Bover, Olympia, Banco de España, Madrid, Spain
Gaussian distribution

Bru, Segundo, Universidad de Valencia, Valencia, Spain
Senior's last hour

Burguet, Roberto, Universitat Autònoma de Barcelona, Barcelona, Spain
Walras's auctioneer and tâtonnement

Cabrillo, Francisco, Universidad Complutense, Madrid, Spain
Coase theorem

Calderón Cuadrado, Reyes, Universidad de Navarra, Pamplona, Spain
Hermann–Schmoller definition

Callealta, Francisco J., Universidad de Alcalá de Henares, Alcalá de Henares, Madrid, Spain
Neyman–Fisher theorem

Calsamiglia, Xavier, Universitat Pompeu Fabra, Barcelona, Spain
Gale–Nikaido theorem

Calzada, Joan, Universitat de Barcelona, Barcelona, Spain
Stolper–Samuelson theorem

Candeal, Jan Carlos, Universidad de Zaragoza, Zaragoza, Spain
Cantor's nested intervals theorem; *Cauchy's sequence*

Carbajo, Alfonso, Confederación Española de Cajas de Ahorro, Madrid, Spain
Director's law

Cardoso, José Luís, Universidad Técnica de Lisboa, Lisboa, Portugal
Gresham's law

Carnero, M. Angeles, Universidad Carlos III, Madrid, Spain
Mann–Wald's theorem

Carrasco, Nicolás, Universidad Carlos III, Madrid, Spain
Cox's test; *White test*

Carrasco, Raquel, Universidad Carlos III, Madrid, Spain
Cournot aggregation condition; *Engel aggregation condition*

Carrera, Carmen, Universidad Complutense, Madrid, Spain
Slutsky equation

Caruana, Guillermo, CEMFI, Madrid, Spain
Hicks composite commodities

Castillo, Ignacio del, Ministerio de Hacienda, Madrid, Spain
Fullarton's principle

Castillo Franquet, Joan, Universitat Autònoma de Barcelona, Barcelona, Spain
Tchébichef's inequality

Castro, Ana Esther, Universidad de Vigo, Vigo, Pontevedra, Spain
Ponzi schemes

Cerdá, Emilio, Universidad Complutense, Madrid, Spain
Bellman's principle of optimality and equations; *Euler's theorem and equations*

Comín, Diego, New York University, New York, USA
Harrod–Domar model

Corchón, Luis, Universidad Carlos III, Madrid, Spain
Maskin mechanism

Costas, Antón, Universitat de Barcelona, Barcelona, Spain
Palmer's Rule; *Peel's Law*

Díaz-Emparanza, Ignacio, Instituto de Economía Aplicada, Universidad del País Vasco-EHU, Bilbao, Spain
Cochrane–Orcutt procedure

Dolado, Juan J., Universidad Carlos III, Madrid, Spain
Bonferroni bound; *Markov switching autoregressive model*

Domenech, Rafael, Universidad de Valencia, Valencia, Spain
Solow's growth model and residual

Echevarría, Cruz Angel, Universidad del País Vasco-EHU, Bilbao, Spain
Okun's law and gap

Escribano, Alvaro, Universidad Carlos III, Madrid, Spain
Engle–Granger method; *Hodrick–Prescott decomposition*

Espasa, Antoni, Universidad Carlos III, Madrid, Spain
Box–Jenkins analysis

Espiga, David, La Caixa-S.I. Gestión Global de Riesgos, Barcelona, Spain
Edgeworth oligopoly model

Esteban, Joan M., Universitat Autònoma de Barcelona, Barcelona, Spain
Pigou–Dalton progressive transfers

Estrada, Angel, Banco de España, Madrid, Spain
Harrod's technical progress; *Hicks's technical progress*

Etxebarria Zubeldía, Gorka, Deloitte & Touche, Madrid, Spain
Montaigne dogma

Fariñas, José C., Universidad Complutense, Madrid, Spain
Dorfman–Steiner condition

Febrero, Ramón, Universidad Complutense, Madrid, Spain
Becker's time allocation model

Fernández, José L., Universidad Autónoma, Madrid, Spain
Cauchy–Schwarz inequality; *Itô's lemma*

Fernández Delgado, Rogelio, Universidad Rey Juan Carlos, Madrid, Spain
Patman effect

Fernández-Macho, F. Javier, Universidad del País Vasco-EHU, Bilbao, Spain
Slutsky–Yule effect

Ferreira, Eva, Universidad del País Vasco-EHU, Bilbao, Spain
Black–Scholes model; *Pareto distribution*; *Sharpe's ratio*

Flores Parra, Jordi, Servicio de Estudios de Caja Madrid, Madrid, Spain and Universidad Carlos III, Madrid, Spain
Samuelson's condition

Franco, Yanna G., Universidad Complutense, Madrid, Spain
Cairnes–Haberler model; *Ricardo–Viner model*

Freire Rubio, Mª Teresa, Escuela Superior de Gestión Comercial y Marketing, Madrid, Spain
Lange–Lerner mechanism

Freixas, Xavier, Universitat Pompeu Fabra, Barcelona, Spain and CEPR
Friedman-Savage hypothesis

Frutos de, M. Angeles, Universidad Carlos III, Madrid, Spain
Hotelling's model of spatial competition

Fuente de la, Angel, Universitat Autònoma de Barcelona, Barcelona, Spain
Swan's model

Gallastegui, Carmen, Universidad del País Vasco-EHU, Bilbao, Spain
Phillip's curve

Gallego, Elena, Universidad Complutense, Madrid, Spain
Robinson-Metzler condition

García, Jaume, Universitat Pompeu Fabra, Barcelona, Spain
Heckman's two-step method

García-Bermejo, Juan C., Universidad Autónoma, Madrid, Spain
Harsanyi's equiprobability model

García-Jurado, Ignacio, Universidad de Santiago de Compostela, Santiago de Compostela, A Coruña, Spain
Selten paradox

García Ferrer, Antonio, Universidad Autónoma, Madrid, Spain
Zellner estimator

García Lapresta, José Luis, Universidad de Valladolid, Valladolid, Spain
Bolean algebras; *Taylor's theorem*

García Pérez, José Ignacio, Fundación CENTRA, Sevilla, Spain
Scitovsky's compensation criterion

García-Ruiz, José L., Universidad Complutense, Madrid, Spain
Harris–Todaro model; *Prebisch–Singer hypothesis*

Gimeno, Juan A., Universidad Nacional de Educación a Distancia, Madrid, Spain
Peacock–Wiseman's displacement effect; *Wagner's law*

Girón, F. Javier, Universidad de Málaga, Málaga, Spain
Gauss–Markov theorem

Gómez Rivas, Léon, Universidad Europea, Madrid, Spain
Longfield's paradox

Graffe, Fritz, Universidad del País Vasco-EHU, Bilbao, Spain
Leontief model

Grifell-Tatjé, E., Universitat Autònoma de Barcelona, Barcelona, Spain
Farrell's technical efficiency measurement

Guisán, M. Cármen, Universidad de Santiago de Compostela, Santiago de Compostela, A Coruña, Spain
Chow's test; *Granger's causality test*

Herce, José A., Universidad Complutense, Madrid, Spain
Cass–Koopmans criterion; *Koopmans's efficiency criterion*

Herguera, Iñigo, Universidad Complutense, Madrid, Spain
Gorman's polar form

Hernández Andreu, Juan, Universidad Complutense, Madrid, Spain
Juglar cycle; *Kitchin cycle*; *Kondratieff long waves*

Herrero, Cármen, Universidad de Alicante, Alicante, Spain
Perron–Frobenius theorem

Herrero, Teresa, Confederación Española de Cajas de Ahorro, Madrid, Spain
Heckscher–Ohlin theorem; *Rybczynski theorem*

Hervés-Beloso, Carlos, Universidad de Vigo, Vigo, Pontevedra, Spain
Sard's theorem

Hoyo, Juan del, Universidad Autónoma, Madrid, Spain
Box–Cox transformation

Huergo, Elena, Universidad Complutense, Madrid, Spain
Stackelberg's oligopoly model

Huerta de Soto, Jesús, Universidad Rey Juan Carlos, Madrid, Spain
Ricardo effect

Ibarrola, Pilar, Universidad Complutense, Madrid, Spain
Ljung–Box statistics

Iglesia, Jesús de la, Universidad Complutense, Madrid, Spain
Tocqueville's cross

de la Iglesia Villasol, Mª Covadonga, Universidad Complutense, Madrid, Spain
Hotelling's theorem

Iñarra, Elena, Universidad deli País Vasco-EHU, Bilbao, Spain
von Neumann–Morgenstern stable set

Induraín, Esteban, Universidad Pública de Navarra, Pamplona, Spain
Hawkins–Simon theorem; *Weierstrass extreme value theorem*

Jimeno, Juan F., Universidad de Alcalá de Henares, Alcalá de Henares, Madrid, Spain
Ramsey model and rule

Justel, Ana, Universidad Autónoma, Madrid, Spain
Gibbs sampling

Lafuente, Alberto, Universidad de Zaragoza, Zaragoza, Spain
Herfindahl–Hirschman index

Lasheras, Miguel A., Grupo CIM, Madrid, Spain
Baumol's contestable markets; *Ramsey's inverse elasticity rule*

Llobet, Gerard, CEMFI, Madrid, Spain
Bertrand competition model; *Cournot's oligopoly model*

Llombart, Vicent, Universidad de Valencia, Valencia, Spain
Turgot–Smith theorem

Llorente Alvarez, J. Guillermo, Universidad Autónoma, Madrid, Spain
Schwarz criterion

López, Salvador, Universitat Autònoma de Barcelona, Barcelona, Spain
Averch–Johnson effect

López Laborda, Julio, Universidad de Zaragoza, Zaragoza, Spain
Kakwani index

Lorences, Joaquín, Universidad de Oviedo, Oviedo, Spain
Cobb–Douglas function

Loscos Fernández, Javier, Universidad Complutense, Madrid, Spain
Hansen–Perloff effect

Lovell, C.A.K., The University of Georgia, Georgia, USA
Farrell's technical efficiency measurement

Lozano Vivas, Ana, Universidad de Málaga, Málaga, Spain
Walras's law

Lucena, Maurici, CDTI, Madrid, Spain
Laffer's curve; *Tobin's tax*

Macho-Stadler, Inés, Universitat Autònoma de Barcelona, Barcelona, Spain
Akerlof's 'lemons'

Malo de Molina, José Luis, Banco de España, Madrid, Spain
Friedman's rule for monetary policy

Manresa, Antonio, Universitat de Barcelona, Barcelona, Spain
Bergson's social indifference curve

Maravall, Agustín, Banco de España, Madrid, Spain
Kalman filter

Marhuenda, Francisco, Universidad Carlos III, Madrid, Spain
Hamiltonian function and Hamilton–Jacobi equations; *Lyapunov stability*

Martín, Carmela, Universidad Complutense, Madrid, Spain
Arrow's learning by doing

Martín Marcos, Ana, Universidad Nacional de Educación de Distancia, Madrid, Spain
Scitovsky's community indifference curve

Martín Martín, Victoriano, Universidad Rey Juan Carlos, Madrid, Spain
Buridan's ass; Occam's razor

Martín-Román, Angel, Universidad de Valladolid, Segovia, Spain
Edgeworth box

Martínez, Diego, Fundación CENTRA, Sevilla, Spain
Lindahl–Samuelson public goods

Martinez Giralt, Xavier, Universitat Autònoma de Barcelona, Barcelona, Spain
Schmeidler's lemma; *Sperner's lemma*

Martínez-Legaz, Juan E., Universitat Autònoma de Barcelona, Barcelona, Spain
Lagrange multipliers; *Banach's contractive mapping principle*

Martínez Parera, Montserrat, Servicio de Estudios del BBVA, Madrid, Spain
Fisher effect

Martínez Turégano, David, AFI, Madrid, Spain
Bowley's law

Mas-Colell, Andreu, Universitat Pompeu Fabra, Barcelona, Spain
Arrow–Debreu general equilibrium model

Mazón, Cristina, Universidad Complutense, Madrid, Spain
Roy's identity; *Shephard's lemma*

Méndez-Ibisate, Fernando, Universidad Complutense, Madrid, Spain
Cantillon effect; *Marshall's symmetallism*; *Marshall–Lerner condition*

Mira, Pedro, CEMFI, Madrid, Spain
Cauchy distribution; *Sargan test*

Molina, José Alberto, Universidad de Zaragoza, Zaragoza, Spain
Lancaster's characteristics

Monasterio, Carlos, Universidad de Oviedo, Oviedo, Spain
Wicksell's benefit principle for the distribution of tax burden

Morán, Manuel, Universidad Complutense, Madrid, Spain
Euclidean spaces; *Hessian matrix and determinant*

Moreira dos Santos, Pedro, Universidad Complutense, Madrid, Spain
Gresham's law in politics

Moreno, Diego, Universidad Carlos III, Madrid, Spain
Gibbard–Satterthwaite theorem

Moreno García, Emma, Universidad de Salamanca, Salamanca, Spain
Minkowski's theorem

Moreno Martín, Lourdes, Universidad Complutense, Madrid, Spain
Chamberlin's oligopoly model

Mulas Granados, Carlos, Universidad Complutense, Madrid, Spain
Ledyard–Clark–Groves mechanism

Naveira, Manuel, BBVA, Madrid, Spain
Gibrat's law; *Marshall's external economies*

Novales, Alfonso, Universidad Complutense, Madrid, Spain
Radner's turnpike property

Núñez, Carmelo, Universidad Carlos III, Madrid, Spain
Lebesgue's measure and integral

Núñez, José J., Universitat Autònoma de Barcelona, Barcelona, Spain
Markov chain model; *Poisson process*

Núñez, Oliver, Universidad Carlos III, Madrid, Spain
Kolmogorov's large numbers law; *Wiener process*

Olcina, Gonzalo, Universidad de Valencia, Valencia, Spain
Rubinstein's model

Ontiveros, Emilio, AFI, Madrid, Spain
Díaz–Alejandro effect; *Tanzi-Olivera effect*

Ortiz-Villajos, José M., Universidad Complutense, Madrid, Spain
Kaldor paradox; *Kaldor's growth laws*; *Ricardo's comparative costs*; *Verdoorn's law*

Padilla, Jorge Atilano, Nera and CEPR
Areeda–Turner predation rule; *Coase conjecture*

Pardo, Leandro, Universidad Complutense, Madrid, Spain
Pearson's chi-squared statistic; *Rao–Blackwell's theorem*

Pascual, Jordi, Universitat de Barcelona, Barcelona, Spain
Babbage's principle; *Bagehot's principle*

Pazó, Consuelo, Universidad de Vigo, Vigo, Pontevedra, Spain
Dixit–Stiglitz monopolistic competition model

Pedraja Chaparro, Francisco, Universidad de Extremadura, Badajoz, Spain
Borda's rule; *Condorcet's criterion*

Peña, Daniel, Universidad Carlos III, Madrid, Spain
Bayes's theorem

Pena Trapero, J.B., Universidad de Alcalá de Henares, Alcalá de Henares, Madrid, Spain
Beveridge–Nelson decomposition

Perdices de Blas, Luis, Universidad Complutense, Madrid, Spain
Becher's principle; *Davenant–King law of demand*

Pérez Quirós, Gabriel, Banco de España, Madrid, Spain
Suits index

Pérez Villareal, J., Universidad de Cantabria, Santander, Spain
Haavelmo balanced budget theorem

Pérez-Castrillo, David, Universidad Autònoma de Barcelona, Barcelona, Spain
Vickrey auction

Pires Jiménez, Luis Eduardo, Universidad Rey Juan Carlos, Madrid, Spain
Gibson paradox

Polo, Clemente, Universitat Autònoma de Barcelona, Barcelona, Spain
Lancaster–Lipsey's second best

Poncela, Pilar, Universidad Autónoma, Madrid, Spain
Johansen's procedure

Pons, Aleix, CEMFI, Madrid, Spain
Graham's demand

Ponsati, Clara, Institut d'Anàlisi Econòmica, CSIC, Barcelona, Spain
Kalai–Smorodinsky bargaining solution

Prat, Albert, Universidad Politécnica de Cataluña, Barcelona, Spain
Hotelling's T^2 *statistics*; *Student t-distribution*

Prieto, Francisco Javier, Universidad Carlos III, Madrid, Spain
Newton–Raphson method; *Pontryagin's maximum principle*

Puch, Luis A., Universidad Complutense, Madrid, Spain
Chipman–Moore–Samuelson compensation criterion; *Hicks compensation criterion*; *Kaldor compensation criterion*

Puig, Pedro, Universitat Autònoma de Barcelona, Barcelona, Spain
Poisson's distribution

Quesada Paloma, Vicente, Universidad Complutense, Madrid, Spain
Edgeworth expansion

Ramos Gorostiza, José Luis, Universidad Complutense, Madrid, Spain
Faustmann–Ohlin theorem

Reeder, John, Universidad Complutense, Madrid, Spain
Adam Smith problem; *Adam Smith's invisible hand*

Regúlez Castillo, Marta, Universidad del País Vasco-EHU, Bilbao, Spain
Hausman's test

Repullo, Rafael, CEMFI, Madrid, Spain
Pareto efficiency; Sonnenschein–Mantel–Debreu theorem

Restoy, Fernando, Banco de España, Madrid, Spain
Ricardian equivalence

Rey, José Manuel, Universidad Complutense, Madrid, Spain
Negishi's stability without recontracting

Ricoy, Carlos J., Universidad de Santiago de Compostela, Santiago de Compostela, A Coruña, Spain
Wicksell effect

Rodero-Cosano, Javier, Fundación CENTRA, Sevilla, Spain
Myerson revelation principle

Rodrigo Fernández, Antonio, Universidad Complutense, Madrid, Spain
Arrow–Pratt's measure of risk aversion

Rodríguez Braun, Carlos, Universidad Complutense, Madrid, Spain
Clark–Fisher hypothesis; *Genberg-Zecher criterion*; *Hume's fork*; *Kelvin's dictum*; *Moore's law*; *Spencer's law*; *Stigler's law of eponymy*; *Wieser's law*

Rodríguez Romero, Luis, Universidad Carlos III, Madrid, Spain
Engel curve

Rodríguez-Gutíerrez, Cesar, Universidad de Oviedo, Oviedo, Spain
Laspeyres index; *Paasche index*

Rojo, Luis Ángel, Universidad Complutense, Madrid, Spain
Keynes's demand for money

Romera, Rosario, Universidad Carlos III, Madrid, Spain
Wiener–Khintchine theorem

Rosado, Ana, Universidad Complutense, Madrid, Spain
Tinbergen's rule

Rosés, Joan R., Universitat Pompeu Fabra, Barcelona, Spain and Universidad Carlos III, Madrid, Spain
Gerschenkron's growth hypothesis; *Kuznets's curve*; *Kuznets's swings*

Ruíz Huerta, Jesús, Universidad Rey Juan Carlos, Madrid, Spain
Edgeworth taxation paradox

Salas, Rafael, Universidad Complutense, Madrid, Spain
Gini's coefficient; *Lorenz's curve*

Salas, Vicente, Universidad de Zaragoza, Zaragoza, Spain
Modigliani–Miller theorem; *Tobin's q*

San Emeterio Martín, Nieves, Universidad Rey Juan Carlos, Madrid, Spain
Lauderdale's paradox

San Julián, Javier, Universitat de Barcelona, Barcelona, Spain
Graham's paradox; *Sargant effect*

Sánchez, Ismael, Universidad Carlos III, Madrid, Spain
Neyman–Pearson test

Sánchez Chóliz, Julio, Universidad de Zaragoza, Zaragoza, Spain
Sraffa's model

Sánchez Hormigo, Alfonso, Universidad de Zaragoza, Zaragoza, Spain
Keynes's plan

Sánchez Maldonado, José, Universidad de Málaga, Málaga, Spain
Musgrave's three branches of the budget

Sancho, Amparo, Universidad de Valencia, Valencia, Spain
Jarque–Bera test

Santacoloma, Jon, Universidad de Deusto, Bilbao, Spain
Duesenberry demonstration effect

Santos-Redondo, Manuel, Universidad Complutense, Madrid, Spain
Schumpeterian entrepeneur; *Schumpeter's vision*; *Veblen effect good*

Sanz, José F., Instituto de Estudios Fiscales, Ministerio de Hacienda, Madrid, Spain
Fullerton-King's effective marginal tax rate

Sastre, Mercedes, Universidad Complutense, Madrid, Spain
Reynolds–Smolensky index

Satorra, Albert, Universitat Pompeu Fabra, Barcelona, Spain
Wald test

Saurina Salas, Jesús, Banco de España, Madrid, Spain
Bernoulli's paradox

Schwartz, Pedro, Universidad San Pablo CEU, Madrid, Spain
Say's law

Sebastián, Carlos, Universidad Complutense, Madrid, Spain
Muth's rational expectations

Sebastián, Miguel, Universidad Complutense, Madrid, Spain
Mundell–Fleming model

Segura, Julio, Universidad Complutense, Madrid, Spain
Baumol–Tobin transactions demand for cash; *Hicksian perfect stability*; *LeChatelier principle*; *Marshall's stability*; *Shapley–Folkman theorem*; *Snedecor F-distribution*

Senra, Eva, Universidad Carlos III, Madrid, Spain
Wold's decomposition

Sosvilla-Rivero, Simón, Universidad Complutense, Madrid, Spain and FEDEA, Madrid, Spain
Dickey–Fuller test; *Phillips–Perron test*

Suarez, Javier, CEMFI, Madrid, Spain
von Neumann–Morgenstern expected utility theorem

Suriñach, Jordi, Universitat de Barcelona, Barcelona, Spain
Aitken's theorem; *Durbin–Watson statistics*

Teixeira, José Francisco, Universidad de Vigo, Vigo, Pontevedra, Spain
Wicksell's cumulative process

Torres, Xavier, Banco de España, Madrid, Spain
Hicksian demand; *Marshallian demand*

Tortella, Gabriel, Universidad de Alcalá de Henares, Alcalá de Henares, Madrid, Spain
Rostow's model

Trincado, Estrella, Universidad Complutense, Madrid, Spain
Hume's law; *Ricardian vice*

Urbano Salvador, Amparo, Universidad de Valencia, Valencia, Spain
Bayesian–Nash equilibrium

Urbanos Garrido, Rosa María, Universidad Complutense, Madrid, Spain
Williams's fair innings argument

Valenciano, Federico, Universidad del País Vasco-EHU, Bilbao, Spain
Nash bargaining solution

Vallés, Javier, Banco de España, Madrid, Spain
Giffen goods

Varela, Juán, Ministerio de Hacienda, Madrid, Spain
Jones's magnification effect

Vázquez, Jesús, Universidad del País Vasco-EHU, Bilbao, Spain
Cagan's hyperinflation model

Vázquez Furelos, Mercedes, Universidad Complutense, Madrid, Spain
Lyapunov's central limit theorem

Vega, Juan, Universidad de Extremadura, Badajoz, Spain
Harberger's triangle

Vega-Redondo, Fernando, Universidad de Alicante, Alicante, Spain
Nash equilibrium

Vegara, David, Ministerio de Economià y Hacienda, Madrid, Spain
Goodhart's law; *Taylor rule*

Vegara-Carrió, Josep Ma, Universitat Autònoma de Barcelona, Barcelona, Spain
von Neumann's growth model; *Pasinetti's paradox*

Villagarcía, Teresa, Universidad Carlos III, Madrid, Spain
Weibull distribution

Viñals, José, Banco de España, Madrid, Spain
Balassa–Samuelson effect

Zaratiegui, Jesús M., Universidad de Navarra, Pamplona, Spain
Thünen's formula

Zarzuelo, José Manuel, Universidad del País Vasco-EHU, Bilbao, Spain
Kuhn–Tucker theorem; *Shapley value*

Zubiri, Ignacio, Universidad del País Vasco-EHU, Bilbao, Spain
Theil index

Preface

Robert K. Merton defined eponymy as 'the practice of affixing the name of the scientist to all or part of what he has found'. Eponymy has fascinating features and can be approached from several different angles, but only a few attempts have been made to tackle the subject lexicographically in science and art, and the present is the first *Eponymous Dictionary of Economics*.

The reader must be warned that this is a modest book, aiming at helpfulness more than erudition. We realized that economics has expanded in this sense too: there are hundreds of eponyms, and the average economist will probably be acquainted with, let alone be able to master, just a number of them. This is the void that the *Dictionary* is expected to fill, and in a manageable volume: delving into the problems of the sociology of science, dispelling all Mertonian multiple discoveries, and tracing the origins, on so many occasions spurious, of each eponym (cf. 'Stigler's Law of Eponymy' *infra*), would have meant editing another book, or rather books.

A dictionary is by definition not complete, and arguably not completable. Perhaps this is even more so in our case. We fancy that we have listed most of the economic eponyms, and also some non-economic, albeit used in our profession, but we are aware of the risk of including non-material or rare entries; in these cases we have tried to select interesting eponyms, or eponyms coined by or referring to interesting thinkers. We hope that the reader will spot few mistakes in the opposite sense; that is, the exclusion of important and widely used eponyms.

The selection has been especially hard in mathematics and econometrics, much more eponymy-prone than any other field connected with economics. The low risk-aversion reader who wishes to uphold the conjecture that eponymy has numerically something to do with scientific relevance will find that the number of eponyms tends to dwindle after the 1960s; whether this means that seminal results have dwindled too is a highly debatable and, owing to the critical time dimension of eponymy, a likely unanswerable question.

In any case, we hasten to invite criticisms and suggestions in order to improve eventual future editions of the dictionary (please find below our e-mail addresses for contacts).

We would like particularly to thank all the contributors, and also other colleagues that have helped us: Emilio Albi, José María Capapé, Toni Espasa, María del Carmen Gallastegui, Cecilia Garcés, Carlos Hervés, Elena Iñarra, Emilio Lamo de Espinosa, Jaime de Salas, Rafael Salas, Vicente Salas Fumás, Cristóbal Torres and Juan Urrutia. We are grateful for the help received from Edward Elgar's staff in all the stages of the book, and especially for Bob Pickens' outstanding job as editor.

Madrid, December 2003

J.S. [jsegura@bde.es]
C.R.B. [crb@ccee.ucm.es]

Mathematical notation

A vector is usually denoted by a lower case italic letter such as x or y, and sometimes is represented with an arrow on top of the letter such as $\vec{x}$ or $\vec{y}$. Sometimes a vector is described by enumeration of its elements; in these cases subscripts are used to denote individual elements of a vector and superscripts to denote a specific one: $x = (x_1, \ldots, x_n)$ means a generic n-dimensional vector and $x^0 = (x_1^0, \ldots, x_n^0)$ a specific n-dimensional vector. As it is usual, $x >> y$ means $x_i > y_i$ (i = 1, . . ., n) and $x > y$ means $x_i \geq y_i$ for all i and, for at least one i, $x_i > y_i$.

A set is denoted by a capital italic letter such as X or Y. If a set is defined by some property of its members, it is written with brackets which contain in the first place the typical element followed by a vertical line and the property: $X = (x/x >> 0)$ is the set of vectors x with positive elements. In particular, R is the set of real numbers, R_+ the set of non-negative real numbers, R_{++} the set of positive real numbers and a superscript denotes the dimension of the set. R_+^n is the set of n-dimensional vectors whose elements are all real non-negative numbers.

Matrices are denoted by capital italic letters such as A or B, or by squared brackets surrounding their typical element $[a_{ij}]$ or $[b_{ij}]$. When necessary, $A(qxm)$ indicates that matrix A has q rows and m columns (is of order qxm).

In equations systems expressed in matricial form it is supposed that dimensions of matrices and vectors are the right ones, therefore we do not use transposition symbols. For example, in the system $y = Ax + u$, with $A(nxn)$, all the three vectors must have n rows and 1 column but they are represented ini the text as $y = (y_1, \ldots, y_n)$, $x = (x_1, \ldots, x_n)$ and $u = (u_1, \ldots, u_n)$. The only exceptions are when expressing a quadratic form such as xAx' or a matricial product such as $(X' X)^{-1}$.

The remaining notation is the standard use for mathematics, and when more specific notation is used it is explained in the text.

A

Adam Smith problem

In the third quarter of the nineteenth century, a series of economists writing in German (Karl Knies, 1853, Lujo Brentano, 1877 and the Polish aristocrat Witold von Skarzynski, 1878) put forward a hypothesis known as the *Umschwungstheorie*. This suggested that Adam Smith's ideas had undergone a turnaround between the publication of his philosophical work, the *Theory of Moral Sentiments* in 1759 and the writing of the *Wealth of Nations*, a turnaround (*umschwung*) which had resulted in the theory of sympathy set out in the first work being replaced by a new 'selfish' approach in his later economic study. Knies, Brentano and Skarzynski argued that this turnaround was to be attributed to the influence of French materialist thinkers, above all Helvétius, with whom Smith had come into contact during his long stay in France (1763–66). Smith was something of a *bête noire* for the new German nationalist economists: previously anti-free trade German economists from List to Hildebrand, defenders of *Nationalökonomie*, had attacked Smith (and *smithianismus*) as an unoriginal prophet of free trade orthodoxies, which constituted in reality a defence of British industrial supremacy.

Thus was born what came to be called *Das Adam Smith Problem*, in its more sophisticated version, the idea that the theory of sympathy set out in the *Theory of Moral Sentiments* is in some way incompatible with the self-interested, profit-maximizing ethic which supposedly underlies the *Wealth of Nations*. Since then there have been repeated denials of this incompatibility, on the part of upholders of the consistency thesis, such as Augustus Oncken in 1897 and the majority of twentieth-century interpreters of Smith's work. More recent readings maintain that the Adam Smith problem is a false one, hingeing on a misinterpretation of such key terms as 'selfishness' and 'self-interest', that is, that self-interest is not the same as selfishness and does not exclude the possibility of altruistic behaviour. Nagging doubts, however, resurface from time to time – Viner, for example, expressed in 1927 the view that 'there are divergences between them [*Moral Sentiments* and *Wealth of Nations*] which are impossible of reconciliation' – and although the *Umschwungstheorie* is highly implausible, one cannot fail to be impressed by the differences in tone and emphasis between the two books.

JOHN REEDER

Bibliography

Montes, Leonidas (2003), '*Das Adam Smith Problem*: its origins, the stages of the current debate and one implication for our understanding of sympathy', *Journal of the History of Economic Thought*, **25** (1), 63–90.

Nieli, Russell (1986), 'Spheres of intimacy and the Adam Smith problem', *Journal of the History of Ideas*, **47** (4), 611–24.

Adam Smith's invisible hand

On three separate occasions in his writings, Adam Smith uses the metaphor of the invisible hand, twice to describe how a spontaneously evolved institution, the competitive market, both coordinates the various interests of the individual economic agents who go to make up society and allocates optimally the different resources in the economy.

The first use of the metaphor by Smith, however, does not refer to the market mechanism. It occurs in the context of Smith's early unfinished philosophical essay on *The History of Astronomy* (1795, III.2, p. 49) in a discussion of the origins of polytheism: 'in all Polytheistic religions, among savages, as well as in the early ages of Heathen antiquity, it is the irregular events of nature only that are ascribed to the agency and power of their gods. Fire burns, and water refreshes; heavy bodies descend and lighter substances fly upwards, by the necessity of their own nature; nor was the invisible hand of Jupiter ever apprehended to be employed in those matters'.

The second reference to the invisible hand is to be found in Smith's major philosophical work, *The Theory of Moral Sentiments* (1759, IV.i.10, p. 184), where, in a passage redolent of a philosopher's distaste for consumerism, Smith stresses the unintended consequences of human actions:

> The produce of the soil maintains at all times nearly that number of inhabitants which it is capable of maintaining. The rich only select from the heap what is most precious and agreeable. They consume little more than the poor, and in spite of their natural selfishness and rapacity, though they mean only their own conveniency, though the sole end which they propose from the labours of all the thousands whom they employ, be the gratification of their own vain and insatiable desires, they divide with the poor the produce of all their improvements. They are led by an invisible hand to make nearly the same distribution of the necessaries of life, which would have been made, had the earth been divided into equal portions among all its inhabitants, and thus without intending it, without knowing it, advance the interests of the society, and afford means to the multiplication of the species.

Finally, in the *Wealth of Nations* (1776, IV.ii.9, p. 456), Smith returns to his invisible hand metaphor to describe explicitly how the market mechanism recycles the pursuit of individual self-interest to the benefit of society as a whole, and *en passant* expresses a deep-rooted scepticism concerning those people (generally not merchants) who affect to 'trade for the publick good':

> As every individual, therefore, endeavours as much as he can both to employ his capital in the support of domestick industry, and so to direct that industry that its produce may be of the greatest value; every individual necessarily labours to render the annual revenue of the society as great as he can. He generally, indeed, neither intends to promote the publick interest, nor knows how much he is promoting it. . . . by directing that industry in such a manner as its produce may be of the greatest value, he intends only his own gain, and he is in this, as in many other cases, led by an invisible hand to promote an end which was no part of his intention. Nor is it always the worse for the society that it was no part of it. By pursuing his own interest he frequently promotes that of the society more effectually than when he really intends to promote it. I have never known much good done by those who affect to trade for the publick good. It is an affectation, indeed, not very common among merchants, and very few words need be employed in dissuading them from it.

More recently, interest in Adam Smith's invisible hand metaphor has enjoyed a revival, thanks in part to the resurfacing of philosophical problems concerning the unintended social outcomes of conscious and intentional human actions as discussed, for example, in the works of Karl Popper and Friedrich von Hayek, and in part to the fascination with the concept of the competitive market as the most efficient means of allocating resources expressed by a new generation of free-market economists.

JOHN REEDER

Bibliography

Macfie, A.L. (1971), 'The invisible hand of Jupiter', *Journal of the History of Ideas*, **32** (4), 593–9.

Smith, Adam (1759), *The Theory of Moral Sentiments*, reprinted in D.D. Raphael and A.L. Macfie (eds) (1982), *The Glasgow Edition of the Works and Correspondence of Adam Smith*, Indianapolis: Liberty Classics.

Smith, Adam (1776), *An Inquiry into the Nature and Causes of the Wealth of Nations*, reprinted in W.B. Todd (ed.) (1981), *The Glasgow Edition of the Works and Correspondence of Adam Smith*, Indianapolis: Liberty Classics.

Smith, Adam (1795), *Essays on Philosophical Subjects*, reprinted in W.P.D. Wightman and J.C. Bryce (eds) (1982), *The Glasgow Edition of the Works and Correspondence of Adam Smith*, Indianapolis: Liberty Classics.

Aitken's theorem

Named after New Zealander mathematician Alexander Craig Aitken (1895–1967), the theorem that shows that the method that provides estimators that are efficient as well as linear and unbiased (that is, of all the methods that provide linear unbiased estimators, the one that presents the least variance) when the disturbance term of the regression model is non-spherical, is a generalized least squares estimation (GLSE). This theory considers as a particular case the Gauss–Markov theorem for the case of regression models with spherical disturbance term and is derived from the definition of a linear unbiased estimator other than that provided by GLSE ($\tilde{\beta} = ((X'\Omega X)^{-1} X'\Omega^{-1} + \mathbf{C})Y$, C being a matrix with (at least) one of its elements other than zero) and demonstrates that its variance is given by $VAR(\tilde{\beta}) = VAR(\hat{\beta}_{GLSE}) + \sigma^2\mathbf{C}\Omega\mathbf{C}'$, where $\sigma^2\mathbf{C}\Omega\mathbf{C}'$ is a positive defined matrix, and therefore that the variances of the $\tilde{\beta}$ estimators are greater than those of the $\hat{\beta}_{GLSE}$ estimators.

JORDI SURINACH

Bibliography

Aitken, A. (1935), 'On least squares and linear combinations of observations', *Proceedings of the Royal Statistical Society*, **55**, 42–8.

See also: Gauss–Markov theorem.

Akerlof's 'lemons'

George A. Akerlof (b.1940) got his B.A. at Yale University, graduated at MIT in 1966 and obtained an assistant professorship at University of California at Berkeley. In his first year at Berkeley he wrote the 'Market for "lemons" ', the work for which he was cited for the Nobel Prize that he obtained in 2001 (jointly with A. Michael Spence and Joseph E. Stiglitz). His main research interest has been (and still is) the consequences for macroeconomic problems of different microeconomic structures such as asymmetric information or staggered contracts. Recently he has been working on the effects of different assumptions regarding fairness and social customs on unemployment.

The used car market captures the essence of the 'Market for "lemons" ' problem. Cars can be good or bad. When a person buys a new car, he/she has an expectation regarding its quality. After using the car for a certain time, the owner has more accurate information on its quality. Owners of bad cars ('lemons') will tend to replace them, while the owners of good cars will more often keep them (this is an argument similar to the one underlying the statement: bad money drives out the good). In addition, in the second-hand market, all sellers will claim that the car they sell is of good quality, while the buyers cannot distinguish good from bad second-hand cars. Hence the price of cars will reflect their expected quality (the average quality) in the second-hand market. However, at this price high-quality cars would be underpriced and the seller might prefer not to sell. This leads to the fact that only lemons will be traded.

In this paper Akerlof demonstrates how adverse selection problems may arise when sellers have more information than buyers about the quality of the product. When the contract includes a single parameter (the price) the problem cannot be avoided and markets cannot work. Many goods may not be traded. In order to address an adverse selection problem (to separate the good from the bad quality items) it is necessary to add ingredients to the contract. For example, the inclusion of guarantees or certifications on the quality may reduce the informational problem in the second-hand cars market.

The approach pioneered by Akerlof has

been extensively applied to the study of many other economic subjects such as financial markets (how asymmetric information between borrowers and lenders may explain very high borrowing rates), public economics (the difficulty for the elderly of contracting private medical insurance), labor economics (the discrimination of minorities) and so on.

INÉS MACHO-STADLER

Bibliography

Akerlof, G.A. (1970), 'The market for "lemons": quality uncertainty and the market mechanism', *Quarterly Journal of Economics*, **89**, 488–500.

Allais paradox

One of the axioms underlying expected utility theory requires that, if A is preferred to B, a lottery assigning a probability p to winning A and $(1-p)$ to C will be preferred to another lottery assigning probability p to B and $(1-p)$ to C, irrespective of what C is. The Allais paradox, due to French economist Maurice Allais (1911–2001, Nobel Prize 1988) challenges this axiom.

Given a choice between one million euro and a gamble offering a 10 per cent chance of receiving five million, an 89 per cent chance of obtaining one million and a 1 per cent chance of receiving nothing, you are likely to pick the former. Nevertheless, you are also likely to prefer a lottery offering a 10 per cent probability of obtaining five million (and 90 per cent of gaining nothing) to another with 11 per cent probability of obtaining one million and 89 per cent of winning nothing.

Now write the outcomes of those gambles as a 4×3 table with probabilities 10 per cent, 89 per cent and 1 per cent heading each column and the corresponding prizes in each row (that is, 1, 1 and 1; 5, 1 and 0; 5, 0 and 0; and 1, 0 and 1, respectively). If the central column, which plays the role of C, is dropped, your choices above (as most people's) are perceptibly inconsistent: if the first row was preferred to the second, the fourth should have been preferred to the third.

For some authors, this paradox illustrates that agents tend to neglect small reductions in risk (in the second gamble above, the risk of nothing is only marginally higher in the first option) unless they completely eliminate it: in the first option of the first gamble you are offered one million for sure. For others, however, it reveals only a sort of 'optical illusion' without any serious implication for economic theory.

JUAN AYUSO

Bibliography

Allais, M. (1953), 'Le Comportement de l'homme rationnel devant la risque: critique des postulats et axioms de l'ecole américaine', *Econometrica*, **21**, 269–90.

See also: Ellsberg paradox, von Neumann–Morgenstern expected utility theorem.

Areeda–Turner predation rule

In 1975, Phillip Areeda (1930–95) and Donald Turner (1921–94), at the time professors at Harvard Law School, published what now everybody regards as a seminal paper, 'Predatory pricing and related practices under Section 2 of the Sherman Act'. In that paper, they provided a rigorous definition of predation and considered how to identify prices that should be condemned under the Sherman Act. For Areeda and Turner, predation is 'the deliberate sacrifice of present revenues for the purpose of driving rivals out of the market and then recouping the losses through higher profits earned in the absence of competition'.

Areeda and Turner advocated the adoption of a *per se* prohibition on pricing below marginal costs, and robustly defended this suggestion against possible alternatives. The basis of their claim was that companies that were maximizing short-run profits would, by definition, not be predating. Those companies would not price below marginal cost. Given the difficulties of estimating marginal costs, Areeda and Turner suggested using average variable costs as a proxy.

The Areeda–Turner rule was quickly adopted by the US courts as early as 1975, in *International Air Industries* v. *American Excelsior Co.* The application of the rule had dramatic effects on success rates for plaintiffs in predatory pricing cases: after the publication of the article, success rates dropped to 8 per cent of cases reported, compared to 77 per cent in preceding years. The number of predatory pricing cases also dropped as a result of the widespread adoption of the Areeda–Turner rule by the courts (Bolton *et al.* 2000).

In Europe, the Areeda–Turner rule becomes firmly established as a central test for predation in 1991, in *AKZO* v. *Commission.* In this case, the court stated that prices below average variable cost should be presumed predatory. However the court added an important second limb to the rule. Areeda and Turner had argued that prices above marginal cost were higher than profit-maximizing ones and so should be considered legal, 'even if they were below average total costs'. The European Court of Justice (ECJ) took a different view. It found AKZO guilty of predatory pricing when its prices were between average variable and average total costs. The court emphasized, however, that such prices could only be found predatory if there was independent evidence that they formed part of a plan to exclude rivals, that is, evidence of exclusionary intent. This is consistent with the emphasis of Areeda and Turner that predatory prices are different from those that the company would set if it were maximizing short-run profits without exclusionary intent.

The adequacy of average variable costs as a proxy for marginal costs has received considerable attention (Williamson, 1977; Joskow and Klevorick, 1979). In 1996, William Baumol made a decisive contribution on this subject in a paper in which he agreed that the two measures may be different, but argued that average variable costs was the more appropriate one. His conclusion was based on reformulating the Areeda–Turner rule. The original rule was based on identifying prices below profit-maximizing ones. Baumol developed instead a rule based on whether prices could exclude equally efficient rivals. He argued that the rule which implemented this was to compare prices to average variable costs or, more generally, to average avoidable costs: if a company's price is above its average avoidable cost, an equally efficient rival that remains in the market will earn a price per unit that exceeds the average costs per unit it would avoid if it ceased production.

There has also been debate about whether the price–cost test in the Areeda–Turner rule is sufficient. On the one hand, the United States Supreme Court has stated in several cases that plaintiffs must *also* demonstrate that the predator has a reasonable prospect of recouping the costs of predation through market power after the exit of the prey. This is the so-called 'recoupment test'. In Europe, on the other hand, the ECJ explicitly rejected the need for a showing of recoupment in *Tetra Pak I* (1996 and 1997).

None of these debates, however, overshadows Areeda and Turner's achievement. They brought discipline to the legal analysis of predation, and the comparison of prices with some measure of costs, which they introduced, remains the cornerstone of practice on both sides of the Atlantic.

JORGE ATILANO PADILLA

Bibliography

Areeda, Phillip and Donald F. Turner (1975), 'Predatory pricing and related practices under Section 2 of the Sherman Act', *Harvard Law Review*, **88**, 697–733.

Baumol, William J. (1996), 'Predation and the logic of the average variable cost test', *Journal of Law and Economics*, **39**, 49–72.

Bolton, Patrick, Joseph F. Brodley and Michael H. Riordan (2000), 'Predatory pricing: strategic theory and legal policy', *Georgetown Law Journal*, **88**, 2239–330.

Joskow, A. and Alvin Klevorick (1979): 'A framework for analyzing predatory pricing policy', *Yale Law Journal*, **89**, 213.

Williamson, Oliver (1977), 'Predatory pricing: a strategic and welfare analysis', *Yale Law Journal*, **87**, 384.

Arrow's impossibility theorem

Kenneth J. Arrow (b.1921, Nobel Prize in Economics 1972) is the author of this celebrated result which first appeared in Chapter V of *Social Choice and Individual Values* (1951). Paradoxically, Arrow called it initially the 'general *possibility* theorem', but it is always referred to as an impossibility theorem, given its essentially negative character. The theorem establishes the incompatibility among several axioms that might be satisfied (or not) by methods to aggregate individual preferences into social preferences. I will express it in formal terms, and will then comment on its interpretations and on its impact in the development of economics and other disciplines.

In fact, the best known and most reproduced version of the theorem is not the one in the original version, but the one that Arrow formulated in Chapter VIII of the 1963 second edition of *Social Choice and Individual Values*. This chapter, entitled 'Notes on the theory of social choice', was added to the original text and constitutes the only change between the two editions. The reformulation of the theorem was partly justified by the simplicity of the new version, and also because Julian Blau (1957) had pointed out that there was a difficulty with the expression of the original result.

Both formulations start from the same formal framework. Consider a society of n agents, which has to express preferences regarding the alternatives in a set A. The preferences of agents are given by complete, reflexive, transitive binary relations on A. Each list of n such relations can be interpreted as the expression of a state of opinion within society. Rules that assign a complete, reflexive, transitive binary relation (a social preference) to each admissible state of opinion are called 'social welfare functions'.

Specifically, Arrow proposes a list of properties, in the form of axioms, and discusses whether or not they may be satisfied by a social welfare function. In his 1963 edition, he puts forward the following axioms:

- Universal domain (U): the domain of the function must include all possible combinations of individual preferences;
- Pareto (P): whenever all agents agree that an alternative x is better than another alternative y, at a given state of opinion, then the corresponding social preference must rank x as better than y;
- Independence of irrelevant alternatives (I): the social ordering of any two alternatives, for any state of opinion, must only depend on the ordering of these two alternatives by individuals;
- Non-dictatorship (D): no single agent must be able to determine the strict social preference at all states of opinion.

Arrow's impossibility theorem (1963) tells that, when society faces three or more alternatives, no social welfare function can simultaneously meet U, P, I and D.

By Arrow's own account, the need to formulate a result in this vein arose when trying to answer a candid question, posed by a researcher at RAND Corporation: does it make sense to speak about social preferences?

A first quick answer would be to say that the preferences of society are those of the majority of its members. But this is not good enough, since the majority relation generated by a society of n voters may be cyclical, as soon as there are more than two alternatives, and thus different from individual preferences, which are usually assumed to be transitive. The majority rule (which otherwise satisfies all of Arrow's requirements), is not a social welfare function, when society faces more than two alternatives. Arrow's theorem generalizes this remark to any other rule: no social welfare function can meet his requirements, and no aggregation method meeting them can be a social welfare function.

Indeed, some of the essential assumptions underlying the theorem are not explicitly stated as axioms. For example, the required transitivity of the social preference, which rules out the majority method, is included in the very definition of a social welfare function. Testing the robustness of Arrow's theorem to alternative versions of its implicit and explicit conditions has been a major activity of social choice theory for more than half a century. Kelly's updated bibliography contains thousands of references inspired by Arrow's impossibility theorem.

The impact of the theorem is due to the richness and variety of its possible interpretations, and the consequences it has on each of its possible readings.

A first interpretation of Arrow's formal framework is as a representation of voting methods. Though he was not fully aware of it in 1951, Arrow's analysis of voting systems falls within a centuries-old tradition of authors who discussed the properties of voting systems, including Plinius the Young, Ramón Llull, Borda, Condorcet, Laplace and Dodgson, among others. Arrow added historical notes on some of these authors in his 1963 edition, and the interested reader can find more details on this tradition in McLean and Urken (1995). Each of these authors studied and proposed different methods of voting, but none of them fully acknowledged the pervasive barriers that are so well expressed by Arrow's theorem: that no method at all can be perfect, because any possible one must violate some of the reasonable requirements imposed by the impossibility theorem. This changes the perspective in voting theory: if a voting method must be selected over others, it must be on the merits and its defects, taken together; none can be presented as an ideal.

Another important reading of Arrow's theorem is the object of Chapter IV in his monograph. Arrow's framework allows us to put into perspective the debate among economists of the first part of the twentieth century, regarding the possibility of a theory of economic welfare that would be devoid of interpersonal comparisons of utility and of any interpretation of utility as a cardinal magnitude. Kaldor, Hicks, Scitovsky, Bergson and Samuelson, among other great economists of the period, were involved in a discussion regarding this possibility, while using conventional tools of economic analysis. Arrow provided a general framework within which he could identify the shared values of these economists as partial requirements on the characteristics of a method to aggregate individual preferences into social orderings. By showing the impossibility of meeting all these requirements simultaneously, Arrow's theorem provided a new focus to the controversies: no one was closer to success than anyone else. Everyone was looking for the impossible. No perfect aggregation method was worth looking for, as it did not exist. Trade-offs between the properties of possible methods had to be the main concern.

Arrow's theorem received immediate attention, both as a methodological criticism of the 'new welfare economics' and because of its voting theory interpretation. But not everyone accepted that it was relevant. In particular, the condition of independence of irrelevant alternatives was not easily accepted as expressing the desiderata of the new welfare economics. Even now, it is a debated axiom. Yet Arrow's theorem has shown a remarkable robustness over more than 50 years, and has been a paradigm for many other results regarding the general difficulties in aggregating preferences, and the importance of concentrating on trade-offs, rather than setting absolute standards.

Arrow left some interesting topics out of his monograph, including issues of aggregation and mechanism design. He mentioned, but did not elaborate on, the possibility that voters might strategically misrepresent their preferences. He did not discuss the reasons why some alternatives are on the table, and others are not, at the time a social decision must be taken. He did not provide a general framework where the possibility of using cardinal information and of performing interpersonal comparisons of utility could be explicitly discussed. These were routes that later authors were to take. But his impossibility theorem, in all its specificity, provided a new way to analyze normative issues and established a research program for generations.

SALVADOR BARBERÀ

Bibliography

Arrow, K.J. (1951), *Social Choice and Individual Values*, New York: John Wiley; 2nd definitive edn 1963.

Blau, Julian H. (1957), 'The existence of social welfare functions', *Econometrica*, **25**, 302–13.

Kelly, Jerry S., 'Social choice theory: a bibliography', http://www.maxwell.syr.edu/maxpages/faculty/jskelly/A.htm.

McLean, Ian and Arnold B. Urken (1995), *Classics of Social Choice*, The University of Michigan Press.

See also: Bergson's social indifference curve, Borda's rule, Chipman–Moore–Samuelson compensation criterion, Condorcet's criterion, Hicks compensation criterion, Kaldor compensation criterion, Scitovski's compensation criterion.

Arrow's learning by doing

This is the key concept in the model developed by Kenneth J. Arrow (b.1921, Nobel Prize 1972) in 1962 with the purpose of explaining the changes in technological knowledge which underlie intertemporal and international shifts in production functions. In this respect, Arrow suggests that, according to many psychologists, the acquisition of knowledge, what is usually termed 'learning', is the product of experience ('doing'). More specifically, he advances the hypothesis that technical change depends upon experience in the activity of production, which he approaches by cumulative gross investment, assuming that new capital goods are better than old ones; that is to say, if we compare a unit of capital goods produced in the time t_1 with one produced at time t_2, the first requires the cooperation of at least as much labour as the second, and produces no more product. Capital equipment comes in units of equal (infinitesimal) size, and the productivity achievable using any unit of equipment depends on how much investment had already occurred when this particular unit was produced.

Arrow's view is, therefore, that at least part of technological progress does not depend on the passage of time as such, but grows out of 'experience' caught by cumulative gross investment; that is, a vehicle for improvements in skill and technical knowledge. His model may be considered as a precursor to the further new or endogenous growth theory. Thus the last paragraph of Arrow's paper reads as follows: 'It has been assumed that learning takes place only as a by-product of ordinary production. In fact, society has created institutions, education and research, whose purpose is to enable learning to take place more rapidly. A fuller model would take account of these as additional variables.' Indeed, this is precisely what more recent growth literature has been doing.

CARMELA MARTÍN

Bibliography

Arrow, K.J. (1962), 'The economics implications of learning by doing', *Review of Economic Studies*, **29** (3), 155–73.

Arrow–Debreu general equilibrium model

Named after K.J. Arrow (b.1921, Nobel Prize 1972) and G. Debreu (b. 1921, Nobel Prize 1983) the model (1954) constitutes a milestone in the path of formalization and generalization of the general equilibrium model of Léon Walras (see Arrow and Hahn, 1971, for both models). An aspect which is characteristic of the contribution of Arrow–Debreu is the introduction of the concept of contingent commodity.

The fundamentals of Walras's general equilibrium theory (McKenzie, 2002) are consumers, consumers' preferences and resources, and the technologies available to society. From this the theory offers an account of firms and of the allocation, by means of markets, of consumers' resources among firms and of final produced commodities among consumers.

Every Walrasian model distinguishes itself by a basic parametric prices hypothesis: 'Prices are fixed parameters for every individual, consumer or firm decision problem.' That is, the terms of trade among commodities are taken as fixed by every individual decision maker ('absence of monopoly power'). There is a variety of circumstances that justify the hypothesis, perhaps approximately: (a) every individual decision maker is an insignificant part of the overall market, (b) some trader – an auctioneer, a possible entrant, a regulator – guarantees by its potential actions the terms of trade in the market.

The Arrow–Debreu model emphasizes a second, market completeness, hypothesis: 'There is a market, hence a price, for every conceivable commodity.' In particular, this holds for contingent commodities, promising to deliver amounts of a (physical) good if a certain state of the world occurs. Of course, for this to be possible, information has to be 'symmetric'. The complete markets hypothesis does, in essence, imply that there is no cost in opening markets (including those that at equilibrium will be inactive).

In any Walrasian model an equilibrium is specified by two components. The first assigns a price to each market. The second attributes an input–output vector to each firm and a vector of demands and supplies to every consumer. Input–output vectors should be profit-maximizing, given the technology, and each vector of demands–supplies must be affordable and preference-maximizing given the budget restriction of the consumer.

Note that, since some of the commodities are contingent, an Arrow–Debreu equilibrium determines a pattern of final risk bearing among consumers.

In a context of convexity hypothesis, or in one with many (bounded) decision makers, an equilibrium is guaranteed to exist. Much more restrictive are the conditions for its uniqueness.

The Arrow–Debreu equilibrium enjoys a key property, called the first welfare theorem: under a minor technical condition (local nonsatiation of preferences) equilibrium allocations are Pareto optimal: it is impossible to reassign inputs, outputs and commodities so that, in the end, no consumer is worse off and at least one is better off. To attempt a purely verbal justification of this, consider a weaker claim: it is impossible to reassign inputs, outputs and commodities so that, in the end, all consumers are better off (for this local non-satiation is not required). Define the concept of gross national product (GNP) at equilibrium as the sum of the aggregate value (for the equilibrium prices) of initial endowments of society plus the aggregate profits of the firms in the economy (that is, the sum over firms of the maximum profits for the equilibrium prices). The GNP is the aggregate amount of income distributed among the different consumers.

Consider now any rearrangement of inputs, outputs and commodities. Evaluated at equilibrium prices, the aggregate value of the rearrangement cannot be higher than the GNP because the total endowments are the same and the individual profits at the rearrangement have to be smaller than or equal to the profit-maximizing value. Therefore the aggregate value (at equilibrium prices) of the consumptions at the rearrangement is not larger than the GNP. Hence there is at least one consumer for which the value of consumption at the rearrangement is not higher than income at equilibrium. Because the equilibrium consumption for this consumer is no worse than any other affordable consumption we conclude that the rearrangement is not an improvement for her.

Under convexity assumptions there is a converse result, known as the second welfare theorem: every Pareto optimum can be sustained as a competitive equilibrium after a lump-sum transfer of income.

The theoretical significance of the Arrow–Debreu model is as a benchmark. It offers, succinctly and elegantly, a structure of markets that guarantees the fundamental property of Pareto optimality. Incidentally, in particular contexts it may suffice to dispose of a 'spanning' set of markets. Thus, in an intertemporal context, it typically suffices that in each period there are spot markets and markets for the exchange of contingent money at the next date. In the modern theory of finance a sufficient market structure to guarantee optimality obtains, under some conditions, if there are a few financial assets that can be traded (possibly short) without any special limit.

Yet it should be recognized that realism is not the strong point of the theory. For example, much relevant information in economics is asymmetric, hence not all contingent markets can exist. The advantage of the theory is that it constitutes a classification tool for the causes according to which a specific market structure may not guarantee final optimality. The causes will fall into two categories: those related to the incompleteness of markets (externalities, insufficient insurance opportunities and so on) and those related to the possession of market power by some decision makers.

ANDREU MAS-COLELL

Bibliography

Arrow K. and G. Debreu (1954), 'Existence of an equilibrium for a competitive economy', *Econometrica*, **22**, 265–90.

Arrow K. and F. Hahn (1971), *General Competitive Analysis*, San Francisco, CA: Holden-Day.

McKenzie, L. (2002), *Classical General Equilibrium Theory*, Cambridge, MA: The MIT Press.

See also: Pareto efficiency, Walras's auctioneer and tâtonnement.

Arrow–Pratt's measure of risk aversion

The extensively used measure of risk aversion, known as the Arrow–Pratt coefficient, was developed simultaneously and independently by K.J. Arrow (see Arrow, 1970) and J.W. Pratt (see Pratt, 1964) in the 1960s. They consider a decision maker, endowed with wealth x and an increasing utility function u, facing a risky choice represented by a random variable z with distribution F. A risk-averse individual is characterized by a concave utility function. The extent of his risk aversion is closely related to the degree of concavity of u. Since $u''(x)$ and the curvature of u are not invariant under positive lineal transformations of u, they are not meaningful measures of concavity in utility theory. They propose instead what is generally known as the Arrow–Pratt measure of risk aversion, namely $r(x) = -u''(x)/u'(x)$.

Assume without loss of generality that $Ez = 0$ and $\sigma_z^2 = Ez^2 < \infty$. Pratt defines the risk premium π by the equation $u(x - \pi) =$

$E(u(x + z))$, which indicates that the individual is indifferent between receiving z and getting the non-random amount $-\pi$. The greater is π the more risk-averse the individual is. However, π depends not only on x and u but also on F, which complicates matters. Assuming that u has a third derivative, which is continuous and bounded over the range of z, and using first and second order expansions of u around x, we can write $\pi(x, F) \cong r(x)\sigma_z^2/2$ for σ_z^2 small enough. Then π is proportional to $r(x)$ and thus $r(x)$ can be used to measure risk aversion 'in the small'. In fact $r(x)$ has global properties and is also valid 'in the large'. Pratt proves that, if a utility function u_1 exhibits everywhere greater local risk aversion than another function u_2, that is, if $r_1(x) > r_2(x)$ for all x, then $\pi_1(x, F) > \pi_2(x, F)$ for every x and F. Hence, u_1 is globally more risk-averse than u_2. The function $r(x)$ is called the absolute measure of risk aversion in contrast to its relative counterpart, $r^*(x) = xr(x)$, defined using the relative risk premium $\pi^*(x, F) = \pi(x, F)/x$.

Arrow uses basically the same approach but, instead of π, he defines the probability $p(x, h)$ which makes the individual indifferent between accepting or rejecting a bet with outcomes $+h$ and $-h$, and probabilities p and $1 - p$, respectively. For h small enough, he proves that

$$p(x, h) \cong \frac{1}{2} + r(x)h/4.$$

The behaviour of the Arrow–Pratt measures as x changes can be used to find utility functions associated with any behaviour towards risk, and this is, in Arrow's words, 'of the greatest importance for the prediction of economic reactions in the presence of uncertainty.'

ANTONIO RODRIGO FERNÁNDEZ

Bibliography

Arrow, K.J. (1970), *Essays in the Theory of Risk-Bearing*, Essay 3, Amsterdam: North-Holland/American Elsevier, pp. 90–120.

Pratt, J.W. (1964), 'Risk aversion in the small and in the large', *Econometrica*, **32**, 122–36.

See also: von Neumann–Morgenstern expected utility theorem.

Atkinson's index

One of the most popular inequality measures, named after the Welsh economist Anthony Barnes Atkinson (b.1944), the index has been extensively used in the normative measurement of inequality. Atkinson (1970) set out the approach to constructing social inequality indices based on the loss of equivalent income. In an initial contribution, another Welsh economist, Edward Hugh Dalton (1887–1962), used a simple utilitarian social welfare function to derive an inequality measure. The same utility function was taken to apply to all individuals, with diminishing marginal utility from income. An equal distribution should maximize social welfare. Inequality should be estimated as the shortfall of the sum-total of utilities from the maximal value. In an extended way, the Atkinson index measures the social loss resulting from unequal income distribution by shortfalls of equivalent incomes. Inequality is measured by the percentage reduction of total income that can be sustained without reducing social welfare, by distributing the new reduced total exactly. The difference of the equally distributed equivalent income with the actual income gives Atkinson's measure of inequality.

The social welfare function considered by Atkinson has the form

$$U(y) = A + B\frac{y^{1-\varepsilon}}{1-\varepsilon}, \varepsilon \neq 1$$

$$U(y) = \log_e(y), \varepsilon = 1$$

and the index takes the form

$$A_\varepsilon = 1 - \left[\frac{1}{n}\sum_{i=1}^{n}\left(\frac{y_i}{\mu}\right)^{1-e}\right]^{\frac{1}{1-e}} \quad \varepsilon \geq 0, \varepsilon \neq 1$$

$$A_1 = 1 - \exp\left[\frac{1}{n}\sum_{i=1}^{n} Ln\left(\frac{y_i}{\mu}\right)\right] \quad \varepsilon = 1$$

where ε is a measure of the degree of inequality aversion or the relative sensitivity of transfers at different income levels. As ε rises, we attach more weight to transfers at the lower end of the distribution and less weight to transfers at the top. The limiting cases at both extremes are $\varepsilon \to \infty$, which only takes account of transfers to the very lowest income group and $\varepsilon \to 0$, giving the linear utility function which ranks distribution solely according to total income.

LUÍS AYALA

Bibliography

Atkinson, A.B. (1970), 'On the measurement of inequality', *Journal of Economic Theory*, **2**, 244–63.
Dalton, H. (1920), 'The measurement of the inequality of incomes', *Economic Journal*, **30**, 348–61.

See also: Gini's coefficient, Theil index.

Averch–Johnson effect

A procedure commonly found to regulate private monopolies in countries such as the United States consists in restraining profits by fixing the maximum or fair return on investment in real terms: after the firm substracts its operating expenses from gross revenues, the remaining revenue should be just sufficient to compensate the firm for its investment in plant and equipment, at a rate which is considered to be fair. The Averch–Johnson effect concerns the inefficiencies caused by such a control system: a firm regulated by just a maximum allowed rate of return on capital will in general find it advantageous to substitute capital for other inputs and to produce in an overly capital-intensive manner. Such a firm will no longer minimize costs. From a normative point of view, and as compared with the unregulated monopoly, some regulation via the fair rate of return is welfare-improving. See Sheshinski (1971), who also derives the optimal degree of regulation.

SALVADOR LÓPEZ

Bibliography

Averch, H.A. and L.L. Johnson, (1962), 'Behavior of the firm under regulatory constraint', *American Economic Review*, **52** (5), 1052–69.
Sheshinski, E. (1971), 'Welfare aspects of a regulatory constraint: note', *American Economic Review*, **61** (1), 175–8.

B

Babbage's principle

The Englishman Charles Babbage (1791–1871) stands out in different subjects: mathematics, economics, science and technology policy. Analyzing the division of labour (1832, ch. XIX), Babbage quotes Adam Smith on the increase of production due to the skill acquired by repeating the same processes, and on the causes of the advantages resulting from the division of labour. After saying that this division perhaps represents the most important economic feature in a manufacturing process, and revising the advantages that usually are considered a product of this division, he adds his principle: 'That the master manufacturer, by dividing the work to be executed into different processes, each requiring different degrees of skill or of force, can purchase exactly that precise quantity of both which is necessary for each process; whereas, if the whole work were executed by one workman, that person must possess sufficient skill to perform the most difficult, and sufficient strength to execute the most laborious, of the operations into which the art is divided' (pp. 175–6). Babbage acknowledges that the principle appeared first in 1815 in Melchiorre Gioja's *Nuovo Prospetto delle Scienze Economiche*.

JORDI PASCUAL

Bibliography

Babbage, Charles (1832), *On the Economy of Machinery and Manufactures*, London: Charles Knight; 4th enlarged edn, 1835; reprinted (1963, 1971), New York: Augustus M. Kelley.

Liso, Nicola de (1998), 'Babbage, Charles', in H.Kurz and N.Salvadori (eds), *The Elgar Companion to Classical Economics*, Cheltenham, UK and Lyme, USA: Edward Elgar, pp. 24–8.

Bagehot's principle

Walter Bagehot (1826–77) was an English historical economist, interested in the interrelation between institutions and the economy, and who applied the theory of selection to political conflicts between nations. The principle that holds his name is about the responsibilities of the central bank (Bank of England), particularly as lender of last resort, a function that he considered it must be prepared to develop. These ideas arose in the course of the debates around the passing of the Banking Act in 1844 and after. In an article published in 1861, Bagehot postulated that the Bank had a national function, keeping the bullion reserve in the country. His opinion on the central bank statesmanship contrasted with the philosophy of laissez-faire, and Bagehot attempted the reconciliation between the service that the Bank of England must render to the British economy and the profit of its stockholders.

In his *Lombard Street* (1873) Bagehot took up his essential ideas published in *The Economist*, and formulated two rules in order to check the possible panic in time of crisis: (1) the 'loans should only be made at a very high rate of interest'; (2) 'at this rate these advances should be made on all good banking securities, and as largely as the public ask for them'.

JORDI PASCUAL

Bibliography

Bagehot, Walter (1861), 'The duty of the Bank of England in times of quietude', *The Economist*, 14 September, p. 1009.

Bagehot, Walter (1873), *Lombard Street: A Description of the Money Market*, reprinted (1962), Homewood, IL: Richard D. Irwin, p. 97.

Fetter, Frank Whitson (1965), *Development of British Monetary Orthodoxy 1797–1875*, Cambridge MA: Harvard University Press, pp. 169, 257–283.

Balassa–Samuelson effect

The pioneering work by Bela Balassa (1928–91) and Paul Samuelson (b.1915, Nobel Prize 1970) in 1964 provided a rigorous explanation for long-term deviations of exchange rates from purchasing power parity by arguing that richer countries tend to have, on average, higher price levels than poorer countries when expressed in terms of a single currency. The so-called 'Balassa–Samuelson theory of exchange rate determination' postulates that this long-term empirical regularity is due to international differences of productivity in the traded goods sector. In a dynamic setting, since productivity gains tend to be concentrated in the traded goods sector (through faster technological progress), the theory explains why faster growing economies tend to have higher rates of overall price increases when expressed in terms of a single currency; that is, appreciating real exchange rates.

The rationale behind the explanation provided by Balassa and Samuelson, which leads to a dismissal of the well-known purchasing power parity theory as a long-term theory of exchange rate determination, runs as follows: countries tend to produce both internationally traded and non-traded goods. International exchanges guarantee that the price of traded goods is equalized across countries when expressed in terms of the same currency. However, the price of non-traded goods tends to be higher in the richer country, thus leading to a higher overall price level there. Specifically, insofar as real wages tend to move in line with labour productivity since the richer country has higher productivity in the manufacture of traded goods, traded goods price equalization leads to both real and nominal wages also being higher in the traded goods sector of the richer country. As internal labour mobility guarantees that a unique nominal wage prevails in each country, nominal wages in the non-traded goods sector will be as high as in the traded goods sector. Moreover, as long as international productivity differentials across non-traded sectors are not very pronounced, this means that the price of the non-traded goods in the richer country will have to be higher given the prevailing higher nominal wage and the lower labour productivity compared to the traded goods sector.

In a dynamic setting, the faster growing economy will have a relatively more rapid growth in the productivity of the traded goods sector, a correspondingly higher rate of increase in non-traded goods prices and, given the equalization of traded goods price increases across countries, a higher rate of increase in the overall price level when expressed in the same currency (the so-called 'Balassa–Samuelson effect').

When examining the propositions put forward by Balassa and Samuelson, it is important to note, first, that it is one among several competing explanations for the driving forces behind the real exchange rate in the long term; second, it is purely a supply-side theory of relative national price levels with demand conditions playing no role; and third, it applies under both fixed and flexible exchange rates since it is a theory of relative prices, not absolute prices.

JOSÉ VIÑALS

Bibliography

Balassa, B. (1964), 'The purchasing power parity doctrine: a reappraisal', *Journal of Political Economy*, **72** (6), 584–96.

Canzoneri, M., R. Cumby and B. Diba (1999), 'Relative labor productivity and the real exchange rate in the long run: evidence from a panel of OECD countries', *Journal of International Economics*, **47**, 245–66.

Samuelson, P.A. (1964), 'Theoretical notes on trade problems', *Review of Economics and Statistics*, **46** (2), 145–54.

Banach's contractive mapping principle

Stefan Banach (1892–1945) was one of the most important mathematicians of the twentieth century and one of the founders of modern functional analysis, several of whose fundamental notions and results, besides Banach's contractive mapping principle, bear his name (Banach spaces, Banach algebras, the Hahn–Banach theorem, the Banach–Steinhaus theorem, the Banach–Alaoglu theorem, the Banach–Tarski paradox, and so on).

The most typical way of proving existence results in economics is by means of fixed point theorems. The classical Brouwer's fixed point theorem for single-valued mappings and its extension to multi-valued mappings due to Kakutani are widely used to prove the existence of an equilibrium in several contexts. Among the many other existing fixed point theorems, one of the oldest, simplest but nevertheless most useful ones is Banach's principle for contractive mappings from a complete metric space into itself.

A metric space is a mathematical structure consisting of a set X and a function d assigning a non-negative real number $d(x, y)$ to each ordered pair x, y of elements in X. We can interpret the number $d(x, y)$ as the distance between x and y, regarded as points. For this interpretation to make sense, the function d should have the properties that a notion of distance is expected to have: it should be symmetric, in the sense that $d(x, y) = d(y, x)$ for any two points x and y, take the value zero when $x = y$ and only in this case, and satisfy the so-called 'triangle inequality': $d(x, y) \leq d(x, z) + d(z, y)$ for any three points x, y and z. Then d is called a distance function and the pair (X, d) is said to be a metric space. A metric space (X, d) is called complete when every sequence $\{x_n\}$ in X with the property that $d(x_n, x_m)$ can be made arbitrarily small by choosing n and m sufficiently large converges to some point $x \in X$, which means that $d(x_n, x) \to 0$ as $n \to \infty$.

Banach's contractive mapping principle refers to mappings $T:X \to X$ that contract distances; that is, such that, for some positive number $\alpha < 1$ one has $d(T(x), T(y)) \leq \alpha d(x, y)$ for every $x, y \in X$. Assuming that the space is complete, the principle establishes the existence of a unique point $x \in X$ with $T(x) = x$. We can say that x is the fixed point of T.

In mathematics, a typical application of Banach's contractive mapping principle is to prove the existence and uniqueness of solutions to initial value problems in differential equations. It is used as well to establish the existence and uniqueness of a solution to Bellman's equation in dynamic programming, so that it constitutes the underlying basic tool in the theoretical analysis of many macroeconomic and growth models. In microeconomics, it has been employed, for instance, to prove the existence and uniqueness of Cournot equilibrium.

JUAN E. MARTÍNEZ LÓPEZ

Bibliography

Banach, Stefan (1922), 'Sur les Opérations dans les ensembles abstraits et leur application aux équations intégrales', *Fundamenta Mathematicae*, **3**, 133–81.

Van Long, Ngo and Antoine Soubeyran (2000), 'Existence and uniqueness of Cournot equilibrium: a contraction mapping approach', *Economic Letters*, **67** (3), 345–8.

See also: Bellman's principle of optimality and equations, Brouwer fixed point theorem, Cournot's oligopoly model, Kakutani's fixed point theorem.

Baumol's contestable markets

Under partial equilibrium theory, monopolistic markets, if there are no economies of scale, drive to higher prices than in the case of effective competition. This conclusion is questioned by the theory of contestable markets. William J. Baumol (b.1922) originally formulated the theory in Baumol (1986) and Baumol *et al.* (1982). Contestable markets theory contends, under certain assumptions, that monopoly and efficiency prices are not so different.

The idea is that, assuming the inexistence of barriers to entry, a monopoly firm has no other choice than to establish prices as close as possible to efficiency or competitive market prices. Otherwise the monopoly would put in danger its continuity as the only firm in the market. In the case where the monopolist chose to raise prices and to obtain extraordinary profits, other investors or firms would consider entering the market to capture all or part of the profits. Under the threat of such a contest, the monopolist prefers to maintain prices close to costs, renouncing extraordinary benefits, but ensuring its permanence as a monopoly without competitors.

The consequence of the theory of contestable markets is that regulating by ignoring control of prices and attending only to the raising of all the barriers to entry is effective in achieving efficiency prices. Although the idea is quite simple, the defence of the underlying assumptions it needs is more difficult.

The assumptions of contestable markets refer, basically, to the inexistence of barriers to entry. Barriers to entry are asymmetric costs that a new entrant has to pay when coming into an industry or market which do not have to be currently supported by the incumbent monopoly. These costs can be related to economic behaviour, technology, administrative procedures or legal rules. For example, if the monopolist behaves by reducing prices below costs temporarily to eliminate competitors (predatory behaviour), new entrants could not afford the temporary losses and would not come into the market. In such a case, prices of the monopolist will sometimes be lower, sometimes higher, than competition prices. Another barrier to entry appears when consumers react not only to prices but also to other market signals. Brand and quality are product attributes different from prices that have an influence on consumers' choice. Monopolies can be protected by a combination of quality and brand signals that are unaffordable to new entrants. Again, without price regulation, prices would differ from competitive or efficiency prices. Generally speaking, sunk costs operate as economic barriers to entry because they impose a heavy burden on the new entrants and indicate the sound commitment of the monopoly to carry on in the industry.

Also the technology used by a monopoly could deter new entrants and constitute a barrier to entry. The existence of different technologies could create asymmetries in costs and prices. Finally, administrative and legal authorizations can also impose a different cost on new entrants vis-à-vis the incumbent monopolies. In all these cases, eliminating the control of monopoly prices will not lead to efficiency prices.

Actually the overwhelming presence of economical, technical and legal barriers to entry in industries formerly organized as monopolies, such as power, natural gas, water or telecommunications, makes almost ineffective the application of the theory of contestable markets to regulatory action in order to suppress price controls.

MIGUEL A. LASHERAS

Bibliography

Baumol, W.J. (1986), 'On the theory of perfectly contestable markets' in J.E. Stiglitz and G.F. Mathewson (eds), *New Developments in the Analysis of Market Structure*, London: Macmillan.

Baumol, W.J., J.C. Panzar and R.D. Willig (1982), *Contestable Markets and the Theory of Industry Structure*, New York: Harcourt Brace Jovanovich.

Baumol's disease

William J. Baumol (b.1922) hypothesized that, because labour productivity in service industries grows less than in other industries, the costs in services end up rising over time as resources move and nominal wages tend to equalize across sectors. His model of unbalanced productivity growth predicts that (1) relative prices in sectors where productivity growth is lower will rise faster; (2) relative employment will tend to rise in sectors with low productivity growth; and (3) productivity growth will tend to fall economy-wide as labour moves to low-productivity sectors, given a persistent demand for services.

The evolution of developed economies has confirmed these predictions. Prices of personal services have risen, the weight of service employment and the size of the service sector have increased substantially, and productivity has grown less in services. Problems are more serious in labour-intensive services, with little room for capital substitution. It has also been argued that they are suffered by many government activities, which would imply growing public expenditures. Solutions that innovate around this trap are often effective but equally often radically alter the nature of the service, by including in it some elements of self-service and routine. Radio, records and television increased the productivity of musical performers, but their new services lacked the personal character and many other qualities of live concerts.

The root of the problem lies in a particular characteristic of services, for many of which consumers are the main input of the production process. This constrains innovation, because consumers often resent efforts to 'industrialize' production. Their complaints range from the depersonalization of medicine to being treated as objects by bureaucracies or protesting at the poor quality of fast food.

BENITO ARRUÑADA

Bibliography

Baumol, William J. (1967), 'Macroeconomics of unbalanced growth: the anatomy of urban crisis', *American Economic Review*, **57** (3), 415–26.

Baumol, William J. and Edward N. Wolff (1984), 'On interindustry differences in absolute productivity', *Journal of Political Economy*, **92** (6), 1017–34.

Baumol, William J., Sue Anne Batey Blackman and Edward N. Wolff (1985), 'Unbalanced growth revisited: asymptotic stagnancy and new evidence', *American Economic Review*, **75** (4), 806–17.

Baumol–Tobin transactions demand for cash

The interest elasticity of the demand for money has played an important role in discussions on the usefulness of monetary policy and on the comparisons between Keynesian, classical and monetarist views. If money is demanded as an alternative asset to other financial assets for precautionary or speculative motives, its demand has evidently negative interest elasticity. But it was the merit of W.J. Baumol (b.1922) and James Tobin (1918–2002, Nobel Prize 1981) to show in the 1950s that the transactions demand for cash exhibits significantly negative interest elasticity. Their idea was to show that, although the *size* of transaction balances depends mainly on the volume of transactions and on the degree of synchronization between individuals' expenditures and receipts, mainly determined by institutional characteristics, the *composition* of transaction balances is ruled by other factors. Even though there is a cost involved in the liquidation of assets, there is also an interest opportunity cost involved in the holding of cash. Therefore individuals may wish to hold part of their transaction balances in income-earning assets, in which case rational behaviour leads them to maximize their net receipts.

Baumol's paper (1952) is an application of a simple model of inventory control to determine the optimal value of each cash withdrawal. Assume that an individual, with a value T of transactions per period, withdraws cash evenly throughout the period in lots of value C. Let b stand for the transaction cost of each withdrawal and i be the opportunity cost of holding cash (the interest rate). Since the individual makes T/C withdrawals per period, his total transaction costs are bT/C. His average cash balance through the period is $C/2$, with an associated opportunity cost of $iC/2$. Therefore the total cost of holding cash for transaction purposes is $bT/C +$

$iC/2$ and the value of C that minimizes it is the well-known expression $C = (2bT/i)^{1/2}$. Hence the interest elasticity of transaction demand for cash equals –0.5.

In some ways Tobin's model (1956) is an extension and generalization of Baumol's to the case in which transactions can take only integral values. Tobin demonstrates that cash withdrawals must be evenly distributed throughout the period (an assumption in Baumol's model) and discusses corner solutions in which, for example, optimal initial investment could be nil. Moreover, Tobin's model allows him to discuss issues related to the transactions velocity of money and to conclude that the interest elasticity of transactions demand for cash depends on the rate of interest, but it is not a constant.

Finally, as in many other cases, the priority of Baumol and Tobin is controversial, because Allais obtained the 'square root' formula in 1947, as Baumol and Tobin recognized in 1989.

JULIO SEGURA

Bibliography

Baumol, W.J. (1952), 'The transactions demand for cash: an inventory theoretic approach', *Quarterly Journal of Economics*, **66**, 545–56.

Baumol, W.J. and J. Tobin (1989), 'The optimal cash balance proposition: Maurice Allais' priority', *Journal of Economic Literature*, **XXVII**, 1160–62.

Tobin J. (1956), 'The interest-elasticity of transactions demand for cash', *Review of Economics and Statistics*, **38**, 241–7.

See also: Hicks–Hansen model, Keynes's demand for money.

Bayes's theorem

This theorem takes its name from the reverend Thomas Bayes (1702–61), a British priest interested in mathematics and astronomy. His theorem, published after his death, applies in the following situation. We have an experiment, its possible outcomes being the events $B, C, D, E \ldots$ For instance, we observe the output of a production process and consider three events: the product is of high quality (B), medium quality (C) or low quality (D). The likelihood of these events depends on an unknown set of causes which we assume are exclusive and exhaustive; that is, one and only one of them must occur. Let A_i be the event whose true cause is the ith and suppose that we have n possible causes $A_1, \ldots, A_n$ which have probabilities $p(A_i)$ where $P(A_1) + \ldots + P(A_n) = 1$. These probabilities are called prior probabilities. For instance, the process could be operating under standard conditions (A_1) or be out of control, requiring some adjustments (A_2). We assume that we know the probabilities $p(B \mid A_i)$ which show the likelihood of the event B given the true cause A_i. For instance, we know the probabilities of obtaining as outcome a high/medium/low-quality product under the two possible causes: the process is operating under standard conditions or the process is out of control. Then we observe the outcome and assume the event B occurs. The theorem indicates how to compute the probabilities $p(A_i \mid B)$, which are called posterior probabilities, when the event B is observed. They are given by

$$p(A_i \mid B) = \frac{p(B \mid A_i)p(A_i)}{P(B)}.$$

Note that the denominator is the same for all the causes A_i and it can be computed by

$$P(B) = \sum_{j=1}^{n} p(B \mid A_j)p(A_j).$$

The theorem states that the posterior probabilities are proportional to the product of the prior probabilities, $p(A_i)$, and the likelihood of the observed event given the cause, $p(B \mid A_i)$.

This theorem is the main tool of the so-called 'Bayesian inference'. In this paradigm all the unknown quantities in an inference problem are random variables with some probability distribution and the inference about the variable of interest is made by using this theorem as follows. We have a model which describes the generation of the data by a density function, $f(x \mid \theta)$, which depends on an unknown parameter θ. The parameter is also a random variable, because it is unknown, and we have a prior distribution on the possible values of this parameter given by the prior density, $p(\theta)$. We observe a sample from this model, X, and want to estimate the parameter that has generated this sample. Then, by Bayes's theorem we have

$$f(\theta \mid X) \propto f(X \mid \theta)p(\theta),$$

which indicates that the posterior density of the parameter given the sample is proportional to the product of the likelihood of the sample and the prior density. The constant of proportionality, required in order that $f(\theta \mid X)$ is a density function and integrates to one, is $f(X)$, the density of the sample, and can be obtained with this condition.

The distribution $f(\theta \mid X)$ includes all the information that the sample can provide with respect to the parameter and can be used to solve all the usual inference problems. If we want a point estimate we can take the mode or the expected value of this distribution. If we want a confidence interval we can obtain it from this posterior distribution $f(\theta \mid X)$ by choosing an interval, which is called the 'credible interval', in which the parameter will be included with a given probability. If we want to test two particular values of the parameter, θ_1, θ_2 we compare the ordinates of both values in the posterior density of the parameter:

$$\frac{f(\theta_1 \mid X)}{f(\theta_2 \mid X)} = \frac{f(X \mid \theta_1)}{f(X \mid \theta_2)} \frac{p(\theta_1)}{p(\theta_2)}.$$

The ratio of the likelihood of the observed data under both parameter values is called the Bayes factor and this equation shows that the ratio of the posterior probabilities of both hypotheses is the product of the Bayes factor and the prior ratio.

The main advantage of Bayesian inference is its generality and conceptual simplicity, as all inference problems are solved by a simple application of the probability rules. Also it allows for the incorporation of prior information in the inference process. This is especially useful in decision making, and the most often used decision theory is based on Bayesian principles. The main drawback is the need to have prior probabilities. When the statistician has no prior information and/or she/he does not want to include her/his opinions in the inference process, a neutral or non-informative prior, sometimes also called a 'reference prior', is required. Although these priors are easy to build in simple problems there is not yet a general agreement as to how to define them in complicated multiparameter problems.

Bayesian inference has become very popular thanks to the recent advances in computation using Monte Carlo methods. These methods make it feasible to obtain samples from the posterior distribution in complicated problems in which an exact expression for this distribution cannot be obtained.

DANIEL PEÑA

Bibliography

Bayes, T. (1763), 'An essay towards solving a problem in the doctrine of chances', *Philosophical Transactions of the Royal Society*, London, **53**, 370–418.

Bayesian–Nash equilibrium

Any Nash equilibrium of the imperfect information representation, or Bayesian game, of a normal-form game with incomplete information is a Bayesian–Nash equilibrium. In a game with incomplete information some or all of the players lack full information about the 'rules of the game' or, equivalently, about its normal form. Let Γ_k be an N-person decision problem with incomplete information, defined by a basic parameter space K; action sets $(A_i)_{i \in N}$ and utility functions u_i: $K \times A \to R$, where $A = \times_{i \in N} A_i$, and it is not indexed by $k \in K$. Problem Γ_k does not correspond to any standard game-theoretical model, since it does not describe the information of the players, or their strategies. $k \in K$ parameterizes the games that the individuals may play and is independent of the players' choices.

Given the parameter space K, we would need to consider not only a player's beliefs over K but also over the other players' beliefs over K, over the other players' beliefs over his own beliefs and so on, which would generate an infinite hierarchy of beliefs. Harsanyi (1967–8) has shown that all this is unnecessary and Γ_k can be transformed into a game with imperfect information Γ_B. In this approach, all the knowledge (or private information) of each player i about all the *independent* variables of Γ_k is summarized by his *type* t_i belonging to a finite set T_i and determined by the realization of a random variable. Nature makes the first move, choosing realizations $t = (t_1, t_2, \ldots, t_N)$ of the random variables according to a marginal distribution P over $T = T_1 \times \ldots \times T_N$ and t_i is secretly transmitted to player i. The joint probability distribution of the t_is, given by $P(t)$, is assumed to be common knowledge among the players.

Then $\Gamma_b = (N, (A_i)_{i \in N}, (T_i)_{i \in N}, P(t), (u_i)_{i \in N})$ denotes a finite Bayesian game with incomplete information. For any $t \in T$, $P(t_{-i} \mid t_i)$ is the probability that player i would assign to the event that $t_{-i} = (t_j)_{j \in N-i}$ is the profile of types for the players other than i if t_i were player i's type. For any $t \in T$ and any $a = (a_j)_{j \in N} \in A$, $u_i(a,t)$ denotes the payoff that player i would get if a were the profile of actions chosen by the players and t were the profile of their actual types.

A pure strategy of player i in Γ_b is a mapping s_i: $T_i \to A_i$, or *decision rule*, $s_i(t_i)$, that gives the player's strategy choice for each realization of his type t_i, and player *i's expected* payoff is

$$\upsilon_i(s_1(t_1), s_2(t_2), \ldots, s_N(t_N))$$
$$= E_t[u_i(s_1(t_1), s_2(t_2), \ldots, s_N(t_N), t_i)].$$

Thus, a profile of decision rules $(s_1(.), \ldots, s_N(.))$ is a Bayesian–Nash equilibrium in Γ_b, if and only if, for all i and all $\bar{t}_i \in T_i$, occurring with positive probability

$$E_{t_{-i}} \mid u_i(s_i(\bar{t}_i), s_{-i}(t_{-i}), \bar{t}_i \mid \bar{t}_i) \mid$$
$$E_{t_{-i}} \mid u_i(s'_i(\bar{t}_i), s_{-i}(t_{-i}), \bar{t}_i \mid \bar{t}_i) \mid$$

for all s'_i, where the expectation is taken over realizations of the other players' random variables conditional on player i's realization of his signal $\bar{t}_i$.

Mertens and Zamir (1985) provided the mathematical foundations of Harsanyi's transformation: a universal beliefs space could be constructed that is always big enough to serve the whole set of types for each player. Then player i's type can be viewed as a belief over the basic parameter and the other players' types.

AMPARO URBANO SALVADOR

Bibliography

Harsanyi, J. (1967–8), 'Games with incomplete information played by Bayesian players', *Management Science*, **14**, 159–82 (Part I); 320–34 (Part II); 486–502 (Part III).

Mertens, J-F. and S. Zamir (1985), 'Formulation of Bayesian analysis for games with incomplete information', *International Journal of Game Theory*, **14**, 1–29.

Becher's principle

One person's expenditure is another person's income. Johann Joachim Becher (1635–82), in common with the majority of his European contemporaries, shared a certain 'fear of goods' and, therefore, like the English mercantilists, he subscribed to the idea that 'it is always better to sell goods to others than to buy goods from others, for the former brings a certain advantage and the latter inevitable damage'. Within the context of his reflections upon monetary affairs, he maintained that people's expenditure on consumption is the 'soul' of economic life; that is, 'one's expenditure is another man's income; or that consumer expenditure generates income'. He weighs up the theoretical possibilities of this observation, but does not develop a system based on this, as Boisguillebert, François Quesnay or John Maynard Keynes were later to do. Becher, one of the most representative cameralists, was a physician and chemist who became adviser to Emperor Leopold I of Austria and director of several state-owned enterprises. He defends interventionist measures by the state to make a country rich and populous, as the title of his main work of 1668 indicates: *Political Discourse – On the actual reasons determining the growth and decline of cities, states, and republics. How to make a state populous and productive and to make it into a real Civil Society.*

LUIS PERDICES DE BLAS

Bibliography

Becher, Johann Joachim (1668), *Politischre Discurs von den eigentlichen Ursachen dess Auff- und Abnehmens der Städt, Länder, und Republicken, in specie, wie ein Land folckreich und nahrhafft zu machen und in eine rechte Societatem civilem zu bringen*; reprinted (1990) in *Bibliothek Klassiker der Nationalökonomie*, Düsseldorf: Verlag Wirtschaft und Finanzen.

Schumpeter, Joseph A. (1954), *History of Economic Analysis*, New York: Oxford University Press.

Becker's time allocation model

Gary Becker's (b.1930, Nobel Prize 1992) approach to consumption theory represents an important departure from conventional theory. The distinguishing feature of Becker's time allocation or household production model is the recognition that consuming market goods takes time. This implies both that market goods are not direct arguments of household utility functions, and that time not spent in the labor market is not leisure any longer in Becker's model.

The new approach introduces a new category of goods, *basic goods*, as the only utility-yielding goods. Basic goods are goods not purchased or sold in the market place. They are instead produced by consumers (for a given state of household technology), using market purchased goods and time (nonworking time) as factor inputs. Now households derive utility from market goods only in an indirect way. Households, then, must make two kinds of decisions: how to produce at the minimum cost and how to consume at the maximum utility level.

Basic goods also exhibit another characteristic. They have no explicit prices, since there are no explicit markets for them. This fact, however, represents no impediment to the development of an operative theory of household behavior, as shadow prices (that is, prices based on home production costs) can always be assigned to basic goods. Unlike market prices, shadow prices reflect the full or effective price of goods. Full prices depend on the price of time, the time and market goods intensities, the price of market goods and the state of household technology. This brings us to a striking conclusion. Two different consumers do not pay (in general) the same price for the same good even if the market under consideration is perfectly competitive.

Regarding time, the crucial variable in Becker's model, the fact that it is an input in total fixed supply used now in both market activities (labor market) and non-market (home) activities has two immediate implications. The first one is that 'time is money'; that is, it has a positive price (an explicit price in market activities and a shadow price, approximated by the market wage rate, in non-market activities) that has to be taken into account when analyzing household behavior. The second is that time not spent working in the labor market is not leisure, but time spent in producing basic goods. These considerations together led Becker to define a new scale variable in the utility maximization problem that households are supposed to solve. It is now 'full income' (that is, the maximum money income a household can achieve when devoting all the time and other resources to earning income) that is the relevant scale variable that limits household choices.

Becker's approach to the study of household behavior implies, then, the maximization of a utility function whose arguments are the quantities of basic goods produced through a well behaved production function whose inputs are the quantities of market goods and the time needed for producing the basic goods. The household faces the conventional budget constraint and also a new time constraint which shows how full income is spent, partly on goods and partly by forgoing earnings to use time in household production.

A number of interesting conclusions can be derived from the comparative statics of Becker's model. A central one concerns the effects of a rise in wages. In the general case of variable proportions technology, unlike conventional theory, an increase in the wage rate now leads to two types of substitution effects. The first one is the conventional substitution effect away from time spent on non-market activities (leisure in the old fashioned theory). This effect leads households to replace time with goods in the production of each basic good. The second type is the new substitution effect created by the changes in the relative full prices (or relative marginal costs) of non-market activities that the increase in the wage rate induces. A rise in the wage rate increases the relative full price of more time-intensive goods and this leads to a substitution effect that moves households away from high to low time-intensive activities. This new effect changes the optimal composition of household production. The two substitution effects reinforce each other, leading to a decline in the total time spent consuming and an increase in the time spent working in the labor market.

It is also of interest to note how the model enables us to evaluate the effects from shocks or differences in environmental variables (age, education, climate and so on). In traditional theory the effects of these variables were reflected in consumers' preferences; in Becker's theory, however, changes in these variables affect households' production functions that cause, in turn, changes in household behavior through income and substitution effects.

Becker's model points out that the relevant measure of global production of an economy is far from being the one estimated by national accounting standards. This model has had applications in areas such as labor supply, the sexual division of labor, income taxation, household technology and the computation of income elasticities. The new consumption theory can explain a great number of everyday facts: for example, why rich people tend to prefer goods low in time-intensity or why women, rather than men, tend to go to the supermarket. Thanks to Becker's work these and other ordinary aspects of households' behavior, attributed to exogenous factors in conventional theory (usually differences in tastes or shifts in preferences), can now be endogenized and related to differences in prices and incomes.

RAMÓN FEBRERO

Bibliography

Becker, G.S. (1965). 'A theory of the allocation of time', *Economic Journal*, **75**, 493–517.

Febrero, R. and P. Schwartz (eds) (1995), *The Essence of Becker*, Stanford, California: Hoover Institution Press.

Bellman's principle of optimality and equations

Richard Bellman (1920–84) received his BA from Brooklyn College in 1941, his MA in mathematics from the University of Wisconsin in 1943 and his PhD from Princeton University in 1946. In 1952 he joined the newly established Rand Corporation in Santa Monica, California, where he became interested in multi-stage decision processes; this led him to the formulation of the principle of optimality and dynamic programming in 1953.

Dynamic programming is an approach developed by Richard Bellman to solve sequential or multi-stage decision problems. This approach is equally applicable for decision problems where sequential property is induced solely for computational convenience. Basically, what the dynamic programming approach does is to solve a multi-variable problem by solving a series of single variable problems.

The essence of dynamic programming is Bellman's principle of optimality. This principle, even without rigorously defining the terms, is intuitive: an optimal policy has the property that whatever the initial state and the initial decisions are, the remaining decisions must constitute an optimal policy with regard to the state resulting from the first decision.

Let us consider the following optimal control problem in discrete time

$$\max_{\{u(k)\}_{k=0}^{N-1}} J = \sum_{k=0}^{N-1} F[x(k), u(k), k] + S[x(N)],$$

subject to $x(k+1) = f[x(k), u(k), k]$, for $k = 0, 1 \ldots, N-1$, with $u(k) \in \Omega(k)$, $x(0) = x_0$.

This problem can be solved by dynamic programming, which proceeds backwards in time from period $N-1$ to period 0: $J_N^*\{x(N)\} = S[x(N)]$, and for each $k \in \{N-1, N-2, \ldots, 1, 0\}$,

$$J^*\{x(k)\} = \max_{u(k)\in\Omega(k)} \{F[x(k), u(k), k] + J_{k+1}^*\{f[x(k), u(k), k]\}\},$$

which are the Bellman's equations for the given problem.

EMILIO CERDÁ

Bibliography

Bellman, R. (1957), *Dynamic Programming*, Princeton, NJ: Princeton University Press.
Bellman, R. and S. Dreyfus (1962), *Applied Dynamic Programming*, Princeton, NJ: Princeton University Press.
Bellman, R. (1984), *Eye of the Hurricane. An Autobiography*, River Edge, NJ: World Scientific Publishing Co.

Bergson's social indifference curve

Let X denote the set of all feasible economic social states that a society may have. An element x of X will be a complete description either of all goods and services that each consumer agent of the economy $i = 1, 2, 3, \ldots N$ may obtain or, in general, how the resources of the economy are allocated. Each consumer of the economy may have a utility function $u(i)$: $X \to R$, where R stands for the real numbers. Consider the following social welfare function G that assigns to each array of utility functions a social utility function W: $X \to R$; that is $F = G\ (u(i), i = 1, 2, 3, \ldots, N)$. The function W will represent the preferences that the society may have on the social states. A social indifference curve will be the set of all x in X such that $W(x) = c$ for some real number c in R, that is, the set of all consumption allocations with respect to which the society will be indifferent. American economist Abram Bergson (1914–2003) was the first to propose the use of social welfare functions as a device to obtain social utility functions in order to solve the problem of how to choose among the different and infinite number of Pareto efficient allocations that the economy may face. To do that, Bergson assumes that a social welfare function is the result of certain value judgments that the economist may explicitly introduce in the analysis of the resource allocation problem. Adopting Bergson's point of view, the economist may choose a particular social state from those with respect to which the society may be indifferent.

However, Arrow (1951) shows that, if individual preferences, represented by utility functions, are ordinal and we assume that they are non-comparable, under certain very reasonable assumptions there is no social welfare function, and so no social utility function can be used to solve Bergson's problem. Nevertheless, if the utility functions of the agents are cardinal and we allow for interpersonal comparisons of utilities, we may have well defined social utility functions. Examples of those functions are the Rawlsian social welfare functions $W = \min(u(i), i = 1, 2, 3, \ldots N)$ and the utilitarian social welfare function, $W = \Sigma u(i)$.

ANTONIO MANRESA

Bibliography

Arrow, K.J. (1951), *Social Choice and Individual Values*, New York: John Wiley.

Bergson, A. (1938), 'A reformulation of certain aspects of welfare economics', *Quarterly Journal of Economics*, **52** (2), 310–34.

See also: Arrow's impossibility theorem.

Bernoulli's paradox

Is it reasonable to be willing to pay for participating in a game less than the expected gain? Consider the following game, known as the St Petersburg paradox: Paul will pay to George €1 if head appears the first time a coin is tossed, €2 if the first time that head appears is the second time the coin is tossed, and so forth. More generally, George will receive €2^{n-1} with probability $(1/2)^{n-1}$ if head appears for the first time at the *n*th toss. The expected gain (that is the mathematical expectation) of the game is the following:

$$E(x) = \frac{1}{2}1 + \frac{1}{4}2 + \ldots$$

Therefore the expected gain for George is infinity. Paradoxically, George, or any other reasonable person, would not pay a large finite amount for joining Paul's game.

One way to escape from the paradox was advanced by Swiss mathematician Daniel Bernoulli (1700–1783) in 1738, although Cramer, in 1728, reached a similar solution. Imagine that George, instead of being concerned about the amount of money, is more interested in the *utility* that money produces for him. Suppose that the utility obtained is the square root of the amount received. In that case, the expected utility of the game would be:

$$E(x) = \frac{1}{2}\sqrt{1} + \frac{1}{4}\sqrt{2} + \ldots = 1 + \frac{\sqrt{2}}{2} \cong 1.71,$$

which, in terms of money, is approximately €2.91. Therefore nobody as reasonable as George, and with the aforementioned utility function, would be prepared to pay more than, say, €3 for entering the game.

In fact, the solution proposed by Bernoulli was a logarithmic utility function and, strictly speaking, it did not solve the paradox. However, his contribution is the key founding stone for the expected utility theory in the sense that individuals maximize expected utility instead of expected value.

JESÚS SAURINA SALAS

Bibliography
Bernoulli, D. (1738), *Specimen theoriae novae de mesura sortis*, English trans. 1954, *Econometrica*, **22**, 23–36.

See also: von Neumann-Morgenstern expected utility theorem.

Berry–Levinsohn–Pakes algorithm (BLP)

This is an iterative routine to estimate the parameters of a model of demand and supply for differentiated products. We have 'too many parameters' when estimating demand for differentiated products. Quantity demanded of each product is decreasing in a firm's own price, and increasing in the price of its rivals. A system of N goods gives N^2 parameters to estimate. Berry (1994) put some structure on the demand problem by making assumptions on consumer utility and the nature of competition to reduce the number of parameters to estimate. Utility of a given consumer for a given product is assumed to depend only on the interaction between consumer attributes and product characteristics, on random consumer 'tastes' and on a small set of parameters to be estimated. This generalizes the multinomial logit model to derive demand systems with plausible substitution patterns (Anderson *et al.* 1992). Firms are assumed to be price setters. The price vector in a Nash pure-strategy interior market equilibrium is a function of marginal costs plus mark-ups. Mark-ups depend on price semi-elasticities, which in turn are functions of the parameters of the demand system.

BLP algorithm estimates jointly the parameters of the nonlinear simultaneous demand and pricing equations. It aggregates by simulation, as suggested by Pakes (1986), individual consumer choices for fitting the estimated market shares and prices to those actually observed using the generalized method of moments. The algorithm estimates the whole distribution of consumer preferences for product characteristics from widely available product-level choice probabilities, price data and aggregate consumer-level data.

JOAN-RAMON BORRELL

Bibliography
Anderson, S., A. de Palma and J. Thisse (1992), *Discrete Choice Theory of Product Differentiation*, Cambridge, MA: MIT Press.
Berry, S.T. (1994), 'Estimating discrete-choice models of product differentiation', *RAND Journal of Economics*, **25** (2), 242–62.
Berry, S.T., J. Levinsohn and A. Pakes (1995), 'Automobile prices in market equilibrium', *Econometrica*, **63** (4), 841–90.
Pakes, A. (1986), 'Patents as options: some estimates of the value of holding European patent stocks', *Econometrica*, **54**, 755–84.

Bertrand competition model

Two classical assumptions are made on the interaction among competitors in oligopolistic markets. If firms choose prices, they are said to compete '*à la* Bertrand'. If instead they choose quantities, they compete '*à la* Cournot'. The reason for this terminology is the work of Cournot, that deals with quantities as strategic variables, and Bertrand's (1883) sanguine review of Cournot's book emphasizing that firms choose prices rather than quantities.

As a matter of fact, the attribution to Bertrand of the price competition among oligopolists is not without controversy (see for example, Magnan de Bornier, 1992). Cournot's book also deals with price competition, but in such a way that it is essentially equivalent to choosing quantities. That is, the model proposed for price competition assumes that each firm takes the quantity produced by the competitors as given. Because the firm is a monopolist over the residual demand – understood as the demand that the firm faces once the competitors have sold – both price and quantity lead to the same outcome.

The contribution of French mathematician Joseph Louis François Bertrand (1822–1900) arises from the criticism of Cournot's assumption that firms choose prices in response to the quantities decided by competitors. Instead, if the good is homogeneous and all firms post a price that represents a commitment to serve any quantity at that price, all consumers should purchase from the firm with the lowest price. Therefore the residual demand curve that each firm faces is discontinuous: it is zero if the firm does not have the lowest price and it corresponds to the total demand otherwise. The results of this assumption are rather striking. Two firms are enough to obtain the competitive outcome if marginal costs are constant and the same for both of them. The reason is that, given any price of the competitors, each firm has incentives to undercut the others in order to take all the market. A successive application of this argument means that the only stable price is marginal cost. Moreover, if firms have fixed costs of production, the previous result also means that only one firm can produce in this market.

If firms differ in marginal costs, but this difference is not too great, the equilibrium price corresponds to the second-lowest marginal cost, meaning that the most efficient firm supplies to the whole market and makes profits corresponding to the cost differential. As a result, when goods are homogeneous, profits under Bertrand competition are substantially lower than when firms compete in quantities.

Edgeworth pointed out that in the short run the commitment to supply unlimited quantities is unlikely to be met. For sufficiently high levels of production, firms might face increasing costs and eventually reach a capacity constraint. Under these conditions, Edgeworth also argued that a pure strategy equilibrium might fail to exist. The following example illustrates this point.

Consider a market with two firms, with marginal cost equal to 0 and a production capacity of, at most, two units. The demand corresponds to four consumers, with valuations of €3, €2, €1 and €0. In this case, both firms will sell up to capacity only if they charge a price of €0, but this price can never be profit-maximizing, since one of them could raise the price to €1 and sell one unit, with positive profits. If instead firms charge positive prices, undercutting by one of them always becomes the optimal strategy.

Models of horizontal differentiation or vertical differentiation, where firms vary the production of a good of various qualities, have extended the term 'Bertrand competition' to differentiated products. In this case, the price–cost margin increases when the products become worse substitutes.

Collusion as a result of the repeated interaction among firms has also been used to relax the results of the Bertrand model. If firms care enough about future profits, they might be interested in not undercutting their rivals if this can lead to a price war and future prices close to marginal cost.

In the case of both homogeneous and heterogeneous goods, the optimal price that a firm charges is increasing in the price chosen by competitors as opposed to the case of competition '*à la* Cournot', where the quantity produced by each firm responds negatively to the quantity chosen by competitors. For this reason, Bertrand competition is also used as an example of the so-called 'strategic complements' while quantity competition is an example of strategic substitutes.

GERARD LLOBET

Bibliography

Bertrand, Joseph (1883), 'Théorie Mathématique de la Richesse Sociale', *Journal des Savants*, **67**, 499–508.

Magnan de Bornier, Jean (1992), 'The Cournot–Bertrand debate: a historical perspective', *History of Political Economy*, **24**, 623–44.

See also: Cournot's oligopoly model, Edgeworth oligopoly model, Hotelling's model of spatial competition.

Beveridge–Nelson decomposition

In the univariate time series analysis, the trend component is the factor that has a permanent effect on the series. The trend may be deterministic when it is completely predictable, and/or stochastic when it shows an unpredictable systematic variation. According to many economic theories, it is important to distinguish between the permanent and the irregular (transitory) movements of the series. If the trend is deterministic, this decomposition is no problem. However, when the trend is stochastic, difficulties may arise because it may be mistaken for an irregular component.

Let us consider the ARIMA (0,1,1) model:

$$Y_t = \alpha + Y_{t-1} + \varepsilon_t + \beta\varepsilon_{t-1}. \qquad (1)$$

Starting from $Y_0 = \varepsilon_0 = 0$ iteration leads to

$$Y_t = \alpha t + (1 + \beta) + \sum_{i=1}^{t} \varepsilon_i + \beta\sum_{j=1}^{t-1}\varepsilon_j$$

or

$$Y_t = \alpha t + (1 + \beta) \sum_{i=1}^{t} \varepsilon_i - \beta\varepsilon_t \qquad (2)$$

In [2] αt is the deterministic trend (DT_t);

$$(1 + \beta)\sum_{i=1}^{t} \varepsilon_i$$

is the stochastic trend (ST_t); $\beta\varepsilon_t$ is the irregular component (C_t). Thus $Y_t = DT_t + ST_t + C_t$, or $Y_t = DT_t + Z_t$, Z_t being the noise function of the series.

On the other hand, $DT_t + ST_t$ is the permanent component and it is possible to prove that this component is a random walk plus drift, so that, if the permanent component is called Y^P:

$$Y^P = \alpha + Y_{t-1} + (1 + \beta)\varepsilon_t$$

This result may be extended to any ARIMA (*p*,1,*q*).

Beveridge and Nelson (1981) show that any ARIMA (*p*,1,*q*) may be represented as a stochastic trend plus a stationary component; that is, a permanent component and an irregular one.

Let us consider the noise function *Z* that follows an ARIMA (*p*,1,*q*) process, that is:

$$A(L)\, Z_t = B(L)\, \varepsilon_t \qquad (3)$$

where $A(L)$ and $B(L)$ are polynomials in the lag operator L of order p and q, respectively and ε_t a sequence of variables of white noise.

Let us suppose that $A(L)$ has a unit root. $A(L) = (1 - L)\, A^*(L)$ with $A^*(L)$ with roots outside the unit circle.

$$\begin{aligned}(1 - L)\, A^*(L)\, Z_t &= A^*(L)\Delta Z_t = B(L)\varepsilon_t\\ \Delta Z_t &= A^*(L)^{-1}B(L)\varepsilon_t\\ &= \psi(L)\varepsilon_\tau\\ &= \{\psi(1) + (1 - L)\,(1 - L)^{-1}\\ &\quad [\psi(L) - \psi(1)]\}\varepsilon_t\\ &= [\psi(1) + (1 - L)\psi^*(L)]\varepsilon_t,\end{aligned}$$

$$\text{where } \psi^*(L) = (1 - L)^{-1}[\psi(L) - \psi(1)]. \qquad (4)$$

Applying operator $(1 - L)$ to both sides of (4), we have

$$Z_t = \psi(1)\sum_{i=1}^{t}\varepsilon_i + \psi^*(L)\varepsilon_t = ST_t + C_t,$$

that allows the decomposition of the noise function into a stochastic trend component (permanent) and an irregular component (transitory).

J.B. PENA TRAPERO

Bibliography

Beveridge, S. and C.R. Nelson (1981), 'A new approach to decomposition of economic time series into permanent and transitory components with particular attention to measurement of the business cycle', *Journal of Monetary Economics*, **7**, 151–74.

Black–Scholes model

Fischer Black (1938–1995) and Myron Scholes (b.1941) asked themselves how to determine the fair price of a financial derivative as, for example, an option on common stock. They began working together at MIT in the late 1960s. Black was a mathematical physicist, recently graduated with a PhD degree from Harvard, and Scholes obtained his doctorate in finance from the University of Chicago. Robert Merton, a teaching assistant in economics with a science degree in mathematical engineering at New York's Columbia University, joined them in 1970. The three of them, young researchers, approached the problem using highly advanced mathematics. The mathematical approach, however, should not be surprising. In the seventeenth century, Pascal and Fermat had shown how to determine the fair price of a bet on some future event.

However, the idea of using mathematics to price derivatives was so revolutionary that Black and Scholes had problems publishing their formula, written in a working paper in 1970. Many senior researchers thought that options trading was just beyond mathematics and the paper was rejected in some journals without being refereed. Finally their work was published in the *Journal of Political Economy* in 1973.

Merton was also very much involved in that research and he published his own extensions to the formula in the same year. Not only did the formula work, the market changed after its publication. Since the beginning of trading at the Chicago Board Options Exchange (CBOE) in 1973, and in the first 20 years of operations, the volume of options traded each day increased from less than 1000 to a million dollars. Six months after the original publication of the Black–Scholes formula, Texas Instruments designed a handheld calculator to produce Black–Scholes option prices and hedge ratios, to be used by CBOE traders. No wonder that the Black–Scholes formula became a Nobel formula. On 14 October 1997, the Royal Swedish Academy of Sciences announced the winners of the 1997 Nobel Prize in Economics. The winners were Robert C. Merton and Myron S. Scholes. Fischer Black had died in 1995.

To understand the Black–Scholes formula, consider a call option of European type. This is a contract between a holder and a writer, which has three fixed clauses: an asset to be purchased, a maturity date T and an exercise price K. The call option gives the holder the right, but not the obligation, to purchase the asset at time T for the exercise price K. The Black–Scholes formula computes the price of such a contract. Conceptually, the formula is simple and it can be read as the discounted expected benefit from acquiring the underlying asset minus the expected cost of exercising the option. To derive the mathematical formula, some assumptions must be made. The key assumption is that the market does not allow for arbitrage strategies, but also that the market is frictionless, the interest rate r remains constant and known, and that the returns on the underlying stock are normally distributed with constant volatility σ. In the Black–Scholes context, the fair price C for an European option at time t is computed as $C = SN(d_1) - Ke^{-r(T-t)}N(d_2)$, where S denotes the current stock price, N is the cumulative standard normal distribution,

$$d_1 = \frac{ln(S/K) + (r + \sigma^2/2)(T - t)}{\sigma\sqrt{T - t}}$$

and $d_2 = d_1 - \sigma\sqrt{t}$.

Technically, this formula arises as the solution to a differential equation, known in physics as the heat equation. This equation is obtained using either an equilibrium model with preferences showing constant relative risk aversion or a hedging argument, as suggested by Merton. Some general remarks can be stated. The option price is always higher than the differential between the current price of the underlying and the present value of the exercise price. The difference gives the price paid for the possibility of a higher stock price at expiration. On the other hand, and this turned out to be very important, the formula can be read in terms of expectations with respect to a so-called 'risk-neutral probability' that reflects not only the probability of a particular state of the world, but also the utility derived from receiving additional money at that state. Interestingly enough, the Black–Scholes formula calculates all these adjustments mathematically. Moreover, as seen from the formula, the standard deviation of the returns is an unknown parameter. If the Black–Scholes model is correct, this parameter is a constant and it can be implicitly derived from market data, being therefore a forward-looking estimate. However, it is also true that the underlying distribution imposed by the assumptions used by the model changes very rapidly during the trading process. This may be the main difficulty associated with the success (or lack of success) that the formula has these days.

EVA FERREIRA

Bibliography

Black, F. and M. Scholes (1973), 'The pricing of options and corporate liabilities', *Journal of Political Economy*, **81** (3), 637–59.

Merton, R.C. (1973), 'Theory of rational option pricing', *Bell Journal of Economics and Management Science*, **4** (1), 141–83.

Bonferroni bound

When constructing a confidence interval I_1 of an estimator β_1 with Type I error α (say, 5 per cent), the confidence coefficient of $1 - \alpha$ (say, 95 per cent) implies that the true value of the parameter will be missed in α per cent of the cases.

If we were to construct confidence intervals for m parameters simultaneously then the confidence coefficient will only be $(1 - \alpha)^m$ if and only if each of the confidence intervals was constructed from an independent sample. This is not the case when the same sample is used to test a joint hypothesis on a set of parameters in, say, a regression model.

The Bonferroni approach, named after the Italian mathematician Emilio Bonferroni (1892–1960), establishes a useful inequality which gives rise to a lower bound of the true significance level of the m tests performed on a given sample of observations. For illustrative purposes, consider the case where $m = 2$, so that I_1 is the confidence interval of β_1 with confidence coefficient $1 - \alpha_1$ whereas I_2 is the confidence interval of β_2 with confidence coefficient $1 - \alpha_2$. Then the inequality says that:

$$P\,[\beta_1 \in I_1\,, \beta_2 \in I_2] \geq 1 - \alpha_1 - \alpha_2.$$

This amounts to a rectangular confidence region for the two parameters jointly with a confidence coefficient at least equal to $1 - \alpha_1 - \alpha_2$. Hence, if $\alpha_1 = \alpha_2 = 0.05$, the Bonferroni bound implies that the rectangular confidence region in the β_1, β_2 plane has a confidence coefficient ≥ 0.9.

Under certain assumptions, in the test of q hypothesis in the standard linear regression model with $k \geq q$ coefficients, the well known $F(q, T - k)$ test yields ellipsoidal confidence regions with an exact confidence coefficient of $(1 - \alpha)$.

A classical reference on the construction of simultaneous confidence intervals is Tukey (1949).

JUAN J. DOLADO

Bibliography

Tukey, J.W. (1949), 'Comparing individual means in the analysis of variance', *Biometrics*, **5**, 99–114.

Boolean algebras

The English mathematician George Boole (1815–64) has been considered the founder of mathematical logic. He approached logic from an algebraic point of view and he introduced a new algebraic structure, called Boolean algebra, that can be applied to several frameworks.

A Boolean algebra is a 6tuple $\langle B, \vee, \wedge, ', 0, 1\rangle$, where B is a non-empty set, $\vee, \wedge$ two binary operations on B (that is, $x \vee y, x \wedge y \in B$ for all $x, y \in B$), $'$ one unary operation on B (that is, $x' \in B$ for all $x \in B$) and $0, 1 \in B$, which satisfies:

1. $x \vee y = y \vee x$ and $x \wedge y = y \wedge x$, for all $x, y \in B$ (commutativity).
2. $x \vee (y \vee z) = (x \vee y) \vee z$ and $x \wedge (y \wedge z) = (x \wedge y) \wedge z$, for all $x, y, z \in B$ (associativity).
3. $x \vee x = x$ and $x \wedge x = x$, for all $x \in B$ (idempotency).
4. $x \vee (x \wedge y) = x$ and $x \wedge (x \vee y) = x$, for all $x, y \in B$ (absortion).
5. $x \wedge (y \vee z) = (x \wedge y) \vee (x \wedge z)$ and $x \vee (y \wedge z) = (x \vee y) \wedge (x \vee z)$, for all $x, y, z \in B$ (distributivity).
6. $x \wedge 0 = 0$ and $x \vee 1 = 1$, for all $x \in B$.
7. $x \wedge x' = 0$ and $x \vee x' = 1$, for all $x \in B$.
   From the definition it follows:
8. $x \wedge y = 0$ and $x \vee y = 1$ imply $x = y'$, for all $x, y \in B$.
9. $(x')' = x$, for all $x \in B$.
10. $(x \vee y)' = x' \wedge y'$ and $(x \wedge y)' = x' \vee y'$, for all $x, y \in B$ (De Morgan's laws).

Typical examples of Boolean algebras are:

- B the class of all the subsets of a nonempty set X; $\vee$ the union, $\cup$; $\wedge$ the intersection, $\cap$; $'$ the complementation, ^{c} (that is, $A^c = \{x \in X \mid x \notin A\}$, for all $A \subseteq X$); 0 the empty set, $\varnothing$ and 1 the total set, X.
- B the class of propositions of the classical propositional logic; $\vee$ the disjunction; $\wedge$ the conjuction; $'$ the negation, $\neg$; 0 the contradiction $p \wedge \neg p$; and 1 the tautology $p \vee \neg p$.
- $B = \{0, 1\}$; $0 \vee 0 = 0$, $0 \vee 1 = 1 \vee 0 = 1 \vee 1 = 1$; $0 \wedge 0 = 0 \wedge 1 = 1 \wedge 0 = 0$, $1 \wedge 1 = 1$; $0' = 1$, $1' = 0$.

JOSÉ LUIS GARCÍA LAPRESTA

Bibliography

Boole, G. (1847), *The Mathematical Analysis of Logic. Being an Essay Towards a Calculus of Deductive Reasoning*, Cambridge: Macmillan.

Boole, G. (1854), *An Investigation of the Laws of Thought, on which are Founded the Mathematical Theories of Logic and Probabilities*, Cambridge: Macmillan.

Borda's rule

This originates in the criticism Jean-Charles de Borda (1733–99) makes about the general opinion according to which plural voting, that is, the election of the candidates preferred by the greater number of voters, reflects the voters' wishes. According to Borda, given more than two candidates (or choices), plural voting could result in errors, inasmuch as candidates with similar positions could divide the vote, allowing a third candidate to receive the greatest number of votes and to win the election. History seems to confirm Borda's concern.

One example may help us to understand this rule. Let us assume 21 voters and three candidates X, Y and Z; seven voters opt for XZY, seven for YZX, six for ZYX and one for XYZ. Plural voting would select X with eight votes, against Y with seven and Z with six, who although receiving fewer votes seems a good compromise solution (those with a preference for X, except 1, prefer Z to Y, and those with a preference for Y prefer, all of them, Z to X).

In order to solve this problem, Borda proposed the election by 'merit order' consisting in that each voter ranks the n-candidates in order, giving n-1 points to the preferred one, n-2 to the second, n-3 to the third, and so on (Borda's count). Once all the points of each candidate are added, Borda's rule ranks the choices from highest to lowest following Borda's count. In the above example, the order would be ZYX (Z 26 points, Y with 21 and X 16), the opposite result to the one obtained from plural voting (XYZ).

The Achilles heel of Borda's rule is, as Condorcet had already put forward, its vulnerability to strategic behaviour. In other words, electors can modify the result of the voting, to their own advantage, by lying over their preference.

Borda admitted this and stated that 'My scheme is only intended for honest men.' In modern theory of social election, starting with Arrow's work, Borda's rule does not comply with the 'independence of irrelevant alternatives' property, which makes this voting subject to manipulation.

FRANCISCO PEDRAJA CHAPARRO

Bibliography

Borda, J-Ch. (1781), 'Mémoire sur les elections au scrutin', *Histoire de l'Académie Royale des Sciences* (1784).

See also: Arrow's impossibility theorem, Condorcet's criterion.

Bowley's law

Income is distributed in a relatively constant share between labour and capital resources. The allocation of factors reflects the maximization of the company's profits subject to the cost function, which leads to selection of their relative amounts based on the relative remuneration of the factors and on the technical progress. If production were more labour (capital)-intensive, the company would hire more workers (capital) for a fixed wage and interest rate, which would lead to an increase in the labour (capital) share. However, what has been observed in several countries through the twentieth century is that this share has been relatively constant in the medium term, in spite of some temporary factors, such as taxation or the cyclical position.

Sir Arthur L. Bowley (1869–1957) registered the constancy of factor shares in his studies for the United Kingdom in the early twentieth century, but many others have accounted later for this face in the economic literature. No doubt technological progress has been present in production processes, leading to an increase in the ratio of capital to labour, but this has been counteracted by the increase in real wages (labour productivity) in comparison with the cost of capital. Proving that the national income is proportionally distributed gives grounds for the acceptance of Cobb–Douglas functions to represent production processes in a macroeconomic sense.

DAVID MARTÍNEZ TURÉGANO

Bibliography

Bowley, A.L. (1920), 'The change in the distribution of the national income: 1880–1913', in *Three Studies on the National Income*, Series of Reprints of Scarce Tracts in Economic and Political Science, The London School of Economics and Political Science (1938).

See also: Cobb–Douglas function.

Box–Cox transformation

The classical linear model (CLM) is specified whenever possible in order to simplify statistical analysis. The Box–Cox (1964) transformation was a significant contribution to finding the required transformation(s) to approximate a model to the requirements of the CLM.

The most used transformation for a variable $z_t > 0$; $t = 1, 2, \ldots, n$, is

$$z_t(\lambda) = \begin{cases} \dfrac{z_t^\lambda - 1}{\lambda} \ ; \lambda \neq 0 \\ \log(z_t) \ ; \lambda = 0, \end{cases} \qquad (1)$$

while for $z_t > -\lambda_2$ it is

$$z_t(\lambda_1, \lambda_2) = \begin{cases} \dfrac{(z_t + \lambda_2)^{\lambda_1} - 1}{\lambda_1} & ; \lambda_1 \neq 0 \\ \log(z_t + \lambda_2) & ; \lambda_1 = 0; \end{cases} \quad (2)$$

therefore the linear model relating the transformed variables is

$$y_t(\lambda) = \beta_0 + \sum_{i=1}^{k} x_{i,t}(\lambda_i)\beta_i + \varepsilon_t. \quad (3)$$

This model is simplified when y_t is the only transformed variable, or when there is a single λ. The Box–Cox transformation is equivalent to the family of power transformations and includes (a) no transformation ($\lambda = 1$), (b) logarithmic ($\lambda = 0$), (c) inverse ($\lambda = -1$), and (d) root square ($\lambda = 0.5$).

The vector $\psi = [\lambda_1 \ldots \lambda_k; \beta_0 \ldots \beta_k; \sigma^2]$, cannot be jointly estimated by non-linear least squares since the residual sum of squares may be arbitrarily made close to zero for $\lambda \to -\infty$ and $\beta \to 0$. The usual solution is maximum likelihood, which prevents nonsensical estimates by introducing the Jacobian terms, but notice that the distributions of the residuals are truncated. For more general transformations, see John and Draper (1980) and Yeo and Johnson (2000).

JUAN DEL HOYO

Bibliography

Box, G.E.P. and D.R. Cox (1964), 'An analysis of transformations', *Journal of the Royal Statistical Society*, B, **26**, 211–43.

John, J.A. and N.R. Draper (1980), 'An alternative family of transformations', *Applied Statistics*, **29**, 190–97.

Yeo, In-Kwon and A. Johnson (2000), 'A new family of transformations to improve normality or symmetry', *Biometrika*, **87**, 954–9.

Box–Jenkins analysis

George E.P. Box (b.1919) and Gwilym M. Jenkins, in their book published in 1970, presented a methodology for building quantitative models, mainly for univariate time series data. The term 'Box–Jenkins methodology' generally refers to single time series.

The methodology proposes a class of models for explaining time series data and a procedure for building a suitable model for a specific time series. The class of models proposed is called ARIMA (autoregressive integrated moving average) models. When dealing with data with seasonal fluctuations, the class is restricted to ARIMA models with a multiplicative scheme.

ARIMA models are designed as relatively general linear structures representing time series with long-run evolution (evolution which tends to perpetuate itself in the future) and zero-mean stationary fluctuations around them. In the absence of future shocks, these stationary fluctuations tend towards zero. In many cases the long-run evolution in economic time series contains trend and seasonal fluctuations. In general, the trend contains one element, level, or two elements, level and growth. In the latter case, the ARIMA model for time series with no seasonal fluctuations takes the form

$$X_t = X_{t-1} + (X_{t-1} - X_{t-2}) + \frac{(1 - \theta_1 L - \ldots - \theta_q L^q)}{(1 - \phi_1 L - \ldots - \phi_p L^p)} a_t, \quad (1)$$

where L is the lag operator and a_t random shocks. The first term of the right-hand of (1) in the previous level of X_t, the second one the past growth of X_t, and the last one its stationary fluctuation level.

In an ARIMA model, the long-run evolution results from the fact that it translates into the future previous level and growth with unit coefficients. These coefficients refer to unit roots in the dynamic difference equation structure that these models have.

With the ARIMA models, Box–Jenkins (1970) synthesized the results of stationary theory and the most useful applied time series procedures known at the time. The theory had been developed over the previous 50 years by Cramer, Kinchin, Kolmogorov, Slutsky, Yule, Walker, Wold and others. The practical procedures had been elaborated in the fields of exponential smoothing forecasting methods by, for example, Brown, Harrison, Holt, Muth and Winter, and of seasonal adjustment at the US Census Bureau. In these two fields trend and seasonality were not considered to be deterministic but stochastic, and it became clear in most cases that the underlying structure was autoregressive with unit roots.

The unit root requirement in an ARIMA model is based on the assumption that, by differentiating the data, their long-run evolution is eliminated, obtaining a stationary transformation of the original time series. Thus from (1), $\Delta^2 X_t$, where $\Delta = (1 - L)$ is the first difference operator, is stationary and the model can be written in a more popular form as

$$(1 - \phi_1 L - \ldots - \phi_p L^p)\, \Delta^2 X_t = (1 - \theta_1 L - \ldots - \theta_q L^q)\, a_t. \qquad (2)$$

In this case differentiating X_t twice, we obtain stationary transformed data. A generalization of the example in (2), maintaining the absence of a constant term, consists of allowing the number of differences required to obtain the stationary transformation to be any integer number d. For d equals zero, the X_t variable itself is stationary. For d equals one, the trend in X_t has stochastic level but no growth. Usually d is no greater than two.

For the process of building an ARIMA model for a given time series, Box and Jenkins propose an iterative strategy with three stages: identification, estimation and diagnostic checking. If model inadequacy is detected in the last stage, appropriate modifications would appear and with them a further iterative cycle would be initiated.

Extensions of the ARIMA model allowing the parameter d to be a real number have been proposed with the fractionally integrated long-memory process. This process (see Granger, 2001) has an 'interesting theory but no useful practical examples in economics'.

Zellner and Palm (1974) and, later, other authors such as Wallis, connected the ARIMA models with econometric models by showing that, under certain assumptions, the ARIMA model is the final form derived for each endogenous variable in a dynamic simultaneous equation model. Therefore the use of an ARIMA model for a certain variable X_t is compatible with the fact that X_t is explained in a wider econometric model.

This connection shows the weakness and potential usefulness of ARIMA models in economics. The limitations come mainly from the fact that univariate models do not consider relationships between variables. Thus Granger (2001) says, 'univariate models are not thought of as relevant models for most important practical purposes in economics, although they are still much used as experimental vehicles to study new models and techniques'. ARIMA models in themselves turned out to be very successful in forecasting and in seasonal adjustment methods. The success in forecasting is (see Clements and Hendry, 1999) especially due to the presence of unit roots. In practice, agents want not only reliable forecasts, but also an explanation of the economic factors which support them. By their nature, ARIMA models are unable to provide this explanation. It requires the congruent econometric models advocated in Clements and Hendry, updating them each time a structural break appears. For the time being, the building of these models for general practice in periodical forecasting could in many cases be complex and costly.

ANTONI ESPASA

Bibliography
Box, G.E.P. and G.M. Jenkins (1970), *Time Series Analysis, Forecasting and Control*, San Francisco: Holden-Day.
Granger, C.W.J. (2001), 'Macroeconometrics – past and future', *Journal of Econometrics*, **100**, 17–19.
Clements, M.P. and D. Hendry (1999), *Forecasting Non-stationary Economic Time Series*, London: MIT Press.
Zellner, A. and F. Palm (1974), 'Time series analysis and simultaneous equation econometric models', *Journal of Econometrics*, **2** (1), 17–54.

Brouwer fixed point theorem

Luitzen Egbertus Jan Brouwer (1881–1966) was a Dutch mathematician whose most important results are characterizations of topological mappings of the Cartesian plane and several fixed point theorems.

This theorem states: let $f : X \rightarrow X$ be a continuous function from a non-empty, compact and convex set $X \subset R^n$ into itself. Then f has a fixed point, that is, there exists $x' \in X$ such that $x' = f(x')$.

This theorem is used in many economic frameworks for proving existence theorems. We mention some of the most relevant. John von Neumann, in 1928, proved the minimax theorem. He established the existence of a pair of equilibrium strategies for zero-sum two-person games; that is, the existence of a saddle-point for the utility of either player. Existence of general equilibrium for a competitive economy was proved by Arrow and Debreu in 1954. Herbert Scarf used it in the computation of economic equilibrium. Hirofumi Uzawa proved, in 1962, the existence of Walrasian equilibrium.

GUSTAVO BERGANTIÑOS

Bibliography
Brouwer, L.E.J. (1912), 'Uber Abbildung von Mannigfaltikeiten', *Mathematische Annalen*, **71**, 97–115.

See also: Arrow–Debreu general equilibrium model; Kakutani's fixed point theorem.

Buchanan's clubs theory

The theory of clubs is part of the theory of impure public goods. When James M. Buchanan (b.1919, Nobel Prize 1986) wrote his seminal piece (1965), the theory of public goods was barely developed, and he was able to fill the Samuelsonian gap between private and pure public goods. Buchanan demonstrated how the conditions of public good provision and club membership interact.

A club good is a particular case of public good, which has the characteristics of excludability and non-rivalry (or partial non-rivalry, depending on the congestion). By contrast, a pure public good has the characteristic of both non-excludability and non-rivalry.

Therefore a club is a voluntary group of individuals deriving mutual benefit from sharing either the cost of production or the members' characteristics or an impure public good. A club good is characterized by excludable benefits. The fundamental characteristic of the club is its voluntary membership. Its members take the decision to belong to the club because they anticipate the benefits of the collective provision from membership.

For this reason, a club good is excludable and this is its main characteristic, because, without exclusion, there would be no incentives to belong to the club and pay fees or rights to enter. Therefore, in contrast to pure public goods, it is possible to prevent its consumption by the people that will not pay for it. However the club good keeps the characteristic of non-rivalry; that is, the consumption of the good by one person does not reduce the consumption of the same good by others, except when congestion happens and the utility of any individual will be affected by the presence of more members of the club. Rivalry and congestion increase when the number of individuals sharing the same club good increases too.

Buchanan's analysis includes the club-size variable for each and every good, which measures the number of persons who are to join in the consumption arrangements for the club good over the relevant time period. The swimming pool is the original example of a club good in Buchanan's article. The users that share a swimming pool suffer rivalry and congestion when the number of members increases.

Another pioneering club model is that of Charles Tiebout (1956) whose 'voting with the feet' hypothesis attempted to show how the jurisdictional size of local governments could be determined by voluntary mobility decisions. In this model, the amount of the shared local public good is fixed and distinct for each governmental jurisdiction and the decentralized decision mechanism allows achieving Pareto optimality for local public goods. Most of the articles analysing the theory of club goods have been written since Buchanan's seminal article; however the roots go back to the 1920s, to A.C. Pigou and Frank Knight, who applied it to the case of tolls for congested roads.

JORDI BACARIA

Bibliography

Buchanan, J.M. (1965), 'An economic theory of clubs', *Economica*, **32**, 1–14.

Tiebout, C.M. (1956), 'A pure theory of local expenditures', *Journal of Political Economy*, **64**, 416–24.

See also: Tiebout's voting with the feet process.

Buridan's ass

Often mentioned in discussions concerning free will and determinism, this refers to an ass placed equidistant from two equal bundles of hay; lacking free will, it cannot choose one or the other and consequcntly starves to death. The paradox is named after the French medieval philosopher Jean Buridan (1300–58), who studied at the University of Paris under nominalist William of Occam, and was later professor and rector of the university. He supported the scholastic scepticism that denied the distinction between the faculties of the soul: will and intellect being the same, man, who has free will, must choose the greatest good, and cannot do it facing two equally desirable alternatives. The theory was ridiculed by his critics with the tale of Buridan's ass, not present in his writings; they stated that the human being has free will, a faculty of the mind that is able to create a preference without sufficient reason. Sen (1997) illustrates the fundamental contrast between maximizing and optimizing behaviour with Buridan's ass and, according to Kahabil (1997) the story suggests that mere logical deduction is insufficient for making any decision, and that risk taking is safer than security seeking.

VICTORIANO MARTÍN MARTÍN

Bibliography

Kahabil, Elias L. (1997), 'Buridan's ass, uncertainty, risk and self-competition: a theory of entrepreneurship', *Kyklos*, **2** (50), 147–64.

Sen, A. (1997), 'Maximization and the act of choice', *Econometrica*, **4** (65), 745–9.

C

Cagan's hyperinflation model

Named after the American economist Phillip D. Cagan (b.1927), this is a monetary model of hyperinflation that rests on three building blocks: first, there is a demand for real money balances that depends only on expected inflation; second, expected inflation is assumed to be determined by an adaptive rule where the expected inflation is revised in each period in proportion to the forecast error made when predicting the rate of inflation in the previous period; third, the money market is always in equilibrium.

The main objective in Cagan's (1956) pioneering paper was identifying a stable demand for money during hyperinflationary episodes. He observed that these are characterized by huge rates of inflation (for instance, monthly rates of inflation higher than 50 per cent) and a sharp fall in real money balances. Cagan postulated that the demand for real money balances is only a function of the expected rate of inflation during hyperinflation; that is, real money balances are inversely related to the expected opportunity cost of holding money instead of other assets. His intuition was that, during hyperinflationary periods, the variation in the real variables determining the demand for real money balances during regular periods (for instance, real income and real interest rate) is negligible compared to the variation of relevant nominal variables. The demand for money can then be isolated from any real variable and can be expressed only in terms of nominal variables during hyperinflation: in particular, in terms of the anticipated rate of inflation.

Specifically, Cagan's money demand postulates that the elasticity of the demand for real money balances is proportional to the expected rate of inflation. An implication of this is that changes in the expected rate of inflation have the same effect on real money balances in percentage terms, regardless of the level of real money balances. Therefore this feature postulates a notion of stability for the demand for real money balances in a scenario characterized by a bizarre behavior of nominal variables. Cagan studied seven hyperinflationary episodes that developed in some central European countries in the 1920s and 1940s. He provided evidence that his simple money demand model fits well with the data from those hyperinflations. Since then, a great number of papers have shown that Cagan's model is a useful approach to understanding hyperinflationary dynamics. More importantly, perhaps, Cagan's model is considered one of the simplest dynamic models used in macroeconomics to study relevant issues. Among other issues, Cagan's model has been used, as a basic framework, to analyze the interaction between monetary and fiscal policies, expectations formation (rational expectations and bounded rationality), multiplicity of equilibria, bubbles and econometric policy evaluation.

JESÚS VÁZQUEZ

Bibliography

Cagan, P.D. (1956), 'Monetary dynamics of hyperinflation', in Milton Friedman (ed.), *Studies in the Quantity Theory of Money*, Chicago: University of Chicago Press.

See also: Baumol–Tobin transactions demand for cash, Keynes's demand for money, Muth's rational expectations.

Cairnes–Haberler model

Named after John E. Cairnes (1823–75) and G. Haberler (1901–95), this model is used for analyzing the gains from international trade in terms of comparative advantage in the very short run. It is formulated as a two countries–two goods–three factors model, on the basis that, in the very short run, it seems reasonable to assume that virtually all factors of production are immobile between sectors. This means that production proportions are fixed, so marginal physical products are constant. As a consequence, if commodity prices are fixed, factor payments will be fixed too. In this context, changes in commodity prices will imply that returns to all factors in an industry change by the same proportion that the price changes.

YANNA G. FRANCO

Bibliography

Krugman, Paul R. and Maurice Obstfeld (2003), *International Economics*, 6th edn, Boston: Addison Wesley, Chapter 2.

Cantillon effect

The Cantillon effect is the temporary and short-run effect on the structure of relative prices when a flow of liquidity (usually specie) gets into the market. Such an effect is related to the monetary theory of Richard Cantillon (1680?–1734) and the use of the quantity of money to explain the price level. In his exposition of the quantity theory, Cantillon distinguished between different ways in which a flow of money (specie) enters the economy. Undoubtedly, the money inflow will finally have as a result an increase in prices, taking into account the volume of output and the velocity of circulation, but until the mechanism acts upon the price level, the money passes through different hands and sectors, depending on the way it has been introduced. In Cantillon's words, Locke 'has clearly seen that the abundance of money makes every thing dear, but he has not considered how it does so. The great difficulty of this question consists in knowing in what way and in what proportion the increase of money rises prices' (Cantillon [1755] 1931, p. 161).

So, although an increase of actual money causes a corresponding increase of consumption which finally brings about increased prices, the process works gradually and, in the short run, money will have different effects on prices if it comes from mining for new gold and silver, if it proceeds from a favourable balance of trade or if it comes from subsidies, transfers (including diplomatic expenses), tourism or international capital movements. In every case, the prices of some products will rise first, and then other prices join the rising process until the increase gradually spreads over all the economy; in each case markets and prices affected in the first place are different. When the general price level goes up, relative prices have been altered previously and this means that all economic decisions and equilibria have changed, so 'Market prices will rise more for certain things than for others however abundant the money may be' (ibid., p. 179). This is the reason why an increased money supply does not raise all prices in the same proportion.

Cantillon applied this effect to his analysis of the interest rate. Although he presents what we may consider a real theory of interest, he accepts that an injection of currency brings down the level of interest, 'because when Money is plentiful it is more easy to find some to borrow'. However, 'This idea is not always true or accurate.' In fact, 'If the abundance of money in the State comes from the hands of money-lenders it will doubtless bring down the current rate of interest . . . but if it comes from the intervention of spenders it will have just the opposite effect and will raise the rate of interest'(ibid., pp. 213, 215). This is an early refutation of the idea that classical economists believed in the neutrality of money.

FERNANDO MÉNDEZ-IBISATE

Bibliography

Cantillon, Richard (1755), *Essai sur la Nature du Commerce en Général*, English translation and other materials by H. Higgs (ed.) (1931), London: Macmillan.

Cantor's nested intervals theorem

Georg Cantor (1845–1918) was a German mathematician (although he was born in St. Petersburg, Russia) who put forward the modern theory on infinite sets by building a hierarchy according to their cardinal number. He strongly contributed to the foundations of mathematics and, in fact, his achievements revolutionized almost every field of mathematics. Here we shall offer two important results of Cantor that are widely used in both pure mathematics and applications.

Nested intervals theorem

Let $[a_n, b_n]_{n \in N}$ be a decreasing sequence of intervals of R, (that is, $[a_{n+1}, b_{n+1}] \subseteq [a_n, b_n]$), such that $\lim_{n\to\infty} [b_n - a_n] = 0$. Then there is a single point that belongs to every interval $[a_n, b_n]$.

This theorem can be generalized to higher dimensions or even to more abstract spaces. In particular, its version for metric spaces is of great relevance. It states that the intersection of a decreasing sequence of non-empty, closed subsets of a complete metric space such that the diameter (roughly speaking, the greatest of the distance among two arbitrary points of the set) of the sets converges to zero consists exactly of one point.

Order type of the rationals

Any numerable totally ordered set that is dense and unbordered is isomorphic to the set of rational numbers, endowed with its natural order.

In simple words, this result says that there is only one numerable totally ordered set that has no gaps and no limits, namely, the set of the rationals. This theorem has a notable significance in the mathematical foundations of decision analysis. In particular, it is used to construct utility functions on certain topological spaces.

JAN CARLOS CANDEAL

Bibliography

Bell, E.T (1986), *Men of Mathematics: The Lives and Achievements of Great Mathematicians from Zeno to Poincaré*, New York: Simon and Schuster.

Bridges, D.S. and G.B. Mehta, (1995), *Representations of Preference Orderings, Lecture Notes in Economics and Mathematical Systems*, Berlin: Springer-Verlag.

Rudin, W. (1976), *Principles of Mathematical Analysis*, 3rd edn, New York: McGraw-Hill.

See also: Cauchy's sequence.

Cass–Koopmans criterion

This is also termed the Ramsey–Cass–Koopmans condition of stationary equilibrium in an economy characterized by a representative consumer that maximizes intertemporal discounted utility subject to a budget constraint and a production constraint. It basically says that, in order to maximize their utility, consumers must increase consumption at a rate equal to the difference between, on the one hand, the rate of return on capital and, on the other hand, the discount rate plus the rate at which technology grows, and save accordingly. At steady-state equilibrium, however, this difference is nil, so that consumption and saving per worker remain constant. Strictly speaking, the Cass–Koopmans criterion refers to the steady-state condition in an economy with endogenous saving.

Formally stated, the above conditions are

$$\frac{dc_t/dt}{c_t} = \frac{1}{\theta}(f'(k_t) - \rho - \theta g),$$

for optimal consumption and saving and $f'(k^*) = \rho + \theta g$ for the steady state where c is consumption, $1/\theta$ is the elasticity of substitution, k is capital per worker, ρ is the time discount rate and g is the growth rate of technology.

David Cass (b.1937) and Tjalling Koopmans (1910–86) developed their models in the early 1960s by adding consumption and savings behaviour to the Solow model developed some years before. The way to do it was already established by Frank Ramsey in his seminal *Economic Journal* paper of 1928. The Cass–Koopmans criterion, incidentally, is related to the Hotelling rule for optimal depletion of an exhaustible resource, as the time discount rate plays a similar role in both.

JOSÉ A. HERCE

Bibliography

Cass D. (1965), 'Optimum growth in an aggregative model of capital accumulation', *Review of Economic Studies*, **32**, 233–40.

Koopmans T.C. (1965), 'On the concept of optimal growth', Cowles Foundation Paper 238, reprinted from *Academiae Scientiarum Scripta Varia*, **28** (1).

Ramsey F.P. (1928), 'A mathematical theory of saving', *Economic Journal*, **38**, 543–59.

See also: Radner's turnpike property, Ramsey model and rule, Solow's growth model and residual.

Cauchy distribution

The Cauchy distribution (Augustin–Louis Cauchy, 1789–1857) has probability density function

$$f(x) = (\pi\lambda)^{-1}\left[1 + \left(\frac{x-\theta}{\lambda}\right)^2\right]^{-1},$$

where θ is the location parameter and λ the scale parameter. This distribution is best known when $\theta = 0$, $\lambda = 1$; the density then reduces to $1/\pi(1 + x^2)$ and is called a 'standard Cauchy'. Its shape is similar to that of a standard normal, but it has longer and fatter tails. For this reason it is often used to study the sensitivity of hypothesis tests which assume normality to heavy-tailed departures from normality. In fact, the standard Cauchy is the same as the t distribution with 1 degree of freedom, or the ratio of two independent standard normals.

The Cauchy distribution is probably best known as an example of a pathological case. In spite of its similarity to the normal distribution, the integrals of the form $\int x^r f(x)dx$ do not converge in absolute value and thus the distribution does not have any finite moments. Because of this, central limit theorems and consistency results for ordinary least squares estimators do not apply. A more intuitive expression of this pathological behaviour is that the sample mean from a random sample of Cauchy variables has exactly the same distribution as each of the sample units, so increasing the sample size does not help us obtain a better estimate of the location parameter.

The distribution became associated with Cauchy after he referred to the breakdown of the large sample justification for least squares in 1853. However, it seems that this and other properties of the standard Cauchy density had been known before.

PEDRO MIRA

Bibliography

Cauchy, A.L. (1853), 'Sur les résultats moyens d'observations de même nature, et sur les résultats les plus probables', *Comptes Rendus de l'Académie des Sciences*, Paris, **37**, 198–206.

Johnson, N.L., S. Kotz and N. Balakrishnan (1994), 'Cauchy distribution', *Continuous Univariate Distributions*, vol. 1, New York: John Wiley, ch. 16.

NIST/SEMATECH e-Handbook of Statistical Methods (2003), 'Cauchy distribution', http://www.itl.nist.gov/div898/handbook/.

Cauchy's sequence

Augustin-Louis Cauchy (1789–1857) was a French mathematician whose contributions include the study of convergence and divergence of sequences and infinite series, differential equations, determinants, probability and mathematical physics. He also founded complex analysis by discovering the

Cauchy–Riemann equations and establishing the so-called 'Cauchy's integral formula' for holomorphic functions.

A sequence $(a_n)_{n \in N}$ is called a 'Cauchy sequence' (or is said to satisfy the Cauchy condition) if, for every $\in > 0$, there exists $p \in N$ such that, for all $m, n \geq p$, $| x_n - x_m | < \in$.

It can be proved that, for a real sequence, the Cauchy condition amounts to the convergence of the sequence. This is interesting since the condition of being a Cauchy sequence can often be verified without any knowledge as to the value of the limit of the sequence.

Both the notions of a Cauchy sequence and the Cauchy criterion also hold in higher (finite or infinite) dimensional spaces where the absolute value function $| . |$ is replaced by the norm function $\| . \|$. Furthermore, a Cauchy sequence can be defined on arbitrary metric spaces where the distance function plays the role of the absolute value function in the above definition. It is easily seen that every convergent sequence of a metric space is a Cauchy sequence. The metric spaces for which the converse also holds are called *complete*. Put into words, a metric space is complete if every Cauchy sequence has a limit. Examples of complete metric spaces include the Euclidean spaces R^n, $n \geq 1$, or much more sophisticated ones like C [0, 1] the Banach space that consists of the continuous real-valued functions defined on [0, 1], endowed with the supremum distance. The notion of Cauchy sequence can also be generalized for uniform topological spaces.

JAN CARLOS CANDEAL

Bibliography

Bell, E.T. (1986), *Men of Mathematics: The Lives and Achievements of Great Mathematicians from Zeno to Poincaré*, New York: Simon and Schuster.

Berberian, S.K. (1994), *A First Course in Real Analysis*, Berlin: Springer-Verlag.

Rudin, W. (1976), *Principles of Mathematical Analysis*, 3rd edn, New York: McGraw-Hill.

See also: Banach's contractive mapping principle, Euclidean spaces.

Cauchy–Schwarz inequality

This inequality bears the names of two of the greatest mathematical analysts of the nineteenth century: Augustin–Louis Cauchy, a Frenchman, and Hermann Amandus Schwarz, a German. A ubiquitous, basic and simple inequality, it is attributed also to Viktor Yakovlevich Bunyakovski, a Russian doctoral student of Cauchy. There are so many names because of different levels of generality, and certain issues of priority.

In its simplest form, the inequality states that, if $(a_i)_{i=1}^n$ and $(b_i)_{i=1}^n$ are lists of real numbers, then:

$$\left(\sum_i^n a_i b_i\right)^2 \leq \left(\sum_i^n a_i^2\right)\left(\sum_i^n b_i^2\right).$$

It is most easily derived by expanding both sides and by using the inequality $2xy \leq (x^2 + y^2)$ (which is another way of writing the obvious $(x - y)^2 \geq 0$) with $x = a_i b_j$ and $y = a_j b_i$. This is actually the argument that appears in Cauchy (1821) in the notes to the volume on algebraic analysis.

The inequality may be viewed as a result about vectors and inner products, because if $\vec{v} = (a_1, a_2, \ldots, a_n)$ and $\vec{w} = (b_1, b_2, \ldots, b_n)$ then it translates into

$$| \vec{v} \cdot \vec{w} | \leq \| \vec{v} \| \| \vec{w} \|$$

Observe that, geometrically, the inequality means that $| \cos \theta | \leq 1$, where θ is the angle between the two vectors. But its real interest rests in that it holds not only for vectors in Euclidean space but for vectors in any vector space where you have defined an inner product and, of those, you have plenty.

For example, we could consider continuous functions f, g in the interval [0, 1] and deduce that

$$(\int_0^1 f(x)g(x)dx) \leq (\int_0^1 f(x)^2dx)^{1/2} (\int_0^1 g(x)^2dx)^{1/2},$$

which is an instance of the more general Hölder's inequality,

$$(\int_0^1 f(x)g(x)dx) \leq (\int_0^1 f(x)^p dx)^{1/p} (\int_0^1 g(x)^q dx)^{1/q},$$

whenever $p, q > 0$ verify

$$\frac{1}{p} + \frac{1}{q} = 1.$$

Or we could consider random variables X and Y (with finite second moments), and deduce the fundamental fact $cov(X, Y) \leq var(X)^{1/2} var(Y)^{1/2}$. The general vector inequality follows by observing that the parabola $y = \| \vec{v} - x\vec{w} \|$ attains its (positive) minimum at $x = (\vec{v} \cdot \vec{w})/\| \vec{w} \|^2$.

What about equality? It can only take place when the two vectors in question are parallel, that is, one is a multiple of the other. Observe that the covariance inequality above simply says that the absolute value of the correlation coefficient is 1 only if one of the random variables is a linear function of the other (but, at most, for a set of zero probability).

Let us consider one particular case of the original inequality: each $b_i = 1$, so that we may write it as:

$$\left| \frac{\sum_i^n a_i}{n} \right| \leq \left| \frac{\sum_i^n a_i^2}{n} \right|^{1/2}$$

and equality may only occur when the a_is are all equal. So the quotient

$$\left| \frac{\sum_i^n a_i^2}{n} \right| \Big/ \left| \frac{\sum_i^n a_i}{n} \right|^2$$

is always at least one and measures how close the sequence $(a_i)_{i=1}^n$ is to being constant. When $a_i = (x_i - \bar{x})^2$, this quotient measures the kurtosis of a sample $(x_i)_{i=1}^n$ with mean $\bar{x}$ (one usually subtracts 3 from the quotient to get the kurtosis).

Suppose, finally, that you have n companies competing in a single market and that company i, say, controls a fraction a_i of that market. Thus $\sum_{i=1}^n a_i = 1$, and the quotient

$$\left| \frac{\sum_i^n a_i^2}{n} \right| \Big/ \left| \frac{\sum_i^n a_i}{n} \right|^2$$

which, in this case, is equal to

$$\left(\sum_i^n a_i^2 \right) n$$

measures how concentrated this market is: a value close to one means almost perfect competition, a value close to n means heavy concentration. This quotient is essentially the Herfindahl index that the Department of Justice of the United States uses in antitrust suits.

JOSÉ L. FERNÁNDEZ

Bibliography

Cauchy, Augustin-Louis (1821), *Cours d'Analyse de L'Ecole Polytechnique*, Paris.

See also: Herfindahl-Hirschman index.

Chamberlin's oligopoly model

The model proposed by Edward Chamberlin (1899–1967) in 1933 analyses a market structure where there is product differentiation. Specifically, he defines a market with a high number of firms, each selling similar but not identical products. Consumers consider those products as imperfect substitutes and therefore their demand curves have significant cross-price elasticities. Each producer is a monopolist of his product facing a demand curve with negative slope. However, he competes in the market with the other varieties produced by the rest of the firms. Chamberlin also assumes free entry and consequently in the long-run equilibrium the profit of all firms is nil. For these characteristics, the market structure defined by Chamberlin is also known as 'monopolistic competition'. This model has been used in many theoretical and empirical papers on international trade.

In the short run, the number of firms and therefore the number of products is fixed. The monopolistic competition equilibrium is very similar to the monopoly equilibrium in the sense that each producer is a price maker of his variety. However, in the context of monopolistic competition, the price that the consumer is willing to pay for the product of each firm depends on the level of production of the other firms. Specifically, the inverse demand function of firm i can be expressed as $p_i = p_i(x_i, x_{-i})$ where

$$x_{-i} = \sum_{\substack{j=1 \\ j \neq 1}}^{N} x_j.$$

In the Chamberlin analysis, each firm assumes a constant behavior of the other firms. That is, each producer assumes that all the producers of other commodities will maintain their prices when he modifies his. However, when competitors react to his price policy, the true demand curve is different from the demand curve facing each firm. In equilibrium, the marginal revenue of both demand curves should be the same for the level of production that maximizes profit. Therefore each firm's forecasts must be compatible with what the other firms actually do. In the equilibrium of monopolistic competition in the short run, $(x^*_1, \ldots, x^*_N)$, it must be satisfied that $MR_i(x^*_i, x^*_{-i}) = MC_i(x^*_i, x^*_{-i})$ $i = 1 \ldots N$. For each firm, its marginal revenue equals its marginal cost, given the actions of all producers.

When the firms obtain positive profits in the short run, new firms will enter the industry, reducing the demand curve of the incumbents. In the long-run equilibrium, the profits of all firms will be zero and therefore the price must equal average cost. As the demand curve facing each has negative slope, the equilibrium is obtained for a level of production which is lower than the minimum average cost that will be the equilibrium without product differentiation (the perfect competition). This result implies that the monopolistic competition equilibrium exhibits *excess capacity*. However, if the products are close substitutes and the firms compete in prices, the demand curve will be very elastic and the excess capacity will be small. On the other hand, although the equilibrium will be inefficient in terms of cost because price exceeds marginal cost, it can be socially beneficial if consumers like product diversity.

LOURDES MORENO MARTÍN

Bibliography

Chamberlin, E.H. (1933), *The Theory of Monopolistic Competition (A Re-orientation of the Theory of Value)*, Oxford University Press.

Dixit, A. and J.E. Stiglitz (1977), 'Monopolistic competition and optimum product diversity', *American Economic Review,* **67**, 297–308.

Spence, M. (1976), 'Product selection, fixed cost and monopolistic competition', *Review of Economic Studies,* **43**, 217–35.

See also: Dixit–Stiglitz monopolistic competition model.

Chipman–Moore–Samuelson compensation criterion

This criterion (hereafter CMS) tries to overcome the relative ease with which inconsistent applications of the Kaldor–Hicks–Scitovski criterion (hereafter KHS) can be obtained. According to this criterion, alternative x is at least as good as alternative y if any alternative potentially feasible from y is Pareto-dominated by some alternative potentially feasible from x. It has the advantage of providing a transitive (although typically incomplete) ranking of sets of alternatives.

The problem with the CMS criterion, contrary to the KHS criterion, is that it does not satisfy the Pareto principle. The CMS criterion is concerned only with potential welfare and it says nothing about actual welfare as evaluated by the Pareto principle.

The non-crossing of utility possibility frontiers is necessary and sufficient for the transitivity of the KHS criterion and for the CMS criterion to be applied in accordance with the Pareto principle without inconsistencias.

LUÍS A. PUCH

Bibliography

Gravel, N. (2001), 'On the difficulty of combining actual and potential criteria for an increase in social welfare', *Economic Theory*, **17** (1), 163–80.

See also: Hicks's compensation criterion, Kaldor compensation criterion, Scitovsky's compensation criterion.

Chow's test

Introduced in 1960 by Gregory Chow (b.1929) to analyse the stability of coefficients in a model and it is based on the comparison of residual sum of squares (RSS), between two periods by means of an F statistic which should have values lower than F_α when the hypothesis of homogeneity of parameters is true. There are two types of Chow's test: one for within-sample comparison, with estimation of a common sample and two separate subsamples; another for post-sample comparison, with a common estimation for sample and post-sample periods and another estimation for the sample period.

The first type consists of estimating three relations, one for all the sample period and one for each of the two subsamples, and compares the value of the statistic $F = (\Delta RSS/dfn)/((RSS_1 + RSS_2)/dfd)$ with the corresponding significant value F_α, being $\Delta RSS = RSS - (RSS1 + RSS2)$, the increase in RSS between the joint sample and the two subsamples, and being dfn/dfd, the degrees of freedom of numerator/denominator, as to say $dfn = (T - k - 1) - (T_1 - k - 1) - (T_2 - k - 1) = k$, and $dfd = (T_1 - k - 1) + (T_2 - k - 1) = T - 2\,(k + 1)$, where $k + 1$ is the number of parameters in the model, and $T = T_1 + T_2$ is the sample size.

The second type consists of the comparison of the value of the statistic $F = [(RSS - RSS_1)/n]/[RSS_1/(T - k - 1)]$, based on the estimation of the common sample of size $T + n$ and a first sample of size T, n being the size of the forecasting period. This second type can also be used for within-sample comparison when the breaking point leaves a very small sample size for the second subsample. The test assumes the existence of homogeneity in the variance of the random shock. This author has had an important influence on the application of both types of test, which have been highly useful for many relevant econometric applications. Generally the lack of stability is due to the omission of one or more relevant variables and the test is of great help to show that problem in order to improve the model specification.

M. CÁRMEN GUISÁN

Bibliography

Chow, G.C. (1960), 'Tests of equality between sets of coefficients in two linear regressions', *Econometrica*, **28**, 591–605.

Clark problem

This refers to J.B. Clark's fast and deep shift from social historicism to neoclassical economics. John Bates Clark (1847–1938) graduated from Amherst College, Massachusetts, in 1875 and then went to Heidelberg, Germany, where he studied under Karl Knies. Back in the USA, Clark taught mainly economics and history in several colleges, and in 1895 obtained a position at Columbia

University. Knies's influence was remarkable in his first writings. Thus, in the midst of the battle between German an English economics in the 1880s and early 1890s, Clark endorsed historicism and institutionalism in opposition to classical theory in his first book (*The Philosophy of Wealth*, 1886), and supported public intervention to subject economic processes to the community's control.

Clark's work through the next decade focused on the theory of functional distribution, leading to *The Distribution of Wealth* (1899), and a great change in Clark's approach: 'Clark had certainly discovered and embraced neoclassical economics; he completely reversed his earlier positions' (Tobin, 1985, p. 29). Although some authors observe a fundamental continuity in Clark's ideas (for example Stabile, 2000), the Clark problem has been adopted as a paradigm of dramatic conversions in economic thought.

GERMÀ BEL

Bibliography

Persky, Joseph (2000), 'The neoclassical advent: American economists at the dawn of the 20th century', *Journal of Economic Perspectives*, **14** (1), 95–108.

Stabile, Donald R. (2000), 'Unions and the natural standard of wages: another look at "the J.B. Clark Problem" ', *History of Political Economy*, **32** (3), 585–606.

Tobin, James (1985), 'Neoclassical Theory in America: J.B. Clark and Fisher', *American Economic Review*, **75** (6), 28–38.

Clark–Fisher hypothesis

This was coined by P.T. Bauer with reference to Colin Clark and Allan G.B. Fisher, who pointed out in the 1930s that economic growth increased the proportion of tertiary activities, trading and other services in underdeveloped countries. Bauer said that official labor statistics were misleading and understated that proportion. Accordingly, the neglect of internal trade in development economics was unwarranted. He concluded: 'the empirical and theoretical bases for the Clark–Fisher hypothesis are insubstantial'.

CARLOS RODRÍGUEZ BRAUN

Bibliography

Bauer, P.T. (1991), *The Development Frontier: Essays in Applied Economics*, London: Harvester-Wheatsheaf.

Bauer, P.T. (2000), *From Subsistence to Exchange and Other Essays*, Princeton, NJ: Princeton University Press, chapter I.

Clark–Knight paradigm

This paradigm can be identified as the explanation of interest as a return to capital, after J.B. Clark (see Clark problem) and Frank H. Knight (1885–1972), one of the founders of the Chicago School of Economics. Classical economists, followed by Karl Marx in his labor theory of value, did not justify incomes other than wages, and American neoclassics searched for the rationale of private property's returns.

In Clark's thought, capital and labor are the two factors that produce aggregate output and their respective returns should be treated in a similar way. Thus rents are the return to existing capital goods, including land. Capital was virtually permanent and 'with a marginal productivity determining its interest rate in much the same way that primary labor's productivity determines its real wage rate and primary land's marginal productivity determines its real rent rate(s)' (Samuelson, 2001, p. 301).

Böhm-Bawerk opposed Clark by arguing that capital involves several time-phasings of labor and land inputs: production uses capital to transform non-produced inputs, such as labor and land. Marginal productivity in determining capital interest rate could not be seen as playing the same role as in land and labor; and the net result of capital derived from the greater value produced by circulating capital. The Clark–Böhm-Bawerk debate was repeated in the 1930s between Hayek and Knight, who argued against capital being measured as a period of production, endorsing Clark's view.

GERMÀ BEL

Bibliography

Leigh, Arthur H. (1974), 'Frank H. Knight as economic theorist', *Journal of Political Economy*, **82** (3), 578–86.

Samuelson, Paul A. (2001), 'A modern post-mortem on Böhm's capital theory: its vital normative flaw shared by pre-Sraffian mainstream capital theory', *Journal of the History of Economic Thought*, **23** (3), 301–17.

Coase conjecture

In a seminal paper published in 1972, Ronald Coase (b.1910, Nobel Prize 1991) challenged economists with a simple, but striking, idea: imagine that someone owned all the land of the United States – at what price would he sell it? Coase 'conjectured' that the only price could be the competitive one. Economists have been considering the implications of the 'Coase conjecture' ever since.

The Coase conjecture concerns a monopoly supplier of a durable good. Conventional thinking suggests the monopolist would maximize profits by restricting supply to only those customers with a high willingness to pay. Yet with durable goods the game is not over. The monopolist now faces the residual consumers who were not willing to pay the initial price. The monopolist can extract more profit by offering them a new, lower, price. Then it will face a new set of residual consumers and can extract more by offering them an even lower price, and so on. However, this reasoning is incomplete. If potential customers know that prices will fall in the future, they will wait, even if they are willing to pay the high initial price.

A monopoly supplier of durable goods creates its own competition and may be unable to exert market power. This has some important policy implications, namely in the fields of antitrust and merger control.

The validity of the Coase conjecture has been confirmed by a number of authors. However it holds only in some circumstances. Suppliers of durable goods can avoid the implications of the Coase conjecture if they can credibly commit themselves not to reduce the price of the durable good in the future. Economists have considered a number of possibilities. First, the supplier could lease, as well as sell, the good (Coase, 1972). Reductions in the future price of durable goods are now costly because they also reduce the value of the leasing contracts. Second, the monopolist may have an incentive to reduce the economic durability of its products by introducing new versions that render the existing ones obsolescent (Bulow, 1986). Third, the supplier could give buy-back guarantees. In this case any reduction in the price of the durable good would be followed by demands that the monopolist buy back the units that were bought at the previous high price. Finally, the supplier could introduce a second product line for non-durable goods that substitute for the durable one (Kühn and Padilla, 1996). Any reduction in the future price of the durable good is now costly because it will cannibalize sales of the non-durable good.

In some markets there may be no need for such strategies because the Coase conjecture fails in any case. Increasing marginal costs of production will cause the conjecture to fail. Consumers can no longer avoid paying a high price by delaying their purchases: if they do so the additional future sales volume will cause the supplier to produce at a higher marginal cost. Another example comes from markets with network externalities. Here the valuation of consumers goes up as the number of users rises over time, so there is no need to reduce future prices to induce additional take-up.

The Coase conjecture has recently played

an important role in the debate on the incentives of companies to integrate vertically. Rey and Tirole show that a monopoly supplier of an upstream input may be unable to exert its monopoly power. One downstream company will pay more for the input if the monopolist restricts supply to the others. However, having sold to one company, the monopolist will have incentives to meet the residual demand from the others, albeit at a lower price. But its inability to commit itself not to do this will deter the first customer from paying a high price. By buying its own downstream company the monopolist can credibly commit itself to restricting sales in the downstream market, because doing so will benefit its affiliate.

Rey and Tirole (2003) demonstrate how important it is to understand the logic of the Coase conjecture to understand the performance of markets where agents' incentives are governed by long-term contracts.

ATILANO JORGE PADILLA

Bibliography

Bulow, Jeremy (1986), 'An economic theory of planned obsolescence', *Quarterly Journal of Economics*, **101**, 729–49.

Carlton, Dennis and Robert Gertner (1989), 'Market power and mergers in durable-good industries', *Journal of Law and Economics*, **32**, 203–26.

Coase, Ronald H. (1972), 'Durability and monopoly', *Journal of Law and Economics*, **15**, 143–9.

Kühn, Kai-Uwe and A. Jorge Padilla (1996), 'Product line decisions and the Coase conjecture', *RAND Journal of Economics*, **27** (2), 391–414.

Rey, P. and J. Tirole (2003), 'A primer on foreclosure', in M. Armstrong and R.H. Porter (eds), *Handbook of Industrial Organization*, vol. 3, New York: North-Holland.

Coase theorem

If transaction costs are zero and no wealth effects exist, private and social costs will be equal; and the initial assignment of property rights will not have any effect on the final allocation of resources. This theorem is based on the ideas developed by Ronald Coase (b.1910, Nobel Prize 1991) first in his 1959 article, and later in his 1960 one. But, as often happens in science when naming theorems, it was not Coase who formulated this one. In Coase (1988) one can read: 'I did not originate the phrase "Coase Theorem", nor its precise formulation, both of which we owe to Stigler', since the theorem was popularized by the third edition of Stigler's book (1966).

Coase's arguments were developed through the study of legal cases in a way perhaps unique in the tradition of modern economics. One of these cases, *Sturges* v. *Bridgman*, a tort case decided in 1879, can be used to illustrate Coase's theory. A confectioner had been using two mortars and pestles for a long time in his premises. A doctor then came to occupy a neighbouring house. At the beginning, the confectioner's machinery did not cause harm to the doctor, but, eight years after occupying the premises, he built a new consulting room at the end of his garden, right against the confectioner's kitchen. It was then found that the noise and vibration caused by the confectioner's machinery prevented the doctor from examining his patients by auscultation and made impossible the practice of medicine.

The doctor went to court and got an injunction forcing the confectioner to stop using his machinery. The court asserted that its judgment was based on the damage caused by the confectioner and the negative effects that an alternative opinion would have on the development of land for residential purposes. But, according to Coase, the case should be presented in a different way. Firstly, a tort should not be understood as a unilateral damage – the confectioner harms the doctor – but as a bilateral problem in which both parts are partially responsible for the damage. And secondly, the relevant question is precisely to determine what is the most efficient use of a plot. Were industry the most efficient use for land, the doctor would have been willing to sell his right and allow the machinery to continue in operation, if the confectioner would have paid him a sum of money greater than the loss of income suffered from having to move his consulting room to some other location or from reducing his activities.

In Coase's words: 'the solution of the problem depends essentially on whether the continued use of the machinery adds more to the confectioner's income than it subtracts from the doctor'. And the efficient solution would be the same if the confectioner had won the case, the only difference being the part selling or buying the property right.

So, according to Coase, if transaction costs are zero, law determines rights, not the allocation of resources. But there is no such thing as a world with zero transaction costs. This simple point has been a significant reason for disagreement between Coase and other economists. Coase has written that the influence of 'The problem of social cost' has been less beneficial than he had hoped, the reason being that the discussion has concentrated on what would happen in a world in which transaction costs were zero. But the relevant problem for institutional economics is to make clear the role that transaction costs play in the fashioning of the institutions which make up the economic systems.

Besides law and economics, the field in which the Coase theorem has been more influential is welfare economics. Coase's analysis involves a strong critique of the conventional Pigouvian approach to externalities, according to which government fiscal policy would be the most convenient tool to equalize private and social costs and private and social benefits, taxing those activities whose social costs are higher than their private costs, and subsidizing those activities whose social benefits are greater than their private benefits. Some important economic problems (pollution is, certainly, the most widely discussed topic, but not the only one) can be explained in a new way from a Coasian perspective. Since contracts allow economic agents to reach efficient solutions, the role of government is substantially reduced whenever a private agreement is possible. Therefore a significant number of cases in which externalities are involved would be solved efficiently if enforcement of property rights were possible. And from this perspective most 'tragedy of the commons'-type problems can be explained, not as market failures, but as institutional failures, in the sense that property rights are a necessary condition for any efficient market to exist.

FRANCISCO CABRILLO

Bibliography

Coase, Ronald H. (1959), 'The Federal Communications Commission', *The Journal of Law and Economics*, **2**, 1–40.

Coase, Ronald H. (1960), 'The problem of social cost', *The Journal of Law and Economics*, **3**, 1–44.

Coase, Ronald H. (1988), 'Notes on the problem of social cost', *The Firm, The Market and the Law*, Chicago and London: University of Chicago Press, pp. 157–85.

Stigler, George, J. (1966), *The Theory of Price*, London: Macmillan.

See also: Pigou tax.

Cobb–Douglas function

Production and utility function, widely used by economists, was introduced by the mathematician C.W. Cobb and the economist P.H. Douglas (1892–1976) in a seminal paper published in 1948 on the distribution of output among production inputs. Its original version can be written as

$$Q = f(L, K) = A \cdot L^a \cdot K^b,$$

where Q is output, L and K denote input quantities, A is a positive parameter often interpreted as a technology index or a measure of technical efficiency, and a and b are positive parameters that can be interpreted as output elasticities (the percentage change in output due to a 1 per cent increase in input use).

It is easy to prove that this function is continuous, monotonic, non-decreasing and concave in inputs. Hence the isoquants of this function are strictly convex. The isoquant's shape allows for input substitution under the assumption that both inputs are essential ($Q = 0$ if $L = 0$ or $K = 0$). An important weakness of this function is that the input substitution elasticities are constant and equal to 1 for any value of inputs. This property implies serious restrictions in economic behaviour, viz. that input ratios and input price ratios always change in the same proportion. As a consequence, in perfect competition, output is distributed among input owners in the same proportion independently of output level or input (price) ratios.

It is obvious that this production function is homogeneous of degree $a + b$, which is very convenient for modelling different returns to scale (decreasing if $a + b < 1$, constant if $a + b = 1$ and increasing if $a + b > 1$). However, since a and b are invariant, returns to scale do not depend on output level. This property precludes the existence of variable returns to scale depending on production scale.

Despite the above-mentioned weaknesses, this production function has been widely used in empirical analysis because its logarithm version is easy to estimate, and in economics teaching since it is quite easy to derive analytical expression for functions describing producer and consumer behaviour (for example, input demand, cost, profit, expenditure and indirect utility).

JOAQUÍN LORENCES

Bibliography

Douglas, P.H. (1948), 'Are there laws of production?', *American Economic Review*, **38**, 1–41.

Cochrane–Orcutt procedure

This is an iterative method that gives an asymptotically efficient estimator for a regression model with autoregressive disturbances. Let the regression model be

$$y_t = \alpha + \beta x_t + u_t,\ t = 1, \ldots, T, \qquad (1)$$

where $u_t = \rho u_{t-1} + \varepsilon_t \quad \varepsilon_t \approx i.i.d.\ (0, \sigma^2_\varepsilon)$.

Given the structure of u_t in (1), we can write

$$y_t - \rho y_{t-1} = \alpha(1 - \rho) + \beta(x_t - \rho x_{t-1}) + \varepsilon_t \quad t = 2, \ldots, T \qquad (2)$$

or

$$y_t - \alpha - \beta x_t = \rho(y_{t-1} - \alpha - \beta x_{t-1}) + \varepsilon_t \quad t = 2, \ldots, T. \qquad (3)$$

The method is given by the following steps:

1. Estimate equation (1) ignoring the existence of autocorrelation.
2. Put the estimated values of α and β in equation (3) and apply OLS to obtain an initial estimate of ρ.
3. Substitute the estimated value of ρ in (2) and, using least squares, update the estimates of the regression coefficients.
4. Use these updated estimates of α and β in (3) to re-estimate the autoregressive parameter.
5. Use this estimate again in equation (2), and so on until convergence is obtained.

The OLS residuals in model (1) are biased towards randomness, having autocorrelations closer to zero than the disturbances u_t, which may make more difficult the estimation of ρ. As a solution, some authors propose to start the iterative process from the estimation of ρ obtained by OLS in the equation $y_t = a_1 + \rho y_{t-1} + a_2 x_t + a_3 x_{t-1} + \varepsilon_t$ (an unrestricted version of (2)).

1. The method is trivially extended to models with more regressor and/or a higher autoregressive order in u_t.
2. For a large enough sample size T, the loss in efficiency originated by the fact that not all of the T observations are being used in (2) and (3) is not significant.
3. In small samples, feasible generalized least squares gives a more efficient estimator.
4. If the model includes a lagged dependent variable as a regressor, it is also possible to obtain asymptotically efficient estimators through the Cochrane–Orcutt procedure. However, in this case to obtain consistency the instrumental variables estimator should be used in the first step.

IGNACIO DÍAZ-EMPARANZA

Bibliography

Cochrane, D. and G. Orcutt (1949), 'Application of least squares regression to relationships containing autocorrelated error terms', *Journal of American Statistical Association*, **4**, 32–61.

Condorcet's criterion

Assuming that majority voting is the best rule to choose between two candidates, the Marquis of Condorcet (1743–94) shares with Borda his misgivings over the adequacy of the plurality rule for more than two candidates. However, in contrast with Borda, his colleague from the French Academy of Sciences, whose rule he criticized, he followed a different path by proposing that the candidates be ranked according to 'the most probable combination of opinions' (maximum likelihood criterion in modern statistical terminology).

The Condorcet criterion consists of choosing the candidate who defeats all others in pairwise elections using majority rule. If such a candidate exists, he receives the name of the *Condorcet winner* in honour of Condorcet's essay (1785), pioneer work in the demonstration of the interest of applying mathematics to social sciences.

The following example makes clear how the criterion works. Let us take voters I, II, and III, whose preferences for candidates A, B and C are expressed in the following table:

	I	II	III
High	A	B	C
	B	C	B
Low	C	A	A

Applying Condorcet's criterion, the 'most probable combination' would be BCA. B is Condorcet's winner because he defeats each of the other two candidates, A and C, by majority.

As Condorcet himself claimed, some configuration of opinions may not possess such a winner. In those cases, the majority rule results in cycles or repeated votes without reaching a decision (*Condorcet's paradox*). In this example, if we modify the preferences of voter III, so that they are CAB, the result is that A beats B, B beats C and C beats A. As Arrow demonstrated in his general impossibility theorem, any voting system applied to an unrestricted collection of voter preferences must have some serious defect. In the case of majority voting, cycles may be the consequence (intransitive collective preferences). One of the early important theorems in public choice was Black's proof that the majority rule produces an equilibrium outcome when voter preferences are single-peaked. This entails relinquishing Arrow's unrestricted domain property.

FRANCISCO PEDRAJA CHAPARRO

Bibliography

Condorcet, Marquis de (1785), 'Essay on the application of mathematics to the theory of decision making', in

K.M. Baker (ed.) (1976), *Condorcet: Selected Writings*, Indianapolis, IN: Bobbs-Merrill.

See also: Arrow's impossibility theorem, Borda's rule.

Cournot aggregation condition

This is a restriction on the derivative of a linear budget constraint of a household demand system with respect to prices. It is the expression of the fact that total expenditure cannot change in response to a change in prices.

Let us consider a static (one time period) model. Assume rational consumers in the sense that the total budget (denoted by x) is spent on different goods. This implies

$$x = \sum_{k=1}^{N} \mathrm{p}_k \mathrm{q}_k,$$

where q_k denotes quantity and p_k denotes prices.

Let us assume that a demand function exists for each good k. These demands can be written as functions of x and the different prices

$$q_i = g_i(x, p) \text{ for } i = 1, \ldots N,$$

where p is the $N \times 1$ vector of prices. These relationships are called 'Marshallian demand functions', representing household consumption behaviour. Substituting these demand functions into the budget constraint gives

$$\sum_{k=1}^{N} \mathrm{p}_k \mathrm{q}_k(x, p) = x.$$

This equation is referred to as the 'adding-up restriction'. Assume that the demand functions are continuous and differentiable. The adding-up restriction can be expressed as restriction on the derivatives of the demand functions, rather than on the functions themselves. Specifically, total differentiation of the adding-up restriction with respect to p requires that

$$\sum_{k=1}^{N} p_k \frac{\partial g_k}{\partial p_i} + q_i = 0,$$

if the adding-up restriction is to continue to apply. This is termed the 'Cournot aggregation condition' in honour of the French economist A. Cournot (1801–77).

The Cournot condition can be rewritten in terms of the elasticity of demand with respect to prices, as follows:

$$\sum_{k=1}^{N} w_k e_{ki} + w_i = 0,$$

where w_k is the share of good k in the consumer's total budget and e_{ki} is the uncompensated cross-price elasticity. This restriction is very useful for empirical work. The estimation of demand systems is of considerable interest to many problems, such as for the estimation of the incidence of commodity and income taxes, for testing economic theories of consumer/household behaviour, or to investigate issues regarding the construction of consumer price indices. One could test the theory of demand by seeing whether the estimates satisfy the Cournot aggregation condition. Alternatively, this assumption of the demand theory can be imposed a priori on the econometric estimates, and statistical tests can be used to test its validity.

RAQUEL CARRASCO

Bibliography

Nicholson, J.L. (1957), 'The general form of the adding-up criterion', *Journal of the Royal Statistical Society*, **120**, 84–5.

Worswick, G.D.N. and D.G. Champernowne (1954), 'A note on the adding-up criterion', *Review of Economic Studies*, **22**, 57–60.

See also: Marshallian demand function.

Cournot's oligopoly model

In oligopoly theory we often assume that firms are Cournot competitors, or that firms compete *à la* Cournot. This term originates from the work of Augustin Cournot (1801–77) in 1838. The model presented in his book, after analyzing the pricing and production decisions of a monopolist, is extended to accommodate the existence of more than one firm and the strategic interaction among them.

The assumption is that firms competing in the market offered a fixed quantity at any price. Firms choose simultaneously and take the quantity of the other firms as exogenous. For a given total production, an auctioneer equates supply and demand, deriving the equilibrium price from this relationship. This price, p, can be written as

$$\frac{p - c_i(q_i)}{p} = \frac{q_i/Q}{\eta},$$

where $c_i(q_i)$ is the marginal cost for firm i of producing q_i units, Q is the total production of all firms and η is the elasticity of demand evaluated when total production is Q. This equation can be rewritten after aggregating for all firms as

$$\frac{p - \sum_{i=1}^{n}(q_i/Q)c_i(q_i)}{p} = \frac{HHI}{\eta},$$

where n is the number of firms and HHI is the Herfindahl–Hirschman concentration index, computed as $HHI = \Sigma_{i=1}^{n}(q_i/Q)^2$. Hence the Cournot model predicts that more concentration or a lower elasticity of demand results in an increase in the percentage margin of firms. In the limit, when concentration is maximum and only one firm produces, the index is $HHI = 1$, and consistently the price corresponds to the monopoly one. In perfect competition $HHI = 0$, and the price equals marginal cost.

This model went unnoticed until a first reference by Joseph Bertrand in 1883. Bertrand criticizes the assumption that firms post quantities instead of prices. Moreover, if firms compete in prices, also known as *à la* Bertrand, and the marginal cost is constant and equal for all firms, the unique equilibrium corresponds to all firms producing at price equal to marginal cost. In other words, two firms would be enough to achieve the competitive outcome. Moreover, depending on the assumptions on cost, the equilibrium might be non-existent or multiple.

Although economists are mainly sympathetic to Bertrand's idea that firms choose prices rather than quantities, there is also some consensus that the predictions of the Cournot model are more coherent with empirical evidence. For this reason an extensive literature has focused on reconciling the two points of view.

In the case of monopoly, the outcome is independent of whether we assume that the firm chooses a price or a quantity. In oligopoly, however, an assumption on the residual demand that a firm faces for a given action by the other firms is required. In the Bertrand model the firm with the lowest price is assumed to produce as much as is necessary to cover the total market demand. Therefore the residual demand of any firm with a higher price is 0. At the opposite end, the Cournot model assumes that the quantity posted by each firm is independent of the price. Moreover, each firm assumes that consumers with the highest valuation are served by its competitors. This is what is denoted as efficient rationing. For this reason, the residual demand is the original demand where the quantity posted by other firms is subtracted. As a result, each firm is a monopolist of his residual demand.

Between these two competition choices a variety of other outcomes can be generated. If, for example, firms post supply functions as in Klemperer and Meyer (1989), the multiplicity of equilibria includes both the Bertrand and the Cournot outcomes as extreme cases.

In general, whether the outcome resembles the Cournot equilibrium or not will depend on the relevant strategic variable in each case. For example, Kreps and Scheinkman (1983) study the case where capacity is fixed in the short run. In their model, firms play in two stages. In the first, they simultaneously choose capacity, while in the second they compete *à la* Bertrand. Despite the choice of prices the equilibrium corresponds to the Cournot outcome. The intuition is that, in the last stage, the capacity is fixed and each firm becomes a monopolist of the residual demand once the other firm has sold its production. Other papers such as Holt and Scheffman (1987) show that most-favored-customer clauses also give rise to Cournot outcomes.

Finally, another reason why the Cournot model has been widely used is that it is a prototypical example in game theory. It derived reaction functions and a notion of equilibrium later formalized by Nash. In recent years, it has also been used as an illustration of supermodular games.

GERARD LLOBET

Bibliography

Cournot, A.A. (1838), *Recherches sur les principes mathématiques de la théorie des richesses*, Paris: L. Hachette.

Holt C. and D. Scheffman (1987), 'Facilitating practices: the effects of advance notice and best-price policies', *Rand Journal of Economics*, **18**, 187–97.

Klemperer, P.D. and M.A. Meyer (1989), 'Supply function equilibria in oligopoly under uncertainty', *Econometrica*, **57** (6), 1243–77.

Kreps, D. and J. Scheinkman (1983), 'Quantity precommitment and Bertrand competition yield Cournot outcomes', *Bell Journal of Economics*, **14**, 326–37.

Vives, X. (1989), 'Cournot and the oligopoly problem', *European Economic Review*, **33**, 503–14.

See also: Bertrand competition model, Edgeworth oligopoly model, Herfindahl–Hirschman index, Nash equilibrium.

Cowles Commission

The Cowles Commission for Research in Economics was set up to undertake econometric research in 1932 by Alfred Cowles (1891–1984), president of Cowles & Co., an investing counselling firm in Colorado Springs, interested in the accuracy of forecasting services, especially after the stock market crash in 1929. The Commission stemmed from an agreement between Cowles and the Econometric Society, created in 1930, in order to link economic theory to mathematics and statistics, particularly in two fields: general equilibrium theory and econometrics. Its first home was Colorado Springs under the directorship of Charles F. Roos, one of the founders of the Econometric Society, but after his resignation the remoteness of Colorado suggested a move. The decision of moving to Chicago in 1939, in spite of the interest of other universities, was associated with the appointment of Theodore O. Yntema as the new research director. Later, under the directorship of Tjalling C. Koopmans, and as the opposition by the Department of Economics at Chicago became more intense, the Commission moved again, to Yale University in 1955.

The change of the Commission's original motto 'Science is Measurement' to 'Theory and Measurement' in 1952 reflected the methodological debates at the time. Frank Knight and his students, including Milton Friedman and Gary Becker, criticized the Commission (Christ, 1994, p. 35). Friedman argued against the econometric brand not only because of the econometric methods but also because of his skeptical view of the Keynesian model and consumption function. There were also financial considerations, and difficulties in finding a new director of research after Koopmans, who was involved in the discussion, left. Once in Yale, James Tobin, who had declined the directorship of the Commission at Chicago, accepted the appointment at Yale (Hildreth, 1986, p.11).

Numerous Cowles associates have won Nobel Prizes for research done while at the Cowles Commission: Koopmans, Haavelmo, Markowitz, Modigliani, Arrow, Debreu, Simon, Klein and Tobin.

MARÍA BLANCO GONZÁLEZ

Bibliography

Christ, Carl (1994), 'The Cowles Commission's contributions to Econometrics at Chicago, 1939–1955', *Journal of Economic Literature*, **32**, 30–59.

Hildreth, Clifford (1986), *The Cowles Commission in Chicago 1939–1955*, Berlin: Springer-Verlag.

Klein, Lawrence (1991), 'Econometric contributions of the Cowles Commission, 1944–1947', *Banca Nazionale del Lavoro Quarterly Review*, **177**, 107–17.

Morgan, Mary (1990), *History of Econometric Ideas*, Cambridge: Cambridge University Press.

Cox's test

In applied econometrics, frequently, there is a need for statistical procedures in order to choose between two non-nested models. Cox's test (Cox, 1961, 1962) is a related set of procedures based on the *likelihood ratio test* that allows us to compare two competing non-nested models.

In the linear hypothesis framework for linear statistical models, consider the following two non-nested models:

$$H_1: Y = X_1\beta_1 + u_1$$
$$H_2: Y = X_2\beta_2 + u_2,$$

where $u_2 \sim N(0, \sigma_2^2 I)$.

These models are non-nested if the regressors under one model are not a subset of the other model even though X_1 y X_2 may have some common variables. In order to test the hypothesis that X_1 vector is the correct set of explanatory variables and X_2 is not, Cox used the following statistic:

$$C_{12} = \frac{T}{2}\ln\left(\frac{\hat{\sigma}_2^2}{\hat{\sigma}_1^2 + \frac{1}{T}\hat{\beta}_1 X'_1 (I - X_2(X'_2X_2)^{-1} X'_2)X_1\hat{\beta}_1}\right)$$

$$= \frac{T}{2}\ln\left(\frac{\hat{\sigma}_2^2}{\hat{\sigma}_{21}^2}\right).$$

Cox demonstrated that, when H_1 is true, C_{12} will be asymptotically normally distributed with mean zero and variance $V(C_{12})$. The small-sample distribution of the test statistic C_{12} depends on unknown parameters and thus cannot be derived. However, if we defined $I - X_2 (X'_2X_2)^{-1} X'_2 = M_2$ and we verified that $M_2 X_1 = 0$, then the models are nested and an exact test exist.

Given the asymptotic variance $V(C_{12})$, under H_1 true, the expression

$$\frac{C_{12}}{(V(C_{12}))^{1/2}}$$

is asymptotically distributed as a standard normal random variable.

Pesaran, in 1974, showed that, if the unknown parameters are replaced by consistent estimators, then

$$\hat{V}(C_{12}) = \left(\frac{\hat{\sigma}_1^2}{\hat{\sigma}_{12}^4}\right)\hat{\beta}_1 X'\, M_2 M_1 M_2 X\hat{\beta}_1$$

can be used to estimate $V(C_{12})$, where M_2 is defined as above and $M_1 = I - X\,(X'X)^{-1} X'$. The test statistic can be run, under H_1 true, by using critical value from the standard normal variable table. A large value of C_{12} is evidence against the null hypothesis (H_1).

NICOLÁS CARRASCO

Bibliography

Cox, D.R. (1961), 'Test of separate families of hypothesis', *Proceedings of the Fourth Berkeley Symposium on Mathematical Statistics and Probability*, vol. 1, Berkeley: University of California Press.

Cox, D.R. (1962), 'Further results on tests of separate families of hypothesis', *Journal of the Royal Statistical Society*, B, **24**, 406–24.

D

Davenant–King law of demand

Empirical study of the inverse relationship between price and quantity. Charles Davenant (1656–1714) and Gregory King (1648–1712) were two British mercantilists who, as followers of William Petty's 'political arithmetic', concerned themselves with quantifying his statements. The former was a public servant and member of parliament (MP) who, amongst other writings on trade, wrote *An Essay on Ways and Means of Supplying the War* (1695), *Essay on the East-India Trade* (1696) and *Discourses on the Public Revenue and on the Trade of England* (1698). The works of the latter were published in 1802, long after his death, and in these appear a number of interesting estimates of population and national income. King (1696) and Davenant (1699), the latter including extracts from the former, establish the inverse relationship between the amount of a good produced and its price. King shows that a reduction in the wheat harvest may be accompanied by an increase in its price in the following proportions:

Reduction of harvest	Increase in price
1 I 10	3 I 10
2 I 10	8 I 10
3 I 10	16 I 10
4 I 10	28 I 10
5 I 10	45 I 10

Davenant, in his work of 1699, states:

> We take it, That a Defect in the Harvest may raise the Price of Corn in the following Proportions:
>
> | *Defect* | | *above the Common Rate* |
> |---|---|---|
> | 1 tenth | | 3 tenths |
> | 2 tenths | | 8 tenths |
> | 3 tenths | } Raises the Price { | 1.6 tenths |
> | 4 tenths | | 2.8 tenths |
> | 5 tenths | | 4.5 tenths |
>
> So that when Corn rises to treble the Common Rate, it may be presumed, that we want above a third of the Common Produce; and if we should want 5 Tenths, or half the Common Produce, the Price would rise to near five times the Common Rate (Davenant [1699] 1995, p. 255).

Later economists such as Arthur Young, Dugald Stewart, Lord Lauderdale, William Stanley Jevons, Philip Henry Wicksteed, Alfred Marshall and Vilfredo Pareto were familiar with King's or Davenant's exposé, or their joint work when they developed their theory of demand.

LUIS PERDICES DE BLAS

Bibliography

Creedy, John (1987), 'On the King–Davenant "law" of demand', *Scottish Journal of Political Economy*, **33** (3), 193–212.

Davenant, Charles (1699), *An Essay Upon the Probable Methods of Making a People Gainers in the Balance of Trade*, reprinted in L. Magnusson (ed.) (1995), *Mercantilism*, vol. III, London and New York: Routledge.

Endres, A.M. (1987), 'The King–Davenant "law" in classical economics', *History of Political Economy*, **19** (4), 621–38.

King, Gregory (1696), *Natural and Political Observations and Conclusions upon the State and Condition of England*, reprinted in P. Laslett (1973), *The Earliest Classics: John Graunt and Gregory King*, Farnborough, Hants: Gregg International Publishers.

Díaz-Alejandro effect

This refers to the paradox that a devaluation may lead to a decrease in domestic output as a consequence of its redistributive effects. This runs counter to the conventional textbook view that devaluations, by encouraging the production of tradable goods, will be expansionary. To understand the effect, assume, for instance, that a country is divided into two classes – wage earners and capitalists – with each class made up of individuals with identical tastes. Since the capitalists' marginal propensity to consume will presumably be lower than the workers', the redistribution of income from wage earners to capitalists brought about by a devaluation will have a contractionary effect on aggregate demand, thereby reducing aggregate output. This contraction will run parallel to the improvement in the trade balance.

When the effect was formulated in 1963, the redistributive effect of devaluations was already well known. But Cuban economist Carlos F. Díaz-Alejandro (1937–85) emphasized the significance and timing of the effect, and its impact on domestic output. He based his insight on the experience of devaluations in Argentina and other semi-industrialized countries during the 1950s, where devaluations had implied a significant transfer of resources from urban workers to landowners.

A review of the literature on this and other effects of devaluations can be found in Kamin and Klau (1998).

EMILIO ONTIVEROS

Bibliography

Díaz-Alejandro, Carlos F. (1963), 'A note on the impact of devaluation and the redistributive effect', *Journal of Political Economy*, **71** (6), 577–80

Kamin, Steven B. and Marc Klau (1998), 'Some multi-country evidence on the effects of real exchange rates on output', *Board of Governors of the Federal Reserve System, International Finance Discussion Papers*, no. 611, May.

Dickey–Fuller test

To apply standard inference procedures in a dynamic time series model we need the various variables to be stationary, since the bulk of econometric theory is built upon the assumption of stationarity. However, in applied research we usually find integrated variables, which are a specific class of non-stationary variables with important economic and statistical properties. These are derived from the presence of unit roots which give rise to stochastic trends, as opposed to pure deterministic trends, with innovations to an integrated process being permanent instead of transient.

Statisticians have been aware for many years of the existence of integrated series and, in fact, Box and Jenkins (1970) argue that a non-stationary series can be transformed into a stationary one by successive differencing of the series. Therefore, from their point of view, the differencing operation seemed to be a prerequisite for econometric modelling from both a univariate and a multivariate perspective.

Several statistical tests for unit roots have been developed to test for stationarity in time series. The most commonly used to test whether a pure AR(1) process (with or without drift) has a unit root are the Dickey–Fuller (DF) statistics. These test statistics were proposed by Dickey and Fuller (1979).

They consider the three following alternative data-generating processes (DGP) of a time series:

$$y_t = \rho_n y_{t-1} + \varepsilon_t \quad (1)$$

$$y_t = \mu_c + \rho_c y_{t-1} + \varepsilon_t \quad (2)$$

$$y_t = \mu_{c\tau} + \gamma_\tau + \rho_{c\tau} y_{t-1} + \varepsilon_t \quad (3)$$

where $\varepsilon_t \sim iid(0, \sigma^2_\varepsilon)$, t is a time trend and the initial condition, y_0 is assumed to be a known constant (zero, without loss of generality). For equation (1), if $\rho_n < 1$, then the DGP is a stationary zero-mean AR(1) process and if $\rho_n = 1$, then the DGP is a pure random walk. For equation (2), if $\rho_c < 1$, then the DGP is a stationary AR(1) process with mean $\mu_c/(1 - \rho_c)$ and if $\rho_n = 1$, then the DGP is a random walk with a drift μ_n. Finally, for equation (3), if $\rho_{c\tau} < 1$, the DGP is a trend-stationary AR(1) process with mean

$$\frac{\mu_{c\tau}}{1 - \rho_{c\tau}} + \gamma_{c\tau}\sum_{j=0}^{t}[\rho_{c\tau}^{j}(t - j)]$$

and if $\rho_{c\tau} = 1$, then the DGP is a random walk with a drift changing over time.

The test is carried out by estimating the following equations

$$\Delta y_t = (\rho_n - 1)y_{t-1} + \varepsilon_t \qquad (1')$$

$$\Delta y_t = \beta_{0c} + (\rho_c - 1)y_{t-1} + \varepsilon_t \qquad (2')$$

$$\Delta y_t = \beta_{0c\tau}t + \beta_{1c\tau}t + (\rho_{c\tau} - 1)y_{t-1} + \varepsilon_t \quad (3')$$

The tests are implemented through the usual t-statistic on the estimated $(\rho - 1)$. They are denoted τ, τ_μ and τ_τ, respectively. Given that, under the null hypothesis, this test statistic does not have the standard t distribution, Dickey and Fuller (1979) simulated critical values for selected sample sizes. More extensive critical values are reported by MacKinnon (1991).

Hitherto, we have assumed that the DGP is a pure AR(1) process. If the series is correlated at higher order lag, the assumption of white noise disturbance is violated. Dickey and Fuller (1979) have shown that we can augment the basic regression models (1′)–(3′) with p lags of Δy_t:

$$\Delta y_t = (\rho_n - 1)y_{t-1} + \sum_{i=1}^{p}\alpha_i\Delta y_{t-i} + \varepsilon_t \qquad (1'')$$

$$\Delta y_t = \beta_{0c} + (\rho_c - 1)y_{t-1} + \sum_{i=1}^{p}\alpha_i\Delta y_{t-i} + \varepsilon_t \quad (2'')$$

$$\Delta y_t = \beta_{0c\tau}t + \beta_{1c\tau}t + (\rho_{c\tau} - 1)y_{t-1} + \sum_{i=1}^{p}\alpha_i\Delta y_{t-i} + \varepsilon_t \qquad (3'')$$

The tests are based on the t-ratio on $(\hat{\rho} - 1)$ and are known as 'augmented Dickey–Fuller' (ADF) statistics. The critical values are the same as those discussed for the DF statistics, since the asymptotic distributions of the t-statistics on $(\hat{\rho} - 1)$ is independent of the number of lagged first differences included in the ADF regression.

SIMÓN SOSVILLA-ROMERO

Bibliography

Box, G.E.P. and G.M. Jenkins (1976), *Time Series Analysis: Forecasting and Control*, rev. edn, Holden-Day.

Dickey, D.A. and W.A. Fuller (1979), 'Distribution of the estimators for autoregressive time series with a unit root', *Journal of the American Statistical Association*, **74**, 427–31.

MacKinnon, J.G. (1991), 'Critical values for cointegration tests', Chapter 13 in R.F. Engle and C.W.J. Granger (eds), *Long-run Economic Relationships: Readings in Cointegration*, Oxford University Press.

See also: Box-Jenkins Analysis, Phillips–Perron test.

Director's law

This is an empirical proposition about the overall effect of government policies on the personal distribution of income. Named after Aaron Director, (1901–2004) Professor of Economics at the Law School of the University of Chicago, it states that, no matter how egalitarian their aims might be, the net effect of government programs is to redistribute income toward the middle class. True to the spirit of the Chicago School and its reliance on the oral tradition, Aaron Director never got to publish his reflections on the positive economics of income redistribution or, indeed, on many other subjects. It is chiefly through his influence on his colleagues and students that his contributions are known. Milton Friedman, George Stigler and others have repeatedly acknowledged their indebtedness to Director's inspiration and criticism.

Stigler, who coined the law, was, more than any other, responsible for bringing

Director's views on redistribution to the attention of the economics profession. Director challenged what is still the dominant view, according to which the progressive income tax and income transfer schemes that figure so prominently in modern fiscal systems effectively operate a redistribution of income from the wealthy to the poorest members of society. He pointed out, according to Stigler, several features of contemporary democracies that account for the unconventional result that governments redistribute income from the tails to the middle of the distribution.

Firstly, under majority voting, in the zero-sum game of cash income redistribution, the minimum winning coalition would comprise the lower half of the distribution. Secondly, one should notice that, as the very poor and destitute do not exercise their voting rights as much as the average citizen, middle-income voters would be overrepresented in the winning coalition. Thirdly, and more relevant, modern governments not only effect pure cash transfers but mostly engage in a variety of actions in response to the pressures of organized interest groups that end up transferring income to the middle class. Agricultural policy transfers income to farmers and affluent landowners; public education (particularly higher education) is a transfer to the well-to-do; subsidies to owner-occupied housing likewise benefit those who are well off; minimum wage legislation favours the lower middle class at the expense of the very poor; professional licensing erects barriers against the most enterprising but less fortunate citizens; lastly, even most programs focused on poverty alleviation, by enlisting the cooperation of social workers, health experts and government officials, create a derived demand for services provided mainly by members of the middle class.

ALFONSO CARBAJO

Bibliography

Riker, W.H. (1962), *The Theory of Political Coalitions*, New Haven: Yale University Press.

Stigler, G.J. (1970), 'Director's law of public income redistribution', *Journal of Law and Economics*, **13** (1), 1–10.

Tullock, G. (1971), 'The charity of the uncharitable', *Western Economic Journal*, **9** (4), 379–92.

Divisia index

The French statistician François Divisia (1889–1964) formulated in a long article published in 1925–6 a new type of index that tried to measure the amount of money held for transaction purposes as an alternative to other indexes, based on the conventional simple-sum aggregates.

Assume that an individual spends a total amount $e(t)$ buying n goods in quantities $(x_1(t), \ldots, x_n(t))$ at prices $(p_1(t), \ldots, p_n(t))$ in period t. Therefore

$$e(t) = \sum_{i=1}^{n} p_i(t)x_i(t).$$

Total log-differentiation of $e(t)$ gives

$$\frac{\dot{e}(t)}{e(t)} = \sum_{i=1}^{n} \frac{p_i(t)x_i(t)}{e(t)} \frac{\dot{p}_i(t)}{p_i(t)} + \sum_{i=1}^{n} \frac{p_i(t)x_i(t)}{e(t)} \frac{\dot{x}_i(t)}{x_i(t)}, \quad (1)$$

where dots over variables indicate derivatives with respect to time. The left side of (1) is the instant growth rate of expenditure and is decomposed into two components: (a) the Divisia index of prices which is the first term of the right-hand side of (1), and (b) the Divisia index of quantities which is the second term of the right-hand side of (1). Therefore the Divisia indexes are weighted averages of the growth rates of individual prices (or quantities), the weight being the respective shares in total expenditure. Although the indexes in (1) are expressed in continuous time, which made them inappropriate for empirical analysis, Törnqvist (1936) solved the problem for approximating (1) to discrete time terms. Törnqvist's solution in the case of prices is

$$\sum_{i=1}^{n} \frac{1}{2}\left[\frac{p_i(t)x_i(t)}{e(t)} + \frac{p_i(t-1)x_i(t-1)}{e(t-1)}\right] \times$$
$$[\log p_i(t) - \log p_i(t-1)],$$

which means that the growth rate of prices is approximated by the logarithmic differences and the weights are approximated by simple averages between two consecutive periods. In the same applied vein, the Divisia indexes can be considered as 'chain indexes' and we can approximate them for Laspeyres or Paasche indexes which change their base in every period.

Although the Divisia indexes have been used in theoretical work for many different problems (industrial and consumption prices, quantities, cost of living and so on) they aimed at avoiding the inconvenience of other monetary aggregates computed as simple sums of components of the monetary quantities, such as currency and demand deposits. That implies perfect substitutability between components of the monetary aggregate, whereas they are not equally useful for all transactions. Therefore simple sum aggregation is inappropriate in consumer demand theory.

Instead of measuring the stock of money held in the economy, the Divisia index assesses the utility the consumer derives from holding a portfolio of different monetary assets. It treats monetary assets as consumer durables such as cars, televisions and houses, yielding a flow of monetary services. These services are performed by different monetary assets to a different degree and are proportional to the stock of monetary assets held. If the consumer's utility function is weakly separable in consumption and monetary assets, the Divisia aggregate can be regarded as a single economic good.

In brief, the objective of the Divisia measure is to construct an index of the flow of monetary services from a group of monetary assets that behave as if they were a single commodity. Divisia monetary aggregates are thus obtained by multiplying each component asset's growth rate by its share weights and adding the products. Every component's share weight depends on the user costs and the quantities of all components assets.

Divisia monetary aggregates can be applied when analysing whether structural change affects the stability of the demand-for-money and supply-of-money functions, under total deregulation and is a good indicator of control on money supply.

MILAGROS AVEDILLO

Bibliography

Bernett, W.A. (1980), 'Economic monetary aggregates: an application of index number and aggregation theory', *Journal of Econometrics*, **14**, 11–48.

Divisia, F. (1925–6), 'L'indice monétaire de la théorie de la monnaie', *Revue d'Economie Politique*, **39** (4), 980–1008; **39** (6), 1121–51; **40** (1), 49–81.

Törnqvist, L. (1936), 'The Bank of Finland's consumption price index', *Bank of Finland Monthly Review*, **10**, 1–8.

See also: Laspeyres index, Paasche index.

Dixit–Stiglitz monopolistic competition model

The model of Avinash K. Dixit and Joseph E. Stiglitz (1977) (DS hereafter) is a benchmark monopolistic competition model which has been widely used in several economic areas such as international economics, growth economics, industrial organization, regional and urban economics and macroeconomics.

The DS model and the similar Spence (1976) model introduced an alternative way to treat product differentiation. In the horizontal and vertical differentiation models a product competes more with some products than with others. In the DS and the Spence models there are no neighboring goods: all products are equally far apart, so every one competes with the rest. This hypothesis requires defining the industry appropriately.

Products must be good substitutes among themselves, but poor substitutes for the other commodities in the economy. Additionally, the preference structure allows modeling directly the desirability of variety, using the convexity of indifference surfaces of a conventional utility function. The representative consumer will purchase a little bit of every available product, varying the proportion of each according to their prices.

The main characteristics of this model are the following. First, there is a representative consumer whose utility function depends on the numeraire commodity, labelled 0, and on all the n commodities of a given industry or sector. The numeraire aggregates the rest of the economy. Using x_0 and x_i, $i = 1, 2 \ldots, n$, to denote the amount of the commodities, the utility function will be

$$u = U(x_0, V(x_1, x_2, \ldots, x_n)),$$

where U is a separable and concave function, and V is a symmetric function. In particular, the central case developed by DS is the constant-elasticity (CES) case, in which

$$V(x_1, x_2, \ldots, x_n) = \left(\sum_{i=1}^{n} x_i^{\rho}\right)^{1/\rho}, \quad 0 < \rho < 1$$

and U is assumed homothetic in its arguments. This implies assuming that the sector expands in proportion to the rest of the economy as the size of the economy changes, which can be very useful in international trade and growth theory. Alternatively, in the Spence model, V is assumed CES and U quasi-linear, which can be very convenient in the context of partial equilibrium analysis.

Second, the consumer budget constraint is

$$x_0 + \sum_{i=1}^{n} p_i x_i = I,$$

where I is the income and p_i is the price of commodity i.

Third, there are n different firms with identical cost functions. Each firm must face some fixed set-up cost and has a constant marginal cost.

Fourth, each firm produces a different commodity.

Fifth, the number of firms, n, is reasonably large and accordingly each firm is negligible, in the sense that it can ignore its impact on, and hence reactions from, other firms, and the cross-elasticity of demand is negligible. In the CES case, for each commodity i it can be checked that demand will be given by $x_i = yq^{\sigma}\, \mathrm{p}_i^{-\sigma}$, where $\sigma = 1/(1 - \rho)$ is the elasticity of substitution between the differentiated products and y and q are quantity and price indices

$$y = \left(\sum_{i=1}^{n} x_i^{\rho}\right)^{1/\rho}, \qquad q = \left(\sum_{i=1}^{n} p_i^{1-\sigma}\right)^{1/(1-\sigma)}.$$

Assuming that each firm is negligible implies that $\partial \log q / \partial \log p_i$ and $\partial \log x_i / \partial \log p_j$, $\forall i \neq j$, both depending on a term of order $1/n$, are negligible.

Finally, firms maximize profits and entry is free.

Monopolistic competition is characterized by solving the representative consumer problem to obtain demand functions, by solving the firm's problems to determine prices, and by taking into account that entry will proceed until the next potential entrant would make a loss.

DS use their model to analyze the optimality of the market solution in the monopolistic equilibrium addressing the question of quantity versus diversity, but their model has been used in a vast number of papers with the most varied purposes. In a collection of essays edited by Brakman and Heijdra (2003), several authors, including Dixit and Stiglitz, present their reflections on the actual state of the theory of monopolistic competition.

CONSUELO PAZÓ

Bibliography

Brakman, S. and B.J. Heijdra (eds) (2003), *The Monopolistic Competition Revolution in Retrospect*, Cambridge University Press.
Dixit, A.K. and J.E. Stiglitz (1977), 'Monopolistic competition and optimum product diversity', *American Economic Review*, **67** (3), 297–308.
Spence, A.M. (1976), 'Product selection, fixed costs and monopolistic competition', *Review of Economic Studies*, **43**, 217–35.

See also: Chamberlin's oligopoly model.

Dorfman–Steiner condition

In their seminal paper on advertising, Robert Dorfman (1916–2002) and Peter O. Steiner show that a profit-maximizing firm chooses the advertising expenditure and price such that the increase in revenue resulting from one additional unit of advertising is equal to the price elasticity of demand for the firm's product. This result has usually been formulated in terms of advertising intensity, the ratio of advertising expenditure to total sales. For this ratio the formula of the Dorfman–Steiner condition is

$$\frac{s}{pq} = \frac{\eta}{\varepsilon},$$

where s denotes the total expenses of advertising, p is the price, q is the quantity, η is the demand elasticity with respect to advertising expenditures and ε is the price elasticity of demand. The equation states that the monopolist's optimal advertising to sales ratio is equal to the relationship between the advertising elasticity of demand and the price elasticity of demand. To obtain the condition two assumptions are required: on the one hand, the demand facing the firm has to be a function of price and advertising and, on the other hand, the cost function has to be additive in output and advertising.

JOSÉ C. FARIÑAS

Bibliography

R. Dorfman and P.O. Steiner (1954), 'Optimal advertising and optimal quality', *American Economic Review*, **44** (5), 826–36.

Duesenberry demonstration effect

In February 1948, James S. Duesenberry (b.1918) presented his doctoral dissertation in the University of Michigan, titled 'The Consumption Function', whose contents were later published with the title *Income, Saving and the Theory of Consumer Behavior* (1949) that was the starting point for the behavior analyses related to consumption and saving until the introduction of the approaches associated with the concepts of permanent income and life cycle.

The expression 'demonstration effect' is specifically stated in section four of the third chapter of the above-mentioned book. This expression overcame the absolute income approach. In this approach the utility index was made dependent on current and future consumption and wealth, but this index was peculiar to every individual and independent of the others. On the contrary, the demonstration effect rejects both the independence between individuals and the temporal reversibility of the decisions taken. It forms the basis of the explanation of the behavior in the interdependence of individuals and the irreversible nature of their temporal decisions.

Thus, on the one hand, it is accepted that individuals aspire to consume better quality goods and in larger quantities when their income increases, but, on the other hand, the utility index of any individual does not depend on the absolute level of their consumption, but on the relation between their expenses and other people's expenses and, taking into account the time dimension, the attitudes towards their future spending will depend on the current levels of consumption, and especially on the maximum level that was previously reached.

What was regarded as the 'fundamental psychological law', namely, every increase in income entails an increase in consumption in a ratio less than the unit, is replaced by another 'psychological postulate' that states that it is more difficult for a family to reduce its expenses from a high level than to refrain from spending big amounts for the first time. Starting from those assumptions, several conclusions can be drawn.

1. The increases in income in the whole population, without altering the distribution, will not alter the average consumption.
2. On the contrary, the increases in income in a certain sector of the population will tend to increase consumption in terms of its absolute value but to decrease average consumption.
3. This last effect is more noticeable in the high-income group (but this is not valid in the low-income groups, where the tendency to consumption is the unit).
4. Changes in the income distribution and/or the population pyramid will affect the performance of consumption and saving.
5. A steady increase in income over time yields, as a result, an average tendency towards stable consumption.
6. A deceleration in economic activity will cause an increase in the average tendency to consume, which will put a brake on the depression.

The demonstration effect also has strong implications for the welfare state since the individual welfare indices will depend (positively or negatively) on incomes and life standards of others. All this alters the efficiency criteria in economic analysis as well as the allocation and fairness criteria, and the fiscal mechanisms required to rectify the inequalities arising from the efficiency criteria based on the strict independence between individuals.

Finally, the demonstration effect shows a considerable explanatory power in relation to the introduction of new goods in the market and the development and structure of the total amount of spending.

JON SANTACOLOMA

Bibliography

Duesenberry, J.S. (1949), *Income, Saving and the Theory of Consumer Behavior*, Cambridge, MA: Harvard University Press.

Durbin–Watson statistic

This determines whether the disturbance term of a regression model presents autocorrelation according to a first-order autoregressive scheme –$AR(1)$–. Its numerical value (which may range from zero to four, both inclusive) is obtained from the residuals (e_t) of the estimation by ordinary least squares of the model. So an expression from which it can be obtained is given by

$$DW = \frac{\sum_{t=2}^{T}(e_t - e_{t-1})^2}{\sum_{t=1}^{T} e_t^2}.$$

Values near zero indicate that the disturbance term presents autocorrelation according to a scheme $AR(1)$ with positive parameter (ρ_1); values near four indicate that the disturbance term presents autocorrelation according to a scheme $AR(1)$ with negative parameter (ρ_1); and values near two indicate that the disturbance term does not present autocorrelation according to a scheme $AR(1)$. Accordingly, one can obtain an approximate value for the Durbin–Watson statistic by means of the expression: $DW = 2(1 - \hat{\rho}_1)$, where $\hat{\rho}_1$ is the estimation of the parameter of the scheme $AR(1)$. Among its drawbacks is the fact that it should not be used if the delayed endogenous variable is among the regressors because in this case the conclusion tends to be that the disturbance term does not present autocorrelation according to a scheme *AR*(1).

JORDI SURINACH

Bibliography

Durbin, J. and G.S. Watson (1950), 'Testing for serial correlation in least squares regression I', *Biometrika*, **37**, 409–28.

Durbin, J. and G.S. Watson (1951), 'Testing for serial correlation in least squares regression II', *Biometrika*, **38**, 159–78.

Durbin, J. and G.S. Watson (1971), 'Testing for serial correlation in least squares regression III', *Biometrika*, **58**, 1–42.

Durbin–Wu–Hausman test

The Durbin–Wu–Hausman test (henceforth DWH test) has been developed as a specification test of the orthogonality assumption in econometrics. In the case of the standard linear regression model, $y = X\beta + u$, this assumption is that the conditional expectation of u given X is zero; that is, $E(u/X) = 0$ or, in large samples,

$$plim \frac{X'u}{T} = 0.$$

The DWH test relies on a quadratic form obtained from the difference between two alternative estimators of the vector of regression coefficients, say $\hat{\beta}_0$ and $\hat{\beta}_1$. $\hat{\beta}_0$ must be consistent and (asymptotically) efficient under the null hypothesis, but it is inconsistent under the alternative hypothesis. On the other hand, $\hat{\beta}_1$ is not asymptotically efficient under the null hypothesis but it is consistent under both the null and the alternative hypotheses. The DWH test is based on $\hat{q} = \hat{\beta}_1 - \hat{\beta}_0$. Under the null hypothesis, $\hat{q}$ converges in probability to zero while, under the alternative hypothesis, this limit is not zero. The idea that one may base a test on the vector of differences between two vectors of estimates dates back to Durbin (1954). Two other relevant papers are Wu (1973) and Hausman (1978). In these papers, the approach is extended to a simultaneous equation econometric model.

ANTONIO AZNAR

Bibliography

Durbin, J. (1954), 'Errors in variables', *Review of the International Statistical Institute*, **22**, 23–32.

Hausman J.A. (1978), 'Specification tests in econometrics', *Econometrica*, **46**, 1251–71.

Wu, D.M. (1973), 'Alternative tests of independence between stochastic regressors and disturbances', *Econometrica*, **41**, 733–50.

E

Edgeworth box

The Edgeworth Box diagram is a conceptual device often used in economics to show how a given basket of goods can be efficiently (and also inefficiently) distributed among a set of individuals. The basic idea of an efficient distribution is that of Pareto-optimality: the goods must be allocated in such a way that no redistribution is possible so that one individual increases his/her utility without someone else decreasing his/hers. The Edgeworth Box illustrates this for the particular case of two individuals (*A* and *B*) and two goods (*X* and *Y*). The box is depicted as a rectangle, the size of which is given by the amount of goods available. The width of the rectangle shows the total amount of *X* and the height shows the total amount of *Y*. Any point in the Edgeworth box (either an interior or a boundary point) shows a possible allocation. The amount of the *X* good assigned to *A* is measured by the horizontal distance from the allocation point to O_A. The vertical distance from the allocation point to O_A shows the amount of *Y* assigned to *A*. Similarly the horizontal and vertical distances from the allocation point to O_B show the amounts of *X* and *Y* that are being assigned to *B*. The indifference maps of both individuals are also represented within the box. *A*'s indifference curves are depicted with reference to O_A, which means that *A*'s utility increases in the north-east direction. *B*'s indifference curves are drawn with reference to O_B. Thus, *B*'s utility increases in the south-west direction.

An efficient allocation, as said before, is one that cannot be improved by any redistribution of goods such that both individuals gain or at least one of them does without the other being hurt. From this definition it follows that an efficient allocation must be a tangency point; that is, a point such that the indifference curves of both individuals are tangent to each other. To illustrate this, let us suppose that each individual has an initial endowment of the goods *X* and *Y* labelled (X_A, Y_A) and (X_B, Y_B), (point *F* in the figure). The tangency condition itself defines a collection of points in the box which are Pareto-efficient. The locus of all efficient allocation is usually called the 'contract curve' or 'conflict curve' (the O_AO_B curve in the figure).

The Edgeworth box is also referred to as the Edgeworth–Bowley diagram. Neither expression (Edgeworth box or Edgeworth–Bowley diagram) is correct if it is to be understood as showing priority of discovery. Francis Y. Edgeworth (1845–1926) in fact never drew the diagram box in its present form. It is true that he elaborated the concept of a contract curve and managed to give a graphical representation of it. Edgeworth (1881, p. 28) used a diagram to illustrate the range of possible final contracts between two isolated individuals in a barter situation with the contract curve depicted in it. However, his contract curve diagram could only be converted into a regular box diagram of specific dimensions if the initial endowments, which Edgeworth deliberately ignored, were made explicit. In any case, Edgeworth's diagram was not a 'box'. Nevertheless, it is worth saying that Edgeworth pointed out the correct solution to the problem of bilateral exchange.

According to Jevons that problem had a unique solution. Edgeworth showed that Jevons's case is the one where the solution is more indeterminate: such a solution will depend on the presence of infinite barterers

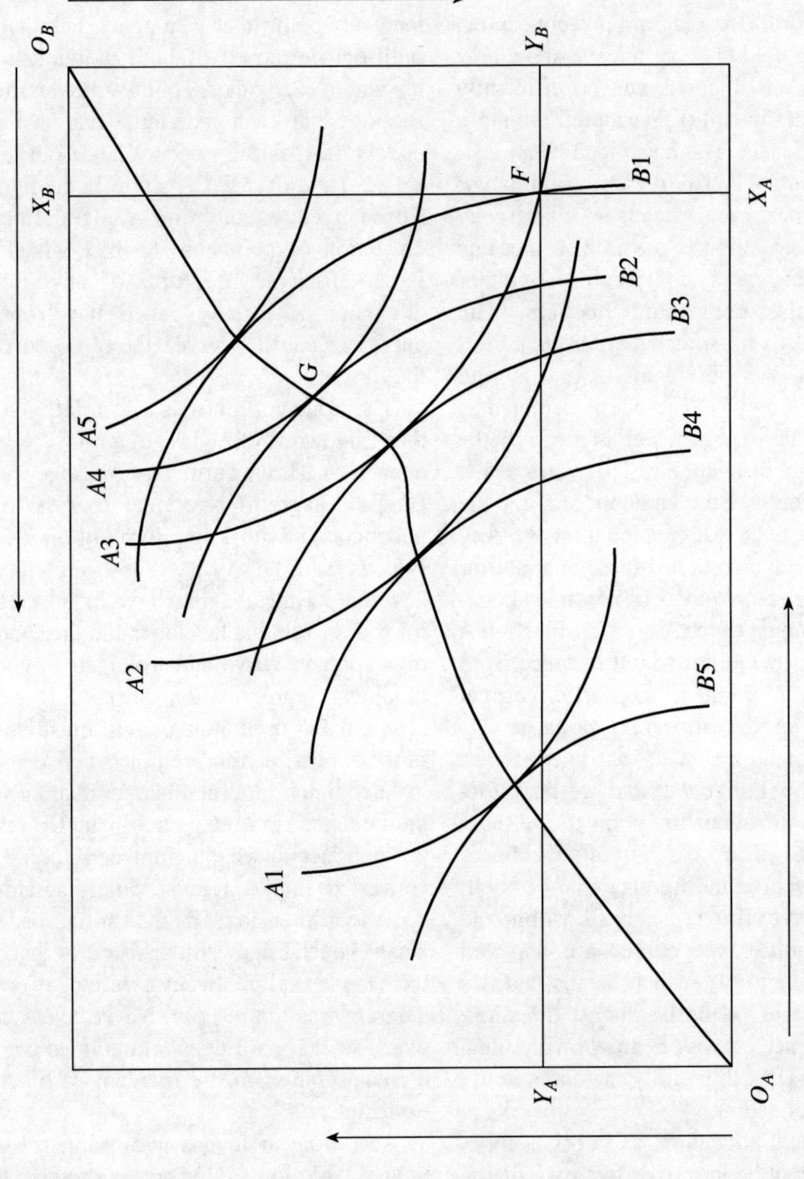

Edgeworth box, or Edgeworth–Bowley diagram

in a setting of perfect competition, which will reduce the contract curve to a sole point. Irving Fisher was the first economist expressly to employ a system of indifference curves for each person in 1892. Twenty one years later Pareto, in a work published in *Encyklopädie der mathematischen Wissenschaften*, used a system of indifference curves (that is, indifference 'maps'). Such a system of curves is a necessary prerequisite for developing the so-called 'box diagram'. The Edgeworth box appeared for the first time in its present form in the 1906 edition of Pareto's *Manuale* (p. 187). In 1924 Arthur Bowley published the first edition of his *Mathematical Groundwork* (p. 5), which contained an elaborate version of the box diagram.

Given that Bowley's book appeared a few years later than Pareto's, the question remains as to whether Bowley's construction was in any sense autonomous. It is quite clear that Bowley had already known Pareto's writings, since he quotes Pareto in his *Mathematical Groundwork*. Bowley's name came to be associated with the box diagram probably because Pareto was virtually unknown in the English-speaking world before the 1930s, and this world became acquainted with the box diagram through Bowley's book. Therefore it is not surprising that, when Bowley popularized the contemporary version of the box diagram to explain two-individual, two-commodity exchange, Edgeworth's name became closely identified with the device. From that moment on this conceptual device has commonly been called the Edgeworth–Bowley box diagram.

ANGEL MARTÍN-ROMÁN

Bibliography

Bowley, Arthur L. (1924), *The Mathematical Groundwork of Economics*, Oxford: The Clarendon Press.

Edgeworth, Francis Y. (1881), *Mathematical Psychics*, London: Kegan Paul.

Pareto, Vilfredo (1906), *Manuale di economia politica con una introduzione alla scienza sociale*, Milan: Piccola Biblioteca Scientifica No. 13. English trans. by A.S. Schwier in A.S. Schwier and A.N. Page (eds) (1971), *Manual of Political Economy*, New York: A.M. Kelley.

Edgeworth expansion

The representation of one distribution function in terms of another is widely used as a technique for obtaining approximations of distributions and density functions.

The Edgeworth representation, introduced at the beginning of the twentieth century, and derived from the theory of errors, was updated by Fisher in 1937 through the use of the Fourier transform.

Let X be a standardized random variable, with density function $f(x)$. Let $\phi(x)$ be the density of the $N(0, 1)$, let k_i $i = 3, 4, \ldots$ be the cumulants of X. The Edgeworth expansion of $f(x)$ is

$$f(x) = \phi(x)(1 + \frac{k_3}{3!} H_3(x) + \frac{k_4}{4!} H_4(x)$$

$$+ \frac{k_5}{5!} H_5(x) + \frac{10k_3 + k_6}{6!} H_6(x) +) \ldots,$$

where the H_j are the Hermite polinomials of order $j = 3, 4, \ldots$, defined as functions of the derivative of the density $\phi(x)$ by $\phi^{k)}(x) = (-1)^k\phi(x)H_k(x)$, or equivalently by recursive equations: $H_{k+1}(x) = xH_k(x) - kH_{k-1}(x)$. As for the function distribution,

$$F(x) = \Phi(x) - \frac{k_3}{3!} H_2(x)\phi(x) - \frac{k_4}{4!} H_3(x)\phi(x)$$

$$- \frac{k_3^2}{6!} H_5(x)\phi(x) + \ldots,$$

where $\Phi(x)$ is the standard normal function distribution. In the case of independent and identically distributed random variables X_i with mean θ_0 and finite variance σ^2, the distribution of the statistic

$$S_n = n^{1/2}(\bar{X} - \theta_0)/\sigma$$

is asymptotically normal and has an Edgeworth expansion as a power series in $n^{\frac{-1}{2}}$:

$$P(S_n \leq x) = \Phi(x) + n^{\frac{-1}{2}}p_1(x)\phi(x) + n^{-1}p_2(x)\phi(x)$$

$$+ \ldots + n^{\frac{-j}{2}}p_j(x)\phi(x) + \ldots,$$

where the p_j are polynomials depending on the cumulants of X and of the Hermite polynomials.

The essential characteristics of the Edge-worth expansion are, first, that it is an orthogonal expansion, due to the biorthogonality between the Hermite polynomials and the derivatives of the normal density

$$\int_{-\infty}^{\infty} H_k(x)\phi^{m)}(x)dx = (-1)^m m!\delta_{km},$$

where δ_{km} is the Kronecker delta; and second, that the coefficients decrease uniformly.

As an application we emphasize its use in the non-parametric estimation of density functions and bootstrap techniques.

VICENTE QUESADA PALOMA

Bibliography

Kendall M. Stuart (1977), *The Avanced Theory of Statistics*, vol. 1, London: Macmillan.

See also: Fourier transform.

Edgeworth oligopoly model

The Francis I. Edgeworth (1845–1926) model (1897) merged the two main oligopolistic behaviour models (quantity and price competition models) by introducing capacity constraints in a two-period game which allowed firms to make decisions on both quantity and price. His new approach to non-cooperative firm competition overcame the basic limitations of previous models and set the standard framework that has been used to develop the oligopoly theory.

The quantity competition model (Cournot, 1838) has been criticized for assuming that firms choose quantities produced and a neutral auctioneer chooses the price that clears the market, which is seen as unrealistic. The price competition model (Bertrand, (1883) assumptions are more plausible, as within this model it is firms who chose prices, but it leads to the counterintuitive Bertrand paradox: only two firms are needed for the competitive equilibrium to be achieved (marginal cost pricing and zero profits for all firms).

Edgeworth set a simple two-stage model. In stage one, firms select their production capacity (more capacity implies a larger fixed cost) and, in stage two, firms choose prices taking into account that they cannot sell more than they are capable of producing. That is, we give up Bertrand's assumption that the firm offering the lowest price covers the whole market. Moreover, the Edgeworth model captures the general belief that price is the main instrument that a firm can change in the short run, while cost structures and production levels can only be altered in the long run.

This model implies that a zero profit solution no longer presents an equilibrium, and it results in a solution with non-competitive prices. The underlying argument is intuitive: since capacity investment is costly, no firm will enter the market to make non-positive profits (or it will just select zero capacity). Thus it is obvious that the equilibrium solution achieves the following: no firm overinvests (in that case, a reduction in capacity investment would increase profits) and profits are, at least, as large as the fixed cost of capacity investment.

To sum up, Edgeworth shows that quantity and price competition models can be integrated in a general model that, depending on the cost structure of a market, will lead to a solution close to Bertrand's (industries with flat marginal costs) or Cournot's (industries with rising marginal costs).

DAVID ESPIGA

Bibliography

Edgeworth, F. (1897), 'La teoria pura del monopolio', *Giornale degli Economisti,* **40**, 13–31; translated as 'The theory of monopoly' in *Papers Relating to Political Economy* (1925), vol. 1, 111–42, London: Macmillan.

See also: Bertrand competition model, Cournot's oligopoly model.

Edgeworth taxation paradox

Francis Y. Edgeworth (1845–1926) described this paradox (1897a, 1897b) according to which the setting of a tax on goods or services can lead to a *reduction* in their market price under certain circumstances. In its original formulation this result was obtained for monopolies jointly producing substitute goods (for instance, first- and second-class railway tickets). It was subsequently extended for complementary goods (that is, passenger transport and luggage for the same example). Years later, Hotelling (1932) put forward a rigorous demonstration that extended these results to include cases of free competition and duopolies, and showed its verisimilitude for real scenarios that went further than the limitations imposed by partial equilibrium analyses and in the face of the resistance it initially aroused (Seligman, 1899), pp. 174, 191, 1921, p. 214, Edgeworth, 1899, 1910).

Also known as the 'Edgeworth–Hotelling paradox', it makes clear the need for taking into account suppositions of joint production that predominate among companies operating in concentrated markets, as opposed to the customary supposition that industry only produces a single good or service. Salinger underlined its implications in the field of the state's regulation of competition by demonstrating that vertical integration processes among successive monopolies do not necessarily ensure that welfare is increased (obtained when there is simple production) when joint production exists.

Similarly, the 'Edgeworth taxation paradox' illustrates the importance of taking into account the interrelationships among different markets, a feature of general equilibrium analysis, with regard to the results of partial equilibrium analyses, as Hines showed. However, analogous results can be obtained within this analytical framework. For instance, Dalton included the possibility of a tax whose amount diminishes as a monopoly's production volume increases. Under certain conditions, the monopoly would tend to increase its production volume while reducing its price and thus transferring part of its extraordinary profits to consumers. In such cases, the monopoly would wholly pay for the tax and therefore reduce the 'social costs' it generates. Sgontz obtained a similar result when he analysed the US Omnibus Budget Reconciliation Act of 1990.

JESÚS RUÍZ HUERTA

Bibliography

Edgeworth, F.Y. (1897a), 'The pure theory of monopoly', reprinted in Edgeworth (1925), vol. I, pp. 111–42.

Edgeworth, F.Y. (1897b), 'The pure theory of taxation', reprinted in Edgeworth (1925), vol. II, pp. 63–125.

Edgeworth, F.Y. (1899), 'Professor Seligman on the theory of monopoly', in Edgeworth (1925), vol. I, pp. 143–71.

Edgeworth, F.Y. (1910), 'Application of probabilities to economics', in Edgeworth (1925), vol. II, pp. 387–428.

Edgeworth, F.Y. (1925), *Papers Relating to Political Economy*, 3 vols, Bristol: Thoemmes Press, 1993.

Hotelling, H. (1932), 'Edgeworth's taxation paradox and the nature of supply and demand functions', *Journal of Political Economy*, **40**, 577–616.

Seligman, E.R.A. (1899, 1910, 1921, 1927), *The Shifting and Incidence of Taxation*, 5th edn, New York: Columbia U.P.; revised, reprinted New York: A.M. Kelley, 1969).

Ellsberg paradox

Expected utility theory requires agents to be able to assign probabilities to the different outcomes of their decisions. In some cases, those probabilities are 'objective', as with tossing a coin. But most real cases involve 'subjective' probabilities, that is, people's perception of the likelihood of certain outcomes occurring. The Ellsberg paradox questions agents' ability to assign subjective probabilities consistent with the assumptions of probability theory.

Assume that there are 300 balls in an urn, 100 of which are red and the rest either blue or green. A ball is to be extracted and you have to choose between receiving one million euros if it is red and winning one million if it is blue. You are likely to choose the former, as most people do. But what if the choice is between one million if the ball is not red and one million if it is not blue? Most people prefer the former. As the prize is the same in all options, these choices have implications in terms of the probability being assigned to each event. Thus the first choice implies that a higher probability is assigned to obtaining a red ball than to obtaining a blue one, while the second implies that, at the same time, the probability assigned to the ball not being red is also higher than that of it not being blue, which is inconsistent.

Regarding the importance of this paradox, some authors interpret it as revealing some aversion to 'uncertainty' – nobody knows how many blue balls are in the urn – in addition to the usual 'risk' aversion: the number of red balls is known to us, but not the colour of the extracted ball. Others, however, consider it a mere 'optical illusion' without serious implications for economic theory.

JUAN AYUSO

Bibliography

Ellsberg, D. (1961), 'Risk, ambiguity and the Savage axioms', *Quarterly Journal of Economics*, **80**, 648–69.

See also: Allais paradox, von Neumann–Morgenstern expected utility theorem.

Engel aggregation condition

This condition is a restriction that has to be satisfied by the household demand elasticity with respect to wealth. It indicates that total expenditure must change by an amount equal to any wealth change.

Let us consider a static (one time period) model. Assume rational consumers in the sense that the total budget (denoted by x) is spent on different goods. This implies

$$x = \sum_{k=1}^{N} \mathrm{p_k q_k},$$

where q_k denotes quantity and p_k denotes prices. Let us assume that a demand function exists for each good k. These demands can be written as functions of x and the different prices,

$$q_i = g_i(x, p) \text{ for } i = 1, \ldots N,$$

where p is the $Nx1$ vector of prices. These relationships are called Marshallian demand functions, representing household consumption behaviour.

Substituting these demand functions into the budget constraint gives

$$\sum_{k=1}^{N} \mathrm{p_k q_k}(x, p) = x.$$

This equation is referred to as the 'adding-up restriction'. Assume that the demand functions are continuous and differentiable. The adding-up restriction can be expressed as a restriction on the derivatives of the demand functions, rather than on the functions themselves. Specifically, total differentiation of the adding-up restriction with respect to x leads to:

$$\sum_{k=1}^{N} p_k \frac{\partial g_k}{\partial x} = 1.$$

This equation is called the 'Engel aggregation condition'. It ensures that additional income will be precisely exhausted by consumers' expenditures.

We can also rewrite this equation in terms of the elasticities of demand with respect to wealth. This is defined by

$$\sum_{k=1}^{N} w_k e_k = 1,$$

where w_k is the share of good k in the consumer's total budget and e_k is the total expenditure elasticity.

Elasticities arise very often in applied work. Many economists consider the estimation of elasticities as one of the main objectives of empirical demand analysis. The Engel aggregation condition is usually imposed a priori on the estimation of demand systems; alternatively it can be tested whether the estimates satisfy the restriction.

RAQUEL CARRASCO

Bibliography

Nicholson, J.L. (1957), 'The general form of the adding-up criterion', *Journal of the Royal Statistical Society*, **120**, 84–5.

Worswick, G.D.N. and D.G. Champernowne (1954), 'A note on the adding-up criterion', *Review of Economic Studies*, **22**, 57–60.

Engel curve

Additionally to his contribution with respect to the so-called Engel's Law, Ernst Engel (1821–96) also introduced what is usually known as the Engel curve. The Engel curve represents the relationship between the household income and its consumption of a given good in a situation of constant prices. Given the results obtained, a good can be classified as 'normal' or 'inferior'. A good is considered as 'normal' when its consumption increases, given an increase in the total household income. On the other hand, a good is considered as 'inferior', if its consumption decreases given an increase in the total income.

Keeping constant all the prices, an increase in the total income of the consumer will imply a parallel movement of the budget restraint up and to the right, reflecting the new possibilities of consumption. For each of the budget restraint lines, it will be an optimal consumption set, defined by the individual preferences. The line derived from these points will be the income consumption curve or income expansion path, which determines the evolution of the consumption of the good for different levels of income. These curves are usually called Engel curves and their conformation for a given good A will follow three possibilities.

In Case 1, the income consumption curve and the Engel curve are straight lines through the origin. The consumer will maintain the same structure of consumption for any level of demand or monetary income.

In Case 2, the income consumption curve is a decreasing function, indicating a reduction in the demand for the good due to an increase in the level of income. The Engel curve is a positive decreasing function of the monetary income, indicating a reduction in the relative presence of the good in the total consumption.

In Case 3, the income consumption curve is an increasing function, indicating an increase on the relative presence of the good on the total consumption. The Engel Curve is a positive increasing function on the monetary income, indicating an increase on the relative presence of the good on the total consumption.

LUÍS RODRÍGUEZ ROMERO

Bibliography

Houthakker, H.S. (1987), 'Engel curve' in P. Newman (ed.), *The New Palgrave Dictionary of Economics and Law*, London: Macmillan.

Varian, H.R (1992), *Microeconomic Analysis*, New York: W.W. Norton.

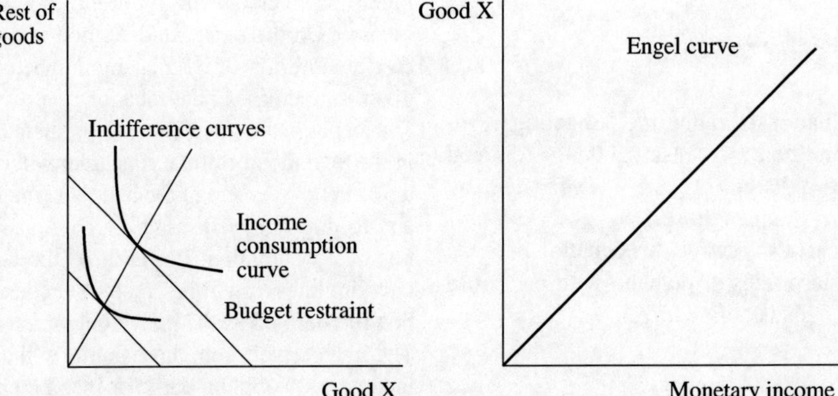

Engel curve Case 1

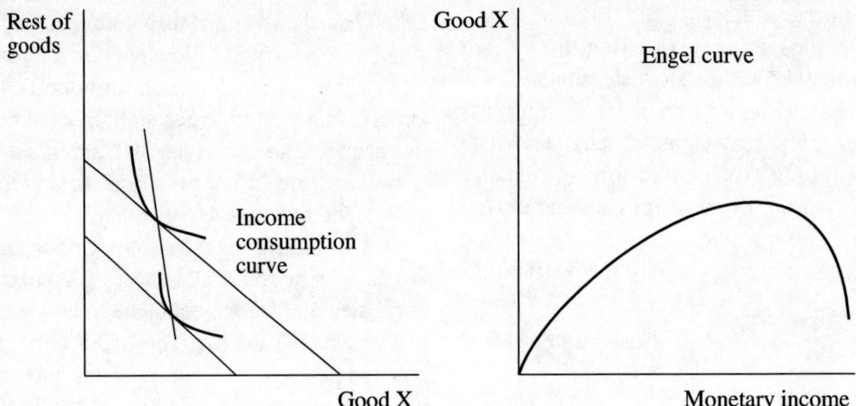

Engel curve Case 2

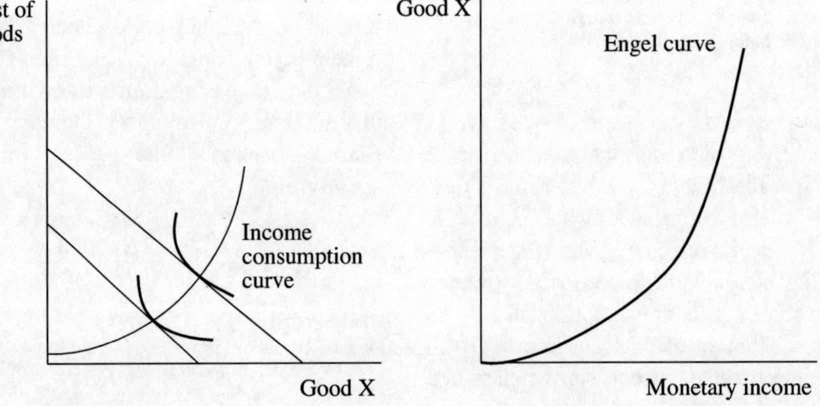

Engel curve Case 3

Engel's law

Formulated in 1857, this law states that households have a regular consumption pattern: the proportion of food in their expenses falls as income rises. German statistician Ernst Engel (1821–96) studied mine engineering first, but soon turned to statistics and social reform. From 1850 to 1882 he was director of the Saxony and Prussian Statistical Bureaus, joined international statistical associations, founded several journals and yearbook collections, and was the main organizer of Germany's modern official statistics. As a social reformer Engel proposed the development of self-help institutions (mortgage insurance, savings banks) and workers' participation in profits; although a founder member of the *Verein für Sozialpolitik*, he maintained firm free-trade convictions (Hacking, 1987).

Engel approached the study of workers' living conditions as a rectification of the minor importance attributed to demand by classical economists, and the weak empirical support of their consumption theories. He added first in nine expense lines the data contributed by Edouard Ducpétiaux and Frédéric Le Play, and suggested that the differences in the food expenditure–income ratio in various geographical areas could be explained by climatic, fiscal or cultural factors. In a second stage, he compared the expenditure structure of three household ranks of earnings, observing that the expenditure proportion on food diminishes when the annual income increases. This 'inductive' relationship, Engel says, is similar to a 'decreasing geometric progression' (Engel 1857, pp. 30–31), which seems to suggest that the income elasticity of food expenditure is less than unity, and that this elasticity decreases when income increases.

Although the empiric relationship based on Belgian workers' consumption was not 'exactly' the same as the hypothetical one (obtained by interpolation), Engel used this model to project the consumption pattern in Saxony. In later studies on 'the value of a human being' Engel refined the aggregation approach of the household expenditure, keeping in mind the number, gender and age of the family members, by means of some physiological equivalences of the annual cost of sustaining a new-born child, a unit that he labelled 'quet' in honour of his master, the Belgian statistician Adolphe Quetelet. Finally Engel (1895, p. 29) acknowledged the denomination 'Engel's law' coined by Carroll D. Wright in 1875, and considered that the law was fully 'confirmed' by new statistical research on the consumption of food and fuel, but it was refuted for clothing consumption and house renting. According to Engel, the first corollary of his contribution is that economic growth implies a lesser weight of food demand and of local agriculture in the composition of total production. He considered that this corollary refuted Malthus's theses (Engel 1857, p. 52). The second corollary points to an inverse relationship between the household's welfare and the share of its expenditure on food (Engel, 1887).

Besides Engel and Wright, other authors (Schwabe, Del Vecchio, Ogburn) studied inductively the expenditure–income relationship between 1868 and 1932. Starting from 1945, the contributions of Working, Houthakker, Theil and others reconciled Engel's law with the Slutsky–Hicks theories, and the revealed preference theories of demand, through different estimates of consumption–income elasticities less than unit (inferior goods) or higher than unit (normal or luxury goods). The modern and generalizated Engel curves, or income consumption curves, are based on consistent aggregation of individual preferences, and the econometric estimates are based on static cross-section analysis, as well as on loglinear, polynomial or nonparametric and special metric (equivalence scales) analysis, in order to study the long-term changes in consumption, inequality and welfare.

SALVADOR ALMENAR

Bibliography

Engel, Ernst (1857), 'Die Productions- und Consumtionsverhältnisse des Königreichs Sachsen', reprinted in *Bulletin de l'Institut International de Statistique*, 1895, **IX** (1), 1–54.

Engel, Ernst (1887), 'La consommation comme mesure du bien-être des individus, des familles et des nations', *Bulletin de l'Institut International de Statistique*, **II** (1), 50–75.

Engel, Ernst (1895), 'Die Lebenkosten Belgicher Arbeiten-Familien frücher und jetzt', *Bulletin de l'Institut International de Statistique*, **IX** (1), 1–124.

Hacking, Ian (1987), 'Prussian numbers 1860–1882', in L. Kruger, L.J. Daston and M. Heidelberger (eds), *The Probabilistic Revolution. Vol 1: Ideas in History*, Cambridge, MA: The MIT Press, pp. 377–94.

Engle–Granger method

The famous 1987 paper by Engle and Granger was one of the main elements that determined the winners of the 2003 Nobel Prize in Economics. This was the seminal paper that proposed a general methodology for estimating long-run relationships among non-stationary series, say velocity of circulation of money and short-term interest rates or short-term and long-term interest rates. They proposed to model the long-run equilibrium (cointegration) together with the short- and medium-term changes by using an error correction model. Such models have all of the variables in first differences, or in rates of growth, but the previous long-run equilibrium errors are in levels.

The Engle–Granger method is a two-step cointegration method that suggests a very simple way of estimating and testing for cointegration. The method works as follows: in the first step, a super-consistent estimator is obtained by running an ordinary least squares (OLS) regression among the variables of the cointegrating relationship, generating estimated equilibrium errors as the residuals. A test for cointegration could also be done by applying a Dickey–Fuller type of test on those residuals. In the second step, those residuals, lagged once, should enter at least one of the dynamic equations specified in first differences. This second step could also be estimated by OLS. The simplicity of the suggested procedure attracted a lot of followers and generated an immense econometric literature extending the two-step procedure to more general cases and to more general estimation procedures. The main limitation of the Engle and Granger method is that it assumes that the number of cointegrating relationships (cointegrating rank) is known a priori.

ALVARO ESCRIBANO

Bibliography

Engle, R.F. and C.J. Granger (1987), 'Cointegration and error correction: representation, estimation and testing', *Econometrica*, **55**, 251–76.

Euclidean spaces

The Euclidean space was introduced by Euclid at the beginning of the third century BC in his *Elements,* perhaps the most famous mathematical book ever written. In its original form, the Euclidean space consisted of a system of five axioms that tried to capture the geometric properties of the space. The German mathematician D. Hilbert (1899) made rigorous the Euclidean space through a system of 21 axioms.

The Euclidean space can be easily presented nowadays in terms of linear algebra as the vector space R^n of n vectors endowed with the inner product

$$\vec{x} \circ \vec{y} = \sum_{i=1}^{n} x_i y_i.$$

The properties of incidence and parallelism depend on the structure of vector space, whilst the inner product gives a definite positive quadratic form $q(\vec{x}) = \vec{x} \circ \vec{x}$, a norm $\| \vec{x} \| =$

$\sqrt{\vec{x} \circ \vec{y}}$, a distance, $d(\vec{x}, \vec{y}) = \sqrt{\| \vec{x} - \vec{y} \|}$, and allows us to define angles and orthogonal projections in spaces of any finite dimension. More generally a Euclidean space can be introduced as a finite dimensional real vector space together with a bilinear symmetric form (inner product), whose associated quadratic form is definite positive.

Alternative non-Euclidean metrics are also possible in spaces of finite dimension, but a distinctive useful feature of a Euclidean space is that it can be identified with its dual space. The metric properties of the Euclidean spaces are also useful in problems of estimation, where a linear manifold or map that minimize the errors of empirical data must be found. The use of the Euclidean metric and orthogonal projections (least squares method) affords concise and elegant solutions. For this reason, the Euclidean metric plays a major role in econometrics.

The non-Euclidean spaces that do not satisfy Euclid's fifth axiom, as the Riemann or Lovachevski spaces, have not played a relevant role in economics yet. Here the most important non-Euclidean spaces are some topological, functional and measure spaces. The first, elementary, approach to economic problems is finite dimensional, static and deterministic. This analysis can be developed in Euclidean spaces. At a higher level, the decision spaces are infinite dimensional (dynamic optimization), and the models are dynamic and stochastic. In these settings non-Euclidean spaces are usually required.

The Euclidean geometry can be easily generalized to infinite dimensional spaces, giving rise to the Hilbert spaces, which play a major role in econometrics and dynamic optimization.

MANUEL MORÁN

Bibliography

Hilbert, D. (1899), *Grundlagen der Geometrie*, Leipzig: Teubner.

Euler's theorem and equations

Leonard Euler (1707–83) entered at age 13 the University of Basle, which had become the mathematical center of Europe under John Bernoulli, who advised Euler to study mathematics on his own and made himself available on Saturday afternoons to help with any difficulties. Euler's official studies were in philosophy and law, and in 1723 he entered the department of theology. However, his interest in mathematics was increasing. In 1727, Euler moved to St Petersburg at the invitation of John Bernoulli's sons, Nicholas and Daniel, who were working there in the new Academy of Sciences. In 1738, he lost the sight of his right eye. In 1740, he moved to Berlin and in 1766 he moved back to St Petersburg. In 1771, he became completely blind, but his flow of publications continued at a greater rate than ever. He produced more than 800 books and articles. He is one of the greatest mathematicians in history and the most prolific.

Euler's theorem states: suppose f is a function of n variables with continuous partial derivatives in an open domain D, where $t > 0$ and $(x_1, x_2, \ldots, x_n) \in D$ imply $(tx_1, tx_2, \ldots, tx_n) \in D$. Then f is homogeneous of degree k in D if and only if the following equation holds for all $(x_1, x_2, \ldots, x_n) \in D$:

$$\sum_{i=1}^{n} x_i \frac{\partial f(x_1, x_2, \ldots, x_n)}{\partial x_i} = kf(x_1, x_2, \ldots, x_n).$$

Euler's equations come from the following calculus of variations problem:

$$\max_{(x_1, x_2, \ldots, x_n) \in \Omega} J = \int_{t_0}^{t_1} F[x_1(t), \ldots, x_n(t), \dot{x}_1, \ldots, \dot{x}_n, t]dt,$$

with

$$x_i(t_0) = x_i^0, \quad x_i(t_1) = x_i^1, \quad \text{for } i = 1, \ldots, n,$$

where F is a real function with $2n + 1$ real variables, of class $C^{(2)}$,

$$\dot{x}_i = \frac{dx_i(t)}{dt}, \text{ for } i = 1, \ldots, n$$

and

$\Omega = \{(x_1, \ldots, x_n) : [t_0, t_1] \to R^n$ such that x_i has first and second continuous derivatives$\}$.

Proposition

A necessary condition for $x^*(t) = (x_1^*(t), \ldots, x_n^*(t))$ to be a local maximum for the problem of calculus of variations is that

$$F_{x_i} - \frac{d}{dt} F_{\dot{x}_i} = 0, \text{ in } [x_1^*(t), \ldots, x_n^*(t), \dot{x}_1^*(t), \ldots, \dot{x}_n^*(t), t], \text{ for } i = 1, \ldots, n,$$

which are the Euler equations. For each i, the Euler equation is in general a second-order nonlinear differential equation.

EMILIO CERDÁ

Bibliography

Chiang, A.C. (1992), *Elements of Dynamic Optimization*, New York: McGraw-Hill.

Silberberg, E. and W. Suen, (2000), *The Structure of Economics. A Mathematical Analysis*, 3rd edn, New York: McGraw-Hill/Irwin.

Sydsaeter, K. and P.J. Hammond (1995), *Mathematics for Economic Analysis*, Englewood Cliffs, NJ: Prentice-Hall.

F

Farrell's technical efficiency measurement

Michael James Farrell (1926–75) was pure Oxbridge, educated at Oxford and employed at Cambridge. During his brief but distinguished academic career he made significant contributions to economic theory, including welfare economics, consumer demand analysis, the profitability of speculation and price formation in public utilities and other imperfectly competitive markets. His interest in business pricing strategy led him to his most lasting achievement, the development in 1957 of a rigorous analysis of the efficiency of business performance. He showed how to measure and compare the technical efficiency of businesses (the avoidance of wasted resources) and their allocative efficiency (the avoidance of resource misallocation in light of their relative prices). He then combined the two to obtain a measure of business cost efficiency. His influence grew slowly at first, and then expanded rapidly, beginning in the 1970s when his work was extended by economists (who used statistical regression techniques) and management scientists (who refined his mathematical programming techniques).

Nearly half a century after his initial investigation, his ideas have gained widespread acceptance. They are used to examine the linkage between the efficiency and profitability of business, and as an early warning business failure predictor. They are used in benchmarking and budget allocation exercises by businesses and government agencies, and to monitor the effectiveness of public service provision, particularly (and controversially) in the UK. They are also used to implement incentive regulation of public utilities in a growing number of countries. At an aggregate level they are used to explore the sources of productivity growth, and they have been adopted by the World Health Organization to monitor the health care delivery performance of its member countries. Farrell's insights have spread far beyond their academic origins.

E. GRIFELL-TATJÉ and C.A.K. LOVELL

Bibliography

Farrell, M.J. (1957), 'The measurement of productive efficiency', *Journal of the Royal Statistical Society*, Series A, **120**, 253–81.

See also: Koopman's efficiency criterion.

Faustmann–Ohlin theorem

A forest stand shall be cut down when the time rate of change of its value ($pf'(t)$) is equal to the forgone interest earnings on the income from current harvest ($ipf(t)$) plus the forgone interest earnings on the value of the forest land (iV):

$$pf'(t) = ipf(t) + iV,$$

where p is the price of timber, i the interest rate, $f(t)$ the stock of timber at time t and V the value of the forest land. In other words, the stand will be cut down when the marginal benefit from postponing the harvest (that is, the net market value of the additional timber) becomes smaller than the opportunity cost of not cutting the stand down (that is, the income flow that could be obtained by investing the net timber value plus the soil value). In 1849, the German forester Martin Faustmann (1822–76) stated the present value of the forest as a function of time

$$(\underset{t}{Max}\, V = \frac{pf(t) - Ce^{it}}{e^{it} - 1}),$$

where C would be the cost of establishment of a new stand). This expression, known as Faustmann's formula, is one of the earliest examples of the application of the net present worth concept (or the principle of discounted cash flow) in a management decision context. But it was Max Robert Pressler (1815–86), another German engineer, who in 1860 solved the maximization problem explicitly and determined the optimal rotation period of a forest, which constitutes a fundamental contribution, not only to natural resources economics, but also to capital theory. In fact, the optimal rotation length is related to the much wider question of finding an optimum rate of turnover of capital stock. The same result obtained by Faustmann and Pressler was reached independently by the Swedish economist Bertil Ohlin in 1917, when he was only 18 years old and participated in Heckscher's seminar as discussant of a paper on the rotation problem. Although other economists, like Hotelling, Fisher or Boulding, tried later to solve this important problem, all failed to find a satisfactory answer.

JOSÉ LUIS RAMOS GOROSTIZA

Bibliography

Faustmann, Martin (1849), 'On the determination of the value which forest land and immature stands possess for forestry'; reprinted in M. Gane (ed.) (1968), 'Martin Faustmann and the evolution of discounted cash flow', Oxford, Commonwealth Forestry Institute, *Oxford Institute Paper*, **42**, 27–55.

Löfgren, Karl G. (1983), 'The Faustmann–Ohlin theorem: a historical note', *History of Political Economy*, **15** (2), 261–4.

Fisher effect

Irving Fisher (1876–1947), one of America's greatest mathematical economists, was the first economist to differentiate clearly between nominal and real interest rates. Fisher, distinguished by an unusual clarity of exposition, wrote on the fields of mathematics, political economy, medicine and public health. A central element of Fisher's contribution to economics is the Fisher effect, which remains the cornerstone of many theoretical models in monetary economics and finance. His theory of interest, labeled by himself the 'impatience and opportunity theory', is explained and also tested in his *Theory of Interest* (1930), a revision of his earlier book, *The Rate of Interest* (1907).

The key issue is that the value of money in terms of goods appreciates or depreciates owing to the inflation rate. This causes a redistribution of purchasing power from creditors to debtors. Accordingly, creditors would require a reaction of the nominal interest rate to changes in the expected inflation rate. It follows that

$$(1 + i) = (1 + r)[1 + E(\pi)]$$

or

$$i = r + E(\pi) + rE(\pi),$$

where i is the nominal interest, r is the real interest and $E(\pi)$ is the expected inflation rate. As the latter term could be negligible in countries where the inflation rate is low, the Fisher effect is usually approximated by $i \approx r + E[\pi]$. Hence, as Fisher pointed out, the real interest is equal to the nominal interest minus the expected inflation rate.

In other words, the Fisher effect suggests that in the long run the nominal interest rate varies, *ceteris paribus*, point for point with the expected inflation rate. That is to say, the real rate is constant in the face of permanent changes in inflation rate.

The Fisher effect has become one of the most studied topics in economics. In general, it has been tested for different countries, yielding mixed results. In fact, Fisher himself attempted to explain why it seems to fail in practice by arguing the presence of some form of money illusion.

MONTSERRAT MARTÍNEZ PARERA

Bibliography

Fisher, I. (1930), *Theory of Interest*, New York: Macmillan.

Fisher–Shiller expectations hypothesis

The expectations hypothesis states that the term structure of interest rates, in particular its slope or difference between long-term and short-term spot rates at a given time, is determined by expectations about future interest rates. Hence a link is established between known spot rates, (given at a certain time, for instance today) on lending up to the end of different terms, and unknown future short-term rates (of which only a probabilistic description can be given) involving lending that occurs at the end of the said terms. A simplified popular version of the expectations hypothesis is that an upward-sloping spot yield curve indicates that short-term interest rates will rise, while a negative slope indicates that they will decline.

While this is an old hypothesis, the first academic discussions are from Fisher (in 1896, later expanded in 1930). While Fisher used a first rigorous version where the rate of interest could be linked to time preferences (marginal rates of substitution between different time instants), it was Shiller who in the 1970s first explored the subject in what is now the accepted standard framework of rational expectations theory, together with its empirical implications (in Shiller's own account in 1990, contributions from many others are noted).

In the modern framework the expectations hypothesis is formulated as a set of statements about term premia (risk premia for future rates), which can be defined, among other choices, as differences between known forward rates and rational expectations of future spot rates. Rational expectations are consistent with premia that may have a term structure but that are constant as time evolves. Hence a modern formulation of the expectations hypothesis would be that the term premia are good forecasts of actual increases in spot rates. Interestingly, in the modern framework the hypothesis is empirically validated for forecasts far into the future of small-term rates, while it is not for forecasts into the near future.

GABRIEL F. BOBADILLA

Bibliography

Fisher, I. (1930), *Theory of Interest*, New York: Macmillan.

Shiller, R.J. (1990), 'The term structure of interest rates', in B.M. Friedman and F.H. Hahn (eds), *Handbook of Monetary Economics*, Amsterdam: North-Holland.

Fourier transform

This ranks among the most powerful tools in modern analysis and one of the greatest innovations in the history of mathematics. The Fourier transform has a wide range of applications in many disciplines, covering almost every field in engineering and science.

The beginnings of Fourier theory date from ancient times with the development of the calendar and the clock. In fact, the idea of using trigonometric sums to describe periodic phenomena such as astronomical events goes back as far as the Babylonians. The modern history of the Fourier transform has one predecessor in the seventeenth century in the figure of Newton, who investigated the reflection of light by a glass prism and found that white light could be decomposed in a mixture of varied coloured rays (namely, the spectrum of the rainbow). His theory was severely criticized since colours were thought at that time to be the result of white light modifications.

In 1748, Euler studied the motion of a

vibrating string and found that its configuration at any time was a linear combination of what he called 'normal modes'. This idea was strongly opposed by Lagrange, who argued that it was impossible to represent functions with corners by just using trigonometric series.

In the year 600 BC, Pythagoras had worked on the laws of musical harmony, which finally found a mathematical expression in terms of the 'wave equation' (which explained phenomena such as heat propagation and diffusion) in the eighteenth century. The problem of finding a solution to this equation was first dealt with by the engineer Jean Baptiste de Fourier (1768–1830) in 1807 by introducing the 'Fourier series' at the French Academy. At that historic meeting Fourier explained how an arbitrary function, defined over a finite interval, could be represented by an infinite sum of cosine and sine functions. His presentation had to confront the general belief that any superposition of these functions could only yield an infinitely differentiable function (an 'analytic function'), as in the case of the Taylor series expansion in terms of powers. However, since the coefficients of a Fourier series expansion are obtained by integration and not by differentiation, it was the global behavior of the function that mattered now and not its local behavior. Thus, while the Taylor series expansion about a point was aimed at predicting exactly the behavior of an infinitely differentiable function in the vicinity of that point, the Fourier series expansion informed on the global behavior of a wider class of functions in their entire domain. The Fourier series was introduced by Fourier as an expansion of a particular class of orthogonal functions, namely the sine and cosine functions. Through misuse of language, this terminology was later applied to any expansion in terms of whatever class of orthogonal functions.

The Fourier series representation of a given periodic function $f(t)$ with fundamental period

$$T = \frac{2\pi}{\omega_0}$$

is given by

$$\tilde{f}(t) = \sum_{k=-\infty}^{\infty} a_k e^{jk\omega_0 t}$$

where the Fourier coefficients, a_k, can be obtained as

$$a_k = \frac{1}{T}\int_{t_0}^{t_0+T} f(t)e^{-jk\omega_0 t}$$

It can be shown that the mean square approximation error (MSE) between $f(t)$ and $\tilde{f}(t)$ becomes zero when $f(t)$ is square integrable. Moreover, $f(t) = \tilde{f}(t)$ pointwise if the so-called 'Dirichlet conditions' are satisfied (boundedness of $f(t)$, finite number of local maxima and minima in one period, and finite number of discontinuities in one period).

While Fourier's initial argument was that any periodic function could be expanded in terms of harmonically related sinusoids, he extended such representation to aperiodic functions, this time in terms of integrals of sinusoids that are not harmonically related. This was called the 'Fourier transform' representation. The Fourier transform $F(\omega)$ of a nonperiodic function $f(t)$ is formally defined as

$$F(\omega) = \int_{-\infty}^{\infty} f(t)e^{-j\omega t}dt$$

Once the value of this function has been obtained for every $\omega \in (0, 2\pi)$, the original function $f(t)$ can be approximated by an integral superposition of the complex sinusoids $\{e^{j\omega t}\}_{0<\omega\leq 2\pi}$ with weights $\{F(\omega)\}_{0<\omega\leq 2\pi}$. The approximating function $\tilde{f}(t)$ is given by

$$\tilde{f}(t) = \frac{1}{2\pi}\int_0^{2\pi} F(\omega)e^{j\omega t}d\omega.$$

It can be shown that the square integrability of $f(t)$ suffices to guarantee a zero MSE. However, in order to have $f(t) = \tilde{f}(t)$ at all values of t, $f(t)$ must satisfy another set of Dirichlet conditions (absolute integrability; finite number of local maxima, minima and discontinuities in any given finite interval; and finite size of the discontinuities).

In many applications only a set of discrete observations of the function are available. In such cases, a 'discrete Fourier transform' (DFT) can be defined which provides an approximation to the Fourier transform of the partially observed function. Under some conditions *(*sampling theorem*)*, it may be possible to recover this Fourier transform from the DFT, which amounts to reconstructing the whole function via interpolation.

FELIPE M. APARICIO-ACOSTA

Bibliography

Giffin, W.C. (1975), *Transform Techniques for Probability Modeling*, New York: Academic Press.

See also: Taylor's theorem.

Friedman's rule for monetary policy

Milton Friedman's (b.1912, Nobel Prize 1976) contribution to economics has been among the most prolific of the twentieth century. He has entered the history of macroeconomic thought as the most prominent figure of the monetarist school. His monetary policy rule is extraordinary for its simplicity. He posits it in a full and orderly fashion in his *A Program for Monetary Stability* as a simplification of a previous, more complex proposal based on the effects of the budgetary balances of a fiscal policy resulting from the free operation of the automatic stabilizers on the monetary base. As he himself put it: 'The simple rule is that the stock of money be increased at a fixed rate year-in and year-out without any variation in the rate of increase to meet cyclical needs' (Friedman, 1959, p. 90).

It is a rule that ties in with the conventional view of the quantitative theory of money whereby an exogenously given one-time change in the stock of money has no lasting effect on real variables but leads ultimately to a proportionate change in the money price of goods. More simply, it declares that, all else being equal, money's value or purchasing power varies with its quantity. Actually, however, Friedman's normative proposal is not derived from a well-defined and formulated monetary model but from an application of a set of general economic principles.

The first of these is the neutrality of money in the long run, such that the trend of real output is governed by forces that cannot be affected in a lasting manner by monetary policy. In the long run money is a veil, but in the short run there is no neutrality and fluctuations in the money stock may, in the presence of price rigidities, prompt fluctuations in output that are, however, transitory and, therefore, consistent with long-term neutrality.

The second principle is the impossibility of harnessing the short-term effects of monetary policy for the purposes of stabilizing output, owing to imperfect knowledge of the transmission mechanisms, to the delays with which relevant information becomes available and to uncertainty over the lags with which monetary impulses operate. Friedman's 1963 book, written in collaboration with Anna J. Schwartz, provides an exhaustive illustration of empirical cases where monetary interventions for stabilizing purposes would themselves have been a source of economic disturbance.

The normative consequence Friedman extracts from these principles is that the monetary authorities should be bound by rules that prevent the destabilizing effects on output and prices of sharp swings in policy and the tendency to overreact. In Friedman's own words: 'In the past, monetary authorities have on occasions moved in the wrong direction – as in the episode of the Great Contraction that I have stressed. More frequently, they have moved in the right direction, albeit often too late, but have erred by moving too far. Too late and too much has been the general practice' (Friedman, 1969, p. 109).

The proposal for a set rule thus stems from a fundamental lack of confidence in the model based on attributing a general stabilization target to an independent central bank, once the chains of the gold standard had been broken. And it involves affirming the superiority of the rule over discretionarity and a reaction to the monetary activism that might derive from certain Keynesian-type models.

Defining the rule in terms of the money stock is warranted not so much by the pre-eminent role of money in the medium- and long-term behaviour of prices as by the fact that it is a variable the central bank can actually control. The main advantage of the rule would stem from the elimination of the uncertainty generated by the discretionarity of the monetary authorities, thus making for a presumably more predictable and transparent environment, so that the private sector adjustment mechanisms might operate without distortions.

In practice, Friedman's rule has not been applied in the strictest sense, given central banks' difficulties in effectively controlling the money in circulation. Rather, it has been used as a basis for monetary aggregate targeting strategies with varying degrees of flexibility. These range from those based on the quantitative theory of money, whereunder the average long-run rate of inflation will equal the average money growth rate, minus the long-run growth rate of real GDP, plus the velocity growth rate, to others that seek to act on changes in the velocity of circulation.

True, these strategies enjoyed considerable prestige during the 1970s and 1980s, but the growing difficulty in defining the monetary aggregate under control, amid rapid financial innovation, and the growing instability of the estimates of its demand function prompted a move towards generally more complex strategies, among which direct inflation or exchange rate targets were predominant, with the formulation of more sophisticated rules derived from an objective function and from the relevant information set available. However, that is a different story, with different names.

JOSÉ LUIS MALO DE MOLINA

Bibliography

Friedman, M. (1959), *A Program for Monetary Stability*, New York: Fordham University Press.

Friedman, M. (1969), *The Optimum Quantity of Money*, London: Macmillan.

Friedman, M. and A.J. Schwartz (1963), *A Monetary History of the United States 1867–1960*, Princeton, NJ: Princeton University Press for the National Bureau of Economic Research.

Friedman–Savage hypothesis

In 1948, Milton Friedman (b.1912, Nobel Prize 1976) and Leonard J. Savage (1917–71) published an influential paper that was to alter the way economists analyse decision taking under uncertainty. Its huge impact was due to the combination of two effects. First, their contribution was a catalyst for the understanding of von Neumann and Morgenstern's recent work on expected utility, at a time when the implications of the expected utility assumption were not yet fully understood. Second, it pointed out a possible explanation of the fact that some economic agents simultaneously buy insurance and participate in lotteries. This fact was seen as a puzzle as gambling is characteristic of risk-loving behaviour while insurance is typical of risk aversion.

As a contribution to the general understanding of decision taking under uncertainty, Friedman and Savage argued that only cardinal utility theory is able to express rational choices under uncertainty, so that the ordinal utility theory has to be abandoned. The criticism of von Neumann and Morgenstern is thus ill-founded.

Instead, their expected utility assumption makes it possible to characterize agents' choices by their degree of risk aversion measured, for given probabilities, by the risk premium they are ready to pay in order to have the expected value of a lottery rather than the lottery itself.

But, of course, assuming risk aversion and a concave utility function implies that agents will buy insurance but they will never resort to gambling. In order to explain this behaviour, the Friedman and Savage hypothesis introduces a utility function that is concave for low levels of income and convex for intermediate levels, becoming concave again for very high incomes. In other words, the Friedman–Savage assumption states that, although agents are risk-averse for small variations in their income, they are risk lovers when it comes to high 'qualitative' increases in their income. This is shown to be consistent with the observed behaviour on insurance and gambling.

XAVIER FREIXAS

Bibliography

Friedman, M. and L.J. Savage (1948), 'The utility analysis of choices involving risk', *Journal of Political Economy*, **56**, 279–304.

See also: von Neuman–Morgenstern expected utility theorem.

Fullarton's principle

This principle was coined by Ludwig von Mises after John Fullarton (1780–1849), who is considered, with Thomas Tooke, the foremost representative of the British Banking School. Having been associated with a bank in Calcutta, he published back in England *On the Regulation of Currencies* (1844), in which he presented Adam Smith's real bills doctrine in its most elaborated form. Fullarton's principle, also called 'the principle of the reflux of banking notes', states that banks do not increase the circulating media if they finance strictly self-liquidating short-term transactions (90 days commercial paper representing the actual sale of commodities). That is, they only exchange existing credit instruments into a more readily circulating form. No overissue of currency or deposits can occur because banks can only raise the volume of money temporarily; the backflow of their automatically self-liquidating, short-term credits limits both the size and the duration of the expansion. The banking mechanism adapts the volume of credit to the flow of goods in an elastic fashion. The unwanted bank notes flow back to the banks that have issued them (reflux), and will be exchanged for gold or for earning assets such as bills of exchange.

The principle was challenged in the nineteenth century, first by Henry Thonton and thereafter by members of the Currency School such as Torrens and Lord Overstone. Their objections were developed in the twentieth century by the supporters of the quantity theory of money, especially with the rediscovery of the banking multiplier by H.J. Davenport, C.A. Phillips and others, who pointed out the fact that a major part of deposits are actually created by the banks themselves. The Austrian theory of the trade cycle, launched by Mises (1912) argued, following Thornton, that circulating credit (notes and deposits) can be over-expanded by cheap money policies. Mises also noted that bank notes could be held for very long periods of time without being presented for redemption at the banks.

JOSÉ IGNACIO DEL CASTILLO

Bibliography

Fullarton, John (1844), *On the Regulation of Currencies*, reprinted (1969) New York: A.M. Kelley, ch. 5, pp. 82ff.

Mises, Ludwig von (1912), *The Theory of Money and Credit*, reprinted (1971) New York: The Foundation for Economic Education, part III, ch. II.

Mises, Ludwig von (1996), *Human Action*, 4th edn, San Francisco: Fox and Wilkes, p. 444.

Fullerton–King's effective marginal tax rate

Don Fullerton studied at Cornell and Berkeley Universities. He taught at Princeton University (1978–84), the University of Virginia (1984–91) and Carnegie Mellon University (1991–4) before joining the University of Texas in 1994. From 1985 to 1987, he served in the US Treasury Department as Deputy Assistant Secretary for Tax Analysis. Mervyn King studied at King's College, Cambridge, and Harvard and taught at Cambridge and Birmingham Universities before spells as visiting professor at both Harvard University and MIT. He was Professor of Economics at the London School of Economics. Since 2002, Mervyn King has been Governor of the Bank of England and Chairman of the Monetary Policy.

Fullerton and King popularized the concept of effective marginal tax rates (EMTR) in 1984. EMTR on an asset provides a measurement of the distortion caused by the tax system in the market of this asset and its substitute goods. EMTR is calculated by dividing the tax wedge (the differential between the gross and net return received by the investor–saver) by the investment yield. The level of effective tax rates enables the identification of arbitrage processes between investments and financing methods, as well as the degree of neutrality in the taxation of investors' returns.

JOSÉ F. SANZ

Bibliography

Fullerton, D. and M. King (1984), *The Taxation of Income and Capital*, Chicago: University of Chicago Press.

G

Gale–Nikaido theorem

This theorem is a key instrument to prove the existence of a competitive equilibrium. The basic objective of general equilibrium theory is to explain prevailing prices and actions as the result of the interaction of independent agents (consumers and producers) in competitive markets. A competitive equilibrium obtains when, at going prices, all firms maximize profits, consumers maximize their preferences subject to the budget constraint, and their actions are mutually compatible: supply equals demand. This can be formally expressed, as Walras did, as a system of $n-1$ equations with $n-1$ unknowns, $Z(p) = 0$. Here Z denotes the vector valued excess demand function, giving the difference between aggregate demand and aggregate supply, and n is the number of commodities.

Concerning the existence of a solution, Walras did not go beyond counting the number of equations and unknowns. However, this condition is neither necessary nor sufficient. A rigorous analysis had to wait for the availability of an important result in combinatorial topology, namely, Brouwer's fixed point theorem.

In the late 1930s, in his paper on maximal growth, von Neumann (1945, English version) used a method of proof that was an extension of Brouwer's fixed point theorem. Later, Kakutani extended the latter from functions to correspondences. Nash used Kakutani's theorem in 1950 to prove the existence of an equilibrium in an N-person game. These were the first applications of fixed point theorems to economics.

In the early 1950s, Arrow and Debreu (1954) began independently, and completed jointly, the pioneering and influential general equilibrium model which included an existence proof based on Kakutani's fixed point theorem. Gale (1955) and Nikaido (1956) followed a different approach and proved independently a mathematical theorem that simplified significantly the original proof given by Arrow and Debreu. It presents the existence of equilibria in the most purified form, namely, the continuity properties of a convex valued correspondence and Walras law.

Excess demand functions $Z(p)$ are the outcome of maximizing choices in budget sets and therefore must be homogeneous in prices and satisfy Walras law: $p.Z(\mathrm{p}) \leq 0$. Given this, if every commodity can be freely dispensed with, a competitive equilibrium can be formally expressed as a price vector p such that $Z(p) \leq 0$. Strict equality is only required in the absence of free goods, when all prices are positive. Since in the general case there are multiple optimal choices, $Z(p)$ is thought to be a correspondence and the theorem is formulated as follows.

Let $Z(p)$ be a non-empty valued correspondence from the standard simplex of R^l into R^n. If $Z(p)$ is upper hemicontinuous, convex valued and satisfies Walras law there exists $\bar{p} \in P$ such that $Z(\bar{p}) \cap R\_ \neq 0$.

Note that, if $Z(p)$ and $R\_$ have a non-empty intersection, there exists a vector of excess demands $\bar{z} \in Z(\bar{p})$ such that $\bar{z} \leq 0$, and an equilibrium exists. The basic intuition of the proof can be illustrated in a simple diagram with excess demands, z_i, in the axes.

The second condition (Walras law) means that, at any price vector, $Z(p)$ is a set of excess demands that lies below the hyperplane H given by $p.z = 0$. If $Z(p)$ intersects the non-positive orthant $R\_$, this price is an equilibrium. If not, the convex set $Z(p)$ must be entirely contained in either R_2 or R_4. Suppose that it is in R_2, as in the picture. If

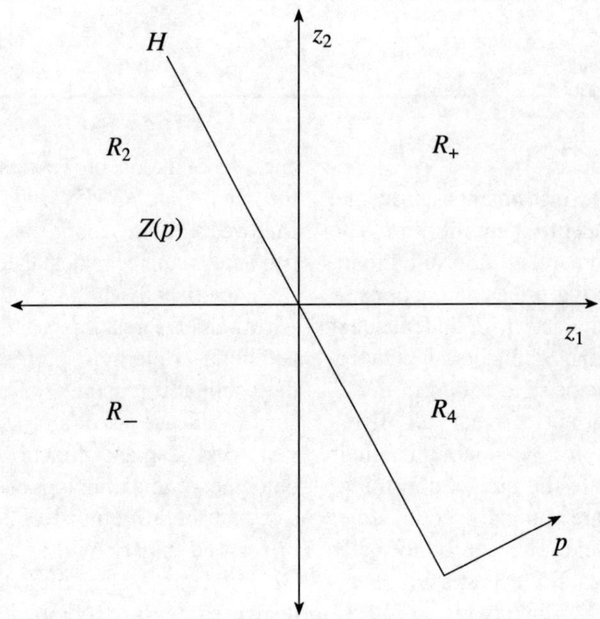

Gale–Nikaido theorem

we change the price vector so that the hyperplane rotates and gets flatter, unless we cross $R\_$ and an equilibrium is found, the new image will be squeezed into a smaller subset of the second orthant, R_2. As we keep changing prices in this way and H tends to the horizontal axis, $Z(p)$ will eventually be in R_4. But if the correspondence has the postulated continuity properties, the set will have to intersect the non-positive orthant $R\_$ at some point and an equilibrium will exist.

This existence proof is based on Brouwer's fixed point theorem. In a remarkable result, Uzawa showed in 1962 that, conversely, Brouwer's fixed-point theorem is implied by the Gale–Nikaido theorem: they are essentially equivalent.

XAVIER CALSAMIGLIA

Bibliography

Arrow, J.K. and G. Debreu (1954), 'Existence of an Equilibrium for a competitve economy', *Econometrica*, **22**, 265–90.

Gale, D. (1955), 'The law of supply and demand', *Mathematics Scandinavica*, **3**, 155–69.

Nash, J. (1950), 'Equilibrium points in N-person games', *Proceedings of the National Academy of Sciences* , **36**, 48–9.

Neumann, J. von (1945), 'A model of general economic equilibrium', *Review of Economic Studies*, **13**, 1–9.

Nikaido, H. (1956), 'On the classical multilateral exchange problem', *Metroeconomica*, **8**, 135–45.

See also: Arrow–Debreu general equilibrium model, Brouwer fixed point theorem, Kakutani's fixed point theorem, von Neumann's growth model.

Gaussian distribution

The Gaussian or normal probability distribution with mean zero and variance 1 is

$$\Phi(x) = \int_{-\infty}^{x} \phi(z)dz,$$

where $\phi(z)$ is the standard normal density function:

$$\phi(z) = \frac{1}{\sqrt{2\pi}} \exp\left(-\frac{1}{2} z^2\right).$$

The curve $\phi(z)$ is symmetric around zero, where it has its maximum, and it displays a familiar bell shape, covering an area that integrates to unity. By extension, any random variable Y that can be expressed as a linear function of a standard normal variable X,

$$Y = \mu + \sigma X,$$

is said to have a normal distribution with mean μ, variance σ^2, and probability (we can take $\sigma > 0$ without loss of generality since, if X is standard normal, so is $-X$):

$$Pr(Y \leq y) = \Phi\left(\frac{y-\mu}{\sigma}\right).$$

This distribution originated in the work of Abraham De Moivre, published in 1733, who introduced it as an approximation to the binomial distribution. Specifically, letting $y_1, \ldots, y_n$ be a sequence of 0–1 independently and identically distributed (iid) random variables, the binomial probability is given by

$$Pr\left(\bar{y} = \frac{r}{n}\right) = \binom{n}{r} p^r (1-p)^{n-r} \ (r = 0, 1, \ldots, n),$$

where $\bar{y} = n^{-1}\Sigma_{i=1}^{n} y_i$ is the relative frequency of ones, p is the corresponding probability, and we have $E(\bar{y}) = p$ and $Var(\bar{y}) = p(1 - p)/n$. De Moivre's theorem established that the probability distribution of the standardized relative frequency converged to $\Phi(x)$ for large n:

$$\lim_{n\to\infty} Pr\left(\frac{\bar{y}-p}{\sqrt{p(1-p)/n}} \leq x\right) = \Phi(x).$$

Seen through modern eyes, this result is a special case of the central limit theorem, which was first presented by Pierre Simon Laplace in 1810 in his memoir to the French Academy.

A completely different perspective on the formula $\phi(z)$ was given by Carl Friedrich Gauss (1777–1855) in 1809. He considered n linear combinations of observable variables $x_{1i}, \ldots, x_{ki}$ and unknown coefficients $\beta_1, \ldots, \beta_k$:

$$\mu_i = \beta_1 x_{1i} + \ldots + \beta_k x_{ki} \quad (i = 1, \ldots, n),$$

which were associated with the observations $y_1, \ldots, y_n$, and the corresponding errors $v_i = y_i - \mu_i$. He also considered the values of the coefficients that minimized the sum of squared errors, say, $\hat{\beta}_1, \ldots, \hat{\beta}_k$. His substantive motivation was to develop a method to estimate a planet's orbit. Gauss posed the following question: if the errors $v_1, \ldots, v_n$ are iid with symmetric probability distribution $f(v)$ and a maximum at $v = 0$, which forms have to have $f(v)$ for $\hat{\beta}_1, \ldots, \hat{\beta}_k$ being the most probable values of the coefficients?

In the special case where the μ_i are constant ($\mu_i = \mu$), there is just one coefficient to determine, whose least squares value is the arithmetic mean of the observations $\bar{y}$. In this case the most probable value of μ for a given probability distribution of the errors $f(v)$ solves

$$\sum_{i=1}^{n} \frac{d\log f(y_i - \mu)}{d\mu} = 0.$$

Because $\bar{y}$ is the solution to $\Sigma_{i=1}^{n} h(y_i - \mu) = 0$ for some constant h, $\bar{y}$ is most probable (or maximum likelihood) when $f(v)$ is proportional to

$$\exp\left(-\frac{h}{2}v^2\right);$$

that is, when the errors are normally distributed. Gauss then argued that, since $\bar{y}$ is a natural way of combining observations, the errors may be taken as normally distributed (c.f. Stigler, 1986). Moreover, in the general case, the assumption of normal errors implies that the least squares values are the most probable.

Gauss also found that, when the errors are normally distributed, the distribution of the least squares estimates is also normal. This was a crucial fact that could be used to assess the precision of the least squares method. Faithful to his publication goal motto 'Ut nihil amplius desiderandum relictum sit' (that nothing further remains to be done), Gauss also considered generalizations of least squares to measurements with unequal but known precisions, and to nonlinear contexts. Nevertheless, he only considered relative precision of his least squares estimates, making no attempt to provide an estimate of the scale *h* of the error distribution.

Laplace's work made the connection between the central limit theorem and linear estimation by providing an alternative rationale for assuming a normal distribution for the errors: namely, if the errors could be regarded as averages of a multiplicity of random effects, the central limit theorem would justify approximate normality.

Gauss's reasoning was flawed because of its circularity: since least squares is *obviously* such a good method it must be the most probable, which in turn implies the errors must be normally distributed; hence we assume normal errors to evaluate the precision of the method. Even today the normality assumption is often invoked as an error curve, very much as Gauss did originally. The persistence of such practice, however, owes much to the central limit theorem, not as a direct justification of normality of errors, but as a justification of an approximate normal distribution for the least squares estimates, even if the errors are not themselves normal.

The distribution is today universally called the 'normal', as first used by Galton, or the 'Gaussian' distribution, although some writers have also referred to it by the name Laplace–Gauss. According to Stephen Stigler, Gauss was used as an eponymic description of the distribution for the first time in the work of F.R. Helmert, published in 1872, and subsequently by J. Bertrand in 1889.

OLYMPIA BOVER

Bibliography

Gauss, C.F. (1809), *Theoria motus corporum celestium in sectionibus conicis solum ambientium*, Hamburg: Perthes et Besser; translated in 1857 as *Theory of Motion of the Heavenly Bodies Moving around the Sun in Conic Sections,* trans. C.H, Davis, Boston, MA: Little, Brown; reprinted (1963), New York: Dover.

Laplace, P.S. (1810), 'Mémoire sur les approximations des formules qui sont fonctions de très grands nombres et sur leur application aux probabilités', *Mémoires de l'Académie des sciences de Paris,* pp. 353–415, 559–65; reprinted in Laplace (1878–1912), *Oeuvres complètes de Laplace,*vol.12, Paris: Gauthier-Villars, pp. 301–53.

Stigler, S.M. (1986), *The History of Statistics. The Measurement of Uncertainty Before 1900,* Cambridge, MA: Harvard University Press.

Gauss–Markov theorem

This is a fundamental theorem in the theory of minimum variance unbiased estimation of parameters in a linear model. The theorem states that, if the error terms in a linear model are homoscedastic and uncorrelated, then the least squares estimates of the regression parameters have minimum variance among the class of all linear unbiased estimates.

The theorem may be stated as follows: if in the linear model of full rank $y = X\theta + \varepsilon$, the error vector satisfies the conditions $E(\varepsilon) = 0$ and $Cov(\varepsilon) = \sigma^2 I$, then the least squares estimate of θ, namely $\hat{\theta} = (X^t X)^{-1} X^t y$, is the minimum variance linear unbiased estimate of θ within the class of unbiased linear estimates.

As a corollary of this theorem, the minimum variance unbiased linear estimate $\hat{\phi}$ of any linear combination $\phi = c^t\theta$ is the same linear combination of the minimum variance unbiased estimates of θ, namely, $\hat{\phi} = c^t\hat{\theta}$.

A slight generalization of the theorem

asserts that, if $\hat{V} = \sigma^2(X^t X)^{-1}$ is the covariance matrix of the least squares estimate $\hat{\theta}$ and $\tilde{V}$ is the covariance matrix of any other linear unbiased estimate, then $\tilde{V} - \hat{V}$ is positive semidefinite.

Carl Friedrich Gauss (1777–1855) was the first to prove the theorem in 1821, and in 1823 he extended the theorem to estimating linear combinations of the regression parameters. Many authors rediscovered the theorem later. In particular, Andrei Andreyevich Markov (1856–1922) gave a proof in 1900. Apparently, the eponymous 'Gauss–Markov theorem' was coined by David and Neyman in 1938, and has remained so known since then.

F. JAVIER GIRÓN

Bibliography

Gauss, K.F. (1821, 1823, 1826), 'Theoria combinationis erroribus minimis obnaxine', parts 1 and 2, and supplement, *Werke*, **4**, 1–108.

Genberg–Zecher criterion

Identified thus by D.N. McCloskey after economists Hans A. Genberg and Richard J. Zecher, the criterion has to do with the standards for measuring international market integration, and focuses on markets within the analysed countries: 'The degree to which prices of bricks, saws, and sweaters move parallel in California and Vermont provides a criterion (the very Genberg–Zecher one) for measuring the degree of integration between America as a whole and Britain.'

CARLOS RODRÍGUEZ BRAUN

Bibliography

McCloskey, D.N. (1986), *The Rhetoric of Economics*, Brighton: Wheatsheaf Books, pp. 145, 156, 159.

Gerschenkron's growth hypothesis

In his *Economic Backwardness in Historical Perspective* (1962), Alexander Gerschenkron (1904–1978) used a comparative history of industrialization in Europe to challenge the evolutionist view according to which backward societies follow the path of the pioneering nations. Denying that every development followed a pattern observable in the first industrialized countries, moving from a common stage of prerequisites into industrial growth, he argued that the development of such backward countries by 'the very virtue of their backwardness' will differ fundamentally from that of advanced countries. Using the concept of 'relative economic backwardness', Gerschenkron organized the disparate national industrialization patterns into coherent universal patterns. However, they do not offer a precise definition of backwardness based on an economic indicator but a rather loose definition based on the combination of savings ratios, literacy, technology, social capital and ideology.

Gerschenkron's core argument is that, when industrialization develops in backward countries there are 'considerable differences' from the same processes in advanced countries. These differences include the speed of industrial growth, and the productive and organizational structures that emerge from the industrialization process. From these two basic differences, Gerschenkron derives up to seven characteristics of industrialization directly related to the levels of backwardness.

Thus he argues that, the more backward the country, the more rapid will be its industrialization, the more it will be based on the capital rather than the consumer goods industry, the larger will be the typical scale of plant or firm, the greater will be the pressure on consumption levels of the population (given the high rate of capital formation during industrialization), the less will be the role of the agricultural sector as a market for industry products and source of rising productivity, the more active will be the role of institutions (like the banks in Germany and the state in Russia) in promoting growth and, finally, the more important will be the industrializing ideologies. Gerschenkron's ideas continue to provide insights for economics in general and economic history in particular; recent developments emphasize the relevance of his hypothesis for understanding the patterns of economic growth.

JOAN R. ROSÉS

Bibliography

Gerschenkron, Alexander (1962), *Economic Backwardness in Historical Perspective*, Cambridge, MA: Harvard University Press.

Sylla, Richard and Gianni Toniolo (eds) (1991), *Patterns of European Industrialization. The Nineteenth Century*, London: Routledge.

Gibbard–Satterthwaite theorem

This theorem establishes that a voting scheme for which three or more outcomes are possible is vulnerable to individual manipulation unless it is dictatorial.

Voting schemes are procedures for public decision making which select an outcome from a feasible set on the basis of the preferences reported by the members of society. An individual can manipulate a voting scheme when, by misrepresenting his preferences, he can induce an outcome he prefers to that selected when he reports his true preferences. Dictatorial voting schemes are those that select outcomes on the basis of the preferences declared by a particular individual. The condition that at least three outcomes must be possible is indispensable: when only two outcomes are possible, majority rule is neither a manipulable nor a dictatorial voting scheme; hence the Gibbard–Satterthwaite theorem does not hold in this case.

The Gibbard–Satterthwaite theorem reveals the difficulties of reconciling individuals' interests in making public decisions. These difficulties can easily become so severe that they cannot be resolved satisfactorily: allowing the choice to include three or more outcomes which every individual may rank in every possible way reduces the set of available voting schemes to those that use the preferences of a single individual as the sole criterion, or are subject to strategic manipulation. Although it is apparent that the requirement that no individual can ever manipulate a voting scheme is very strong (it imposes the condition that reporting one's true preferences must be an optimal strategy whatever preferences the others report), it is somewhat surprising that only dictatorial voting schemes satisfy this requirement.

The theorem was independently established by Allan Gibbard and Mark Satterthwaite. In their formulation, voting schemes must decide on a universal domain of preference profiles. Later authors have established that, on restricted domains of preferences, there are voting schemes that are neither manipulable nor dictatorial; for example, Hervé Moulin has shown that, if there is an order on the set of feasible outcomes according to which admissible preferences are single-peaked (that is, such that an outcome is less preferred than any outcome located in the order between this outcome and the most preferred outcome), then the set of voting schemes that are not manipulable coincides with the class of median voters.

Versions of the Gibbard–Satterthwaite theorem have been established in settings motivated by economic considerations; that is, when the decision includes dimensions of public interest but may also include other dimensions of interest only to some individuals or even to single individuals. In these settings the theorem has been established for the domains of preferences usually associated with economic environments (for example, when admissible preferences are those that can be represented by utility functions that are continuous, increasing and quasi-concave).

The original proofs of the Gibbard–Satterthwaite theorem rely on Arrow's impossibility theorem. Indeed, recent literature has shown that both Arrow's and Gibbard–Satterthwaite's theorems are corollaries of a deeper result that reveals the irreconcilable nature of the conflict of interest present in a social decision problem.

DIEGO MORENO

Bibliography

Gibbard, A. (1973), 'Manipulation of voting schemes: a general result', *Econometrica*, **41**, 587–601.

Satterthwaite, M. (1975), 'Strategy-proofness and Arrow's Conditions: existence and correspondence for voting procedures and social welfare functions', *Journal of Economic Theory*, **10**, 187–216.

See also: Arrow's impossibility theorem.

Gibbs sampling

This is a simulation algorithm, the most popular in the family of the Monte Carlo Markov Chain algorithms. The intense attention that Gibbs sampling has received in applied work is due to its mild implementation requirements, together with its programming simplicity. In a Bayesian parametric model, this algorithm provides an accurate estimation of the marginal posterior densities, or summaries of these distributions, by sampling from the conditional parameter distributions. Furthermore, the algorithm converges independently of the initial conditions. The basic requirement for the Gibbs sampler is to be able to draw samples from all the conditional distributions for the parameters in the model. Starting from an arbitrary vector of initial values, a sequence of samples from the conditional parameter distributions is iteratively generated, and it converges in distribution to the joint parameter distribution, independently of the initial values selection. As an estimation method, Gibbs sampling is less efficient than the direct simulation from the distribution; however the number of problems where the distribution is known is too small, compared with the numerous cases for the Gibbs sampling application.

The Gibbs sampling name suggests that the algorithm was invented by the eminent professor of Yale, the mathematician Josiah Willard Gibbs (1839–1903). However, for the origin of the Gibbs sampling algorithm, we need look no further than 1953, when a group of scientists proposed the Metropolis algorithm for the simulation of complex systems in solid-state physics (Metropolis *et al.*, 1953). The Gibbs sampling is a particular case of this algorithm. Some years later, Hastings (1970) proposed a version of the algorithm for generating random variables; he could introduce the algorithm ideas into the statisticians' world, but unfortunately he was ignored. Finally, Geman and Geman (1984) published the Gibbs sampling algorithm in a computational journal, using the algorithm for image reconstruction and simulation of Markov random fields, a particular case of the Gibbs distribution, and this is the real origin of the present name for the algorithm.

The great importance of Gibbs sampling now is due to Gelfand and Smith (1990), who suggested the application of Gibbs sampling to the resolution of Bayesian statistical models. Since this paper was published, a large literature has developed. The applications cover a wide variety of areas, such as the economy, genetics and paleontology.

ANA JUSTEL

Bibliography

Gelfand, A.E. and A.F.M. Smith (1990), 'Sampling-based approaches to calculating marginal densities', *Journal of the American Statistical Association*, **85**, 398–409.

Geman, S. and D. Geman (1984), 'Stochastic relaxation, Gibbs distributions and the Bayesian restoration of images', *IEEE Transaction on Pattern Analysis and Machine Intelligence*, **6**, 721–41.

Hastings, W.K. (1970), 'Monte-Carlo sampling methods using Markov chains and their applications', *Biometrika*, **57**, 97–109.

Metropolis, N., A.W. Rosenbluth, M.N Rosenbluth, A.H. Teller and E. Teller (1953), 'Equations of state calculations by fast computing machines', *Journal of Chemical Physics*, **21**, 1087–91.

Gibrat's law

Robert Gibrat (1904–1980), formulated the 'law of proportionate effect' in 1931. It states that the expected growth rate of a firm is independent of its size. That is, the probability of a given proportionate change in size during a specified period is the same for all firms in a given industry, no matter their size at the beginning of the period.

Economists have interpreted Gibrat's law in at least three different ways: some of them think it holds for all firms in a given industry, including those which have exited during the period examined, while others state that it refers only to firms that survive over the entire period; finally, others assume it holds only for firms large enough to have overcome the minimum efficient scale of a given industry.

Extensive empirical research has repeatedly rejected the law, but many studies show that this rejection may be due to the fact that smaller firms are more likely to die than bigger ones: it is not that size has no bearing on growth, but, having survived, the biggest and oldest grow the most slowly. In economic terms, young firms entering the industry at suboptimal scale experience decreasing average costs and enjoy rapid growth, whereas mature big firms can go through a flattening average cost curve.

Gibrat's law has also been tested in city growth processes. Despite variation in growth rates as a function of city size, empirical work does not support Gibrat's law.

MANUEL NAVEIRA

Bibliography

Gibrat, Robert (1931), *Les Inégalités Économiques*, Paris: Librairie du Recueil Sirey.

Sutton, John (1997), 'Gibrat's legacy', *Journal of Economic Literature*, **35**, 40–59.

Gibson's paradox

A.H. Gibson was an economist who specialized in British finance and who published an article (Gibson, 1923) showing the close correlation between the nominal interest rates and the price level over a period of more than a hundred years (1791–1924). Keynes focused on Gibson's figures (Keynes, 1930, vol. 2, pp. 198–208) to explain what Keynes himself called 'the Gibson paradox'. It is a paradox because, in the long term, classical monetary theory suggests that nominal interest rates should move with the rate of change in prices, rather than the price level itself.

In the 1930s, Keynes, Fisher, Wicksell and others attempted to solve the Gibson paradox, using the Fisher effect; that is, the concept of the market rate of interest as a sum of the expected rate of inflation and the natural rate of interest. Thus the high prices cause, through the expectation of more inflation, a rise in the market rate of interest and a higher inflation. In the long term, the price level will move in the same direction as the rate of interest whenever the market rate of interest moves in the same direction and below the natural rate of interest. Nevertheless, many economists consider that the empirical phenomenon of the Gibson paradox has not yet found a satisfactory theorical explanation. One recent study (Barsky and Summers, 1988) links the paradox to the classical gold standard period. If we consider gold as a durable asset, besides acting as money, its price should move inversely to the real interest rate in a free market. Thus interest rates are related to the general price level, as the Gibson paradox shows, because the level of prices is the reciprocal of the price of gold in terms of goods.

LUIS EDUARDO PIRES JIMÉNEZ

Bibliography

Barsky, Robert B. and Lawrence H. Summers (1988), 'Gibson's paradox and the gold standard', *Journal of Political Economy*, **96** (3), 528–50.

Gibson, A.H. (1923), 'The future course of high-class investment values', *Bankers', Insurance Managers', and Agents' Magazine*, London, January, pp. 15–34.
Keynes, John Maynard (1930), *A Treatise on Money*, 2 vols, London: Macmillan.

See also: Fisher effect.

Giffen goods

Sir Robert Giffen (1837–1910) was educated at Glasgow University. He held various positions in the government and was a prolific writer on economics and on financial and statistical subjects.

One of the main tenets of neoclassical economics is the 'law of demand', which states that, as the price of goods falls, the quantity bought by the consumer increases, that is, the demand curve slopes downwards. To identify the full effect of a price reduction on the demand for a commodity, it should be borne in mind that this can be decomposed into two effects: the income effect and the substitution effect. In the presence of an inferior good, the income effect is positive and works against the negative substitution effect. If the income effect is sufficiently sizable and outweighs the substitution effect, the fall in price will cause the quantity demanded to fall, contradicting the law of demand. This is called the 'Giffen paradox'.

The most cited reference to Giffen goods is found in the 1964 edition of Samuelson's famous textbook, *Economics*. It mentions how the 1845 Irish famine greatly raised the price of potatoes, and poor families that consumed a lot of potatoes ended up consuming more rather than less of the high-price potatoes. Nevertheless, the first reference to the Giffen paradox was not attributable to Samuelson but to Marshall: 'a rise in the price of bread makes so large a drain on the resources of the poorer labouring families and raises so much the marginal utility of money to them, that they are forced to curtail their consumption of meat and the more expensive farinaceous foods' (Marshall, 1895, p. 208).

Both Marshall's and Samuelson's texts mention events that occurred in the British Isles during the nineteenth century and refer to Giffen, although neither indicates the source of Giffen's observation. But researchers of his work have failed to find a statement of the paradox.

It is possible that the Giffen observation refers more to English bread eaters than to Irish potato famines, but the empirical evidence does not support either Marshall's or Samuelson's claim. Thus it seems that the Giffen paradox is more of a myth than an empirical fact. Still, we should acknowledge its importance in establishing the limitations of the neoclassical paradigm with respect to the law of demand.

JAVIER VALLÉS

Bibliography

Marshall, A. (1895), *Principles of Economics*, 3rd edn, London: Macmillan.

Gini's coefficient

This is a summary inequality measure linked with the Lorenz curve. Normally, this coefficient is applied to measure the income or wealth inequality. The Gini coefficient (G) is defined as the relative mean difference, that is, the mean of income differences between all possible pairs of individuals, divided by the mean income value μ,

$$G = \frac{\sum_{i=1}^{n} \sum_{j=1}^{n} | x_j - x_i |}{2n^2\mu},$$

where x_i is the income level of the ith individual and n, the total population. This value coincides with twice the area that lies between the Lorenz curve and the diagonal line of perfect equality. This formula is unfeasible for a large enough number of individuals. Alternatively, once income data have been ordered in an increasing way, G can be written as:

$$G = \frac{\sum_{i=1}^{n} (2i - n - 1)x_i^*}{n^2\mu},$$

where x_i^* is the income level of the ordered ith individual. G value ranks from zero (when there is no inequality) to a potential maximum value of one (when all income is earned by only one person, in an infinite population). It can be proved that, for finite samples, G must be multiplied by a factor $n/(n-1)$ to obtain unbiased estimators.

RAFAEL SALAS

Bibliography

Gini, C. (1914), 'Sulla misera della concentrazione e della variabilità dei caratteri', *Atti del R. Instituto Veneto*, **73**, 1913–14. There is an English version, 'Measurement of inequality of incomes' (1921), *Economic Journal*, **31**, 124–6.

See also: Kakwani index, Lorenz's curve, Reynolds–Smolensky index.

Goodhart's law

The pound had finished its postwar peg with the dollar by 1971. Some alternative to the US currency as a nominal anchor and some guiding principles for monetary policy were needed in the UK. Research had been indicating that there was a stable money demand function in the UK. The implication for monetary policy was deemed to be that the relationship could be used to control monetary growth via the setting of short-term interest rates.

It was thought that a particular rate of growth of the money stock could be achieved by inverting the money demand equation that had (apparently) existed under a different regime. But in the 1971–3 period this policy did not work in the UK and money growth went out of control. Previously estimated relationships seemed to have broken down.

In this context, Charles A.F. Goodhart (b.1936) proposed his 'law': 'Any observed statistical regularity will tend to collapse once pressure is placed upon it for control purposes.' Goodhart's law does not refer to the inexistence of a money demand function that depends on the interest rate (nor to the long-run stability of this function), but to the fact that, when monetary policy makers want to use a statistical relationship for control purposes, changes in behaviour of economic agents will make it useless. Although a statistical relationship may have the appearance of a regularity, it has a tendency to break down when it ceases to be an ex post observation of related variables (given private sector behaviour) and becomes instead an ex ante rule for monetary policy purposes.

Readers familiar with the Lucas critique and the invariance principle will recognize some of the arguments. Though contemporary and arrived at independently of the Lucas critique, in some sense it could be argued that Goodhart's law and the Lucas critique are essentially the same thing. As Goodhart himself put it in 1989, 'Goodhart's Law is a mixture of the Lucas Critique and Murphy's Law.'

DAVID VEGARA

Bibliography

Goodhart, C.A.E. (1975), 'Monetary relationships: a view from Threadneedle Street', *Papers in Monetary Economics*, vol. I, Reserve Bank of Australia.

Goodhart, C.A.E. (1984), *Monetary Theory and Practice: The U.K. Experience*, London: Macmillan.

See also: Lucas critique

Gorman's polar form

The relationship between individual preferences and market behavior marked a constant research line in the life of William Gorman (1923–2003) who was born in Ireland, graduated from Trinity College Dublin and taught in Birmingham, London and Oxford. A key problem that Gorman solved was aggregating individual preferences in order to obtain a preference map of a whole group or society. Under what conditions of the underlying individual preferences can we derive a representative consumer?

Gorman proposed one solution: we need the Engel curves of the individuals (the relationship between income levels and consumption) to be parallel straight lines in order to construct an aggregate preference relationship. For the aggregation to be possible, what was needed was that the individuals' response to an income change had to be equal across consumers, while each response to a price change could take different forms.

More specifically, Gorman focused on the functional form needed in the individual preference relationships so that we can derive from them straight-line Engel curves. He answered this with indirect utility functions for each consumer of the form,

$$V_i(p, w_i) = a_i(p) + b(p)w_i, \qquad (1)$$

where w_i is each individual's income and p is the vector of prices he faces. The key insight was the subscript i to denote each consumer and to note that the function $b(p)$ is independent of each consumer. This condition allows us to go a lot further in the aggregation of preferences, or in the justification of social welfare functions that arise from a representative consumer. In fact, using the functional form in (1), it is possible to find a solution to the central planner's problem of finding a wealth (or income) distribution that solves for the maximization of a utilitarian social welfare function where its solution provides a representative consumer for the aggregate demand which takes the simple form of the sum of the individual demands, $x(p, w) = \sum_i x_i(p, w_i(p, w))$.

One important interpretation of this result is that, in general, we know that the properties of aggregate demand (and social welfare) functions depend crucially on the way wealth is distributed. Gorman provided a set of conditions on individual preferences such that the social welfare function obtained is valid under any type of wealth distribution.

Gorman advanced the duality approach (1959) to consumer theory; in fact, in expression (1), the dual of the utility function has already been used. His work led to important advances not only in the theory of consumption and social choice but even in empirical applications. Gorman imposed the requirement that aggregate demand function behave as the sum of the individual demand functions. This restriction proved to be very demanding, but similar ones provided years after the seminal work of Gorman turned out to be very useful, as the contributions of Deaton and Muellbauer (1980) showed.

One crucial assumption already used in the indirect utility function (1) is separability. For Gorman, separability was basic in the context of the method of analysis for an economist. He used separability as a coherent way of making clear on what factors to focus a study and what to ignore, and applied separability to the intertemporal utility function under uncertainty in order to achieve a linear aggregate utility function useful for dynamic analysis and estimation procedures, as well as on pioneer work on goods' characteristics and demand theory.

IÑIGO HERGUERA

Bibliography

Deaton A.S. and J. Muellbauer (1980), *Economics and Consumer Behaviour*, Cambridge: Cambridge University Press.

Gorman, W.M. (1959), 'Separable utility and aggregation', *Econometrica*, **27** (3), 469–81.

See also: Engel curve.

Gossen's laws

German economist and precursor of marginalism, Hermann Heinrich Gossen (1810–58), in his *Entwicklung der Gesetze des menschlichen Verkehrs* (1854) on the theory of consumption, defined the principle of falling marginal utility and the conditions of consumer equilibrium, rediscovered by Jevons, Menger and Walras in the 1870s. The book remained almost unknown until it was reprinted in 1889. The term 'Gossen's laws' was coined in 1895 by Wilhelm Lexis, an economist close to the historical school, one of the founders of the Verein für Sozialpolitik, and editor of the *Jahrbücher für Natianälökonomie und Statistik*, though in fact Lexis was critical of Gossen's contribution. Gossen's laws are the fundamental laws of demand theory. The first law states that all human necessity diminishes in intensity as one finds satisfaction; in Gossen's words: 'The magnitude of a given pleasure decreases continuously if we continue to satisfy this pleasure without interruption until satiety is ultimately reached' (Gossen, 1983, p. 6; 1889, p. 4). Gossen's second law states that any individual, to obtain his maximum satisfaction, has to distribute the goods that he consumes in such a way that the marginal utility obtained from each one of them is the same; in Gossen's words: 'The magnitude of each single pleasure at the moment when its enjoyment is broken off shall be the same for all pleasures' (Gossen, 1983, p. 14; 1889, p. 12). Gossen illustrated these laws with diagrams similar to the ones that Jevons was to draw later, but instead of curves he used the simpler form of straight lines. In the case of the first law, utility is represented on the y axis, while time of consumption, a form of measuring enjoyment of a good, is measured on the x axis.

Jevons was introduced to Gossen's book by Robert Adamson, also professor of political economy at Manchester, and he told Walras of his discovery. From that point onwards, Gossen figured as one of the fathers of the marginalist revolution, and a co-founder of marginal utility theory: indeed, his two laws constitute the core of the marginalist revolution. Although antecedents of the first law are found in previous writers on decreasing marginal utility, the authorship of the second law lies entirely with Gossen. Like von Thünen, Gossen believed in the importance of his discoveries, and he compared them to those of Copernicus. His starting point was an extreme utilitarianism according to which men always search for the maximum satisfaction, which Gossen believed to be of divine origin. This utilitarianism, highly suited to the cultural environment of England, was largely neglected in a Germany dominated by historicism.

Gossen also proposed a division of goods into three classes: consumption goods, goods that had to be transformed in order to be consumed, and goods such as fuel that are used up in the act of production. His laws were applicable to the first type of goods and, indirectly, to the other two classes as well; in the latter case, the diagram would show quantities used and not time of enjoyment.

LLUÍS ARGEMÍ

Bibliography

Gossen, Hermann Heinrich (1854), *Entwicklung der Gesetze des menschlichen Verkehrs, und der daraus fliessenden Regeln für menschliches Handeln*, 2nd edn, Berlin: Prager, 1889.

Gossen, Hermann Heinrich (1950), *Sviluppo delle leggi del commercio umano*, Padua: Cedam.

Gossen, Hermann Heinrich (1983), *The Laws of Human Relations and the Rules of Human Action Derived Therefrom*, Cambridge: MIT Press.

Jevons, William Stanley (1879), *Theory of Political Economy*, 2nd edn, London: MacMillan; preface reprinted (1970) Harmondsworth: Penguin.

Walras, Léon (1874), *Éléments d'Économie Politique Pure*, Paris: Guillaumin; preface, 16ème leçon, reprinted (1952) Paris: Libraire Générale.

Walras, Léon (1896), *Études d'Économie Sociale*, Lausanne: Rouge, pp. 351–74.

Graham's demand

Frank Dunstone Graham (1890–1949) is mainly known for his work in the theory of international trade. He regarded his attack on the doctrines of the classical trade theory as his principal contribution to economic thought.

In his work of 1923, Graham argued that John Stuart Mill's two-country and two-commodity model reached unjustifiable conclusions on the effect of changes in international demand on the commodity terms of trade. According to Mill, the pattern of international prices is governed by the intensities of demand of the goods of other countries. By showing that international values depend upon international prices, while domestic values depend upon costs, Mill supported Ricardo's thesis concerning the difference between the theory of international trade and the theory of trade within a single country.

Retaining Mill's assumptions of costless transport, free trade and constant cost per 'unit of productive power', Graham showed that the adjusting process in response to a shift in international demand is not essentially different from the Ricardian adjusting process within a single country once a trade between many countries and many commodities has been established. He repeatedly emphasized the fact that this process is as dependent upon conditions of supply as upon conditions of demand.

If the average cost ratios among the various commodities are always the same regardless of how a country's resources are employed, it is possible to consider each commodity as the equivalent to a certain number of units of homogeneous productive power, and a reciprocal demand can then be derived for that commodity. Such a demand schedule will have a 'kink' at any point at which a country ceases to produce any given commodity and begins to import the entire supply of it from abroad, and at any point at which the country begins to import something it has formerly produced entirely for itself. Some segments of the demand schedule, corresponding to terms of trade at which a country is both an importer and a domestic producer of a given commodity, will be infinitely elastic, while other segments will have a much lower elasticity.

Two of his disciples extended his work. Within (1953) illustrated the model geometrically and reached the conclusion that Graham's model anticipated linear programming. One year later, McKenzie's (1954) proved the existence of competitive equilibrium in Graham's theory of international trade under any assumed continuous demand function using Kakutani's fixed point theorem. He found that this solution becomes unique for the demand functions actually used by Graham.

ALEIX PONS

Bibliography

Graham, F.D. (1923), 'The theory of international values re-examined', *Quarterly Journal of Economics*, **38**, 54–86.

McKenzie, L.W. (1954), 'On equilibrium in Graham's model of world trade and other competitive systems', *Econometrica*, **22**, 147–61.

Within, T.M. (1953), 'Classical theory, Graham's theory and linear programming in international trade', *Quarterly Journal of Economics*, **67**, 520–44.

See also: Graham's paradox, Kakutani's fixed point theorem.

Graham's paradox

This is a situation described by Frank Graham (1890–1949) in which Ricardian classical international free trade theory of specialization along lines of comparative advantage leads to a net welfare loss in one of the countries involved. Influenced by Marshall, Graham rejects the classical assumption of constant costs, and attempts to prove that, in some cases, free trade is not the best commercial policy choice, and protection could be desirable.

His model considers two commodities (wheat and watches) and two countries, England (producing both commodities under constant costs), and the USA (producing wheat with increasing costs and watches with decreasing costs). England has a comparative advantage in watches and the USA in wheat. The USA obtains the best possible terms in its trade with England. According to the specialization model, in the USA wheat output increases and watch output decreases, raising unit costs in both. This loss of productivity is more than compensated by the gain due to favourable terms of trade, but if specialization continues, this compensatory effect will eventually vanish, driving the USA to a net welfare loss under free trade compared to autarky. The USA will reach this point before totally losing its cost advantage (Graham, 1925, pp. 326–8). So it will be advisable for the country specializing in the decreasing return commodity to protect its increasing return industry, even if this industry is never able to survive without protection (Graham, 1923, pp. 202–3). He concludes that comparative advantage is by no means an infallible guide for international trade policy (ibid. p. 213).

Graham considered that his theory could explain why regions with slender natural resources devoted to manufactures are often more prosperous than others with abundant resources. He also warned that, although his opinion would give some support to US protectionists, all the economic advantages of protection in that country had already been realized. At the time, American comparative advantage tended towards manufactures, which would benefit from free trade, like Britain in the first Industrial Revolution (ibid., pp. 215, 225–7).

Although Graham's model was not very precise and some aspects remained unclear, his thesis caused a controversy which was ended in 1937 by Viner, who stated that Graham's arguments were correct but useless in practice (Bobulescu, 2002, pp. 402–3, 419). Graham's model was rediscovered at the end of the 1970s, in the revival of the protectionism–free trade debate. It was reexamined by Krugman, Helpman, Ethier and Panagariya in the 1980s, and reformulated by Chipman in 2000 and Bobulescu in 2002.

JAVIER SAN JULIÁN

Bibliography

Bobulescu, R. (2002), 'The "paradox" of F. Graham (1890–1949): a study in the theory of International trade', *European Journal of History of Economic Thought*, **9** (3), 402–29.

Graham, F.D. (1923), 'Some aspects of protection further considered', *Quarterly Journal of Economics*, **37**, 199–227.

Graham, F.D. (1925), 'Some fallacies in the interpretation of social costs. A reply', *Quarterly Journal of Economics*, **39**, 324–30.

See also: Ricardo's comparative costs.

Granger's causality test

This test, which was introduced by Granger (1969), has been very popular for several decades. The test consists of analysing the causal relation between two variables *X* and *Y*, by means of a model with two equations that relates the present value of each variable in moment *t* to lagged values of both variables, as in VAR models, testing the joint significance of all the coefficients of *X* in the equation of *Y* and the joint significance of all the coefficients of *Y* in the equation of *X*. In the case of two lags the relations are

$$Y/X(-1)\ X(-2)\ Y(-1)\ Y(-2), \qquad (1)$$

$$X/Y(-1)\ Y(-2)\ X(-1)\ X(-2) \qquad (2)$$

and the hypothesis '*Y* is not Granger caused by *X*' is rejected if the *F* statistic corresponding to the joint nullity of parameters β_1 and β_2 in relation (1) is higher than the critical value. A similar procedure is applied to relation (2) to test '*X* is not Granger caused by *Y*'. The results may vary from no significant relation to a unilateral/bilateral relation.

The test interpretation is sometimes misguided because many researchers identify non-rejection of nullity with acceptance, but in cases of a high degree of multicollinearity, specially frequent with several lags, the confidence intervals of the parameters are very wide and the non-rejection could simply mean uncertainty and it should not be confused with evidence in favour of acceptance. Guisan (2001) shows that, even with only one lag, the problem of uncertainty very often does not disappear, because a very common real situation is the existence of a causal relation between Y and X in the form of a mixed dynamic model like

$$Y = \alpha_1 D(X) + \alpha_2 Y(-1) + \varepsilon, \quad (3)$$

with X linearly related to $X(-1)$, for example $X = \delta X(-1)$, where D means first difference and δ has a value a little higher/lower than 1. And in those cases the estimation of the relation

$$Y = \beta_1 X(-1) + \beta_2 Y(-1) + \varepsilon, \quad (4)$$

leads to testing the hypothesis of nullity of $\beta_1 = \alpha_1(1 - \delta)$, being the value of β_1, nearly zero, even when α_1 is clearly different from zero, as the value of $(1 - \delta)$ is very often close to zero. The linear correlation existing between $X(-1)$ and $Y(-1)$ explains the rest, provoking a degree of uncertainty in the estimation that does not allow the rejection of the null hypothesis. Granger's idea of testing the impact of changes in the explanatory variable, given the lagged value of the one explained, is a valid one but it is surely better performed by testing the nullity of α_1 in relation (3) than testing the nullity of β_1 in relation (4). This conclusion favours the Cowles Commission approach of contemporaneous relations between variables.

M. CARMEN GUISAN

Bibliography

Granger, C.W. (1969), 'Investigating causal relations by econometric models and cross-spectral methods', *Econometrica*, **37**, 424–38.

Guisan, M.C. (2001), 'Causality and cointegration between consumption and GDP in 25 OECD countries: limitations of the cointegration approach', *Applied Econometrics and International Development*, **1** (1), 39–61.

Gresham's law

'Bad money drives out good money', so the story goes. Not always, however, do men have control over the use made of their name, as in the case of Sir Thomas Gresham (1519–79), an important English merchant and businessman, best known for his activity as a royal agent in Antwerp. There is no evidence that, in conducting negotiations for royal loans with Flemish merchants or in the recommendations made to Queen Elizabeth for monetary reform, he ever used the expression that now bears his name. But it is likely that the sense of the law had already intuitively been understood by him, since it is related to the spontaneous teachings of everyday commercial and financial life, as experienced by someone dealing with different types of currencies in circulation, coupled with the needs for hoarding and making payments abroad.

It was H.D. MacLeod who, in 1858, gave the idea Sir Thomas's name, but, had he been more painstaking in his reading of the texts in which the same teaching is conveyed, he would have encountered antecedents two centuries earlier, in the writings of Nicolas Oresme. Even Aristophanes would not have escaped a mention for also having come close to understanding the significance of a law that is today an integral part of everyday economic language.

The idea is very rudimentary, almost self-evident, and is applied to any means of payment used under a system of perfect substitutability, at a fixed relative price, parity or exchange rate, determined by the government or by the monetary authority in a given country or currency zone. The law operates only when there is such a compulsory regime fixing the value of the currencies at a price different from the result of a free market trading. In the simplest situation, if the same face value is attributed to two metallic means of payment of different intrinsic values (either because they contain a smaller amount of the same metal or because they were minted in different quality metals), the holder of such means of payment will prefer to use the currency with the lower intrinsic value (bad money) in his transactions, thereby tending to drive the currency of higher value (good money) out of circulation. Bad money is preferred by economic agents who keep it in use and circulation for trading on the internal market, whilst good money is hoarded, melted down or exported to foreign countries.

The debate about the validity of Gresham's law proved to be particularly relevant when discussing the advantages and disadvantages of monetary regimes based on a single standard. In the 1860s and 1870s, the controversy over accepting either French bimetallism or the English gold standard provided the perfect opportunity for using Gresham's law to justify the phenomena that occur in the circulation of money.

JOSÉ LUÍS CARDOSO

Bibliography

Kindleberger, Charles (1984), *The Financial History of Western Europe*, London: George Allen & Unwin.

MacLeod, Henry D. (1858), *The Elements of Political Economy*, London: Longmans, Green & Co, p. 477.

Redish, Angela (2000), *Bimetallism. An Economic and Historical Analysis*, Cambridge and New York: Cambridge University Press.

Roover, Raymond de (1949), *Gresham on Foreign Exchange: An Essay on Early English Mercantilism with the Text of Sir Thomas Gresham's Memorandum for the Understanding of the Exchange*, Cambridge, MA: Harvard University Press.

Gresham's law in politics

The import of Gresham's law to the analysis of political phenomena is recent. Geoffrey Brennan and James Buchanan, in the fourth chapter of their *The Reason of Rules: Constitutional Political Economy* (1985), applied the old concept devised by Gresham to these phenomena and, notably, to politicians' behaviour. The authors support the idea that the *Homo economicus* construction of classical and neoclassical political economy is the most appropriate to study the behaviour of individuals in what they call 'constitutional analysis'. Gresham's law in politics states that 'bad politicians drive out good ones', as bad money does with good or, quoting Brennan and Buchanan, 'Gresham's Law in social interactions [means] that bad behaviour drives out good and that all persons will be led themselves by the presence of even a few self-seekers to adopt self-interested behaviour.'

PEDRO MOREIRA DOS SANTOS

Bibliography

Brennan, Geoffrey and Buchanan, James (1985), *The Reason of Rules: Constitutional Political Economy*; reprinted (2000) in *Collected Works of James M. Buchanan*, vol. 10, Indianapolis: Liberty Fund, pp. 68–75.

See also: Gresham's Law.

H

Haavelmo balanced budget theorem

The Norwegian economist Trygve Magnus Haavelmo (1911–98) was awarded the Nobel Prize in 1989 for his pioneering work in the field of econometrics in the 1940s. However, his contribution to economic science goes beyond that field, as is shown by his stimulating research in fiscal policy.

Must there be a deficit in public budgeting in order to provide a remedy for unemployment? This issue was rigorously analysed by Haavelmo (1945) who proved the following theorem: 'If the consumption function is linear, and total private investment is a constant, a tax, T, that is fully spent will raise total gross national income by an amount T and leave total private net income and consumption unchanged. And this holds regardless of the numerical value of the marginal propensity to consume, α'(p. 315).

The proof is based on a simple Keynesian closed economy in which private investment V is assumed to remain constant and private consumption expenditure is given by $C = \beta + \alpha (Y - T)$, where $0 < \alpha < 1$ denotes marginal propensity to consume disposable income, $Y - T$, and the parameter $\beta > 0$ accounts for other factors affecting C. If government spending G is matched by an equal rise in taxes T, total gross national income Y (= $C + V + G$) is then determined implicitly by $Y = \beta + \alpha (Y - T) + V + T$, which gives

$$Y^* = \frac{\beta + V}{1 - \alpha} + T.$$

Comparing Y^* with the level (Y^0) corresponding to a economy where $T = G = 0$ we have $\Delta Y = Y - Y^0 = T = G$. In this way, regardless of the numerical value of α, a balanced budget results in a multiplier that is not only positive but also equal to unity ($\Delta Y/T = 1$), leaving private net income ($Y - T$) and consumption (C) unchanged at levels Y^0 and C^0 (= $\beta + \alpha Y^0$), respectively.

Thus it is not essential that there is a budget deficit to stimulate the economy, because the balanced budget policy is not neutral with regard to national income and employment. It is misleading to claim that government would only take back with one hand (by taxing) what it gives with the other (by spending). In the Keynesian consumption function, only part of the income is consumed; taxes decrease this private spending, but the consequent negative effect on the total national expenditure is more than offset by the rise in the governmental spending. Moreover, the non-neutrality of such a policy is strengthened by the fact that it also affects the structure of national income, since the public share has increased.

The expansionary effect of a balanced budget had been pointed out before, but Haavelmo was the first to analyse it in a rigorous theoretical way. For this reason his work provoked an exciting and enriching literature on the multiplier theory, with Baumol and Peston (1955) deserving special mention. According to these authors, unity is a poor approximation to the multiplier associated with any balanced tax–expenditure programme which a government may be expected to undertake. They consider plausible cases in which the balanced budget multiplier might be not only different from one but also negative, depending on the nature of the spending and the taxation involved.

For instance, let us suppose an increase in public expenditure only a fraction of which is devoted to domestically produced goods, with the remainder being spent on imports, or on transfer payments which merely redistribute income, or on capital purchases which affect the old owner by increasing his liquidity rather than his income; these leakages in spending reduce the power of the multiplier. On the other hand, the effects of taxation also depend on the categories of both taxes and taxpayers. For example, consumption taxation is more contracting than income taxation; the impacts of an income tax increase depend on whether it is levied on firms or households; and the propensity to consume of taxpayers may not be the same as that of the recipients of the expenditures. The unity multiplier argument is also weakened when private investment is directly or indirectly affected by the tax–expenditure programme and when goods prices rise as aggregate demand expands.

The Haavelmo theorem, though correctly deduced from its premises, has been questioned in various ways as more realistic frameworks have been considered. Nevertheless, what is still reasonable is the idea that balanced budget policy is not neutral or, in other words, that the expansionary or contractionary bias of fiscal policy is not properly captured by the mere difference between government spending and taxes. In this sense the core of the theorem remains strong.

J. PÉREZ VILLAREAL

Bibliography

Haavelmo, T. (1945), 'Multiplier effects of a balanced budget', *Econometrica*, **13**, 311–18.

Baumol, W.J. and M.H. Peston, (1955), 'More on the multiplier effects of a balanced budget', *American Economic Review*, **45**, 140–8.

Hamiltonian function and Hamilton–Jacobi equations

Many economical laws can be expressed in terms of variation principles; that is, many economic models evolve in such a way that their trajectory maximizes or minimizes some functional, which is given by integrating a function

$$J(y) = \int_{x_0}^{x_1} F(y(x), y'(x), x)dx,$$

where $y(x)$ represents the value of the economic data at time x and the function F relates this magnitude to its derivative $y'(x)$. Lagrange's principle provides a set of second-order differential equations, the Euler–Lagrange equations, which are satisfied by the extremals of the given functional. Alternatively, the Irish mathematician William Rowan Hamilton (1805–65) method provides, by means of the Legendre transformation,

$$p = \frac{\partial F}{\partial y'},$$

(which replaces the variable y' with the new variable p) a remarkably symmetrical system of first-order differential equations, called the Hamiltonian system of equations (or 'canonical equations'),

$$\frac{dy}{dx} = \frac{\partial H}{\partial p} \quad \frac{dp}{dx} = -\frac{\partial H}{\partial y},$$

where $H(x, y, p) = -F + y'p$ is the Hamiltonian function. It is understood that, in the Hamiltonian, y' is considered as a function of p by means of the Legendre transformation. Hamilton's canonical equations are equivalent to the Euler–Lagrange equations. In addition, Hamilton's formulation via the Poisson brackets makes it clear that the conserved quantities $z(y, p)$ along the extremal path are precisely those whose bracket with the Hamiltonian

$$[z, H] = \frac{\partial z}{\partial y}\frac{\partial H}{\partial p} - \frac{\partial z}{\partial p}\frac{\partial H}{\partial y}$$

vanishes.

The Hamilton–Jacobi theorem states that, under certain regularity conditions, if $S(x, y, \alpha)$ is a solution to the Hamilton–Jacobi equations,

$$\frac{\partial S}{\partial x} + H(x, y, \frac{\partial S}{\partial y}) = 0,$$

depending on the parameter of integration α, then for any real value β, the function $y(x, \alpha, \beta)$ defined by

$$\frac{\partial S}{\partial x} = \beta,$$

together with the function

$$p = \frac{\partial S}{\partial y}$$

is a solution of Hamilton's canonical equations. And all the solutions of the canonical equations are obtained this way.

FRANCISCO MARHUENDA

Bibliography

Gelfand, I.M. and S.V. Fomin (1963), *Calculus of Variations*, Englewood Cliffs, NJ: Prentice-Hall.

See also: Euler's theorem and equations.

Hansen–Perloff effect

This refers to the procyclical behaviour of local government finances found by Alvin H. Hansen (1887–1975) and Harvey Perloff (in 1944) for the United States in the 1930s. The normative economic theory of fiscal federalism provides a justification for this behaviour, stating that, as a general rule, the interjurisdictional distribution of competences in multi-level economies should assign responsibility for stabilization policy to the highest (or central) level of public finance rather than to the different sub-central (regional, local) jurisdictions. The sub-central economies' higher degree of openness causes a reduction in the multipliers of Keynesian fiscal policy and spillover effects on neighbouring jurisdictions, thus providing an incentive for free-rider behaviour, in addition to a reduced commitment to stabilization policy objectives. Financial constraints could also reinforce this procyclical effect, thereby favouring a decrease in local current and investment expenditure during periods of recession.

The empirical evidence for this 'fiscal perversity' hypothesis proves that this kind of procyclical behaviour has been observed in several countries (Pascha and Robarschik, 2001, p. 4). Nevertheless, significant exceptions and differences exist among different countries (Pascha and Robarschik, 2001), kinds of expenditure (Hagen, 1992) and business conditions (countercyclical behaviour is stronger and more likely to occur during recessions).

JAVIER LOSCOS FERNÁNDEZ

Bibliography

Haggen, J. von (1992), 'Fiscal arrangements in a monetary union: evidence from the U.S.', in D.E. Fair and C. de Boissieu (eds), *Fiscal Policy, Taxation, and the Financial System in an Increasingly Integrated Europe*, Dordrecht: Kluwer Academic Publishers, pp. 337–59.

Hansen, A. and H.S. Perloff (1944), *State and Local Finance in the National Economy*, New York: W.W. Norton & Company.

Pascha, W. and F. Robaschik (2001), 'The role of Japanese local governments in stabilisation policy', *Duisburg Working Papers on East Asian Studies*, no. 40/2001, Duisburg: Institut für Ostasienwissenschaften, Gerhard-Mercator-Universität Duisburg. (Accessible on the Internet.)

Snyder, W.W. (1973), 'Are the budgets of state and local governments destabilizing? A six country comparison', *European Economic Review*, **4**, 197–213.

Harberger's triangle

This concept was developed in 1954 by Arnold Carl Harberger (b.1924) and centred on aspects of the analysis of welfare under monopoly and of resource allocation. Its basic contribution is that it provides a simple way to measure the irretrievable loss of efficiency due to monopoly, that is, to calculate monopoly's social costs. The traditional method (the Harberger triangle) is based on prices in the presence of market power being higher than the marginal cost, implying allocative inefficiency in the Pareto sense. In particular, the calculation estimates the loss of consumers' surplus (net of gains in the monopolist's surplus) when there is a deviation from competitive prices in a situation of monopolistic prices. The triangle is the area corresponding to the differences in these surpluses.

Using a sample of 2046 companies in 73 US industries during the period 1924–8, Harberger considered an economy in equilibrium in which companies act on their long-term cost curves and obtain normal rates of return on their invested assets. The problems involved with the price elasticity of demand were simplified by setting the elasticity equal to unity. This theoretical scheme allowed Harberger to claim that welfare losses under monopoly could be evaluated by observing the deviations in the rates of return with respect to the competitive levels; that is, high rates of return would indicate constraints on output and a failure to fully use resources. The triangle that Harberger calculated (the welfare loss) represented only 0.1 per cent of the US gross national product of the 1920s, and he concluded that either competitive conditions were the general rule in that economy or the effect of the misallocation of resources under monopolies was insignificant.

JUAN VEGA

Bibliography

Harberger, A.C. (1954), 'Monopoly and resource allocation', *American Economic Review, Papers and Proceedings*, **44**, 77–87.

See also: Tullock's trapezoid.

Harris–Todaro model

John R. Harris (b.1934), professor of economics at Boston University, and Michael P. Todaro (b.1942), professor of economics at New York University, challenged the traditional view of labor markets and migration in Todaro (1969) and Harris and Todaro (1970), arguing that, in the formal sector of the urban labor market, wage rates are institutionally determined and set at levels too high to clear the market. According to Harris and Todaro, rural residents would migrate or not, depending on the prospects for formal sector employment. Such jobs could only be secured, however, after a period of open unemployment and job search that would commence upon the migrant's arrival. In this framework an incentive to migrate persists until urban expected wages come to equal the rural wage. Because urban formal sector wages are fixed, additional migration to cities can only serve to achieve a 'migration equilibrium' with urban unemployment. The Harris–Todaro model implied that urban growth in less developed countries could be excessive and policy should be aimed at curbing an 'urban bias'.

Some key assumptions of the model have met criticism. First, it could be reasonable to assume high wages in the formal sector in the immediate post-independence era, when trade union pressure was effective in setting minimum wages in some urban sectors of the developing countries; unions were particularly vigorous in East Africa, a region well known by Harris and Todaro and which influenced their work. But many case studies have found it difficult to find high and rigid urban wages elsewhere than in government jobs. Moreover, in this sector large workforces have been maintained frequently by allowing salaries to decline, although compensated with some non-wage benefits. In addition, the view that urban labor markets can be divided into formal and informal sectors, with the first offering high wages and long tenure, and the informal low wages and insecure employment, is now recognized as too simplistic. The two sectors often overlap and several studies have failed to find any clear formal sector wage advantage for comparable workers.

Urban open unemployment has likewise proved difficult to identify. The evidence has generally shown that many migrants have few means to sustain themselves without work of some kind. The supposed migrants' strategy 'move first, then search' is open to question. In many cases jobs have been lined up before they move, with chain migration providing information about jobs. It is not surprising that a migrant would draw on information from family, social support networks and other contacts before deciding to leave home.

The Harris–Todaro model has been extended to address these shortcomings (for example, to include some urban real wage flexibility or add urban agglomeration effects and the impact of subsidies) and it continues to provide a useful basic framework for studying labor transfers.

JOSÉ L. GARCÍA-RUIZ

Bibliography

Harris, J.R. and M.P. Todaro (1970), 'Migration, unemployment and development: a two-sector analysis', *American Economic Review*, **60** (1), 126–42.

Todaro, M.P. (1969), 'A model of labor migration and urban unemployment in less developed countries', *American Economic Review*, **59** (1), 139–48.

Harrod's technical progress

Technological progress is one of the basic ingredients, along with the productive inputs, of any production function. From a formal perspective and using just two inputs (labour, L, and capital, K) for the sake of simplicity, a general specification of the production function would be

$$Y_t = F(A_t, K_t, L_t),$$

where Y is total output, F is a homogeneous function of degree γ and A the state of technology. Thus technological progress (changes in the level of technology) can be understood as the gain in efficiency accruing to the productive factors as knowledge and experience accumulate. From an empirical point of view, technological progress is usually calculated residually as that part of output growth which is not explained by the simple accumulation of the productive inputs: log-differentiating the previous expression, technological progress is formally obtained as follows

$$\Delta a_t = \Delta y_t - \frac{F_L L_t}{Y_t} \Delta l_t - \frac{F_K K_t}{Y_t} \Delta k_t,$$

where lower-case variables are the logs of the corresponding upper-case variables, Δ is the first difference operator and F_x is the marginal factor productivity.

There are a number of ways in which this technological progress can be characterized. According to its impact on the intensity the productive inputs are used. The main property of the one labelled, after Roy F. Harrod (1900–1978) 'Harrod-neutral' (or 'labour-augmenting') technological progress is that it alters at least one of the possible pairs of marginal productivity ratios among the inputs considered in the production function. This means that the improvement in efficiency favours a particular factor. Formally, this concept can be represented by the following production function

$$Y_t = F(A_t L_t, K_t).$$

In this case, the marginal productivity of labour is $A_t F_L(A_t L_t, K_t)$ and that of capital $F_K(A_t L_t, K_t)$. From these expressions, it is clear that the ratio of marginal productivities depends on A, the technology. This means that technological progress changes the relative demand for productive factors even in the absence of changes in their relative cost.

ANGEL ESTRADA

Bibliography

Harrod, R.F. (1948), *Towards a Dynamic Economics. Some Recent Developments of Economic Theory and their Applications to Policy*, London and New York: Macmillan.

See also: Hicks's technical progress.

Harrod–Domar model

Roy F. Harrod (1900–1978) in 1939 and Evsey Domar (1914–97) in 1946 attempted to analyze the relation between investment, employment and growth. They recognized the dynamic effects that a higher employment rate has on capital through income and savings, and developed models where these dynamics lead almost certainly to the underutilization of the resources of production.

The three basic assumptions of the Harrod–Domar model are: Leontief aggregate production function, no technological progress, and a constant savings rate. Let K and L denote respectively the level of capital and labor in the economy. Output (Y) is produced with the following Leontief technology:

$$Y = \min [AK, BL] \tag{1}$$

with A, B strictly positive and constant, which implies that there is no technological change.

I use capital letters to denote aggregate levels, lower-case to denote per worker levels

$$(x \equiv X/L),$$

and a dot to denote the time derivative of a variable

$$(\dot{X} \equiv dX/dt).$$

To analyze the static allocation of resources, let $\bar{L}$ be the constant full employment level. With the production technology in (1), if $AK > BL$, only $B\bar{L}/A$ units of capital will be utilized and, therefore, $K - B\bar{L}/A$ units of capital will be idle in the economy. Conversely, if $AK < BL$, $\bar{L} - AK/B$, workers will be unemployed. Only in the knife-edge case where $AK = B\bar{L}$ is there full utilization of all the factors of production.

To analyze the dynamics of the economy, it proves simple to focus on the centralized version. The central planner devotes a fraction s of output to accumulate capital. This in turn depreciates at the constant rate δ. The resulting law of motion for capital per employed worker is

$$\dot{k} = s \min [Ak, B] - \delta k.$$

Dividing both sides by k, we obtain the expression for the growth rate of capital per employed worker,

$$\dot{k}/k = s \min [Ak, B/k] - \delta.$$

There are two cases depending on the relationship between δ and sA. If $\delta < sA$, for low levels of capital per worker, the rate of gross savings per unit of capital is higher than the depreciation rate and therefore the capital stock per worker grows initially at a positive and constant rate. Eventually, the economy reaches the full employment level and, from that moment on, the accumulated capital does not create further output. As a result, the ratio of gross savings per unit of capital starts to decline until the economy reaches the steady-state level of capital per employed worker, $k^* = sB/\delta$. If the economy starts with a higher level of capital per worker than k^*, the gross savings per unit of capital will fall short of the depreciation rate and the economy will decumulate capital until reaching the steady-state level.

If $sA < \delta$, sA is so low that there is always decumulation of capital for all the levels of capital per worker. This implies that the economy implodes: it converges to a zero level of capital per worker and to an unemployment rate of 100 per cent of the population.

Hence the combination of the three assumptions implies that, unless we are in the knife-edge case where sA is exactly equal to δ, the economy will converge to a state with underutilization of some of the factors of production.

DIEGO COMÍN

Bibliography

Domar, E. (1946), 'Capital expansion, rate of growth, and employment', *Econometrica,* **14** (2), 137–47.

Harrod, R. (1939), 'An essay in dynamic theory', *Economic Journal,* **49**, 14–33.

Harsanyi's equiprobability model

The model approaches the question of the mathematical form of an individual's social welfare function *W*. J.C. Harsanyi (b.1920, Nobel Prize 1999) concludes that if the model's postulates are satisfied, then *W* is a weighted sum of the utilities of all the individuals U_i that is, *W* takes the form $W = \Sigma_{i=1}^{N}\alpha_i U_i$, where α_i is the value of *W* when $U_i = 1$ and $U_j = 0$ for all $j \neq i$. In sum, *W*'s form is very close to that of the utilitarian social welfare function.

One of the best known elements in the model is the distinction made by Harsanyi between moral or ethical preferences, represented by individuals' social functions, and their personal or subjective preferences, represented by their utility functions. In this respect, the main issue is Harsanyi's interpretation of moral preferences as those satisfying the following impersonality or impartiality requirement:

> an individual's preferences satisfy this requirement of impersonality if they indicate what social situation he would choose if he did not know what his personal position would be in the new situation chosen (and in any of its alternatives) but rather had an equal chance of obtaining any of the social positions existing in *this* situation, from the highest down to the lowest. (Harsanyi, 1955, p. 14)

As a consequence of this, a choice based on such preferences would be an instance of a 'choice involving risk' (Harsanyi, 1953, p. 4).

Harsanyi assumes also that moral and personal preferences satisfy Marschak's postulates about choices under uncertainty, and that every two Pareto-indifferent prospects are socially also indifferent.

Given that interpersonal comparisons of utility are presupposed by the model, Harsanyi argues, against Robbins's known position, in support of their legitimacy. Regarding such comparisons, Harsanyi sees the lack of the needed factual information as the main problem in making them. From his point of view, the more complete this information, the more the different individuals' social welfare functions will tend to be the utilitarian one.

JUAN C. GARCÍA-BERMEJO

Bibliography

Harsanyi, John C. (1953), 'Cardinal utility in welfare economics and in the theory of risk-taking', reprinted (1976) in *Essays on Ethics, Social Behavior and Scientific Explanation*, Dordrecht: D. Reidel Publishing Company, pp. 4–6.

Harsanyi, John C. (1955), 'Cardinal welfare, individualistic ethics, and interpersonal comparisons of utility', reprinted (1976) in *Essays on Ethics, Social Behavior and Scientific Explanation*, Dordrecht: D. Reidel Publishing Company, pp. 6–23.

Hausman's test

J.A. Hausman proposed a general form of specification test for the assumption $E(u/X) = 0$ or, in large samples, $\text{plim}\frac{1}{T}X'u = 0$, sometimes called the 'orthogonality assumption' in the standard regression framework, $y = X\beta + u$. The main idea of the test is to find two estimators of β, $\hat{\beta}_0$ and $\hat{\beta}_1$ such that (a) under the (null) hypothesis of no misspecification (H_0) $\hat{\beta}_0$ is consistent, asymptotically normal and asymptotically efficient (it attains the asymptotic Cramer–Rao bound). Under the alternative hypothesis of misspecification (H_1), this estimator will be biased and inconsistent; and (b) there is another estimator $\hat{\beta}_1$ that is consistent both under the null and under the alternative, but it will not be asymptotically efficient under the null hypothesis.

The test statistic considers the difference between the two estimates $\hat{q} = \hat{\beta}_1 - \hat{\beta}_0$. If there is no misspecification, plim $\hat{q} = 0$, being different from zero if there is misspecification. Given that $\hat{\beta}_0$ is asymptotically efficient under H_0, it is uncorrelated with $\hat{q}$, so that the asymptotic variance of $\sqrt{T}\hat{q}$ is easily calculated as $V_{\hat{q}} = V_1 - V_0$, where V_1 and V_0 are the asymptotic variance of $\sqrt{T}\hat{\beta}_1$ and $\sqrt{T}\hat{\beta}_0$, respectively, under H_0.

Under H_0, the test statistic

$$m = T\,\hat{q}'(\hat{V}_{\hat{q}})^{-1}\,\hat{q} \xrightarrow{d} \chi^2_{(k)},$$

where $\hat{V}_{\hat{q}}$ is a consistent estimate (under H_0) of $\hat{V}_{\hat{q}}$ using $\hat{\beta}_1$ and $\hat{\beta}_0$, and k is the number of unknown parameters in β when no misspecification is present.

Hausman (1978) applies this test to three different settings. The first is the errors in variables problem. In this case the ordinary least squares (OLS) estimator is $\hat{\beta}_0$ and an instrumental variables (IV) estimator will be $\hat{\beta}_1$. An alternative way of carrying out the test for errors in variables is to test H_0: $\alpha = 0$ in the regression

$$y = X_1\beta_1 + X_2\beta_2 + \hat{X}_1\alpha + u,$$

where $\hat{X}_1 = Z(Z'Z)^{-1}Z'X_1$ and Z is a matrix of instruments which should include X_2 if those variables are known to be uncorrelated with the error term. Sometimes the problem is to find a valid matrix of instruments.

The second setting involves panel data: random effects versus fixed effects models. The difference between the two specifications is the treatment of the individual effect, μ_1. The fixed effects model treats μ_1 as a fixed but unknown constant, differing across individuals. The random effects or variance components model assumes that μ_1 is a random variable that is uncorrelated with the regressors. The specification issue is whether this last assumption is or is not true.

Under the (null) hypothesis of the random effects specification, the feasible generalized least squares (GLS) estimator is the asymptotically efficient estimator ($\hat{\beta}_0$) while the fixed effects (FE) estimator ($\hat{\beta}_1$) is consistent but not efficient. If the assumption is not true, the GLS or random effects estimator is inconsistent while the FE estimator remains consistent. Thus the specification test statistic compares both estimators.

The third setting, with simultaneous equation systems, involves testing the system specification. The test compares two-stage least squares (2SLS) and three-stage least squares (3SLS) of the structural parameters of the system. Under the null hypothesis of correct specification, 3SLS is asymptotically efficient but yields inconsistent estimates of all equations if any of them is misspecified. On the other hand, 2SLS is not as efficient as 3SLS, but only the incorrectly specified equation is inconsistently estimated under misspecification.

MARTA REGÚLEZ CASTILLO

Bibliography

Hausman, J.A. (1978), 'Specification tests in econometrics', *Econometrica*, **46** (6), 1251–71.

Hawkins–Simon theorem

In the input–output analysis of economic models concerning the production of commodities, there often appears the problem of characterizing the positivity of some of the existing solutions of a system of linear equations. That is, even when a given system is compatible (a fact characterized by Rouché's theorem), some extra conditions must be given to guarantee the existence of solutions whose coordinates are all non-negative. This happens, for instance, when we are dealing with quantities or prices.

That problem was solved with the help of the Hawkins–Simon theorem, now a powerful tool in matrix analysis. The theorem states, as follows: Let $A = (a_{ij})i,j = 1, \ldots, n$ be a n x n matrix of non-negative real numbers, such that $a_{ii} \leq 1$, for any element a_{ii} $(i = 1, \ldots, n)$ in the main diagonal of A.

The following statements are equivalent:

1. There exists a vector C whose coordinates are all positive, associated with which there exists a vector X whose coordinates are all non-negative, satisfying that $(I - A) X = C$.
2. For every vector C whose coordinates are all non-negative, there exists a vector X whose coordinates are all non-negative too, such that $(I - A) X = C$.
3. All the leading principal subdeterminants of the matrix $I - A$ are positive.

(Here I denote the $n \times n$ identity matrix).

ESTEBAN INDURAÍN

Bibliography

Hawkins, D. and H.K. Simon (1949), 'Note: some conditions of macroeconomic stability', *Econometrica*, **17**, 245–8.

See also: Leontief model.

Hayekian triangle

The essential relationship between final output, resulting from the production process, and the time which is necessary to generate it, can be represented graphically by a right triangle. Named after Friedrich A. von Hayek (1899–1992, Nobel Prize 1974) (1931, p.36), it is a heuristic device that gives analytical support to a theory of business cycles first offered by Ludwig von Mises in 1912. Triangles of different shapes provide a convenient way of describing changes in the intertemporal pattern of the economy's capital structure. Thus the Hayekian triangle is the most relevant graphic tool of capital-based Austrian macroeconomics.

In the Hayekian triangle, production time involves a sequence of stages which are represented along its lower 'time axis'. While the horizontal segment represents the time dimension (production stages) that characterizes the production process, the vertical one represents the monetary value of spending on consumer goods (or, equivalently, the monetary value of final output), as can be seen in the figure (Garrison, 2001, p. 47). Finally, the vertical distances from the 'time axis' to the hypotenuse of the Hayekian triangle shows the value of intermediate goods.

In a fundamental sense, the Hayekian triangle illustrates a trade-off recognized by Carl Menger and emphasized by Eugen von Böhm-Bawerk: in the absence of resource idleness, investment is made at the expense of consumption. Moreover, it is a suitable tool to capture the heterogeneity and the intertemporal dimension of capital (or, in the same way, the intertemporal structure of production).

The first theorist to propose a similar representation was William Stanley Jevons in *The Theory of Political Economy* (1871). The Jevonian investment figures, which were the core of Jevons's writings on capital, showed capital value rising linearly with time as production proceeded from inception to completion. Years later, in *Kapital und Kapitalzins*, vol. II (1889), Böhm-Bawerk would develop a graphical exposition of multi-stage production, the so-called

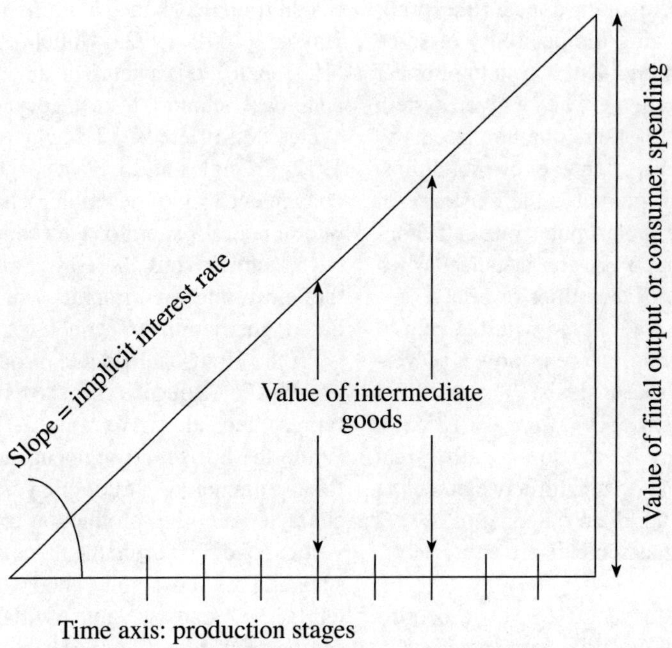

Hayekian triangle

'bull's-eye' figure. Instead of using triangles to show the stages, he used annual concentric rings, each one representing overlapping productive stages. Production began in the center with the use of the original means (land and labor) and the process emanated outwards over time. The final product emerged at the outermost ring.

In essence, Böhm-Bawerk was doing the same thing that Hayek would do in 1931. However, Böhm-Bawerk did not add monetary considerations. Moreover, his representation of the intertemporality of the production process was not very precise. These problems would be solved in 1931 by Hayek, in the first edition of *Prices and Production*, including a very similar representation to that showed in the figure. However, a more precise and elegant representation would be utilized by Hayek in 1941, in *The Pure Theory of Capital* (p. 109).

The Hayekian triangle is an essential tool to explain the Austrian theory of business cycles, and has been found relevant as an alternative way of analyzing the economic fluctuations of some developed countries.

MIGUEL ÁNGEL ALONSO NEIRA

Bibliography

Garrison, R. (1994), 'Hayekian triangles and beyond', in J. Birner and R. van Zijp (eds), *Hayek, Coordination and Evolution: His Legacy in Philosophy, Politics, Economics, and the History of Ideas*, London: Routledge.

Garrison, R. (2001), *Time and Money. The Macroeconomics of Capital Structure*, London: Routledge.

Hayek, F.A. (1931), *Prices and Production*, London: Routledge.

Hayek, F.A. (1941), *The Pure Theory of Capital*, London: Routledge.

Heckman's two-step method

This is a two-step method of estimation of regression models with sample selection, due to J.J. Heckman (b.1944, Nobel Prize 2000). This is the case when trying to estimate a wage equation (regression model), having only information on wages for those who are working (selected sample), but not for those who are not.

In general, in those cases the expected value of the error term conditional on the selected sample is not zero. Consequently, the estimation by ordinary least squares of this model will be inconsistent. This sample selection bias can be interpreted as the result of an omitted variables problem because the element which appears in the expected value of the error term is not included as an explanatory variable. This term is known as the inverse of Mill's ratio. This correction term, under the normality assumptions considered by Heckman, is a non-linear function of the explanatory variables in the equation corresponding to the selection criterion (whether the individual works or not in the above example of the wage equation).

Heckman proposed a consistent estimation method based on first estimating (first step) the discrete choice model (a Probit model in his proposal) corresponding to the selection criterion, using the whole sample (both those working and those not in our example). From this estimation we can obtain an adjusted value for the correction term corresponding to the expected value of the error term and, then, (second step) we can estimate the model by ordinary least squares, using only the selected sample (only those who are working) including as an additional regressor the above-mentioned correction term. This estimation method will be consistent but not efficient.

This method is also known in the literature as Heckit ('Heck' from Heckman and 'it' from probit, tobit, logit . . .).

JAUME GARCÍA

Bibliography

Heckman, J.J. (1976), 'The common structure of statistical models of truncation, sample selection and limited dependent variables and a simple estimator for such models', *Annals of Economic and Social Management*, **5**, 475–92.

Heckman, J.J. (1979), 'Sample selection bias as a specification error', *Econometrica*, **47**, 153–61.

Heckscher–Ohlin theorem

Based on the original insights of Eli Heckscher (1879–1952), developed by his student Bertin Ohlin (1899–1979) and formalized later by Samuelson (1948), the theorem asserts that the pattern of trade in goods is determined by the differences in factor endowments between countries. In its most common version, the two countries, two goods and two factors model, also known as the Heckscher–Ohlin–Samuelson model, the theorem states that each country will tend to specialize and export the good that uses intensively its relatively abundant factor.

The model assumes the existence of two countries (*A* and *B*), each one producing two homogeneous goods (*X* and *Y*) by employing two factors, labor (*L*) and capital (*K*), under identical, constant returns to scale technologies; factor endowments are fixed in each country but different across countries; factors are perfectly mobile across sectors but immobile across countries; there are no transaction costs or taxes and competition prevails throughout. Assuming *X* is the capital-intensive good (*Y* is the labor-intensive one), if *A* is the relatively capital-abundant country (*B* the relatively labor-abundant one), the theorem states that *A* will export good *X* (import *Y*), while *B* will export good *Y* (import *X*).

There are two ways of defining factor abundance: in terms of physical units of factors and in terms of relative factor prices. According to the price definition, *A* is relatively capital-abundant compared to *B*, if capital is relatively cheaper in *A* than in *B*.

Denoting by w and r the prices of labor and capital, respectively, this says that $r_A/w_A < r_B/w_B$. On the other hand, the physical definition maintains that country A is relatively capital-abundant if the ratio of the physical capital stock to labor is larger in country A than in country B ($K_A/L_A > K_B/L_B$). While the former allows for a unique relationship between factor endowments and relative factor prices in autarchy, the latter requires additional restrictions on demand conditions (identical and homothetic preferences across countries) in order to ensure that the conclusions of the theorem are valid.

Lines $X_A - Y_A$ and $X_B - Y_B$ in the figure represent the possibility production frontier of country A and country B, respectively. Due to their different factor endowments, the frontier of country A is biased in favour of producing the labour-intensive good when comparing to country B. Identity of tastes means that the countries face the same social indifference curve (I_o). A_o and B_o are the equilibrium points of consumption (and production) in the autarchy of A and B, respectively, where the marginal transformation rate in production (the slope of the frontier) equals the marginal substitution rate in consumption (the slope of the indifference curve I_o) and the internal terms of trade for each country (R_a and R_b).

The slope of the frontier at point B_o (R_b) is steeper than the slope of country A (R_a) at A_o, implying that in autarchy the relative price of X is lower in A than in B, so that country A has a comparative advantage in the production of X, while country B has a comparative advantage in the production of Y. In a free trade situation, international terms of trade are represented by the line R_I ($R_{A<}$ $R_{I<}$ R_B) and countries will produce at points A_1 and B_1 on their frontier while they will consume at $C_{1.}$ Therefore country A will export ZA_1 of good X and will import HC_1 of good Y, while country B will export HB_1 of good Y and will import ZC_1 of good Y. Notice that there is no

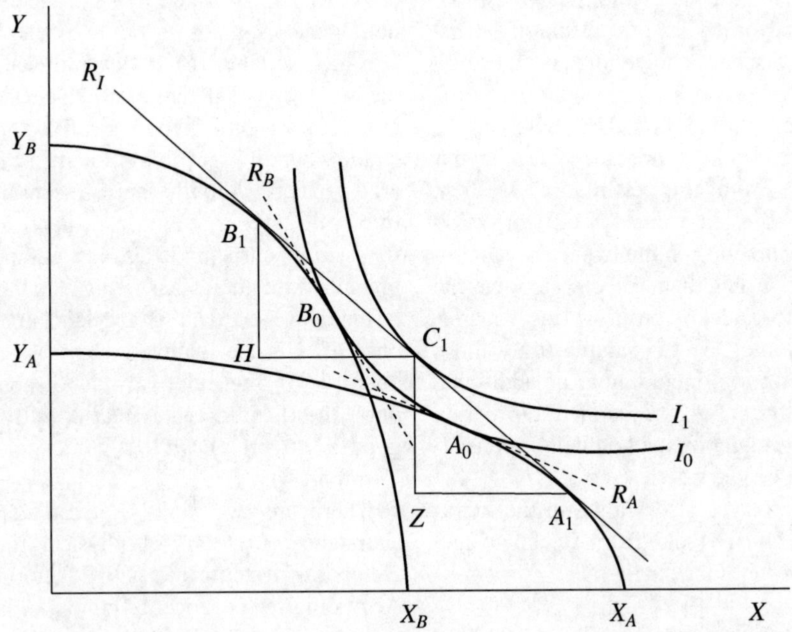

Heckscher–Ohlin theorem

world excess in demand or supply in any of the goods (as expected from the perfect competition assumption), so that R_I represents the equilibrium terms of trade.

Therefore international trade expands until relative commodity prices are equalized across countries, allowing, under previous assumptions, the equalization of relative and absolute factor prices. This result, that follows directly from Heckscher–Ohlin, is known as the 'factor price equalization theorem' or the Heckscher–Ohlin–Samuelson theorem and implies that free international trade in goods is a perfect substitute for the international mobility of factors.

TERESA HERRERO

Bibliography

Bhagwati, Jagdish, A. Panagariya, and T.N. Srinivasan, (1998), *Lectures on International Trade*, Cambridge, MA: MIT Press, pp. 50–79.

Heckscher, Eli (1919), 'The effect of foreign trade on the distribution of income', *Economisk Tidskrift*, **21**, 1–32. Reprinted in H.S. Ellis and L.A. Metzler (eds) (1949), *Readings in the Theory of International Trade*, Philadelphia: Blakiston.

Ohlin, Bertil (1933), *Interregional and International Trade*, Cambridge, MA: Harvard University Press, esp. pp. 27–45.

Samuelson, Paul (1948), 'International trade and the equalization of factor prices', *Economic Journal*, **58**, 163–84.

Herfindahl–Hirschman index

The Herfindhal–Hirschman index (HHI) is defined as the sum of the squares of the market shares (expressed in percentages) of each individual firm. As such, it can range from 0 to 10 000, from markets with a very large number of small firms to those with a single monopolistic producer. Decreases in HHI value generally indicate a loss of pricing power and an increase in competition, whereas increases imply the opposite. The index is commonly used as a measure of industry concentration. For instance, it has been shown theoretically that collusion among firms can be more easily enforced in an industry with high HHI. In addition, many researchers have proposed this index as a good indicator of the price–cost margin and, thus, social welfare.

Worldwide, antitrust commissions evaluate mergers according to their anticipated effects upon competition. In the United States, a merger that leaves the market with an HHI value below 1000 should not be opposed, while a merger that leaves the market with an HHI value that is greater than 1800 should always be opposed. If the merger leaves the market with an HHI value between 1000 and 1800, it should only be opposed if it causes HHI to increase by more than 100 points.

The index was first introduced by Albert O. Hirschman (b.1915) as a measure of concentration of a country's trade in commodities. Orris C. Herfindahl (b.1918) proposed the same index in 1950 for measuring concentration in the steel industry and acknowledged Hirschman's work in a footnote. Nevertheless, when the index is used, it is now usually referred to as the Herfindhal index. 'Well, it's a cruel world,' was Hirschman's response to this.

ALBERTO LAFUENTE

Bibliography

Herfindahl, O.C. (1950), 'Concentration in the US steel industry', unpublished doctoral dissertation, Columbia University.

Hirschman, A.O. (1945), *National Power and the Structure of Foreign Trade*, Berkeley, CA: University of California Bureau of Business and Economic Research.

Hirschman, A.O. (1964), 'The paternity of an index', *American Economic Review*, **54**, 761.

Hermann–Schmoller definition

Net income was defined by Hermann (1832, p. 112) and in the same way by Schmoller (1904, pp. 177–8) thus: 'The flow of rent produced by a capital without itself suffering any diminution in exchange value' (Schumpeter, pp. 503, 628). Friedrich B.W.

von Hermann (1795–1868) was a Bavarian civil servant, political economist and professor at the University of Munich, where he studied income and consumption and published *Staatswirtschaftliche Untersuchungen* in 1832. Gustav von Schmoller (1838–1917), professor at Halle, Strassburg and Berlin, was the leader of the German 'younger' Historical School who engaged in a methodological dispute or *methodenstreit* with Carl Menger, the founder of the Austrian School, and upheld an inductivist approach in many books and essays.

According to Hermann, with respect to capital goods, 'rent can be conceived as a good in itself . . . and may acquire an exchange value of its own . . . retaining the exchange value of capital' (1832, pp. 56–7). Schmoller shared this view: capital should not be identified with accumulated wealth but with patrimony/property. For both authors the first meaning of capital is net income.

REYES CALDERÓN CUADRADO

Bibliography

Hermann, F. von (1832), *Staatswirtschaftliche Untersuchungen über Bermogen, Wirtschaft, Productivitat der Arbeiten, Kapital, Preis, Gewinn, Einkommen und Berbrauch*, reprinted (1987), Frankfurt: Wirtschaft und Finanzen.

Schmoller, G. von (1904), *Grundriss der Allgemeinen Volkswirtschaftslehre*, vol. II, reprinted (1989), Düsseldorf: Wirtschaft und Finanzen.

Schumpeter, J.A. (1954), *History of Economic Analysis*, New York: Oxford University Press.

Hessian matrix and determinant

The Hessian matrix $H(f(\vec{x}_0))$ of a smooth real function $f(\vec{x})$, $\vec{x} \in R^n$, is the square matrix with (i, j) entry given by $\partial^2 f(\vec{x}_0)/\partial x_j \partial x_i$. It was introduced by the German mathematician L.O. Hesse (1811–74) as a tool in problems of analytic geometry.

If f belongs to the class C^2 (that is, all its second order derivatives are continuous) in an open neighbourhood U of $\vec{x}_0$, then the Hessian $H(f(\vec{x}_0))$ is a symmetric matrix. If U is a convex domain and $H(f(\vec{x}))$ is positive semidefinite (definite) for all $\vec{x} \in U$, then f is a convex (strictly convex respectively) function on U. If $H(f(\vec{x}))$ is negative semidefinite (definite), then f is concave (strictly concave) on U.

If $\vec{x}_0$ is a critical point ($\nabla f(\vec{x}_0) = 0$) and $H(f(\vec{x}_0))$ is positive (negative) definite, then $\vec{x}_0$ is a local minimum (maximum). This result may be generalized to obtain sufficient second-order conditions in constrained optimization problems if we replace the objective function f with the Lagrangian $L(\vec{x}, \vec{\lambda}) = f(\vec{x}) - \vec{\lambda} \circ (\vec{g}(\vec{x}) - \vec{b})$, where $\vec{g}(\vec{x}) = \vec{b}$ are the constraints of the problem. The Hessian matrix of the Lagrangian is called the 'bordered Hessian matrix', and it plays an analogous role to the ordinary Hessian matrix in non-constrained problems.

The determinant of the Hessian matrix often arises in problems of economic analysis. For instance, the first-order necessary conditions of consumption and production optimization problems take the form $\nabla f(\vec{x}_0, \vec{p}_0) = \vec{0}$ where $\vec{p}_0$ is some parameter vector, usually the price vector of consumption goods or production factors. In order to obtain from this system of (non-linear) equations the demand functions, which give the optimal quantities of goods or production factors to be consumed as a function of the parameter vector in a neighbourhood of $(\vec{x}_0, \vec{p}_0)$, we must ensure that the Jacobian of $\nabla f(\vec{x}, \vec{p})$, which is the Hessian determinant, does not vanish at $(\vec{x}_0, \vec{p}_0)$. This is, therefore, a necessary condition for the existence of demand functions in these problems. The positive or negative definiteness of the Hessian matrix in $(\vec{x}_0, \vec{p}_0)$ provides sufficient second-order conditions which ensure that the demand functions obtained in this way indeed give (local) optimal consumptions.

MANUEL MORÁN

Bibliography
Simons, C.P. and L. Blume (1994), *Mathematics for Economists*, New York and London: W.W. Norton.

Hicks compensation criterion

The so-called 'Hicks compensation criterion' is nothing but the *inverse factor* of the binary relation proposed originally by Kaldor.

LUÍS A. PUCH

Bibliography
Hicks, J.R. (1939), 'The foundations of welfare economics', *Economic Journal*, **49**, 696–712.

See also: Chipman–Moore–Samuelson compensation criterion, Kaldor compensation criterion, Scitovski's compensation criterion.

Hicks composite commodities

Almost any study in economics, in order to make it tractable, implicitly or explicitly, involves certain doses of aggregation of the goods considered (think of food, labour, capital and so on). John R. Hicks (1904–89, Nobel Prize 1972) provided in 1936 the first set of conditions under which one could consider different goods as a unique composite good (normally called the *numeraire*). Citing Hicks, 'if the prices of a group of goods change in the same proportion, that group of goods behaves just as if it were a single commodity'. In other words, what is needed is that the relative prices in this set of commodities remain unchanged.

Formally, consider a consumer with wealth w and a utility function $u(x, y)$ over two sets of commodities x and y, with corresponding prices p and q. Assume that the prices for good y always vary in proportion to one another, so that $q = \alpha y$. Then, for any $z > 0$, we can define

$$v(x, z) = \underset{y}{MaxU}(x, y)$$
$$s.t.: \alpha y \leq z$$

and reconsider the original consumption problem as defined over the goods x and the single composite commodity z with corresponding prices p and α, and with the utility function $v(x, z)$ (which inherits all the well-behaved properties of the original one).

There are two essential reasons for the importance of this result. First, as already said, it facilitates the aggregate study of broad categories by lumping together similar goods (think, for instance, of the consumption–leisure decision, or the intertemporal consumption problem). Second, it also provides solid ground for the justification of partial equilibrium analysis. If we are interested in the study of a single market that constitutes a small portion of the overall economy, we can consider the rest of goods' prices as fixed, and therefore treat the expenditure on these other goods as a single composite commodity.

GUILLERMO CARUANA

Bibliography
Hicks, J.R. (1936), *Value and Capital*, Oxford University Press.

Hicks's technical progress

Technical progress is one of the basic ingredients, along with the productive inputs, of any aggregate production function. From a formal perspective and using just two inputs (labour, L, and capital, K) for the sake of simplicity, a general specification of the production function would be

$$Y_t = F(A_t, L_t, K_t),$$

where Y is total output, F is a homogeneous function of degree γ and A the state of technology. Thus technological progress (changes in the level of technology) can be understood as the gains in efficiency accruing to the productive factors as knowledge and experience accumulate. From an empirical point of view, technological progress is usually calculated residually as that part of output growth which is not explained by the simple accumulation of the productive inputs; log-differentiating the previous expression, technological progress is formally obtained as follows

$$\Delta a_t = \Delta y_t - \frac{F_L L_t}{Y_t} \Delta l_t - \frac{F_K K_t}{Y_t} \Delta k_t$$

where lower-case variables are the logs of the corresponding upper-case variables, Δ is the first differences operator and F_x is the marginal factor productivity.

There are a number of ways in which this technological progress can be characterized, according to its impact on the intensity with which the productive inputs are used. The main property of the one named after John R. Hicks (1904–89, Nobel Prize 1972) as Hicks-neutral technological progress is that it does not alter any of the possible pairs of marginal productivity ratios among the different inputs that are included in the production function. This means that the improvement in efficiency resulting from technological progress is transmitted equally to all the productive factors. From a formal perspective, Hicks-neutral technological progress can be represented by the following production function:

$$Y_t = A_t F(L_t, K_t).$$

In such a case, the marginal productivity of labour would be $A_t F_L(L_t, K_t)$, and that of capital $A_t F_K(L_t, K_t)$. As can be seen, the ratio of these two expressions does not depend on A, the technology, implying that technological progress itself does not affect the relative demand for productive inputs.

ANGEL ESTRADA

Bibliography

Hicks, J.R. (1932), *The Theory of Wages*, London: MacMillan.

See also: Harrod's technical progress.

Hicksian demand

John R. Hicks (1904–89) was one of the leading figures in the development of economic theory. He made seminal contributions to several branches of economics, including the theory of wages, value theory, welfare analysis, monetary economics and growth theory. He shared the Nobel Prize in Economics with K.J. Arrow in 1972. His paper with R.G.D. Allen (1934), showed that the main results of consumer theory can be obtained from utility maximization and introduced the decomposition of demand into substitution and income effects. In this paper, he defined what is known as 'Hicksian demand', which is obtained by changing the wealth as the level of price changes, keeping an index of utility constant.

Formally, Hicksian demand is the outcome of the expenditure minimization problem that computes the minimum level of wealth required to obtain a fixed level of utility u_0, taking the price vector $p \in R^n_{++}$ as given. This problem can be written as follows:

$$\begin{array}{l} Min_{x \geq 0}\, px \\ s.t.\ u(x) \geq u_0. \end{array}$$

Under the usual assumption of monotone preferences, the solution to this problem exists. The optimal consumption bundle is known as the (unobservable) Hicksian demand, which is usually denoted by $h(p, u) \in R^n_+$. As prices change, $h(p, u)$ indicates the demand that would arise if consumers' wealth was adjusted to keep their level of utility constant. This contrasts with Marshallian demand, which keeps wealth fixed but allows utility to change. Hence wealth effects are absent and $h(p, u)$ measures only the cross-substitution effects of price changes. This explains why Hicksian demand is also known as 'compensated demand'.

The expenditure minimization problem that yields the Hicksian demand is the dual of the utility maximization problem. If the usual assumptions about preferences hold, $u(x)$ is a continuous and monotonic utility function representing these preferences and $p >> 0$, then the solutions to both problems coincide. In particular, if x^* is optimal in the utility maximization problem when wealth is w^*, x^* is also the solution to the expenditure minimization problem when $u_0 = u(x^*)$ and the level of expenditure in equilibrium is w^*. Therefore, under the above assumptions, Marshallian and Hicksian demands are identical.

XAVIER TORRES

Bibliography

Hicks, J.R. and R.G.D. Allen (1934), 'A reconsideration of the theory of value', Parts I and II, *Economica*, N.S., Feb. I (1), 52–76; May II (2), 196–219.

Mas-Colell, A., M.D. Whinston and J.R. Green (1995), *Microeconomic Theory*, Oxford University Press.

See also: Marshallian demand, Slutsky equation.

Hicksian perfect stability

Contrary to Marshall's 'applied economics' interest in market stability, the motivation behind Sir John R. Hicks's (1904–89, Nobel Prize 1972) analysis of this issue was a theoretical one. In the opening paragraph of Chapter V of *Value and Capital*, one can read

> The laws of change of the price-system [. . .] have to be derived from stability conditions. We first examine what conditions are necessary in order that a given equilibrium system should be stable; then we make an assumption of regularity, that positions in the neighbourhood of the equilibrium position will be stable also; and thence we deduce rules about the way in which the price-system will react to changes in tastes and resources' (Hicks, 1939, p. 62).

In other words, if stability is taken for granted we can do comparative static analyses for changes in the relevant parameters.

Hicks's concept of 'perfect stability' is a generalization of the Walrasian stability condition (through *tâtonnement*) in which price changes are governed by excess demands. This issue had been successfully settled by Walras but only for the case of two commodities in a pure exchange economy. According to Hicks, a price system is perfectly stable if the rise (fall) of the price of any good above (below) its equilibrium level generates an excess supply (demand) of that good, regardless of whether or not the prices of other commodities are fixed or adjusted to ensure equilibrium in their respective markets.

The original proof (Hicks, 1939, mathematical appendix to Chapter V, pp. 315–19) in the case of n goods and N consumers consists of the determination of mathematical conditions ensuring the negative sign of the derivatives of every good's excess demand function with respect to its own price when (i) all other prices remain constant, (ii) another price adjusts so as to maintain equilibrium in each market but all other prices remain unchanged, (iii) any other two prices adjust so as to maintain equilibrium in both of their respective markets but all other prices remain unchanged . . . until all prices are adjusted except for the price of the numeraire good which is always unity. The well-known necessary condition is that the value of the determinants of the principal minors of the Jacobian matrix of the excess demand functions must be alternatively negative and positive. The only possible cause of instability in a pure exchange economy is the asymmetry of consumer income effects.

One obvious limitation of Hicksian stability, besides its local nature, is that it is a short-term ('within the week' in Hicks's own words) analysis. But the most important weakness, as Samuelson (1947) pointed out, is its lack of a specified dynamic adjustment process for the economy as a whole. The Hicksian condition is neither necessary nor sufficient for dynamic stability. Nevertheless, the usefulness of the Hicksian concept in comparative static has generated a lot of research on the relationship between the conditions for perfect stability and for true dynamic stability. It was shown that they often coincide (Metzler, 1945). They do so, for example, particularly when the Jacobian matrix of excess demand is symmetric or quasi-negative definite and also when all goods are gross substitutes.

JULIO SEGURA

Bibliography

Hicks, J.R. (1939), *Value and Capital*, Oxford: Oxford University Press (2nd edn 1946).

Metzler, L. (1945), 'Stability of multiple markets: the Hicks conditions', *Econometrica*, **13**, 277–92.

Samuelson, P.A. (1947), *Foundations of Economic Analysis*, Cambridge, MA: Harvard University Press.

See also: Lange–Lerner mechanism, Lyapunov stability, Marshall's stability, Walras's auctioneer and tâtonnement.

Hicks–Hansen model

The Hicks–Hansen or IS–LM model, developed by Sir John R. Hicks (1904–89, Nobel Prize 1972) and Alvin H. Hansen (1887–1975), was the leading framework of macroeconomic analysis from the 1940s to the mid-1970s.

Hicks introduced the IS–LM model in his 1937 article as a device for clarifying the relationship between classical theory and *The General Theory of Employment Interest and Money* (1936) of John Maynard Keynes. Hicks saw as Keynes's main contribution the joint determination of income and the interest rate in goods and financial markets. His early mathematical formalization of an important but very difficult book provided the fulcrum for the development of Keynesian theory, while spurring endless debates on whether it captured Keynes's ideas adequately. Hansen (1949, 1953) extended the model by adding, among other things, taxes and government spending.

The simplest IS–LM model has three blocks. In the goods market, aggregate demand is given by the sum of consumption as a function of disposable income, investment as a function of income and the interest rate, and government spending. In equilibrium, aggregate demand equals aggregate supply and so investment equals saving, yielding the *IS* curve. In money market equilibrium, money demand, which depends on income and the interest rate, equals money supply, giving rise to the *LM* curve (liquidity preference – as Keynes called money demand – equals money). In the third block employment is determined by output through an aggregate production function, with unemployment appearing if downward rigidity of the nominal wage is assumed. Joint equilibrium in the output–interest rate space appears in the figure below. The analysis of monetary and fiscal policies is straightforward: lower taxes and higher government spending shift the *IS* curve out (having a multiplier effect) and higher money supply shifts the *LM* curve out.

The IS–LM model represents a static, short-run equilibrium. Not only the capital stock but also wages and prices are fixed, and expectations (crucial in Keynesian theory as 'animal spirits') play virtually no role. Given that the IS captures a flow equilibrium and the LM a stock equilibrium, the joint time frame is unclear. There is no economic foundation for either aggregate demand components or money demand, and output is demand-determined. These

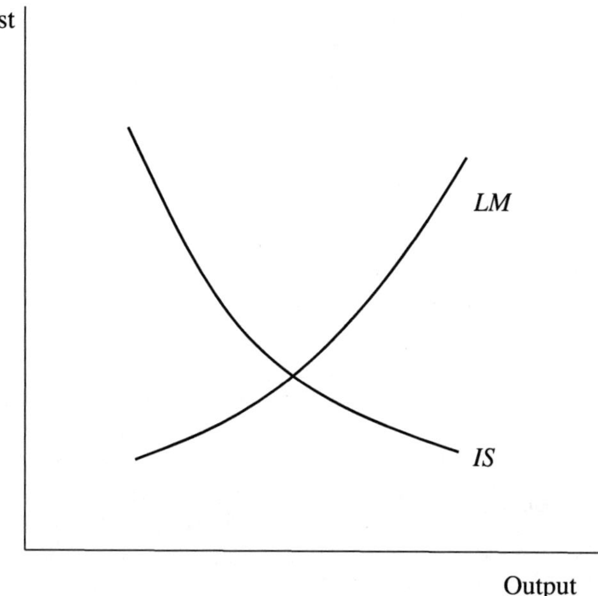

Hicks–Hansen, or IS–LM, model

limitations stimulated the rise of modern macroeconomics.

In the 1950s, Franco Modigliani and Milton Friedman developed theories of consumption, and James Tobin developed theories of investment and money demand. The lack of dynamics was tackled by adding a supply block constituted by the Phillips curve, an empirical relationship apparently implying a reliable trade-off between the unemployment rate and price inflation. In the 1960s, the IS–LM was enlarged by Robert Mundell and Marcus Fleming to encompass the open economy.

The extended IS–LM, called the 'neoclassical synthesis' or, later, the 'Aggregate supply–aggregate demand model', gave rise to large macroeconometric models, such as the MPS model, led by Franco Modigliani in the 1960s. It was seen and used as a reliable tool for forecasting and for conducting policy in fine-tuning the economy, this in spite of continuing criticism from the monetarists, led by Milton Friedman, who argued that there was no long-run inflation–unemployment trade-off and that monetary policy rather than fiscal policy had the strongest impact on output, but also that, since it could be destabilizing, it should stick to a constant money growth rule.

The IS–LM model is still the backbone of many introductory macroeconomics textbooks and the predictions of its extended version are consistent with many empirical facts present in market economies. However, it is now largely absent from macroeconomic research. Its demise was brought about both by its inability to account for the simultaneous high inflation and unemployment rates experienced in the late 1970s, owing to its non-modelling of the supply side, and by its forecasting failures, which lent support to the Lucas critique, which stated that macroeconometric models which estimate economic relationships based on past policies without modelling expectations as rational are not reliable for forecasting under new policies. Current macroeconomic research is conducted using dynamic general equilibrium models with microeconomic foundations which integrate the analyses of business cycles and long-term growth. However, the idea that wage and price rigidities help explain why money affects output and that they can have important effects on business cycle fluctuations, a foundation of the IS–LM model, survives in so-called 'new Keynesian' macroeconomics.

SAMUEL BENTOLILA

Bibliography

Hansen, A.H. (1949), *Monetary Theory and Fiscal Policy*, New York: McGraw-Hill.
Hansen, A.H. (1953), *A Guide to Keynes*, New York: McGraw-Hill.
Hicks, J.R. (1937), 'Mr. Keynes and the "Classics"; a suggested interpretation', *Econometrica*, **5** (2), 147–59.
Keynes, J.M. (1936), *The General Theory of Employment Interest and Money*, New York: Macmillan.

See also: Friedman's rule for monetary policy, Keynes's demand for money, Lucas critique, Mundell–Fleming model, Phillips curve.

Hodrick–Prescott decomposition

The evolution of the economic activity of industrialized countries indicates that aggregate production grows, oscillating around a trend. One of the problems that attracted most attention in the history of economics is how to decompose the aggregate production into the two basic components: the trend and the cycle (business cycle). Until very recently, different economic models were used to explain the evolution of each component. However, modern real business cycle theory tries to explain both components with the same type of models (stochastic growth models, for example). In order to evaluate or calibrate the economic implications of those models it is necessary to define each component.

The Hodrick and Prescott (Edward C. Prescott, b. 1940, Nobel Prize 2004) (1980) paper, published in 1997, represents an interesting approach, known as the Hodrick–Prescott (HP) filter. The filter works as follows: first, the trend component is generated for a given value of λ and, second, the cycle is obtained as the difference between the actual value and the trend. This parameter λ is fixed exogenously as a function of the periodicity of the data of each country (quarterly, annually, and so on). For a value of $\lambda = 0$ the economic series is a pure stochastic trend with no cycle and for large values of λ (say $\lambda > 100\,000$) the series fluctuates (cyclically) around a linear deterministic trend. In the US economy the values most commonly used are $\lambda = 400$ for annual data and $\lambda = 1.600$ for quarterly data. With those values the cyclical component obtained eliminates certain low frequencies components, those that generate cycles of more than eight years' duration.

ALVARO ESCRIBANO

Bibliography

Hodrick R. and E.C. Prescott (1997), 'Postwar U.S. business cycles: a descriptive empirical investigation', *Journal of Money, Credit and Banking*, **29** (1), 1–16; discussion paper 451, Northwestern University (1980).

Hotelling's model of spatial competition

Harold Hotelling (1929) formulated a two-stage model of spatial competition in which two sellers first simultaneously choose locations in the unit interval, and then simultaneously choose prices. Sellers offer a homogeneous good produced at zero cost. Consumers are evenly distributed along the interval, and each of them buys one unit of the good from the seller for which price plus travel cost is lowest. Another interpretation of this model is that consumers have different tastes, with the line representing its distribution, and they face a utility loss from not consuming their preferred commodity.

In Hotelling's original formulation, travel costs are proportional to distance, and for this setting he claimed that both sellers will tend to locate at the centre of the interval (principle of minimum differentiation). This statement has been proved to be invalid as, with linear transport costs, no price equilibrium exists when sellers are not far enough away from each other. Minimum differentiation may not hold. Fixing the location of one seller, the other has incentives to move closer so as to capture more consumers. But since price is chosen after locations are set, sellers that are close will compete aggressively, having the incentive to locate apart so as to weaken this competition.

To circumvent the problem of non-existence of equilibrium, Hotelling's model has been thoroughly worked through in terms of altering the basic assumptions in the model. In particular, D'Aspremont *et al.* (1979) have shown the existence of an equilibrium for any location of the two firms when transport costs are quadratic. For this version, there is a tendency for both sellers to maximize their differentiation (principle of maximum differentiation).

Hotelling's (1929) model has been shown to provide an appealing framework to address the nature of equilibrium in characteristic space and in geographic space, and it has also played an important role in political science to address parties' competition.

M. ANGELES DE FRUTOS

Bibliography

D'Aspremont, C., J.J. Gabszewicz and J.F. Thisse (1979), 'On Hotelling's "Stability in Competition" ', *Econometrica*, **47**, 1145–50.

Hotelling, H. (1929), 'Stability in competition', *Economic Journal*, **39**, 41–57.

Hotelling's T² statistic

The statistic known as Hotelling's T^2 was first introduced by Hotelling (1931) in the context of comparing the means of two samples from a multivariate distribution. We are going to present T^2 in the one sample problem in order to better understand this important statistic.

Let us start by recalling the univariate theory for testing the null hypothesis H_0; $\mu = \mu_0$ against H_1; $\mu \neq \mu_0$. If $x_1, x_2, \ldots, x_n$ is a random sample from a normal population $N(\mu, \sigma)$, the test statistics is

$$t = \frac{(\bar{x} - \mu_0)}{\frac{S}{\sqrt{n}}},$$

with $\bar{x}$ and S being the sample mean and the sample standard deviation.

Under the null hypothesis, t has a Student t distribution with $v = n - 1$ degrees of freedom. One rejects H_0 when $|t|$ exceeds a specified percentage point of the t-distribution or, equivalently, when the p value corresponding to t is small enough. Rejecting H_0 when $|t|$ is large is equivalent to rejecting H_0 when its square,

$$t^2 = \frac{(\bar{x} - \mu_0)^2}{\frac{S^2}{n}} = n(\bar{x} - \mu_0)\,(S^2)^{-1}\,(\bar{x} - \mu_0),$$

is large.

In the context of one sample from a multivariate population, the natural generalization of this squared distance is Hotelling's T^2 statistic:

$$T^2 = n(\bar{x} - \mu_0)^1\,(\bar{S})^{-1}\,(\bar{x} - \mu_0), \qquad (1)$$

where

$$\bar{x} = \frac{1}{n}\sum_{j=1}^{n} x_j$$

is a p-dimensional column vector of sample means of a sample of size n ($n > p$) drawn from a multivariate normal population of dimension p. $N_p(\mu; \Sigma)$ with mean μ and covariance matrix Σ.

S is the sample covariance matrix estimated with $n - 1$ degrees of freedom

$$S = \frac{1}{n-1}\sum_{j=1}^{n}(x_j - \bar{x})(x_j - \bar{x})'.$$

A vector is denoted u, a matrix A and A^{-1} and A' are the inverse and the transpose of A.

The statistic (1) is used for testing the null hypothesis H_0: $\mu = \mu_0$ versus H_1: $\mu = \mu_1 \neq \mu_0$. If the null hypothesis is true, the distribution of

$$\frac{(n-p)}{p(n-1)}T^2$$

is the F distribution with degrees of freedom p and $n - p$.

Departures of μ from μ_0 can only increase the mean of T^2 and the decision rule for a test of significance level α is

$$\text{reject } H_0\text{: } \mu = \mu_0 \text{ if } T^2 > \frac{p(n-1)}{n-p}F_{\alpha,p,n-p}.$$

ALBERT PRAT

Bibliography

Hotelling H. (1931), 'The generalization of Student's ratio', *Annals of Mathematical Statistics*, **2**, 360–78.

Hotelling's theorem

Named after Harold Hotelling (1895–1973), and containing important implications for consumers' duality, the theorem establishes that, if the expenditure functions can be differenced, the Hicksian demand functions (in which the consumer's rent is compensated to achieve a certain utility level) are the partial derivatives of the expenditure functions with respect to the corresponding prices.

If $h(p, U)$ is the Hicksian demand vector that solves the consumer's dual optimization problem, the expenditure function, $e(p, U)$ is defined as the minimum cost needed to obtain a fixed utility level with given prices:

$$e(p, U) = p \cdot h(p, U) = \sum_i p_i h_i(p, U) \quad \forall i = 1 \ldots n.$$

Differencing the expenditure function by Hotelling's theorem we have

$$\frac{\partial e(p, U)}{\partial p_i} = h_i(p, U) \quad \forall i = 1 \ldots n.$$

The theorem has implications on consumer's duality. It allows us to deduce some of the Hicksians demand properties from the expenditure function properties. If this function is first degree homogeneous in the price vector (p), Hicksian demands are zero degree homogeneous, that is to say, demands do not vary if all the goods' prices change in the same proportion. If the expenditure function is concave in the price vector (p), this indicates the decreasing of a good's Hicksian demand with respect to its own price, and establishes the negative sign of the substitution effect of this price's variation:

$$\frac{\partial^2 e(p, U)}{\partial p_i^2} = \frac{\partial h_i(p, U)}{\partial p_i} < 0 \quad \forall i = 1 \ldots n.$$

On the other hand, Hotelling's theorem, together with the basic duality that postulates the identity of primal and dual solutions if they exist, solves the integrability problem. So, whenever the expenditure function and its properties and the Hicksian demands verify the symmetry condition of the cross substitution effects of a price change,

$$\frac{\partial h_i(p, U)}{\partial p_j} = \frac{\partial h_j(p, U)}{\partial p_i} \quad \forall i \neq j,$$

it is possible to deduce the only utility function from which they derive, that underlies the consumer's optimization problem and satisfies the axioms of consumer's choice.

M^A COVADONGA DE LA IGLESIA VILLASOL

Bibliography

Hotelling H. (1932), 'Edgworth's taxation paradox and the nature of demand and supply functions', *Journal of Political Economy*, **40** (5), 578–616.

See also: Hicksian demand, Slutsky equation.

Hume's fork

All knowledge is analytic or empirical. Scottish philosopher David Hume (1711–76) distinguished between matters of fact, that could only be proved empirically, and relations between ideas, that could only be proved logically. The distinction, known as Hume's fork, rules out any knowledge not rooted in ideas or impressions, and has to do with philosophical discussions about the scientific reliability of induction–synthesis versus deduction–analysis. It is thus stated in the last paragraph of his *Enquiry concerning Human Understanding*:

> When we run over libraries, persuaded of these principles, what havoc must we make? If we take in our hand any volume – of divinity or school metaphysics, for instance – let us ask, *Does it contain any abstract reasoning concerning quantity or number?* No. *Does it contain any experimental reasoning concerning matter of fact and existence?* No. Commit it then to the flames: For it can contain nothing but sophistry and illusion.

D.N. McCloskey mentioned Hume's fork as the golden rule of methodological modernism in economics, and strongly criticized its validity.

CARLOS RODRÍGUEZ BRAUN

Bibliography

Hume, David (1748), *An Enquiry Concerning Human Understanding*, first published under this title in 1758; reprinted in T.H. Green and T.H. Grose (eds) (1882), *David Hume. Philosophical Works*, vol. 4, p. 135.

McCloskey, D.N. (1986), *The Rhetoric of Economics*, Brighton: Wheatsheaf Books, pp. 8, 16.

Hume's law

This refers to the automatic adjustment of a competitive market balance of international payments based on specie standard. Although the basic components had already been stated by notable predecessors, as Thomas Mun (1630), Isaac Gervaise (1720) or Richard Cantillon (1734) tried to systematize them, the influential exposition of the mechanism was presented by the Scottish philosopher and historian David Hume (1711–76) in the essay 'Of the balance of trade', published in 1752. The law was broadly accepted and inspired classical economics, as it proved that the mercantilistic target of a persistently positive balance of trade and consequent accumulation of gold was unsustainable.

Hume's law is an application of the quantity theory of money. Starting from an equilibrium in the balance of trade, in a pure gold standard an increase in the money stock leads to a proportionate rise in the price level, absolute and relative to other countries. As the domestic goods become less competitive, the country will increase its imports and decrease its exports, and the gold outflow will reduce prices until the international price differentials are eliminated.

The conclusion is that money is a 'veil' that hides the real functioning of the economic system. The amount of money in a nation is irrelevant, as the price level adjusts to it. Nonetheless, Hume recognized that specie flow was indirectly a causal factor that promotes economic development as it changes demand and saving patterns. In the short run, before it increases all prices, money can promote wealth. For this reason, Adam Smith denied Hume's argument as, in the end, it demonstrated that specie *was* wealth (Smith, 1896, p. 507).

Although it is sometimes referred to as the specie-flow mechanism, Humes's law was specifically a *price*–specie–flow mechanism. It has been objected that the mechanism assigns a crucial role to differences between domestic and foreign prices, but it would work 'even if perfect commodity arbitrage prevented any international price differential from emerging' (Niehans, 1990, p. 55). But the model, even as a price mechanism, has been found problematic. For example, the self-correction of the trade balance depends on the demand elasticities of our exports in other countries and of our imports in our own country. When, say, the foreign demand elasticity of our exports is sufficiently small, the rise of prices can increase, instead of decreasing, the trade surplus, as the exports' value increases. The consequent specie inflow can result in a cumulative increase in prices and export values. Besides, we can imagine other price self-regulatory mechanisms. For instance, when there is a specie inflow, the prices of the internationally traded goods will not increase to the same extent as those of the non-internationally tradables, as the decrease in the demand for them in the countries that are losing specie neutralizes the price increases. Domestic consumers will prefer the now cheaper international goods, absorbing exportables; and producers will prefer the now dearer non-internationally tradables, reducing the exports balance. This mechanism will continue until the trade balance is adjusted.

ESTRELLA TRINCADO

Bibliography

Hume, David (1752), 'Of the balance of trade'; reprinted in E. Rotwein (ed.) (1970), *David Hume: Writings on Economics*, Madison: University of Wisconsin Press.

Niehans, Jürg (1990), *A History of Economic Theory. Classic Contributions 1720–1980*, Baltimore and London: The Johns Hopkins University Press.

Smith, Adam (1896), *Lectures on Jurisprudence*, reprinted in R.L. Meek, D.D. Raphael and P.G. Stein (eds) (1978), *The Glasgow Edition of the Works and Correspondence of Adam Smith*, vol. V, Oxford: Oxford University Press.

I

Itô's lemma

In mathematical models of evolution, we prescribe rules to determine the next position of a system in terms of its present position. If we know the starting position, we may calculate the position of the system at any further time T by applying recursively that rule. If the model is a continuous time model, the evolution rule will be a differential equation, and differential calculus, particularly the chain rule, will allow us to resolve in a formula the position at time T.

If we incorporate uncertainty in the modelling by prescribing that the next position is to be decided by means of a drawing from a particular probability distribution then we have a stochastic differential equation.

The Japanese mathematician Kiyoshi Itô completed the construction of a whole theory of stochastic differential equations based on Brownian motion, almost single-handedly. He was mainly motivated by his desire to provide a firm basis to the naive modelling of financial markets that had been proposed by Louis Bachelier at the beginning of the twentieth century in his celebrated doctoral dissertation, *Théorie de la Spéculation* which may be considered the origin of mathematical finance.

Itô was born in 1915 in Mie, in the southern part of the island of Honshu, the main island of Japan, and studied mathematics at the Imperial University of Tokyo. He worked from 1938 to 1943 at the Bureau of Statistics, which he left to start his academic career at the Imperial University at Nagoya. It was during his stay at the Bureau of Statistics that he established the foundations of stochastic calculus.

Itô's lemma is one of the main tools of stochastic calculus. To explain its meaning, we start with a deterministic rule of evolution, such as $dx = a(x)dt$, and consider the transformation, $y = f(x)$.

The chain rule tells us that the evolution of y will be given by $dy = f'(x)a(x)dt$. However, in a stochastic context, the rule governing the evolution is of the form $dx = a(x)dt + b(x)dW_t$. The term dW_t is responsible for randomness and represents a drawing from a normal distribution with mean zero and variance dt, with the understanding that successive drawings are independent. The notation W honours Norbert Wiener, who provided the foundations of the mathematical theory of Brownian motion, that is, the continuous drawing of independent normal variables. What is the evolution of $y = f(x)$? How does it relate to the evolution of x? Candidly, one may think that it should be $dy = f'(x)a(x)dt + f'(x)b(x)dW_t$. However, Itô's lemma, so surprising at first sight, tells us that the evolution of y is given by

$$dy = f'(x)a(x)dt + \frac{1}{2} f''(x)b^2(x)dt$$
$$+ f'(x)b(x)dW_t.$$

The puzzling additional term

$$\frac{1}{2} f''(x)b^2(x)dt,$$

so characteristic of stochastic calculus, comes from the fact that the size of dW_t is, on average and in absolute value, $\sqrt{dt}$. By way of example, let us assume that the value or the price of a certain good evolves according to $dx = x\ (rdt + \sigma\ dW_t)$, where r and σ are certain constants. This rule prescribes an instantaneous return that oscillates randomly around a certain value r.

The (continuous) return R that accumulates from time 0 to time T is given by

$$R = \frac{1}{T}\ln(x(T)/100).$$

Let us compare what happens in a deterministic situation, when $\sigma = 0$, with the general stochastic situation. If $\sigma = 0$, we consider the transformation $y = \ln(x)$ and, with the help of the chain rule, deduce, as expected, that $R = r$. But, in general, the same argument, but using now Itô's lemma, tells us that the random variable R is

$$R = \left(r - \frac{\sigma^2}{2}\right) + \frac{\sigma}{\sqrt{T}}Z,$$

where Z is a drawing from a standard normal variable. One discovers that, *on average*,

$$R = \left(r - \frac{\sigma^2}{2}\right)$$

and not r, as the deterministic case could have led us to believe: a lower return, on average, than expected at first sight.

In general, Itô's lemma is important because, when modelling uncertainty, it allows us to focus on the fundamental variables, since the evolution of all other variables which depend upon them can be directly deduced by means of the lemma.

JOSÉ L. FERNÁNDEZ

Bibliography

Itô, K. (1944), 'Stochastic integral', *Proc. Imp. Acad. Tokyo*, **20**, 519–21.

J

Jarque–Bera test

This test consists of applying an asymptotically efficient score test (Lagrange multiplier – LM – test) to derive a test which allows us to verify the normality of observations.

Considering a set of N independent observations of a random variable v_i $i = 1, 2, 3 \ldots N$ with mean $\mu = E[v_i]$ and $v_i = \mu + u_i$, and assuming that the probability density function of u_i is a member of the Pearson family (this is not a very restrictive assumption, given that a wide range of distributions are encompassed in it), the likelihood for this distribution will be given by the expression

$$df(u_i)/du_i = (c_1 - u_i)f(u_i)/(c_0 - c_1u_i + c_2u_i^2) \quad (-\infty < u_i < \infty).$$

The logarithm of the likelihood function for N observations is

$$l(\mu, c_0, c_1, c_2) = -N \log\left[\int_{-\infty}^{\infty}\exp\left[\int \frac{c_1 - u_i}{c_0 - c_1u_i + c_2u_i^2}du_i\right]du_i\right] + \sum_{i=1}^{N}\left[\int \frac{c_1 - u_1}{c_0 - c_1u_i + c_2u_i^2}du_i\right].$$

The assumption of normality implies testing H_0: $c_1 = c_2 = 0$ and, if the null hypothesis is true, the LM test is given by

$$LM = N\left[\frac{(m_3^2/m_2^3)^2}{6} + \frac{((m_4/m_2^2) - 3)^2}{24}\right] = \text{JB},$$

where $m_j = \Sigma(v_j - \bar{v})^j/N$ and $\bar{v} = \Sigma v_i/N$. The expression m_3^2/m_2^3 is the skewness and m_4/m_2^2 is the kurtosis sample coefficient. This expression is asymptotically distributed as $\chi^2_{(2)}$ (chi-squared distribution with two degrees of freedom) under H_0 that the observations are normally distributed.

This test can be applied in the regression model $y_i = x_i'\beta + u_i$, in order to test the normality of regression disturbances $u_1, u_2, \ldots u_N$. For this purpose, ordinary least squares residuals are used and the LM test, in the case of linear models with a constant term, is obtained with the skewness and the kurtosis of the OLS residuals.

Since, for a normal distribution, the value of skewness is zero and the kurtosis is 3, when the residuals are normally distributed, the Jarque-Bera statistic has an $\chi^2_{(2)}$ distribution. If the value of Jarque-Bera is greater than the significance point of $\chi^2_{(2)}$, the normality assumption is rejected.

AMPARO SANCHO

Bibliography

Jarque, C.M. and A. Bera (1987), 'A test for normality of observations and regression residuals', *International Statistical Review*, **55**, 163–72.

See also: Lagrange multiplier test.

Johansen's procedure

Soren Johansen has developed the likelihood analysis of vector cointegrated autoregressive models in a set of publications (1988, 1991, 1995 are probably the most cited).

Let $\mathbf{y}_t$ be a vector of m time series integrated of order 1. They are cointegrated of rank r if there are $r < m$ linear combinations of them that are stationary. In this case, the dynamics of the time series can be represented by a vector error correction model,

$$\nabla y_t = \Pi y_{t-1} + \Gamma_1\nabla y_{t-1} + \ldots + \Gamma_k\nabla y_{t-k} + \Phi D_t + \varepsilon_t,\ t = 1, \ldots, T,$$

where ∇ is the first difference operator such that $\nabla y_t = y_t - y_{t-1}$, D_t is a vector of deterministic regressors (constant, linear term, seasonal dummies . . .), ε_t are independently and identically distributed (iid). Gaussain errors $(0, \Sigma)$ and $\Pi, \Gamma_1, \ldots, \Gamma_k$ are $m \times m$ parameter matrices, being $\Pi = \alpha\beta'$ where α and β are $m \times r$ matrices. This model has gained popularity because it can capture the short-run dynamic properties as well as the long-run equilibrium behaviour of many series.

Johansen's procedure determines the cointegration rank r of the previous model by testing the number of zero canonical correlations between ∇y_t and y_{t-1}, once you have corrected for autocorrelation. Let λ_i be the ith largest eigenvalue of the matrix

$$M = S_{ii}^{-i} S_{ij} S_{jj}^{-1} S_{ji},$$

where $S_{ij} = T^{-1}\Sigma R_{it}R'_{jt}$, $i, j = 0, 1$ and R_{0t} and R_{1t} are the residuals of the least squares regression of ∇y_t and y_{t-1} over k lags of ∇y_t and D_t. The test statistic for r versus m cointegration relations is

$$l(r \mid m) = -T\sum_{i=r+1}^{m} \log(1 - \lambda_i).$$

The distribution of the test is non-standard owing to the non-stationarity of the vector of time series and the percentiles of the distribution have been tabulated by simulation.

PILAR PONCELA

Bibliography

Johansen, S. (1988), 'Statistical analysis of cointegration vectors', *Journal of Economic Dynamics and Control*, **12**, 231–54.

Johansen, S. (1991), 'Estimation and hypothesis testing of cointegration vectors in Gaussian vector autoregressive models', *Econometrica*, **59**, 1551–80.

Jones's magnification effect

The magnification effect is one of the properties of the Heckscher–Ohlin model. It was enounced by Ronald W. Jones (1965).

Actually there are two magnification effects: one concerning the effects of changes in factor endowments on outputs and the other concerning the effects of changes in commodity prices on factor prices. In the first case, the magnification effect is a generalization of the Rybczynski theorem and in the second it is a generalization of the Stolper–Samuelson theorem.

As regards factor endowments, the magnification effect says that, if factor endowments expand at different rates, the commodity intensive in the use of the fastest growing factor expands at a greater rate than either factor, and the other commodity grows (if at all) at a slower rate than either factor.

As regards commodity prices, the magnification effect says that, if commodity prices increase at different rates, the price of the factor used more intensively in the production of the commodity with the fastest rising price grows at a greater rate than either commodity price, and the price of the other factor grows (if at all) at a slower rate than either commodity price.

JUAN VARELA

Bibliography

Jones, R.W. (1965), 'The structure of simple general equilibrium models', *Journal of Political Economy*, **73**, 557–72.

See also: Heckscher–Ohlin theorem, Rybczynski thorem, Stolper–Samuelson theorem.

Juglar cycle

This is an economic cycle lasting nine or ten years, covering the period of expansion followed by a crisis that leads to a depression. It was discovered by the French economist Clément Juglar (1819–1905), who in 1848 abandoned his medical studies, turned his attention to economics and demography, and was the first to develop a theory of trade crises in the context of economic cycles. He believed that such crises could be predicted, but not avoided; like organic illness, they appeared to be a condition for the existence of commercial and industrial societies. Juglar published studies on birth, death and marriage statistics of his native country, and also on financial variables. His most noteworthy book was *Des crises commerciales* (1862), where he looked to monetary conditions to explain the origin and nature of crises. In his view, the increase of domestic and foreign trade at prices inflated by speculation was one of the chief causes of demand crises. Juglar's work gained acceptance thanks to the positive appraisals of Mitchell and Schumpeter.

JUAN HERNÁNDEZ ANDREU

Bibliography

Juglar, Clément (1862), *Des crises commerciales et leur retour périodique en France, en Angleterre et aux Etats-Unis*, Paris: Librairie Guillaumin & Cie; presented in the Académie de Sciences Morales et Politiques in 1860; 2nd edn 1889; a third edition was translated into English by W. Thom.

O'Brien, D.P. (ed.) (1997), *The Foundations of Business Cycle Theory*, Cheltenham, UK and Lyme, USA: Edward Elgar, vol. I.

Schumpeter, J.A. (1968), *History of Economic Analysis*, New York: Oxford University Press, p. 1124.

See also: Kitchen cycle, Kondratieff long waves.

K

Kakutani's fixed point theorem

Shizuo Kakutani (b.1911), a Japanese mathematician, was a professor at the universities of Osaka (Japan) and Yale (USA). Among the areas of mathematics on which he has written papers we may mention analysis, topology, measure theory and fixed point theorems. Kakutani's theorem is as follows.

Let $f: X \to X$ be an upper semicontinuous correspondence from a non-empty, compact and convex set $X \subset R^n$ into itself such that, for all $x \in X$, the set $f(x)$ is non-empty and convex. Then f has a fixed point, that is, there exists $x' \in X$ such that $x' \in f(x')$.

This theorem is used in many economic frameworks for proving existence theorems. We mention some of the most relevant. John Nash proved, in 1950, the existence of Nash equilibria in non-cooperative n-person games. The existence of a competitive equilibrium in an exchange economy was proved by Kenneth Arrow and Gerard Debreu in 1954. Lionel McKenzie proved, in 1954, the existence of equilibrium in a model of world trade and other competitive systems.

GUSTAVO BERGANTIÑOS

Bibliography

Kakutani, S. (1941), 'A generalization of Brouwer's fixed point theorem', *Duke Mathematical Journal*, **8**, 457–9.

See also: Arrow–Debreu general equilibrium model, Graham's demand, Nash equilibrium.

Kakwani index

This is a measure of tax progressivity. A progressive tax introduces disproportionality into the distribution of the tax burden and induces a redistributive effect on the distribution of income. We can measure these effects along the income scale. Such measures are called indices of local or structural progression: liability progression is the elasticity of the tax liability with respect to pre-tax income; residual progression is the elasticity of post-tax income with respect to pre-tax income.

But we can also quantify the effects of a progressive tax, once the income distribution to which it will be applied is known. Progressivity indices (or effective progression indices) summarize the tax function and pre-tax income distribution in a single number. The Kakwani index is one such progressivity index. It measures the disproportionality in the distribution of the tax burden, that is, the part of the tax burden that is shifted from low to high pre-tax income recipients. Deviation from proportionality is evidenced by the separation of the Lorenz curve for pre-tax income, and the concentration curve for tax liabilities. If we denote C to be the concentration index of taxes and G the Gini index of the pre-tax income, the Kakwani index, P, can be written $P = C - G$.

A progressive tax implies a positive value of P. Departure from proportionality is closely related to the redistributive effect: a progressive tax also shifts part of the post-tax income from high to low-income recipients. Kakwani has shown that the index of redistributive effect, R, is determined by disproportionality and the overall average tax rate, t. Neglecting re-ranking (that is, reversals in the ranking of incomes in the transition from pre-tax to post-tax),

$$R = \frac{t}{1-t} P$$

Effective progression indices satisfy a consistency property with local or structural indices: for every pre-tax income distribution, increases in liability progression imply enhanced deviation from proportionality, and increases in residual progression imply enhanced redistributive effect.

JULIO LÓPEZ LABORDA

Bibliography

Kakwani, N.C. (1977), 'Applications of Lorenz curves in economic analysis', *Econometrica*, **45**, 719–27.
Kakwani, N.C. (1977), 'Measurement of tax progressivity: an international comparison', *Economic Journal*, **87**, 71–80.

See also: Reynolds–Smolensky index, Suits index.

Kalai–Smorodinsky bargaining solution

This is a solution, axiomatically founded, proposed by E. Kalai and M. Smorodinsky (1975), to the 'bargaining problem' as an alternative to the Nash bargaining solution.

A two-person bargaining problem is summarized by a pair (S, d), where $S \subset R^2$ represents the feasible set that consists of all utility pairs attainable by an agreement, and $d \in R^2$ is the disagreement point, the utility pair that results if disagreement prevails. It is assumed that $d \in S$, and S is compact, convex, comprehensive and contains some point that strictly dominates d. A bargaining solution is a function Φ that associates with each bargaining problem a point $\Phi(S, d)$ in its feasible set.

Nash initiated the present formalization of bargaining problems and proposed the most celebrated of bargaining solutions, the Nash bargaining solution, providing its axiomatic characterization. Claiming that a bargaining solution must be compatible with axioms of efficiency, symmetry, independence of affine transformations and independence of irrelevant alternatives, he proved that the unique solution compatible with these four axioms selects the point maximizing the product of utility gains from d among all points of S dominating d.

The independence of irrelevant alternatives is somewhat controversial. Moreover, the Nash bargaining solution lacks monotonicity: when the set of feasible agreements is expanded, while the disagreement point and the maximal aspiration of one of the players $\alpha_i(S, d) = \max\{s_i \mid s \in S \text{ and } s_j \geq d_j\}$ and are unchanged, it is not assured that the other bargainer receives a better allocation.

On the basis of these observations Kalai and Smorodinsky claim that, instead of the independence of irrelevant alternatives, a solution ought to satisfy monotonicity: for all (S, d) and (T, d), $S \subset T$ and $\alpha_i(S, d) = \alpha_i(T, d)$, $\Phi_j(S, d) \leq \Phi_j(T, d)$.

The Kalai–Somorodinsky solution that selects the maximal point of S in the segment connecting d to the maximal aspirations point $\alpha(S, d)$ satisfies monotonicity. It satisfies efficiency, symmetry and independence of affine transformations as well; and no other solution is compatible with these four axioms.

CLARA PONSATI

Bibliography

Kalai, E. and M. Smorodinsky (1975), 'Other solutions to Nash's bargaining problem', *Econometrica*, **43**, 513–18.

See also: Nash bargaining solution.

Kaldor compensation criterion

The so-called 'Kaldor compensation criterion', named after Nicholas Kaldor (1908–86), ranks economic alternative x above economic alternative y if there exists, in the set of alternatives potentially achievable from x, an economic alternative z (not necessarily distinct from x) which Pareto denominates y.

By including the Pareto criterion as a subrelation, the Kaldor criterion clearly satisfies the Pareto principle. The strong Pareto principle asserts that a sufficient condition for ranking an economic alternative above another is when no one in society strictly prefers the latter and at least one person prefers the former. Economists like to think that, with this principle, they have at their disposal a non-controversial criterion to assess whether or not economic transformations are worth doing. A major problem with this criterion is that the domain of cases to which it can be applied is rather narrow.

The motivation behind the Kaldor compensation criterion is to overcome this difficulty, without invoking other ethical principles, by suggesting that the domain of cases to which the Pareto principle can be applied should be extended from actual cases to potential or hypothetical ones. It is a natural translation of the idea of giving priority to actual considerations while resorting to potential considerations when actual ones are not conclusive. Those rankings of economic alternatives that are the result of such an idea are known in welfare economics as compensation criteria *à la* Kaldor–Hicks–Scitovsky (KHS).

The KHS criterion serves even today as a justification for using many tools of applied welfare economics such as consumer surpluses. It is also commonly used in cost–benefit analysis. Of course, almost certainly, unethical interpersonal comparisons of utility emerge implicitly when the KHS criterion is applied without any actual compensation occurring.

The usual argument in favour of the KHS criterion is that it extends (albeit incompletely) the power of the Pareto principle at a low cost in terms of ethical defensibility. However, the relevance of hypothetical situations for assessing the social desirability of actual ones is certainly not a principle that is well established. Further, the KHS criterion can lead to contradictory (intransitive) policy recommendations.

LUÍS A. PUCH

Bibliography

Kaldor, N. (1939), 'Welfare propositions in economics and interpersonal comparisons of utility', *Economic Journal*, **49**, 549–52.

See also: Chipman–Moore–Samuelson compensation criterion, Hicks compensation criterion, Scitovski's compensation criterion.

Kaldor paradox

This term refers to the positive correlation observed between the international competitiveness of several countries and their relative unit labour costs. This paradox was noted first by Nicholas Kaldor (1908–86) while he was looking for the causes of the British exports share decline in international markets after the 1960s. Economic theory had traditionally predicted that export success depends on a low level of prices. But Kaldor observed that Britain's international trade share had been declining together with its relative unit labour costs, while in other countries (Japan, Germany) export trade shares were increasing together with their relative unit labour costs. That is to say, higher wages, costs and prices were not weakening the competitive position of Japan and Germany, but, on the contrary, were contributing to their growing competitiveness.

This apparent contradiction was explained by the 'non-price' factors of competitiveness: the increase of the relative German and Japanese export prices was accompanied by improvements on other quality factors that offset the negative effect of price increase. The 'non-price' factors have proved to be crucial for maintaining and increasing the competitiveness of industrial economies with high wage levels. This important observation increased the attention given by economists and policy makers to R&D and educational investments as the proper ways to assure a developed country's competitiveness in the long term.

JOSÉ M. ORTIZ-VILLAJOS

Bibliography

Kaldor, N. (1978), 'The effects of devaluation on trade', *Further Essays on Economic Policy*, London: Duckworth.

Kaldor, N. (1981), 'The role of increasing returns, technical progress and cumulative causation in the theory of international trade and economic growth', *Économie Appliquée*, **34** (4), 593–617.

Kaldor's growth laws

In 1966, Nicholas Kaldor (1908–86) published a study where he tried to explain the 'causes of the slow rate of economic growth in the United Kingdom', which was an empirical and comparative analysis based on three theoretical formulations, known as Kaldor's growth laws. The first law states that the rates of economic growth are closely associated with the rates of growth of the secondary sector. According to Kaldor, this is a characteristic of an economy in transition from 'immaturity' to 'maturity'. The second law, also known as the Kaldor–Verdoorn law, says that the productivity growth in the industrial sector is positively correlated to the growth of industrial output. It is an early formulation of the endogenous growth theory, based on the idea that output increase leads to the development of new methods of production (learning-by-doing), which increases productivity. This fosters competitiveness and exports and, thus, economic growth, introducing the economy into a virtuous circle of cumulative causation.

The third law gives a special relevance to the labour factor: economic growth leads to wage increases, so the only way for mature economies to maintain or increase their competitiveness is by shifting their way of competing from price to quality factors. This requires a structural change, which needs a labour transference from the primary to the secondary sector.

JOSÉ M. ORTIZ-VILLAJOS

Bibliography

Kaldor, N. (1966), *Causes of the Slow Rate of Economic Growth of the United Kingdom*, Cambridge: Cambridge University Press.

Kaldor, N. (1967), *Strategic Factors in Economic Development*, Ithaca: Cornell University; Frank W. Pierce Memorial Lectures, October 1966, Geneva, New York: W.F. Humphrey Press.

Thirlwall, A.P. (1983): 'A plain man's guide to Kaldor's growth laws', *Journal of Post Keynesian Economics*, **5** (3), 345–58.

See also: Verdoorn's law.

Kaldor–Meade expenditure tax

The idea of an expenditure tax dates back at least as far as the seventeenth century, in the works of Thomas Hobbes. Nicholas Kaldor (1908–86) proposed his famous 'expenditure tax' (1955) that was implemented in India and Sri Lanka, when Kaldor worked as an advisor to both countries. Most recently, in the UK, it was considered in 1978 by a committee headed by the British economist James Meade (1907–95, Nobel Prize 1977). The Meade Committee issued a lengthy report of their findings.

An expenditure tax is a direct tax in which the tax base is expenditure rather than income. Income taxes have sometimes been criticized on the grounds that they involve the 'double taxation of savings'. To the extent that income tax does penalize savings, it can be argued to reduce savings in the economy and by doing so to reduce the funds available for investment. An expenditure tax, on the other hand, taxes savings only once, at the point at which they are spent. Expenditure taxation is not the equivalent of indirect taxes such as value added tax. As with other direct taxes, it could be levied at progressive rates, whereas indirect taxes are almost inevitably regressive in their effects. Personal allowances could also be built into an expenditure tax regime as in income tax.

Imposing an expenditure tax would not require people to keep a record of every item of expenditure. The usual approach suggested is to start with a person's gross income (income + capital receipts + borrowing) and then subtract spending on capital assets, lending and repayment of debt. Consumption expenditure = income + capital receipts + borrowing – lending – repayment of debt – spending on capital assets.

Expenditure taxation avoids need for valuation of wealth, but information on earned income and net transactions in registered assets is necessary. Some of the advantages of the expenditure tax are the avoidance of double taxation of savings and the inexistence of distortion of intertemporal consumption decisions due to taxation of interest. But a political cost has to be highlighted: since savings are not included in the tax base, tax rates on the remaining base must be higher. Also one of the main problems is the transition from income taxation: it is really important to register assets at the outset. If assets could escape registration, expenditure from subsequent sale of these assets would be untaxed. Taxation of entrepreneurial incomes could be a problem as well, since income from a small business consists partly of the proprietor's earned income, and partly return on the proprietor's capital invested.

NURIA BADENES PLÁ

Bibliography

Kaldor, N. (1955), *An Expenditure Tax*, London: Unwin University Books.

Meade Committee (1978), *The Structure and Reform of Direct Taxation*, London: Institute for Fiscal Studies (report of a committee chaired by Professor J.E. Meade), London: Allen and Unwin.

Kalman filter

The Kalman filter (KF), named after the Hungarian mathematician Rudolf Emil Kalman (b.1930), is an algorithm to estimate trajectories in stochastic dynamic systems, intensively used in fields such as engineering, statistics, physics or economics. Its origins are the work of Gauss on conditional expectations and projections, of Fisher on the maximum likelihood method, and of Wiener and Kolmogorov on minimum mean squared error (MMSE) estimation theory. The explosion in computational methods provided the catalyst. A standard original reference is Kalman (1960), although Bucy should also be mentioned.

The KF is an efficient algorithm for MMSE estimation of a state variable vector, which is the output of a dynamic model, when the model and the observations are perturbed by noise. (In econometrics, the noise perturbing the model is often called 'shock'; that perturbing the measurement, 'error'.) The filter requires the model to be set in state space (SS) format, which consists of two sets of equations. The first set (the dynamic or transition equation) specifies the dynamics of the state variables. The second set (the measurement equation) relates the state variables to the observations.

A standard SS representation (among the many suggested) is the following. Let x_t denote a vector of observations, and z_t a vector of (in general, unobserved) variables describing the state. The transition and measurement equations are

$$z_{t+1} = A_t z_t + \eta_t,$$

$$x_t = M_t z_t + \varepsilon_t,$$

where A_t and M_t and are the transition and measurement matrices of the system (assumed non-stochastic), and the vectors η_t and ε_t represent stochastic noise. Although the filter extends to the continuous time case, the discrete time case will be considered. Let $x_t = (x_1, x_2, \ldots, x_t)'$ denote the vector of observations available at time t (for some periods observations may be missing). Given x_t, the filter yields the MMSE linear estimator $\hat{z}_t$ of the state vector z_t.

Assuming (a) an initial state vector, x_0,

distributed N(Ex_0, Σ_0); (b) variables η_t, ε_t distributed $N(0, Q_t)$ and $N(0, R_t)$, respectively, and (c) mutually uncorrelated x_0, η_t and ε_t, the estimator $\hat{z}_t$ is obtained through the recursive equations:

$$\hat{z}_0 = E\, z_0,$$

$$\hat{z}_t = A_{t-1}\, \hat{z}_{t-1} + G_t\, (\mathbf{x}_t - A_{t-1}\, \hat{z}_{t-1}) \text{ for } t = 1, 2, \ldots$$

The matrix G_t is the 'Kalman gain', obtained recursively through

$$\Sigma_{0|0} = \Sigma_0$$

$$\Sigma_{t|t-1} = A_{t-1}\, \Sigma_{t-1|t-1}\, A'_{t-1} + Q_{t-1}$$

$$G_t = \Sigma_{t|t-1}\, M'_t\, (M_t \Sigma_{t|t-1}\, M'_t + R_t)^{-1}$$

$$\Sigma_{t|t} = (I - G_t\, M_t)\Sigma_{t|t-1}\ (t = 1, 2, \ldots)$$

and $\Sigma_{t|t-1}$ is the covariance of the prediction error $(z_t - A_{t-1}\, \hat{z}_{t-1})$.

The KF consists of the previous full set of recursions. Under the assumptions made, it provides the MMSE estimator of z_t, equal to the conditional expectation of the unobserved state given the available observations, $E(z_t \mid x_t)$. (When the series is non-Gaussian, the KF does not yield the conditional expectation, but still provides the MMSE linear estimator). At each step of the filter, only the estimate of the last period and the data for the present period are needed, therefore the filter storage requirements are small. Further, all equations are linear and simply involve matrix addition, multiplication and one single inversion. Thus the filter is straightforward to apply and computationally efficient.

An advantage of the KF is the flexibility of the SS format to accommodate a large variety of models that may include, for example, econometric simultaneous equations models or time series models of the Box and Jenkins ARIMA family. It provides a natural format for 'unobserved components' models.

When some of the parameters in the matrices of the model need to be estimated from x_t, the KF computes efficiently the likelihood through its 'prediction error decomposition'. Given the parameters, the KF can then be applied for a variety of purposes, such as prediction of future values, interpolation of missing observations and smoothing of the series (seasonal adjustment or trend-cycle estimation).

Proper SS representation of a model requires that certain assumptions on the state variable size and the behavior of the system matrices be satisfied. Besides, the standard KF relies on a set of stochastic assumptions that may not be met. The filter has been extended in many directions. For example, the KF can handle non-stationary series (for which appropriate initial conditions need to be set), non-Gaussian models (either for some distributions, such as the *t*, or through 'robust' versions of the filter) and many types of model non-linearities (perhaps using an 'approximate KF').

AGUSTÍN MARAVALL

Bibliography

Anderson, B. and J. Moore (1979), *Optimal Filtering*, Englewood Cliffs, NJ: Prentice Hall.

Harvey, A.C. (1989), *Forecasting Structural Time Series and the Kalman Filter*, Cambridge: Cambridge University Press.

Kalman, R.E. (1960), 'A new approach to linear filtering and prediction problems', *Journal of Basic Engineering, Transactions ASME,* Series D **82**, 35–45.

Kelvin's dictum

'When you cannot express it in numbers, your knowledge is of a meagre and unsatisfactory kind.' Written by William Thompson, Lord Kelvin (1824–1907), in 1883, this dictum was discussed in the methodology of science by T.S. Kuhn and in economics by D.N. McCloskey, who included it in the Ten

Commandments of modernism in economic and other sciences. McCloskey, who criticizes the abuse of the dictum in economics, notes that, although something similar to it is inscribed on the front of the Social Science Research Building at the University of Chicago, Jacob Viner, the celebrated Chicago economist, once retorted: 'Yes, and when you *can* express it in numbers your knowledge is of a meagre and unsatisfactory kind.'

CARLOS RODRÍGUEZ BRAUN

Bibliography

McCloskey, D.N. (1986), *The Rhetoric of Economics*, Brighton: Wheatsheaf Books, pp. 7–8, 16, 54.

Keynes effect

Described by John Maynard Keynes in the *General Theory*, and so called to distinguish it from the Pigou effect, this states that a decrease in price levels and money wages will reduce the demand for money and interest rates, eventually driving the economy to full employment. A fall in prices and wages will reduce the liquidity preference in real terms (demand for real cash balances), releasing money for transaction purposes, and for speculative motives to acquire bonds and financial assets, the demand for which will be increased in turn. As a consequence, the rate of interest falls, stimulating investment and employment (Blaug, 1997, p. 661).

Keynes observed that this mechanism would involve some real income redistribution from wage earners to non-wage earners whose remuneration has not been reduced, and from entrepreneurs to rentiers, with the effect of decreasing the marginal propensity to consume (Keynes [1936] 1973, p. 262). The Keynes effect shifts the *LM* curve to the right. Added to the Pigou effect, it produces what is known as the 'real balance effect': a fall in prices and wages shifts both the *IS* and the *LM* curves to the right until they intersect at a full employment income level (Blaug, 1997, pp. 669–70).

ELSA BOLADO

Bibliography

Blaug, Mark (1997), *Economic Theory in Retrospect*, 5th edn, Cambridge: Cambridge University Press.
Keynes, John Maynard (1936), *The General Theory of Employment Interest and Money*, London: Macmillan; reprinted 1973.

See also: Keynes demand for money, Pigou effect.

Keynes's demand for money

In the inter-war period, John Maynard Keynes's (1883–1946) monetary thought experienced a major change from the prevailing Cambridge quantitativism, a legacy of Marshall and Pigou, to the liquidity preference theory, a fundamental key of his *General Theory*.

The process resulted in the formulation of a macroeconomic model for an economy where individuals have often to make decisions referring to an uncertain future, which introduced important instability elements in the aggregate demand for goods and services, particularly in its investment component; a model of an economy with prices subjected in the short term to major inertial features that blocked its movements, especially downwards, and where the aggregate demand's weakening could lead to production and employment contractions, the rapid correction of which could not be trusted to non-flexible prices; a model, finally, of an economy where money supply and demand determined the market interest rate while the general price level was the result of the pressure of the aggregate demand for goods and services, given production conditions and the negotiated value of nominal wages.

Keynes's attention was in those days concentrated on examining the ways to stimulate aggregate demand in a depressed economy. This in the monetary field was equivalent to asking how the interest rate could cooperate with that stimulus, and the answer required the study of the public's demand for money.

That study's content was the liquidity preference theory, in which money is viewed simultaneously as a general medium of payment and as a fully liquid asset, and its demand is the selection of an optimal portfolio with two assets: money and a fixed-return asset (bonds). The interest rate is the liquidity premium on money, and Keynes named three motives to explain why individuals decide to keep part of their wealth in an asset like money, fully liquid but with no (or with a very low) return.

First, the public finds convenient the possession of money, the generally accepted medium of payment, for transacting and hedging the usual gaps between income and payment flows. This is the 'transaction motive' for the demand for money that, according to Keynes, depends on the level of income with a stable and roughly proportional relation. Second, the public finds it prudent to keep additional money balances to face unforeseen expiration of liabilities, buying occasions stemming from favourable prices and sudden emergencies from various causes. This is the 'precautionary motive' for the demand for money, and Keynes says it depends, like the transaction one, on the level of income. Keynes admits that the demand for money due to these two motives will show some elasticity with respect to the return of the alternative financial asset (bonds), but says that it will be of small relevance.

On the contrary, the interest rate on bonds and its uncertain future play a fundamental role in the third component of the demand for money, that Keynes calls the 'speculative motive'. Bonds as an alternative to money are fixed-yield securities, and so their expected return has two parts: the actual interest rate and the capital gain or loss resulting from the decrease or increase in the expected future interest rate. A person expecting a lower interest rate, and thus a capital gain that, added to the present rate, announces a positive return on the bonds, will abstain from keeping speculative money balances; but if he expects a future higher interest rate, inducing a capital loss larger than the rent accruing from the present rate, he will tend to keep all his speculative balances in money. As each person's expectations of the future are normally not precise, and as these expectations are not unanimous through the very large number of agents participating in the market, it can be expected that as the present interest rate descends, the number of people that expect a higher rate in the future will increase, and so will the speculative demand for money.

Adding the balances demanded for the three motives, the *General Theory* obtains the following aggregate function of the demand for money: $Md = L1\ (P.y;\ r) + L2(r)$, where $L1$ is the demand due to the transaction and precautionary motives, $L2$ to the speculative motive, P is the general level of prices, y the real output and r the interest rate. Money income variations determine the behaviour of $L1$, which is not sensitive to the interest rate; $L2$ is a decreasing function of the market interest rate, with a high elasticity with respect to this variable, an elasticity that is larger the larger is the fall in the interest rate and the quicker is the increase in the number of persons expecting a future rise in the interest rate; this elasticity can rise to infinity at a very low interest rate (liquidity trap). Revisions of the public's expectations on the interest rate will introduce, moreover, an instability element in the speculative demand for money function. Finally, the equality between the money supplied by the authorities and the public's total aggregate demand for money, for a level of money income and expectations of the future interest rate, determines the interest rate that establishes the simultaneous equilibrium in the markets for money and bonds.

From this theoretical perspective, Keynes offered a reply to the above-mentioned question about the possible role of the interest rate in the recovery of an economy dragged into a contraction. If this induces a fall in prices, the consequent reduction in money income and accordingly of the transaction and precautionary demands for money will reduce the interest rate (with the reservation to be noted immediately), and this will tend to stimulate the effective demand for goods and services.

However, Keynes's scepticism regarding the price lowering made him distrustful of this kind of readjustment; he thought that, if a lower interest rate was wanted, an easier and more rapid way would be an expansive monetary policy. But he also had a limited confidence in such a policy: the lower interest rate derived from an increase in the quantity of money could be frustrated or obstructed as a result of an upward revision of the public's expectations on the future interest rate and a high elasticity of the demand for money with respect to the present interest rate. And even if the reduction could be accomplished, the expansive effect could be weak or nil as a consequence of the low elasticities of consumption and investment demands with respect to the interest rate, resulting from the collapse of investment's marginal efficiency in a depressed economy.

In conclusion, Keynes clearly favoured fiscal policy rather than monetary policy as an economy's stabilization resource, although admitting that the effects of the former could be partially neutralized by an upward movement in the interest rate. The liquidity preference theory was revised and perfected in the following decades by economists such as Baumol, Tobin and Patinkin, but Keynesianism continued to relegate monetary policy to a secondary position as a stabilization tool until the 1970s.

LUIS ÁNGEL ROJO

Bibliography

Keynes, John M. (1930), *A Treatise on Money*, London: Macmillan.

Keynes, John M. (1936), *The General Theory of Employment Interest and Money*, London: Macmillan.

See also: Baumol–Tobin transactions demand for cash, Friedman's rule for monetary policy, Hicks–Hansen model, Keynes effect, Pigou effect.

Keynes's plan

In the early 1940s, John Maynard Keynes was delegated by the British government to devise a plan based on the creation of an international world currency, to be denominated Bancor, with a value to be fixed to gold, and with which the member states of a projected monetary union could equilibrate their currencies. Bancor would be accepted to settle payments in an International Clearing Union, a sort of liquidating bank, that would tackle the foreign deficits and surpluses of the different countries without demanding the use of real resources. The limits of the international currency creation would be defined by the maximum of the debtors' balances according to the quotas attributed to each country. Keynes conceived this Union as purely technical, apart from political pressures. The plan aimed at alleviating the war's economic effects and generating the liquidity needed for postwar reconstruction.

The Americans were not in favour of this expansive scheme, and Harry D. White, Assistant Secretary of the Treasury, worked out an alternative plan finally approved in July 1944 at Bretton Woods, where the International Monetary Fund and the World Bank were launched. The Americans wanted a monetary system which would eliminate multiple exchange rates and bilateral payment agreements, and in the end would result in a reduction of commercial barriers, which would foster economic development. Contrary to Keynes's plan, they pushed for the use of the dollar, with a fixed rate against gold, as the international form of payment, which created an imbalance in favour of the United States. Against Keynes's flexible exchanges system, they proposed another one based on fixed but adjustable exchange rates, which favoured the level of certainty and confidence in international commercial relations and permitted a larger manoeuvre margin. Keynes suggested balances of payments financing with public funds, and capital movements controlled on a short-term basis; White reduced the importance of public financing, although he thought it necessary to establish certain controls on capital movements.

After long arguments, the Americans only gave in on the so-called 'scarce currency' clause, according to which debtor nations could adopt discriminatory methods to limit the demand for goods and services, which protected countries like Great Britain from the incipient American hegemony. The relative strengths of the parties left no other option to the British but to accept the American plan. Keynes defended the agreements in the House of Lords, considering that at least three principles had been achieved: the external value of the pound sterling would adjust to its internal value, Britain would control her own internal interest rate, and would not be forced to accept new deflation processes triggered by external influences. Keynes could not impose his plan, but his ideas helped to create the new international order, and he saw an old wish fulfilled: the gold standard had come to an end.

ALFONSO SÁNCHEZ HORMIGO

Bibliography

Hirschman, A.O. (1989), 'How the Keynesian revolution was exported from the United States, and other comments', in Peter A. Hall (ed.), *The Political Power of Economic Ideas. Keynesianism Across Nations*, Princeton, NJ: Princeton University Press, pp. 347–59.

Keynes, J.M. (1980), *The Collected Writings of John Maynard Keynes, Volume XXV*, (ed.) D.E. Moggridge, London: Macmillan, pp. 238–448.

Moggridge, D.E. (1992), *Maynard Keynes, An Economist's Biography*, London: Routledge, pp. 720–55.

Kitchin cycle

This is a short cycle, lasting about 40 months, discovered by Joseph Kitchin (1861–1932), who worked in the mining industry and in international institutions, and came to be an authority on money and precious metals statistics. His most important work, published in 1923, was a study of cycles in Britain and the United States in the 1890–1922 period, where he discerned cycles of 40 months, long cycles of 7–11 years, and trends linked to changes in world money supply. The series he studied were those of the clearing houses, food prices and interest rates in the two countries, connecting them with good or poor harvests and other cyclical fluctuations. Regarding the fundamental movements or trends, Kitchin held that they are not cyclical or rhythmical, but depend on changes in the total amount of money in the world.

JUAN HERNÁNDEZ ANDREU

Bibliography

Diebold, Francis and Glenn D. Rudebusch (1997), *Business Cycles. Durations, Dynamics and Forecasting*, Princeton, NJ: Princeton University Press.

Kitchin, Joseph (1923), 'Cycles and trends in economic factors', *Review of Economics and Statistics*, **5** (1), 10–17.

See also: Juglar cycle, Kondratieff long waves.

Kolmogorov's large numbers law

The strong law of large numbers which appeared in the Russian mathematician

Andre Nikolaievich Kolmogorov's (1903–87) famous report (1933), states that the behavior of the arithmetic mean of a random sequence is strongly influenced by the existence of an expectation.

Theorem: let $X_1, X_2, \ldots$ be a sequence of independent and identically distributed random variables with finite expectation $\mu = E(X_1)$, then with probability one, the arithmetic mean $\bar{X}_n = (X_1 + X_2 + \ldots + X_n)n^{-1}$ converges to μ, as n goes to infinity. If μ does not exist, the sequence $\{\bar{X}_n: n \geq 1\}$ is unbounded with probability one.

The theorem is true with just pairwise independence instead of the full independence assumed here (Durrett, 1996, p. 56 (mathematical formula 7.1)) and also has an important generalization to stationary sequences (the ergodic theorem: ibid., p. 341).

If the 'strong law' of large numbers holds true, so does 'the weak law'. The converse does not necessarily hold. Roughly speaking, the 'strong law' says that the sequence of estimates $\{\bar{X}_n: n \geq 1\}$ will get closer to μ as n increases, while the 'weak law' simply says that it is possible to extract subsequences from $\{\bar{X}_n: n \geq 1\}$ that will get closer to μ. The following example provides another way to understand this difference. Let $X_1, X_2, \ldots, X_n, \ldots$ be a sequence of independent Bernoulli random variables with $P(X_n = 0) = 1 - p_n$. Then $X_n \to 0$ in probability if and only if $p_n \to 0$, while $X_n \to 0$ almost surely (or strongly) if and only if $\sum_n p_n < \infty$.

OLIVER NUÑEZ

Bibliography

Durrett, R. (1996), *Probability: Theory and Examples*, 2nd edn, Belmont, CA: Duxbury Press.

Kolmogorov, A.N. (1933), *Grundbegriffe der Wahrscheinlichkeitsrechnung*, Berlin: Springer Verlag.

Kolmogorov–Smirnov test

Let $X_1, \ldots, X_n$ be a simple random sample drawn from a distribution F. The goal of the Kolmogorov–Smirnov goodness of fit test is to test the null hypothesis H_0: $F = F_0$, where F_0 is a fixed continuous distribution function. The test was introduced by Kolmogorov (1933) and studied afterwards by Smirnov (1939a, 1939b) in detail. The basic idea of the test is to compare the theoretical distribution function under the null hypothesis, F_0, with the empirical distribution function corresponding to the sample, $F_n(x) = \#\{i: X_i \leq x\}/n$. The comparison is carried out using the Kolmogorov–Smirnov statistic,

$$K_n \doteq \sup_x | F_n(x) - F_0(x) | = \| F_n - F_0 \|_\infty$$

that is, the biggest difference between both distribution functions. If the null hypothesis is true, then by the Glivenko–Cantelli theorem, we know that $K_n \to 0$, as $n \to \infty$, almost certainly. Therefore it is reasonable to reject H_0 whenever K_n is large enough for a fixed significance level.

To establish which values of K_n are large enough for rejection, we need to study the distribution of K_n under H_0. Fortunately, it can be shown that this distribution is the same for any continuous distribution F_0. As a consequence, the critical values $K_{n,\alpha}$ such that

$$P_{H_0}(K_n > K_{n,\alpha}) = \alpha$$

do not depend on F_0, and we can define the critical region of the test as $R = \{K_n > K_{n,\alpha}\}$, so that the significance level is α for any F_0. Many textbooks provide tables including $K_{n,\alpha}$, for selected values of n and α, so that the effective application of the test is quite simple.

When the sample size is large, we can also construct an approximate critical region using the asymptotic distribution of $\sqrt{n}\, K_n$, derived by Smirnov. In fact, $\sqrt{n}\, K_n$ converges in distribution to K, where

$$P(K > x) = 2\sum_{j=1}^{\infty}(-1)^{j+1} \exp(-2j^2x^2).$$

Compared with other goodness of fit tests, such as those based on the χ^2 distribution, the Kolmogorov–Smirnov test presents the following advantages: (a) the critical region is exact, it is not based on asymptotic results, and (b) it does not require arranging the observations in classes, so that the test makes an efficient use of the information in the sample. On the other hand, its main limitations are that (a) it can only be applied to continuous distributions, and (b) the distribution F_0 must be completely specified. For instance, the critical region that we have defined above would not be valid (without further modification) to test whether the observations come from a generic normal distribution (with arbitrary expectation and variance).

JOSÉ R. BERRENDERO

Bibliography

Kolmogorov, A. (1933), 'Sulla determinazione empirica di una legge di distribuzione', *Giornale dell'Instituto Italiana degli Attuari*, **4**, 83–91.

Smirnov, N. (1939a), 'Sur les écarts de la courbe de distribution empirique', *Matematicheskii Sbornik*, **48**, 3–26.

Smirnov, N. (1939b), 'On the estimation of the discrepancy between empirical curves of distribution for two independent samples', *Bulletin mathématique de l'Université de Moscou*, **2**, part 2, 1–16.

Kondratieff long waves

These are long-duration movements encompassing an expansive and a contractive phase, each lasting some 20–25 years; hence the entire cycle or 'long wave' is a half-century long. Nikolai Kondratieff (1892–1931?) was a member of the Russian Agriculture Academy and the Moscow Business Research Institute, and was one of the authors of the first Five-year Plan for Soviet agriculture.

Employing statistical methods that were just coming into use in the United States to analyse economic fluctuations, Kondratieff first advanced in 1922 his hypothesis of 'long waves' of a cyclical nature in economic performance. This hypothesis and his defence of it led to Kondratieff's detention and deportation to Siberia in 1930, where he died on an unknown date. The idea that economic activity is subject to periodic rises and falls of long duration was regarded as contrary to Marxist dogma, which held that, once capitalism's expansive force had been exhausted, it would necessarily decline and give way to socialism.

Kondratieff's work regained attention in the late 1930s, thanks chiefly to the use made of it by Schumpeter, who advanced the three-cycle model to describe the capitalist process after the end of the eighteenth century. Schumpeter proposed a movement reflecting the combination of long, medium and short cycles, and named each after the economist who first described it systematically: Kondratieff, Juglar and Kitchin, respectively. The origins of the long economic waves are ascribed to external causes such as changes in technology or in trading networks. Kondratieff's conclusions were accepted by Mitchell and Schumpeter, and later scholars such as Kindleberger, Rostow, Lewis and Maddison observed the continuity of long cycles into our times.

JUAN HERNÁNDEZ ANDREU

Bibliography

Kondratieff, Nikolai D. (1935), 'The long waves in economic life', *Review of Economics and Statistics*, **17** (6), 105–15; first published by the Economics Institute of the Russian Association of Social Science Research Institutes on 6 February 1926.

Louça, F. and Ran Reijnders (1999), *The Foundations of Long Wave Theory*, vol. I, Cheltenham, UK and Northampton, MA: USA: Edward Elgar.

Maddison, A. (1982), *Phases of Capitalist Development*, Oxford: Oxford University Press.

Schumpeter, Joseph A. (1939), *Business Cycles. A Theoretical, Historical and Statistical Analysis of the Capitalist Process*, 2 vols, New York and London: McGraw-Hill.

See also: Juglar cycle, Kitchin cycle.

Koopmans's efficiency criterion

Named after Tjalling Charles Koopmans (1910–85, Nobel Prize 1975), this is also called the 'Pareto–Koopmans efficiency criterion' and is widely used in efficiency analysis. Efficiency analysis consists of the evaluation of the efficiency of any given input–output combination. Efficiency can be stated in technical terms or in economic terms, the former being a necessary condition for the latter. The Koopmans criterion refers to technical efficiency and states that, in a given production possibility set, a pair of input and output vectors is technically (input) efficient if there cannot be found another input vector that uses fewer amounts of all inputs to obtain the same output vector. Alternatively, technical efficiency in the Koopmans sense can be output-based to state that, in a given production possibility set, a pair of input and output vectors is technically (output) efficient if there cannot be obtained another output vector that has more of every output using the same input vector.

More formally, if $(\bar{x}, \bar{y})$ is a feasible input–output combination belonging to production set T, input-based technical efficiency is reached at a measure $\theta^* = \min \theta$: $(\theta\bar{x}, y) \in T$. Alternatively, output-based technical efficiency is reached at a measure

$$\frac{1}{\varphi^*} = \frac{1}{\max \varphi: (\bar{x}, \varphi\bar{y}) \in T}.$$

These two measures can be combined to compute the Koopmans efficiency ratio of any input–output pair $(\bar{x}, \bar{y})$ as

$$\Gamma^* = \frac{\theta^*}{\varphi^*}.$$

The maximum value of Γ^* is unity and the less efficient the bundle the lower Γ^*.

Efficiency frontier analysis (EFA) and data envelopment analysis (DEA) are standard variants of efficiency analysis that make extensive use of linear programming techniques. Also game-theoretic foundations or extensions and duality theorems have been proposed to accompany the conventional Koopmans ratio.

Koopmans wrote his seminal paper in 1951. What he did was to apply the Paretian concept of 'welfare efficiency' to production economics by simply requiring minimum inputs for given outputs or maximum outputs for given inputs within an established technological set. Further refinements were brought by G. Debreu and M.J. Farrell soon after, and it is customary to refer to the Debreu–Farrell measure as an empirical counterpart to the Koopmans criterion.

JOSÉ A. HERCE

Bibliography

Farrell M.J. (1957), 'The measurement of productive efficiency', *Journal of the Royal Statistical Society*, Series A, *120*, 253–81.

Koopmans, T.C. (1951), 'Analysis of production as an efficient combination of activities', in T.C. Koopmans (ed.), *Activity Analysis of Production and Allocation*, New York: Wiley, pp. 33–97.

See also: Farrell's technical efficiency measurement.

Kuhn–Tucker theorem

The optimality conditions for non-linear programming were developed in 1951 by two Princeton mathematicians: the Canadian Albert W. Tucker (1905–95) and the American Harold W. Kuhn (b.1925). Recently they have also become known as KKT conditions after William Karush, who obtained these conditions earlier in his master thesis in 1939, although this was never published.

A non-linear program can be stated as follows:

$$\max_x f(x) \text{ subject to } g_i(x) \leq b_i \text{ for } i = 1, \ldots, m,$$

where f, g_i are functions from R^n to R. A point $x^* \in R^n$ satisfies the Kuhn–Tucker (KT) conditions if there exist 'multipliers' $\lambda_1, \ldots, \lambda_m \in R$, such that

$$\nabla f(x^*) + \sum_{i=1}^{m} \lambda_i \nabla g_i(x^*) = 0$$

and

$$\forall i = 1, \ldots, m: \begin{cases} \lambda_i(g_i(x^*) - b_i) = 0 \\ g_i(x^*) \leq b_i \\ \lambda_i \geq 0 \end{cases}$$

The KT theorem states that these conditions are necessary and/or sufficient for the optimality of point x^*, depending on rather moderate regularity conditions about the differentiability and convexity of the functions f, g_i.

KT conditions imply that $\nabla f(x^*)$ belongs to the cone spanned by the gradients of the binding constraints at x^*. Thus this theorem can be seen as an extension of Lagrange's multiplier theorem. This last theorem deals only with equality constraints, in contrast with KT, which considers problems with inequality constraints, more realistic from an economic point of view.

The real numbers $\lambda_1, \ldots, \lambda_m$ are called 'Lagrange multipliers' (also KT multipliers) and have an interesting economic interpretation: these multipliers indicate the change in the optimal value with respect to the parameters b_i. Sometimes the real number b_i represents the availability of some resource, and then λ_i allows us to know how the optimal value is affected when there is a shift in the status of this resource.

JOSÉ M. ZARZUELO

Bibliography

Kuhn H.W. and A.W. Tucker (1951), 'Non-linear programming', in J. Neyman (ed.), *Proceedings of the Second Berkeley Symposium on Mathematical Statistics and Probability*, Berkeley: University of California Press, pp. 481–92.

See also: Lagrange multipliers.

Kuznets's curve

Nobel Prize-winner Simon Kuznets (1901–85) argued that income inequality grew during the first decades of industrialization, reaching a maximum before dropping as the economy drives to maturity, and so takes the form of an inverted U. His seductive explanation was that the U-shaped curve could be accounted for merely by the expansion of (new) better-paid jobs. Modern economic growth is characterized by a shift of labour from a sector with low wages and productivity (agriculture) to new sectors (industry and services) with high wages and productivity. If we assume that the wage gap between low- and high-productivity sectors remains the same during this transition, the diffusion of better-paid jobs in the new sectors will increase inequality and generate the upswing of Kuznets's curve.

The main empirical predictions of Simon Kuznets seemed consistent with the evidence, and several studies found a similar inverted-U trend in Britain, the United States, Germany, Denmark, the Netherlands, Japan and Sweden. However, all is not right for the Kuznets inverted-U hypothesis. Data on less developed countries are not clear, and later studies have concluded that the course of income inequality might be more complex than his hypothesis suggests. In addition, Kuznets's model did not predict, and cannot explain, the recent inequality rises in mature OECD countries. There have been big increases in inequality in the United States and in Britain, while other countries (especially those in continental Europe) have experienced similar but less intense trends. Finally, and more prominently, Kuznets's explanation has major theoretical and empirical flaws. Jeffrey Williamson (1985, p. 82) has pointed out two: (1) 'The diffusion argument does not offer a true explanation of the Kuznets Curve, since the spread of the high-paying jobs should itself be an endogenous event in any satisfactory theory of growth and distribution.' And (2) 'It is not true that the inequality history of Britain (and the rest of the countries) can be characterized by fixed incomes (as Kuznets argued).'

JOAN R. ROSÉS

Bibliography

Kuznets, Simon (1955), 'Economic growth and income inequality', *American Economic Review*, **45** (1), 1–28.

Williamson, J.G. (1985), *Did British Capitalism Breed Inequality?*, London: Allen & Unwin.

Kuznets's swings

These swings, also known as Kuznets's cycles, named after Simon Kuznets's initial work on the empirical analysis of business cycles in the 1930s, are long-term (15–20 year) transport and building cycles. They are usually associated with the demand for consumer durable goods and longer-lived capital goods, like houses, factories, warehouses, office buildings, railway carriages, aircraft and ships.

JOAN R. ROSÉS

Bibliography

Kuznets, Simon (1930), 'Equilibrium economics and business cycle theory', *Quarterly Journal of Economics*, **44** (1), 381–415.

Solomou, Solomos (1998), *Economic Cycles: Long Cycles, Business Cycles Since 1870*, Manchester: Manchester University Press.

L

Laffer's curve

Arthur Laffer (b.1940), a university professor and consultant, became popular in the second half of the 1970s when he suggested that it was possible to increase tax revenue while cutting taxes. Laffer, a member of Ronald Reagan's Economic Policy Advisory Board (1981–9), has been one of the most salient members of the so-called 'supply-side' economists. Basically, supply-siders argue that economic booms and recessions are driven by incentives of tax policy and believe that demand-side policies, in particular monetary policy, are irrelevant.

Given that there is no tax revenue either when tax rate is zero or when it is 100 per cent (a worker will choose not to work if he knows he must pay all his earnings to the government), Laffer inferred a specific shape of the tax revenue function between these two values. He established as most likely that, starting from a zero tax rate, the resources collected go up as tax rate increases, and then reach a solitary maximum, from which tax revenue decreases until it becomes zero when the tax rate is 100 per cent. Therefore, in Laffer's view, the tax revenue function would have an inverted U-shape. The reasoning behind the Laffer's curve, based on the effects of economic incentives, is simple and theoretically impeccable: if tax rates are sufficiently high, to raise them will be to introduce such disincentives to factors supply that, in the end, financial resources collected will lower.

In the context of real economic choices, fiscal policy decisions based on Laffer's curve have come to be seen as highly questionable, for at least two reasons. First, Laffer's curve ignores dynamic features of fiscal reductions: it usually takes some time for economic agents to change their behaviour when tax rates decrease. And second, it is difficult to determine empirically at which tax rate the revenue function reaches its maximum; at the beginning of the 1980s the Reagan administration, under the wing of Laffer's theories, cut tax rates drastically, which instead of expanding tax revenue made public deficits substantially higher.

MAURICI LUCENA

Bibliography

Canto, V.A., D.H. Joines and A.B. Laffer (eds) (1982), *Foundations of Supply-Side Economics – Theory and Evidence,* New York: Academic Press.

Lagrange multipliers

Joseph Louis Lagrange (1736–1813) was a French mathematician of the eighteenth century. He was one of the main contributors to the calculus of variations, a branch of optimization, in which the objective functionals are integrals, which was starting to develop at that time. Using this and other tools, he succeeded in giving a suitable mathematical formulation of mechanics in his book (1788), thus being the creator of analytical mechanics.

Most models in modern economic theory assume that agents behave in an optimal way according to some criterion. In mathematical terms, they maximize (or minimize) a function $f(x_1, \ldots, x_n)$ of their decision variables $x_1, \ldots, x_n$. In general they are not fully free to decide the values of the x'_js, since these variables should satisfy some constraints, usually expressed by a system of equations $g_1(x_1, \ldots, x_n) = b_1, \ldots, g_m(x_1, \ldots, x_n) = b_m$. It is classically assumed that all functions f, $g_1, \ldots, g_m$ have continuous first-order derivatives. In the absence of constraints, a local maximum $(\bar{x}_1, \ldots, \bar{x}_n)$ of f must be a point at which the gradient (the vector of partial derivatives) $\nabla f(\bar{x}_1, \ldots, \bar{x}_n)$ vanishes; however this condition is too strong to be necessary in the case of constrained problems. Instead, a necessary condition for a feasible point $(\bar{x}_1, \ldots, \bar{x}_n)$ (that is, a point satisfying all the constraints) to be a local maximum of the constrained problem is for this gradient to be orthogonal to the surface defined by the constraints. Under the regularity condition that the vectors $\nabla g_1(\bar{x}_1, \ldots, \bar{x}_n), \ldots \nabla g_m(\bar{x}_1, \ldots, \bar{x}_n)$ are linearly independent, this amounts to the existence of real numbers $\lambda_1, \ldots, \lambda_m$, called Lagrange multipliers, such that

$$\nabla f(\bar{x}_1, \ldots, \bar{x}_n) = \lambda_1 \nabla g_1(\bar{x}_1, \ldots, \bar{x}_n) + \ldots + \lambda_m \nabla g_m(\bar{x}_1, \ldots, \bar{x}_n).$$

Since this vector equation in fact consists of n scalar equations, to solve the maximization problem by using this condition one actually has to solve a system of $n + m$ equations (as the m constraints are also to be taken into account) in the $n + m$ unknowns $\bar{x}_1, \ldots, \bar{x}_n, \lambda_1, \ldots, \lambda_m$.

Although in the method described above the Lagrange multipliers appear to be mere auxiliary variables, it turns out that they have a very important interpretation: under suitably stronger regularity assumptions, λ_i coincides with the partial derivative of the so-called 'value function',

$$V(b_1, \ldots, b_m) = \max\{f(x_1, \ldots, x_n)/g_1(x_1, \ldots, x_n) = b_1, \ldots, g_m(x_1, \ldots, x_n) = b_m\},$$

with respect to b_i at the point $(\bar{x}_1, \ldots, \bar{x}_n)$. This interpretation is particularly interesting in the case of economic problems. Supposing, for instance, that $x_1, \ldots, x_n$ represent the levels of n different outputs that can be produced from m inputs, the available amounts of which are $b_1, \ldots, b_m$, $f(x_1, \ldots, x_n)$ is the profit yielded by those levels and the constraints represent technological restrictions (one for each input). Then λi represents the marginal value of input i, in the sense that it measures the rate of change in the maximal profit $V(b_1, \ldots, b_m)$ due to a slight variation of b_i. In economic terms, λ_i is the so-called 'shadow price' of input i.

The Lagrange multipliers theorem was extended to deal with constrained optimization problems in the second half of the twentieth century, giving rise to the so-called 'Kuhn–Tucker' conditions. This extension is particularly relevant in economics, where inequalities often describe the constraints more appropriately than equalities do.

Mainly motivated by its applications to optimization, in the last decades of the twentieth century a new branch of mathematical analysis, called 'non-smooth analysis', has been extensively developed. It deals with generalized notions of derivatives that are applicable to non-differentiable functions.

JUAN E. MARTÍNEZ-LEGAZ

Bibliography

Bussotti, P. (2003), 'On the genesis of the Lagrange multipliers', *Journal of Optimization Theory and Applications*, **117** (3), 453–9.

Lagrange, Joseph L. (1788), *Méchanique analitique*, Paris, Veuve Desaint.

See also: Kuhn–Tucker theorem.

Lagrange multiplier test

The Lagrange multiplier (LM) test is a general principle for testing hypotheses about parameters in a likelihood framework. The hypothesis under test is expressed as one or more constraints on the values of parameters. To perform an LM test, only estimation of the parameters subject to the restrictions is required. This is in contrast to Wald tests, which are based on unrestricted estimates, and likelihood ratio tests, which require both restricted and unrestricted estimates.

The name of the test derives from the fact that it can be regarded as testing whether the Lagrange multipliers involved in enforcing the restrictions are significantly different from zero. The term 'Lagrange multiplier' itself is a wider mathematical term coined after the work of the eighteenth-century mathematician Joseph Louis Lagrange.

The LM testing principle has found wide applicability to many problems of interest in econometrics. Moreover, the notion of testing the cost of imposing the restrictions, although originally formulated in a likelihood framework, has been extended to other estimation environments, including method of moments and robust estimation.

Let $L(\theta)$ be a log-likelihood function of a $k \times 1$ parameter vector θ, and let the score function and the information matrix be

$$q(\theta) = \frac{\partial L(\theta)}{\partial \theta},$$

$$I(\theta) = -E\left[\frac{\partial^2 L(\theta)}{\partial \theta \partial \theta'}\right].$$

Let $\tilde{\theta}$ be the maximum likelihood estimator (MLE) of θ subject to an $r \times 1$ vector of constraints $h(\theta) = 0$. If we consider the Lagrangian function $L = L(\theta) - \lambda' h(\theta)$, where λ is an $r \times 1$ vector of Lagrange multipliers, the first-order conditions for $\tilde{\theta}$ are

$$\frac{\partial L}{\partial \theta} = q(\tilde{\theta}) - \mathrm{H}(\tilde{\theta})\tilde{\lambda} = 0$$

$$\frac{\partial L}{\partial \lambda} = h(\tilde{\theta}) = 0$$

where $H(\theta) = \partial h(\theta)'/\partial \theta$.

The Lagrange multiplier test statistic is given by

$$LM = \tilde{q}'\tilde{I}^{-1}\tilde{q} = \tilde{\lambda}'\tilde{H}'\tilde{I}^{-1}\tilde{H}\tilde{\lambda},$$

where $\tilde{q} = q(\tilde{\theta})$, $\tilde{I} = I(\tilde{\theta})$ and $\tilde{H} = H(\tilde{\theta})$. The term $\tilde{q}'\tilde{I}^{-1}\tilde{q}$ is the score form of the statistic, whereas $\tilde{\lambda}'\tilde{H}'\tilde{I}^{-1}\tilde{H}\tilde{\lambda}$ is the Lagrange multiplier form of the statistic. They correspond to two different interpretations of the same quantity.

The score function $q(\theta)$ is exactly equal to zero when evaluated at the unrestricted MLE of θ, but not when evaluated at $\tilde{\theta}$. If the constraints are true, we would expect both $\tilde{q}$ and $\tilde{\lambda}$ to be small quantities, so that the region of rejection of the null hypothesis $H_0{:}h(\theta) = 0$ is associated with large values of LM.

Under suitable regularity conditions, the large-sample distribution of the LM statistic converges to a chi-square distribution with $k - r$ degrees of freedom, provided the constraints $h(\theta) = 0$ are satisfied. This result is used to determine asymptotic rejection intervals and p values for the test.

The name 'Lagrangian multiplier test' was first used by S. David Silvey in 1959. Silvey motivated the method as a large-sample significance test of $\tilde{\lambda}$. His work provided a definitive treatment for testing problems in which the null hypothesis is specified by constraints. Silvey related the LM, Wald and likelihood ratio principles, and established their asymptotic equivalence under the null and local alternatives. The score form of the statistic had been considered 11 years earlier, in C.R. Rao (1948). Because of this the test is also known as Rao's score test, although LM is a more popular name in econometrics (cf. Bera and Bilias, 2001). It was first used in econometrics by R.P. Byron in 1968 and 1970 in two articles on the estimation of systems of demand equations subject to restrictions. T.S. Breusch and A.R. Pagan published in 1980 an influential exposition of applications of the LM test to model specification in econometrics.

MANUEL ARELLANO

Bibliography
Bera, A.K. and Y. Bilias (2001), 'Rao's score, Neyman's C (α) and Silvey's LM tests: an essay on historical developments and some new results', *Journal of Statistical Planning and Inference*, **97**, 9–44.
Rao, C.R. (1948), 'Large sample tests of statistical hypotheses concerning several parameters with applications to problems of estimation', *Proc. Cambridge Philos. Soc.*, **44**, 50–57.
Silvey, S.D. (1959), 'The Lagrangian multiplier test', *Annals of Mathematical Statistics,* **30**, 389–407.

See also: Lagrange multipliers.

Lancaster's characteristics

Kelvin John Lancaster (1924–99), an Australian economist best known for his contribution to the integration of variety into economic theory and his second best theorem, influenced his profession's conceptions of free trade, consumer demand, industrial structure and regulation, and played a crucial role in shaping government economic policy.

Lancaster revised economists' perceptions of consumer behaviour and noted how consumers do not choose between different goods, but rather between different characteristics that the goods provide. He used this to justify the replacement of old by new goods. Similarly, he emphasized the use of basic preferences, such as horse power or fuel economy for cars, to determine consumer demand. These contributions helped to explain trade flows between countries, gave economists tools to understand consumer reactions to new goods, and laid the analytical foundations for the new trade theory of imperfect competition.

ALBERTO MOLINA

Bibliography
Lancaster, K.J. (1966), 'A new approach to consumer theory', *Journal of Political Economy*, **74**, 132–57.
Lancaster, K.J. (1979), *Variety, Equity and Efficiency: Product Variety in an Industrial Society*, New York: Columbia University Press.

See also: Lancaster–Lipsey's second best.

Lancaster–Lipsey's second best

By the early 1950s, several authors had examined particular instances in rather different branches of economics that seemed to question the work accomplished in welfare economics in the 1930s and 1940s. A Pareto-efficient allocation cannot be attained when countries set tariffs on trade, but the creation of a customs union by a subset of those countries, or the unilateral elimination of tariffs by one of them, may not result in a better outcome. The presence of leisure in the utility function prevents a Pareto optimum being attained in the presence of commodity taxes or an income tax, but one cannot say which situation is more desirable given that, in both cases, several necessary conditions for attaining a Pareto-efficient allocation are violated. Although profit maximization requires equating marginal cost to marginal revenue, a firm may not be able to do so when a factor is indivisible, it then being necessary, in order to maximize profits, not to equate marginal cost and marginal revenue for the other factors.

It is the merit of Richard G. Lipsey (b.1928) and Kelvin Lancaster (1924–99) to have clearly stated and proved, in 1956, under particular assumptions on the nature of the distortion, the general principle underlying all specific cases described above. It was well known for 'standard' economies that a Pareto-efficient allocation must simultaneously satisfy certain conditions that imply, among other things, aggregate efficiency in production. The second best theorem states that, in the presence of at least one more additional constraint (boundaries, indivisibilities, monopolies, taxes and so on) that prevents the satisfaction of some of those conditions, the attainment of a (constrained) Pareto-efficient allocation requires departing from all the remaining conditions. It is an apparently robust result with profound policy implications. In particular, it follows that one cannot take for granted that the elimination of one constraint when several are present leads to a Pareto superior outcome. Neither is there a simple set of sufficient conditions to achieve an increase in welfare when a maximum cannot be obtained. Altogether, the results were a serious blow to the foundations of cost–benefit analysis and seemed to make 'piecemeal' policy reforms futile.

The 'new' second best theory developed by Diamond and Mirrlees in the late 1960s and published in 1971 was far more enduring. These authors provided sufficient conditions to ensure that any second-best optimum of a Paretian social welfare function entails efficiency in production. The result was proved for rather general economies with private and public producers, many finite consumers with continuous single-valued demand functions, without lump-sum transfers but with linear taxes or subsidies on each commodity which can be set independently, poll taxes or linear progressive income taxes. The desirability of aggregate efficiency implies, among other things, that a project whose benefits exceed its costs (all evaluated at the appropriate prices) should be undertaken. Recently the Diamond–Mirlees result has been generalized to economies with indivisibilities, non-convexities and some forms of non-linear pricing for consumers. And this is good news for cost–benefit analysis.

CLEMENTE POLO

Bibliography

Lipsey, R.G. and K. Lancaster (1956), 'The general theory of second best', *Review of Economic Studies*, **24**, 11–32.

Diamond, P.A. and J.A. Mirlees (1971), 'Optimal taxation and public production I: production efficiency' and 'II: tax rules', *American Economic Review*, **61**, 8–27 (Part I) and 261–78 (Part II).

See also: Pareto efficiency

Lange–Lerner mechanism

This concerns a much-debated market-oriented socialism devised by Oskar Ryszard Lange (1904–65) and complemented by Abba Ptachya Lerner (1903–82) in the mid-1930s, based on the public ownership of the means of production but with free choice of consumption and employment, and consumer preferences through demand prices as the decisive criterion of production and resource allocation. With these assumptions, Lange and Lerner argued that there exists a real market for consumer goods and labour services, although prices of capital goods and all other productive resources except labour are set by a Central Planning Board as indicators of existing alternatives established for the purpose of economic calculus. So, apart from market prices, there are also 'accounting prices' and both are used by enterprise and industry managers, who are public officials, in order to make their choices. Production decisions are taken subject to two conditions: first, managers must pick a combination of factors that minimizes average cost and, second, they must determine a given industry's total output at a level at which marginal cost equals the product price. These ideas were refuted in their own time by several authors, such as Mises and Hayek, who stressed the non-existence of a price system in such a planning mechanism, leading to inefficiency in resource allocation, and challenged the very possibility of economic calculus under socialism.

Mª TERESA FREIRE RUBIO

Bibliography

Lange, Oskar (1936–7), 'On the economic theory of socialism', *Review of Economic Studies*, Part I, **4** (1), October 1936, 53–71; Part II, **4** (2), February 1937, 123–42.

Lange, O. and F.M. Taylor (1938), *On the Economic Theory of Socialism*, Minneapolis: University of Minnesota Press.

Lerner, Abba P. (1936), 'A note on socialist economics', *Review of Economic Studies*, **4** (1), 72–6.

Laspeyres index

The Laspeyres price index, L_p, is a weighted aggregate index proposed by German economist E. Laspeyres (1834–1913), defined as

$$L_p = \frac{\sum_{i=1}^{n} p_{it} q_{i0}}{\sum_{i=1}^{n} p_{i0} q_{i0}},$$

where p_{it} is the price of commodity i ($i = 1, \ldots, n$) in period t, and q_{i0} is the quantity of such a commodity in period 0, which is taken as the base period. The numerator of L_p shows the cost of a basket of goods purchased in the base year at prices of year t, whereas the denominator displays the cost of the same basket of goods at the base year prices. Therefore this index allows computing the rate of variation of the value of a given basket of goods by the simple fact of changing nominal prices. As the weights (q_{i0}) remain fixed through time, L_p is the more accurate index to use on a continuing basis. So it is not surprising that the main economic application of the Laspeyres index is the construction of the consumer price index (CPI), and the price inflation rate is measured by rate of change in the CPI. As a criticism, the L_p index tends to overestimate the effect of a price increase. With a price increase, the quantity would be expected to decrease. However, this index keeps the base year quantities unchanged.

If prices are used as weights instead of quantities, it is possible to compute the Laspeyres quantity index, L_q, defined as

$$L_q = \frac{\sum_{i=1}^{n} q_{it} p_{i0}}{\sum_{i=1}^{n} q_{i0} p_{i0}},$$

This index is used in consumer theory to find out whether the individual welfare varies from period 0 to period t. If L_q is less than 1, it is possible to state that the consumer welfare was greater in the base year than in the year t.

CESAR RODRÍGUEZ-GUTIÉRREZ

Bibliography

Allen, R.G.D. (1975), *Index Numbers in Theory and Practice*, Chicago: Aldine Publishing Company.

See also: Divisia index, Paasche index.

Lauderdale's paradox

The maximization of private riches does not maximize public wealth and welfare. Although Lauderdale has often been recognized as a pioneer dissenter of the Turgot–Smith theorem, the paradox refers to another proposition, against Adam Smith, the doctrine of natural harmony: acquisitive individual activity would lead to maximum social welfare (Paglin, 1961, p. 44). In his major work, *An Inquiry into the Nature and Origin of Public Wealth* (1804), James Maitland, 8th Earl of Lauderdale (1759–1839), applied his theory of value to the discussion. He rejects the labour theory, both as a cause and as a measure of value: value depends on utility and scarcity. He distinguishes between 'private riches' and 'public wealth'. Public wealth 'consists of all that man desires that is useful or delightful to him'. Private riches consist of 'all that man desires that is useful or delightful to him, which exists in a degree of scarcity' (Lauderdale, 1804, pp. 56–7). Scarcity is necessary for a commodity to have exchange value. Use value is sufficient for something to be classed as public wealth, but not as private riches. The latter require exchange value as well.

Lauderdale presents a situation in which water ceases to be a free good and the only source is controlled by a man who proposes to create a scarcity. Water will then have exchange value, and the mass of individual riches, but not public wealth, will be increased. He concludes: 'It seems, therefore, that increase in the mass of individuals' riches does not necessarily increase the national wealth' (p. 47). As a practical matter, the argument attacked monopoly and the tendency of businessmen to resort to restrictions on supply. Unfortunately, Lauderdale overlooked Smith's postulate of free competition as a necessary condition for the natural harmony of private and public interest. Ricardo also argued against Lauderdale in a couple of paragraphs in the *Principles* (Ricardo, 1823, pp. 276–7).

NIEVES SAN EMETERIO MARTÍN

Bibliography

Maitland, J., 8th Earl of Lauderdale (1804), *An Inquiry into The Nature and Origin of Public Wealth*; reprinted (1966), New York: A.M. Kelley.

Paglin, M. (1961), *Malthus and Lauderdale: The Anti-Ricardian Tradition*, New York: A.M. Kelley.

Ricardo, D. (1823), *Principles of Political Economy and Taxation*, reprinted in P. Sraffa (ed.) (1951), Cambridge: Cambridge University Press.

Learned Hand formula

Used for determining breach in negligence cases, this derives from the decision of US Justice Billing Learned Hand (1872–1961) in *United States* v. *Caroll Towing Co* (159F.2d 169 [2d.Cir.1947]). The question before the court was whether or not the owner of a barge owed the duty to keep an attendant on board while his boat was moored. Judge Learned Hand defined the owner's duty as a function of three variables: the probability that she will break away (P), the gravity of the resulting injury, if she does (L) and the burden of adequate precautions (B). Using a negligence standard, Hand determined that the owner would be negligent if B < PL, or if the burden of precaution was less than the product of the probability of the accident and the damages if the accident occurred.

In short, according to this formula, a court will assess the severity of potential harm from a failure to take certain steps and the probability of that harm occurring. The court will then weigh these factors against the costs of avoiding that harm: if the avoidance costs are greater than the probability and gravity of the harm, a defendant who did not pay them would not breach the standard of care. If the probability and gravity of the harm are greater than the avoidance costs, the defendant will be found to have breached the standard of care if he or she did not take those steps. So negligence occurs when the cost of investing in accident prevention is less then the expected liability. Likewise, if the cost is greater than the expected liability, the defendant would not be negligent.

Conceptually this formula makes sense, and its similarity to modern cost–benefit test analysis formulae is readily apparent. Additionally, it is a guideline that allows for a great amount of flexibility. But, of course, it suffers from the same problem that plagues all cost–benefit and cost-effectiveness analyses, that is, the difficulty of applying it. Adequate figures are rarely available because it is difficult to measure the cost of precaution properly. Critics argue that it is a heuristic device but not a very useful scientific tool.

ROCÍO ALBERT LÓPEZ-IBOR

Bibliography

Cooter, R. and T. Ulen, (2000), *Law and Economics*, 3rd edn, Harlow: Addison Wesley Longman, pp. 313–16.

Posner, R.A. (1992), *Economic Analysis of Law*, 4th edn, Boston: Little Brown and Company, pp. 163–75.

Lebesgue's measure and integral

In his PhD thesis, 'Intégrale, Longueur, Aire' (1902), French mathematician Henri-Léon Lebesgue introduced the most useful notions to date of the concepts of measure and integral, leaving behind the old ideas of Cauchy and Riemann. Although some improper

Riemann integrable functions are not Lebesgue integrable, the latter is the standard model used in economic theory today, thanks to the fact that the Lebesgue integral has very good properties with respect to sequential convergence, differentiation of an integral function and topology of vector spaces of integrable functions.

Lebesgue's name is connected, among others, to the following results:

1. Lebesgue's characterization of Riemann integrable functions: a bounded function f defined on a compact interval is Riemann integrable if and only if the set of points where f is not continuous is a null set.
2. Characterization of Lebesgue (finite) measurable sets: a subset of the real line has finite measure if and only if it can be approximated (except by a set of outer measure arbitrarily small) by a finite union of (open or closed) intervals.
3. Characterization of Lebesgue integrable functions: a function defined on a measurable subset of the real line is Lebesgue integrable if and only if both the positive and the negative parts of f are the limit of pointwise convergent sequences of simple functions, provided that the sequences of integrals are bounded.
4. Lebesgue convergence theorem: the limit of a sequence of integrals of functions is the integral of the pointwise limit of these functions, provided that their absolute values are uniformly bounded by a common integrable function.
5. Lebesgue differentation theorem: any increasing function can be interpreted (in a unique way) as the sum of three different increasing functions: the first is absolutely continuous, the second is continuous and singular, and the third one is a jump function.

CARMELO NÚÑEZ

Bibliography

Royden, H.L. (1988), *Real Analysis*, 3rd edn, London: Macmillan.

LeChatelier principle

This is a heuristic principle used in thermodynamics to explain qualitative differences in the change in volume with respect to a change in pressure when temperature is held constant and when entropy is held constant and temperature is allowed to vary. Samuelson (1947), when analyzing the effect of additional constraints to equilibrium, first applied it to economics: 'How is the equilibrium displaced when there are no auxiliary constraints as compared to the case when constraints are imposed?' (Samuelson, 1947, p. 37).

From a mathematical point of view, the problem is one of comparing

$$\max f(x_1, \ldots, x_n) - \sum_{j=1}^{n} \alpha_j x_j, \qquad (1)$$

where all xs are allowed to vary, with the maximum of (1) subject to a set of s linear constraints:

$$\max f(x_1, \ldots, x_n) - \sum_{j=1}^{n} \alpha_j x_j$$

$$\text{s.t.} \sum_{r=1}^{n} \beta_{rj}(x_r - x_r^0) = 0 \quad (j = 1, \ldots, s), \qquad (2)$$

where $(x_1^0, \ldots, x_n^0)$ is the solution of (1) and the matrix $[\beta_{rj}]$ is of rank s $(s \leq n - 1)$.

Samuelson demonstrated that

$$\left(\frac{dx_r}{d\alpha_r}\right)_0 \leq \left(\frac{dx_r}{d\alpha_r}\right)_1 \leq \ldots \leq \left(\frac{dx_r}{d\alpha_r}\right)_{n-1} \leq 0 \quad (r = 1, \ldots, n), \qquad (3)$$

where the subscript indicates the number of constraints in (2). The theorem indicates that the change in any variable with respect to its own parameter is always negative and that it is more negative when there are no constraints than when there is one, more negative when there is one than when there are two, and so forth. The economic interpretation of the LeChatelier principle is straightforward: if (1) defines the equilibrium of an individual agent (for instance, *f*(.) is the production function and as the factor prices), (3) could be interpreted in terms of the changes in the demand of a production factor due to a change in its own price.

Samuelson (1947, ch. 3) applied (3) to prove (i) that a decrease in a price cannot result in a decrease in the quantity in the factor used, (ii) that a compensated change in the price of a good induces a change in the amount demanded of that good greater if the consumer is not subject to rationing, and (iii) that the introduction of each new constraint will make demand more elastic. Later on, Samuelson (1960) extended the LeChatelier principle to Leontief–Metzler–Mosak systems and to multisectorial Keynesian multiplier systems. Other examples of relevant extensions of the LeChatelier principle are those of T. Hatta to general extremum problems, and A. Deaton and J. Muellbauer to the analysis of commodities demand functions with quantity restrictions.

JULIO SEGURA

Bibliography

Samuelson, P.A. (1947), *Foundations of Economic Analysis*, Cambridge: Harvard University Press.

Samuelson, P.A. (1960), 'An extension of the LeChatelier Principle', *Econometrica*, **28** (2), 368–79.

Ledyard–Clark–Groves mechanism

This is a mechanism in which the principal designs a game arbitrarily to extract the agent's private information in contexts of asymmetric information. In this case the method used to make agents act according to some desired behaviour is to introduce payments into the game. This mechanism is designed to maximize the sum of utilities of all agents, by choosing an optimal 'social choice' that affects everybody. In such a mechanism, everybody is paid according to the sum of all others' utilities calculated according to their declarations. Since the organizer of the system (say the state or social planner) is maximizing the sum of utilities, and your overall utility is your real utility plus the others' declared utility, your own utility coincides with whatever the organizer is trying to maximize. Therefore, in this context, the dominant strategy for any agent is to tell the truth and count on the organizer to maximize your 'own' utility.

The application of this mechanism to the provision of public goods is straightforward and contributes to solving the Pareto-inefficient outcomes that asymmetric information tends to produce. Consider a government's decision on whether to build a bridge. Different people might have different valuations for the bridge (it would be very valuable for some, some people might think it is nice but not worth the cost, and others might be downright annoyed by it). All this is private information. The social planner should only build the bridge if the overall value for society is positive. But how can you tell? The Ledyard–Clark–Groves mechanism induces the people to tell the truth, and helps the social planner to make the correct decision.

CARLOS MULAS-GRANADOS

Bibliography

Clark, E. (1971), 'Multipart pricing of public goods', *Public Choice*, **18**, 19–33.

Groves, T. (1973), 'Incentives in teams', *Econometrica*, **41** (1), 617–31.

Groves, T. and J. Ledyard (1977), 'Optimal allocation of public goods: a solution to the "free rider" problem', *Econometrica*, **45** (4), 783–809.

See also: Lindahl–Samuelson public goods.

Leontief model

Wassily Leontief's (1906–99, Nobel Prize 1973) most important contribution to economics lies in his work, *The Structure of American Economy, 1919–1939*, which gave rise to what is now known as the Leontief model. There are two versions of the model.

The static model

Also known as the input–output model, this is a particular version of Walras's general equilibrium model. In its simplest version, it is based on the assumption that production in an economic system takes place in n industries, each of which produces a single good that can be used in the production of other industries, in the production of the same industry and to meet the exogenously determined needs of consumers. Given that the model is static, it is assumed that there is no good in the production system that is used in producing other goods for more than one period of time; that is, there are no capital goods.

Denote by X_i production in industry i, by X_{ij} the quantity of goods produced by industry i and used in the production of industry j; denote by d_i that quantity of the production of industry i that is demanded by consumers. We then have the following equation:

$$X_i = \sum_{j=1}^{j=n} x_{ij} + d_i \quad \text{for } i = 1, \ldots, n, \quad (1)$$

which expresses the equilibrium between supply and demand for the production of industry i. Since the number of industries is n, the simultaneous equilibrium for the n industries is expressed by n equations like the above.

A crucial assumption in the model is that there is a single production technique in each industry, which implies that one production factor cannot be replaced by another, so for each industry i the quantity used from the production of industry j is given by the following relationship: $x_{ij} = a_{ij}X_j$ and the set of equation (1) can be expressed as

$$X_i = \sum_{j=1}^{j=n} a_{ij}X_j + d_i \quad \text{for } i = 1, \ldots, n.$$

Given that the quantities of the various goods produced and demanded are non-negative, the *as* are also non-negative. Given that demands are given exogenously and assuming freedom of entry, in this basic Leontief model the price of goods is determined by the cost of production. If we denote by p_i the price of good i and by w the wage rate, which is determined exogenously, then

$$p_i = \sum_{j=1}^{j=n} a_{ji}p_i + wl_i \quad \text{for } i = 1, \ldots, n, \, (2)$$

where l_i is the quantity of the labour required to produce one unit of good i. The system of equations (1) and (2) has non-negative solutions in quantities and prices, provided that the production system is non-decomposable, that is, if it is not possible to partition the production system in such a way that there exists one set of sectors that is essential to the rest, but that set does not need the production of the others to produce its goods.

The dynamic model

A version of the model is obtained by making the following modifications to the above model: (1) production of goods is dated, the quantities produced in one period are available in the next; (2) production is not constant over time, and to increase production from one period to the next an additional quantity of inputs is required; and (3) the quantities of each good demanded are a constant proportion of the employment level. The equilibrium between production and demand for each good is given by the equation

$$X_i(t) = \sum_{j=1}^{j=n} a_{ij}X_j + \sum_{j=1}^{j=n} b_{ij}[X_j(t+1) - X_j(t)] + \delta_i \sum_{j=1}^{j=n} l_i X_i(t),$$

where b_{ij} denotes the quantity of good i required to increase production of good j by one unit and δ_i is the relationship between demand for good *i* and the employment level.

As in the static version of the model, for each good there is an equation that expresses the formation of prices in the economy. Given that inputs required to cover the increase in production from one period to the next must be available before the increase takes place, we must add the cost of capital investment to the cost of current inputs; so in perfect competition we have

$$p_i = \sum_{j=1}^{j=n} a_{ji} p_j + r \sum_{j=1}^{j=n} b_{ji} p_j + w l_i,$$

where *r* is the interest rate in the economy.

The two questions posed are (a) is there a solution in which we can have balanced growth of the production system, where the production of each sector grows at the same rate, and (b) what relationship is there between growth rate and interest rate in the model? The answers, which are of great mathematical beauty, are (a) if the average propensity to consumption is no greater than one and the production system is non-decomposable, then there is a single balanced growth rate; and (b) if the average propensity to consumption is equal to one, then the growth rate coincides with the interest rate.

FRITZ GRAFFE

Bibliography

Kurz, H.D., E. Dietzenbacher and Ch. Lager, (1998), *Input–Output Analysis*, Cheltenham, UK and Lyme, USA: Edward Elgar.

Leontief, W.W. (1951), *The Structure of American Economy, 1919–39*, New York: Oxford University Press.

Morishima, M. (1988), *Equilibrium, Stability and Growth*, Oxford: Clarendon Press.

See also: Hawkins–Simon theorem, Perron–Frobenius theorem.

Leontief paradox

This term has been applied to the empirical result, published by Wassily Leontief (1906–99, Nobel Prize 1973) in 1953, showing that the United States exported labour-intensive commodities while importing capital-intensive commodities. This result is paradoxical because the Heckscher–Ohlin model for international trade predicts just the opposite, that is, capital-abundant countries (like the United States) will export capital-intensive goods and will import commodities in the production of which labour is widely used.

Russian-born Wassily Leontief became Professor of Economics at Harvard and New York Universities. Among his important findings, the development of input–output analysis and its applications to economics is pre-eminent and earned him the Nobel Prize. With respect to international trade, besides the empirical refutation of the Heckscher–Ohlin model, he was also the first to use indifference curves to explain the advantages of international trade between countries.

To carry out his 1953 study, Leontief used the 1947 input–output table for the American economy. He sorted enterprises into industrial sectors depending on whether their production entered international trade or not. He also classified production factors used by enterprises in two groups, labour and capital. Afterwards, he evaluated which was the amount of capital and labour that was needed to produce the typical American million dollars of imports and exports. The result he obtained was that American imports were 30 per cent more capital-intensive than exports.

Since the publication of Leontief's study, many attempts have been made to find an explanation of the paradox that was compatible with the implications of the Heckscher–Olhin model. Here are some of the most popular ones:

- *Demand conditions* A capital-abundant country may import capital-intensive goods if consumers' preferences for those commodities increase prices enough.

- *Factor intensity reversal* Depending on the prices of factors and commodities, the same commodity may be capital-intensive in one country and labour-intensive in another. In other words, it depends on factors' elasticity of substitution.
- *Different labour productivity between countries* An explanation for the paradox could be that the productivity of American workers is higher for a given capital/labour ratio, thanks to (following Leontief's own reasoning) a better organizational structure or to workers' higher economic incentives.
- *Human capital* If the higher educational level of the American workers is considered as capital, results may change.

Nevertheless, none of these explanations on its own has been able to counter the fact that empirical evidence sometimes runs against the Heckscher–Ohlin model's predicted results. This problem has triggered a theoretical debate about the model, which is still used to explain international trade's distributive effects.

JOAQUÍN ARTÉS CASELLES

Bibliography

Chacholiades, M. (1990), *International Economics*, New York and London: McGraw-Hill, pp. 90–97.

Leontief, W. (1953), 'Domestic production and foreign trade: the American capital position re-examined', *Proceedings of the American Philosophical Society*, **97**, 331–49; reprinted in J. Bhagwati (ed.) (1969), *International Trade: Selected Readings*, Harmondsworth: Penguin Books, pp. 93–139.

See also: Heckscher–Ohlin theorem.

Lerner index

The Lerner index (after Abba P. Lerner, 1903–82) attempts to measure a firm's market power, that is, its ability to maintain prices above competitive levels at its profit-maximizing level of output. It does so by subtracting a firm's marginal cost from its price, and then dividing the result by the firm's price. Thus the Lerner index (LI) for a firm is defined as

$$LI = \frac{(p - mc)}{p},$$

where p and mc are the price and the marginal cost of the firm, respectively.

Because the marginal cost is greater than or equal to zero and the optimal price is greater than or equal to the marginal cost, $0 \leq p - mc \leq p$ and the *LI* is bound between 0 and 1 for a profit-maximizing firm. Firms that lack market power show ratios close to zero. In fact, for a competitive firm, the *LI* would be zero since such a firm prices at marginal cost. On the other hand, if the *LI* is closer to 1, the more pricing power the firm has. The *LI* also tells how much of each dollar spent is mark-up over *mc*. From the definition of *LI*, it can be easily obtained that

$$\frac{p}{mc} = \frac{1}{1 - LI}.$$

For a monopolist, the *LI* can be shown to be the inverse of the elasticity of demand. In this case, the marginal revenue (*mr*) of selling an additional unit of output can be written as

$$mr = p + \frac{dp}{dq}q,$$

where q is the quantity of the good. To maximize profits, the monopolist sets marginal revenue equal to marginal cost. Rearranging and dividing by p, we obtain

$$\frac{p - mc}{p} = -\frac{dp}{dq}\frac{q}{p},$$

where the term on the right-hand side is the inverse of the elasticity of demand (η). Therefore

$$LI = \frac{1}{\eta}.$$

The less elastic is demand, or the smaller is η, the greater is the difference between market price and marginal cost of production in the monopoly outcome, and the mark-up will increase.

For an industry of more than one but not a large number of firms, measuring the *LI* is more complicated and requires obtaining some average index. If we assume that the good in question is homogeneous (so that all firms sell at exactly the same price), we can measure a market-wide *LI* as

$$LI = \frac{p - \sum_{i=1}^{n} s_i mc_i}{p},$$

where s_i is firm *i*'s market share.

From an empirical point of view, there are practical difficulties in using the Lerner index as a measure of market power. The most significant practical obstacle is determining the firm's marginal cost of production at any given point in time. A crude approximation to the *LI* which has been used in the empirical literature is sales minus payroll and material costs divided by sales, because this magnitude is easy to compute. However, this is not a good approximation in industries where labour costs are not proportional to output because, when output rises, the ratio of labour cost to revenues falls and, *ceteris paribus*, price–cost margins rise.

JUAN CARLOS BERGANZA

Bibliography

Lerner, A.P. (1934), 'The concept of monopoly and the measurement of monopoly power', *Review of Economic Studies*, **1** (3), 157–75.

Lindahl–Samuelson public goods

The Lindahl–Samuelson condition is a theoretical contribution to determine the optimal level of public goods. This kind of goods presents two properties: firstly, non-rivalry in use, that is, they are not used up when economic agents consume or utilize them, and secondly, no exclusion, that is, potential users cannot be costlessly excluded from the consumption of public goods even though they have not paid for it. Given these characteristics, it can be proved that the competitive equilibrium yields an inefficient allocation of this type of goods; that is, a market failure is produced.

The Lindahl–Samuelson contribution has become one of the main blocks of the theory of public finance, involving issues related to welfare economics, public choice or fiscal federalism. On the other hand, there are different versions of this rule, depending on whether distorting taxation is considered, whether a public good provides productive services or whether the government pursues aims different from social welfare.

Assume an economy with two types of goods: a private good (*X*) and a public good (*G*) that satisfies the properties of no rivalry and no exclusion. Let *N* be the number of individuals who live in that economy. The preferences of each individual *i* are represented by the well-behaved utility function $U_i(x_i, G)$, where x_i is the individual *i*'s consumption of good *X*. In order to characterize the set of Pareto-optimal allocations, we must solve the following problem:

$$\max_{x_1, G} U_1(x_1, G)$$

$$\text{s.t. } U_i(x_i, G) - \bar{u}_i \geq 0, \quad \text{for} \quad i = 2, 3, \ldots, N$$
$$F(X, G) = 0.$$

Assuming that $\bar{u}_i$ is the minimum utility constraint for individual *i* and *F* is a strictly convex production possibility set, which is non-decreasing in its arguments, the solution for the optimal level of public good *G* is:

$$\sum_{i=1}^{N} \frac{\partial U_i(x_i, G)/\partial G}{\partial U_i(x_i, G)/\partial x_i} = \frac{\partial F/\partial G}{\partial F/\partial X}.$$

The economic interpretation of this expression is straightforward: the efficient quantity of public good G occurs when the sum of the private goods that consumers would be willing to give up for an additional unit of the public good just equals the quantity of the private good required to produce that additional unit of the public good. In other words, given the non-rivalry nature of the consumption of the public good, the optimal level of G must take into account the sum of the marginal rates of substitution of the N agents instead of the individual marginal utility used in the case of the private goods. This rule is mainly concerned with no rivalry of the public goods, while the property of no exclusion is not considered explicitly. One of the differences between Samuelson's and Lindahl's approaches is the way they deal with this last characteristic.

The study of the provision of public goods has been tackled from several theoretical viewpoints. Although there are authors who have worked on this topic before, the Scandinavian Erik Lindahl was one of the first economists to deal with problems of the decentralized pricing system in order to define optimally the level of public good to be provided. Lindahl (1919) suggested a theoretical framework where the preferences of each agent are revealed through a pseudo-demand curve of a public good. Assuming only two consumers, the optimal level of public good is determined by the intersection of the two pseudo-demands; moreover, this solution shows what price each agent has to pay according to the marginal utility he derives from the consumption of the public good. The sum of these two prices (the so-called 'Lindahl prices') equals the production cost of the public good.

However, Lindahl's approach has a crucial shortcoming: the individuals have no incentives to reveal their preferences because they know that the price they must pay will depend on the utility they receive. Hence a free-rider situation appears. Before Lindahl, Knut Wicksell proposed that a political process should be considered in order to know agents' preferences on public goods. Still, there are substantial difficulties to designing a well-defined mechanism for voting. Paul A. Samuelson (1954, 1955) was the author who avoided the free-rider problem and got the optimal set of solutions for private and public goods allocations by means of a benevolent planner. It is assumed that this omniscient agent knows individual preferences and may proceed to the efficient solution directly.

Distributional problems about the charge to finance the public good are solved in Samuelson's view by applying a social welfare function.

DIEGO MARTÍNEZ

Bibliography

Lindahl, E. (1919), 'Just taxation – a positive solution', reprinted in R.A. Musgrave, and A.T. Peacock (eds) (1958), *Classics in the Theory of Public Finance*, London: Macmillan.

Samuelson, P.A. (1954), 'The pure theory of public expenditure', *Review of Economics and Statistics*, **36**, 387–9.

Samuelson, P.A. (1955), 'Diagrammatic exposition of a theory of public expenditure', *Review of Economics and Statistics*, **37**, 350–56.

See also: Ledyard–Clark–Groves mechanism.

Ljung–Box statistics

One aim of time-series modeling, given an observed series $\{w_t\}$, is to test the adequacy of fit of the model, considering the estimated residual series $\{\hat{a}_t\}$.Usually we assume that the theoric residuals series $\{a_t\}$ is a white noise and hence that the variables $\{a_t\}$ are incorrelated; the goal of Ljung–Box statistics, introduced by these authors in 1978, is to test this incorrelation starting from the estimators $\hat{a}_t$.

The model considered by Ljung and Box is an ARIMA $\Phi(B)w_t = \Theta(B)a_t$ where $\Phi(B) = 1 - \phi_1 B - \ldots - \phi_p B^p$, $\Theta(B) = 1 - \theta_1 B - \ldots - \theta_q B^q$, $\{a_t\}$ is a sequence of independent and identically distributed random variables $N(0, \sigma)$ and $\{w_t\}$ are observable random variables.

If the variables $\{a_t\}$ could be observed, we could consider the residual correlations from a sample $(a_1, \ldots, a_n)$

$$r_k = \frac{\sum_{t=k+1}^{n} a_t a_{t-k}}{\sum_{t=1}^{n} a_t^2} \qquad (k = 1, \ldots m)$$

and the statistic

$$Q(r) = n(n+2)\sum_{k=1}^{m}(n-k)^{-1} r_k^2.$$

$Q(r)$ is asymptotically distributed as χ_m^2 since the limiting distribution of $r = (r_1, \ldots, r_m)$ is multivariate normal with mean vector zero,

$$\text{var}(r_k) = \frac{(n-k)}{n(n+2)}$$

and $\text{cov}(r_k, r_l) = 0$, $l \neq k$ (Anderson and Walker, 1964).

If the hypotheses of the white noise are true, we will expect small r_k, and for a significance level α we will accept the incorrelation hypothesis if $Q < \chi_m^2(\alpha)$.

Unfortunately, since the variables $\{a_t\}$ are not observable, we will consider the estimated residual series $\hat{a}_t$, obtained from the estimations of the parameters $\hat{\Phi}(B)$, $\hat{\Theta}(B)$, and the residual correlations

$$\hat{r}_k = \frac{\sum_{t=k+1}^{n} \hat{a}_t \hat{a}_{t-k}}{\sum_{t=1}^{n} \hat{a}_t^2} \qquad (k = 1, \ldots m),$$

introducing finally the Ljung–Box statistic

$$\tilde{Q}(\hat{r}) = n(n+2)\sum_{k=1}^{m}(n-k)^{-1} \hat{r}_k^2.$$

Ljung and Box proved that, if n is large with respect to m, $E(\tilde{Q}(\hat{r})) \approx m - p - q$; this fact suggested to them that the distribution of $\tilde{Q}(\hat{r})$ might be approximated by the χ^2_{m-p-q}. Indeed this approximation and the following test which accept the incorrelation hypothesis if $\tilde{Q}(\hat{r}) < \chi^2_{m-p-q}(\alpha)$, will turn out well in practice and actually are included in almost every program about Box–Jenkins methodology.

PILAR IBARROLA

Bibliography

Anderson, T.W. and A.M. Walker (1967), 'On the asymptotic distribution of the autocorrelations of a sample for a linear stochastic process', *Annals of Mathematical Statistics*, **35**, 1296–303.

Ljung G.M. and G.E.P. Box (1978), 'On a measure of lack of fit in time series models', *Biometrika*, **65** (2), 297–303

Longfield paradox

'The poor are not at all helped as a result of being able to purchase food at half the market price' (Johnson, 1999, 676). Samuel Mountifort Longfield (1802–84) served as a property lawyer and a judge of the Irish court. In 1832 he became the first holder of the Whatley Chair in Political Economy at Trinity College, Dublin. In his *Lectures on Political Economy* (1834), he deprecated the practice of trying to help the poor during times of famine by reducing the price of basic food, referring to the ancient custom of charitable people buying food at the ordinary price and reselling it to the poor at a cheaper price. This action may initially reduce prices and increase consumption by the poor; but there will be a feedback effect on market price, pushing it up to twice its former level, so the poor pay precisely what they did before: 'Persons of more benevolence than judgment purchase quantities of the ordinary food of the country, and sell them again to the poor at half price . . . It induces the farmers and dealers to send their stock more speedily to the market . . . Whenever this mode of charity is adopted, prices will necessarily rise' (Longfield, 1834, pp. 56–7).

LEÓN GÓMEZ RIVAS

Bibliography

Johnson, Dennis A. (1999), 'Paradox lost: Mountifort Longfield and the poor', *History of Political Economy*, **31** (4), 675–97.
Longfield, Mountifort (1834), *Lectures on Political Economy*, Dublin: Richard Milliken and Son.

Lorenz's curve

Named after Max O. Lorenz (1880–1962), this is a graphical tool that measures the dispersion of a variable, such as income or wealth. This curve is closely related to the Gini coefficient. The Lorenz curve is defined as a cumulated proportion of the variable (income or wealth) that corresponds to the cumulated proportion of individuals, increasingly ordered by income. Given a sample of n individuals ordered by income levels, $x_1^* \leq x_2^* \ldots \leq x_n^*$, the Lorenz curve is the one that connects the values $(h/n, L_h/L_n)$, where $h = 0, 1, 2, \ldots n$; $L_0 = 0$ and $L_h = \Sigma_{i=1}^h x_i^*$. Alternatively, adopting a continuous notation, the Lorenz curve can be written as

$$L(y) = \frac{\int_0^v xf(x)dx}{\mu},$$

where $0 \leq y \leq \infty$, and $f(y)$ is the relative density function.

The Lorenz curve coincides with the diagonal line (perfect equality line) when all individuals have the same income level. The Lorenz curve lies below the diagonal line when there exists some income inequality. Hence total area between both curves would be a potential inequality measure. In particular, if we multiply this area by two, in order to normalize the measure between zero and one, we obtain the Gini coefficient. The Lorenz curve is the basis for the second-order stochastic or welfare dominance criterion (Atkinson, 1970) and it is commonly used in welfare comparisons when ranking income distributions.

RAFAEL SALAS

Bibliography

Atkinson, A.B. (1970), 'On the measurement of inequality', *Journal of Economic Theory*, **2**, 244–63.
Lorenz, M.O. (1905), 'Methods of measuring concentration and wealth', *Journal of The American Statistical Association*, **9**, 209–19.

See also: Atkinson's index, Gini's coefficient.

Lucas critique

In his seminal work of 1976, Robert E. Lucas (b.1937, Nobel Prize 1995) asserts that macroeconometric models are based on optimal behaviour or decision rules of economic agents that vary systematically with changes in the time path of government policy variables. That is to say, agents' optimal behaviour depends on their expectations about government decisions. Thus traditional economic policy evaluation is not possible because the parameters of models are not invariant (that is, the econometric models are not structural) and so any change in policy variables will alter the actual value of the estimated parameters. The main conclusion of Lucas's work is that policy evaluation in not feasible.

AURORA ALONSO

Bibliography

Lucas, R.E. Jr. (1976), 'Econometric policy evaluation: a critique', in K. Bruner and A.H. Metzler (eds), *The Phillips Curve and Labor Market*, Carnegie-Rochester Conference Series on Public Policy, vol. 1, Amsterdam: North-Holland, pp. 19–46.

See also: Muth's rational expectations.

Lyapunov's central limit theorem

Central limit theorems have been the subject of much research. They basically analyse the asymptotic behaviour of the total effect produced by a large number of individual random factors, each one of them having a negligible effect on their sum. The possible convergence in distribution of this sum was a problem profusely analysed in the nineteenth century. Mathematicians focused their efforts on finding conditions not too restrictive but sufficient to ensure that the distribution function of this sum converges to the normal distribution. Although Laplace formulated the problem, it was Lyapunov who proved the theorem rigorously under rather general conditions. He proceeded as follows:

Let $x_1, x_2, \ldots, x_n$ be a sequence of independent random variables, with $E(x_k) = \mu_k$ and $E(x_k - \mu_k)^2 = \sigma_k^2 < \infty$, and let F_n be the distribution function of the random variable,

$$\frac{\sum_{k=1}^{n}(x_k - \mu_k)}{s_n}, \qquad (1)$$

where

$$s_n^2 = \sum_{k=1}^{n}\sigma_k^2.$$

If there exists a $\delta > 0$ such that

$$\frac{\sum_{k=1}^{n} E|x_k - \mu_k|^{2+\delta}}{s_n^{2+\delta}} \to 0 \text{ as } n \to \infty, \qquad (2)$$

then $F_n \to \Phi$, where Φ denotes the normal distribution with zero mean and unit variance. Thus the sum of a large number of independent random variables is asymptotically normally distributed.

It can be proved that condition (2), called the Lyapunov condition, implies that, for any $\tau > 0$,

$$P\left[Max_{1\leq k\leq n}\left|\frac{x_k - \mu_k}{s_n}\right| \geq \tau\right] \to 0, \qquad \text{as } n \to \infty.$$

That is, the contribution of each element in the sum (1) above is uniformly insignificant but the total effect has a Gaussian distribution. In his revolutionary articles on normal convergence, Lyapunov not only established general sufficient conditions for the convergence in distribution of that sum to the normal distribution, but also provided an upper limit for the term $|F_n - \Phi|$.

Lyapunov proved the central limit theorem using characteristic functions, adding besides the first proof of a continuity theorem of such functions for the normal case. This considerably facilitated further developments of limit theorems no longer checked by overwhelmingly complex calculations.

MERCEDES VÁZQUEZ FURELOS

Bibliography

Lyapunov, A.A. (1900), 'Sur une proposition de la Théorie des probabilités', *Bulletin. Académie Sci. St-Petersbourg,* **13**, 359–86.

Lyapunov, A.A. (1901), 'Nouvelle forme du Théorème sur la limite des probabilités', *Mémoires de L'Académie de St-Petersbourg*, **12**, 1–24.

See also: Gaussian distribution.

Lyapunov stability

Lyapunov stability theory is used to draw conclusions about trajectories of a system of differential equations $\dot{x} = f(x)$ without solving the differential equations. Here, f is a function from Euclidean space into itself.

Lyapunov's theorem states that, if there is a differentiable function V (called a Lyapunov function) from Euclidean space into the real numbers such that (i) $V(0) = 0$, (ii) $V(x) > 0$ for $x \neq 0$ and (iii) $\nabla V(x) \cdot f(x) \leq 0$ for $x \neq 0$, then 0 is a stable point of the above system of differential equations. Furthermore, if in addition $\nabla V(x) \cdot f(x) < 0$ for $x \neq 0$, then 0 is asymptotically stable. In either case, the sublevel sets $\{x: V(x) \leq \alpha\}$ are invariant under the flow of f.

The name of Lyapunov is also associated with continuum economies, where it guarantees the convexity of the aggregate through the following result. Let (Ω, Σ) be a measure space and let $\mu_1, \ldots, \mu_n$ be finite non-atomic measures on (Ω, Σ). Then the set$\{(\mu_1(\sigma), \ldots, \mu_n(\sigma)): \sigma \in \Sigma\}$ is compact and convex.

FRANCISCO MARHUENDA

Bibliography

M.W. Hirsch and S. Smale (1972), *Differential Equations, Dynamical Systems, and Linear Algebra*, Boston, MA: Academic Press.

See also: Negishi's stability without recontracting.

M

Mann–Wald's theorem

This theorem extends the conditions under which consistency and asymptotic normality of ordinary least squares (OLS) estimators occur. This result is very useful in economics, where the general regression model is commonly used. When the regressors are stochastic variables, under the assumption that they are independent on the error term, OLS estimators have the same properties as in the case of deterministic regressors: lack of bias, consistency and asymptotic normality. However, a common situation in econometric analysis is the case of stochastic regressors which are not independent of innovation, for example time series data. In these circumstances, OLS estimators lose their properties in finite samples since they are biased.

Nevertheless, Henry Berthold Mann (1905–2000) and his master Abraham Wald (1902–50) showed in 1943 that the asymptotic properties of the OLS estimators hold even though there is some degree of dependence between the regressors and the innovation process. A formal state of the theorem can be found, for example, in Hendry (1995). Mann and Wald's theorem proves that it is possible to have consistency and asymptotic normality for the OLS estimators under the following assumptions: the regressors are weakly stationary, ergodic and contemporaneously uncorrelated with the innovation, and the innovation is an independently and identically distributed (iid) process with zero mean and finite moments of all orders. In other words, the regressors and the error term can be correlated at some lags and leads, as for example, with the case where the regressors are lags of the dependent variable, and still have the well known asymptotic properties of the OLS estimators and therefore the usual inference, OLS standard errors, t statistics, F statistics and so on are asymptotically valid.

M. ANGELES CARNERO

Bibliography

Hendry, D.F. (1995), *Dynamic Econometrics*, Advanced Texts in Econometrics, Oxford: Oxford University Press.

Mann, H. and A. Wald (1943), 'On the statistical treatment of linear stochastic difference equations', *Econometrica*, **11**, 173–220.

Markov chain model

Andrey Andreyevich Markov (1856–1922) introduced his chain model in 1906. His paper was related to the 'weak law of large numbers' extension to sums of dependent random variables. Markovian dependence is the key concept. Roughly speaking, it expresses the view that the current distribution of one random variable, once its entire history is known, only depends on the latest available information, disregarding the rest.

A chain is defined as any sequence of discrete random variables, and each of its values is a state. The set including all these states is called the 'state space' (S). If S is finite, then the chain is said to be a finite chain. Thus a Markov chain will be a chain with the Markovian dependence as a property.

Formally, let $\{X_t, t = 0, 1, 2, \ldots\}$ be a sequence of discrete random variables with values in S (state space). It will be a Markov chain when

$$P(X_t = i_t/X_1 = i_1, \ldots X_{t-1} = i_{t-1}) = P(X_t = i_t/X_{t-1} = i_{t-1}), \forall t \in \{1, 2, \ldots\}, \forall i_1, \ldots, i_t \in S.$$

At each instant t, the chain position is defined through the state vector

$$V_t = (p_i(t), i \in S), \forall t \in T = \{0, 1, 2, \ldots\},$$

where $p_i(t) = P(X_t = i)$, and the probabilistic dynamic of the model is described by the matrix of transition probabilities:

$$P(s, t) = (p_{ij}(s, t); i, j \in S), \forall s, t \in T: s < t, \text{ with } p_{ij}(s, t) = P(X_t = j/X_s = i).$$

It is easy to prove that the evolution of the state vector of the Markov chain follows this pattern:

$$V_t = V_s \cdot P(s, t), \quad \forall s, t \in T: s < t.$$

One of the most important properties of these transition matrices is the Chapman–Kolmogorov equation, common to all the stochastic processes with the Markov property. In the above circumstances,

$$P(s, t) = P(s, r) \cdot P(r, t), \forall s, r, t \in T: s < r < t.$$

This fact provides a transition matrix decomposition into a product of one-step transition probabilities matrices, by the recursive use of the Chapman–Kolmogorov equation,

$$P(s, t) = P(s, s + 1) \cdot P(s + 1, s + 2) \cdot \ldots \cdot P(t - 1, t) \ \forall s, t \in T: s < t.$$

It is very useful to assume that one-step transition probabilities are invariant across time. In such a case, the Markov chain will be called homogeneous;

$$P(t, t + 1) = P, \forall t \in T, \text{ and so } V_t = V_0 \cdot P^t, \forall t \in T,$$

and the whole dynamic of the model can be described using only V_0 and P.

Nevertheless, the easiest case is determined when the one-step transition matrix is a regular one (each state is accessible from the others in a given number of steps). A simple sufficient condition is that all the elements of the one-step transition matrix are strictly positive. In such a case, the Markov chain model is called ergodic; that is, it reaches a stationary limit distribution. Formally,

$$\pi \cdot P = \pi; \sum_{i \in S} \pi_i = 1 \text{ satisfies:}$$

$$\lim_{t \to \infty} V_t = \lim_{t \to \infty} V_0 \cdot P^t = \pi,$$

whatever the initial state vector (V_0) is, and the convergence rate is geometric.

There are more complex models of Markov chains, according to the accessibility characteristics of the states, such as the periodic and reducible cases. On the other hand, the extension to time-continuous Markov chains is not difficult. Furthermore, the model displayed here is the first-order one, whereas the high-order extension is also possible.

Markov chain models may be considered as a very versatile tool and they have been employed in many fields, including successful applications in economics and sociology, among others.

JOSÉ J. NÚÑEZ

Bibliography

Markov, A.A. (1906), 'Rasprostraneniye zakona bol'shikh chisel na velichiny, zavisyashchiye drug ot druga' (Extension of the law of large numbers to quantities dependent on each other), *Izvestiya Fiz.-Matem. o-va pro Kazanskom un-te* (2), **15**, 135–56.

Parzen, E. (1962), *Stochastic Processes,* San Francisco: Holden-Day.

Markov switching autoregressive model

Many macroeconomic or financial time series are characterized by sizeable changes in their behaviour when observed for a long period. For example, if the series is characterized by an AR (1) process whose unconditional mean changes after period T^*, then prior to T^* we might use the model

$$y_t - \mu_1 = \rho(y_{t-1} - \mu_1) + \varepsilon_t,$$

whereas after T* the corresponding model is

$$y_t - \mu_2 = \rho(y_{t-1} - \mu_2) + \varepsilon_t,$$

where $I \rho I < 1$ and $\mu_1 \neq \mu_2$ and ε_t, is an iid error term.

Since the process has changed in the past, the prospect that it may change in the future should be taken into account when constructing forecasts of y_t. The change in regime should not be regarded as the outcome of a foreseeable determinist event. Thus a complete time series model would include a description of the probability law governing the regime change from μ_1 to μ_2. This observation suggests considering an unobserved random state variable, s_t^*, which takes two values (say, 0 and 1), determining under which regime is the time series (say, state 1 with $\mu = \mu_1$ or state 2 with $\mu = \mu_2$), so that the model becomes

$$y_t - \mu\,(s_t^*) = \rho[y_{t-1} - \mu(s_t^*)] + \varepsilon_t.$$

Hamilton (1989) has proposed modelling (s_t^*) as a two-state Markov chain with probabilities p_{ij} of moving from state i to state j (i, j = 1, 2). Thus $p_{12} = 1 - p_{11}$ and $p_{21} = 1 - p_{22}$. Interpreting this model as a mixture of two distributions, namely $N(\mu_1, \sigma^2)$ and $N(\mu_2, \sigma^2)$ under regimes 1 and 2, respectively, the EM optimization algorithm can be used to maximize the likelihood of the joint density of y_t and s_t^* given by $f(y_t, s_t^* = k, \theta)$ with $k = i, j$ and $\theta = \{\mu_1, \mu_2, \rho, \sigma^2\}$.

This modelling strategy, known as the Markov switching (MS) autoregressive model, allows us to estimate θ and the transition probabilities so that one can compute forecasts conditions in any given state. The basics of the procedure can also be extended to cases where $\rho_1 \neq \rho_2$ and $\sigma_1^2 \neq \sigma_2^2$, and to multivariate set-ups. A useful application of this procedure is to estimate the effect of one variable on another depending on the business cycle phase of the economy.

JUAN J. DOLADO

Bibliography

Hamilton, J.D. (1989), 'A new approach to the study of nonstationary time series and the business cycle', *Econometrica*, **57**, 357–84.

Markowitz portfolio selection model

Harry Markowitz (b.1927, Nobel Prize 1990) presented in his 1952 paper the portfolio selection model, which marks the beginning of finance and investment theory as we know it today. The model focuses on rational decision making on a whole portfolio of assets, instead of on individual assets, thus concerning itself with total investor's wealth.

The mathematical formulation is as follows. Consider a collection of individual assets (securities) and their returns at the end of a given time horizon, modelled as random variables characterized by their respective means and their covariance matrix. Markowitz hypothesized a mean-variance decision framework: investors favour as much expected return as possible, while considering variance of returns as negative. Risk (what investors dislike in returns) is identified with variance. The problem is to determine what are rational portfolio choices, where a portfolio is defined by a set of weights on individual assets. In this decision, rational investors would only be concerned with their final (end of horizon) wealth. The desired portfolios should provide the highest possible expected return given a maximum level of admissible portfolio variance, and (dually) the minimum possible variance given a required level of expected return.

Markowitz saw that the solution was not a

single portfolio, but that there would be a set of efficient portfolios (the 'efficient frontier') fulfilling these conditions. In order to compute the solution, it is necessary to solve a set of quadratic programming problems subject to linear constraints, a demanding task at the time but amenable today to very efficient implementation.

Markowitz himself extended the original model in his 1959 book, addressing the choice by an individual investor of one specific optimal portfolio along the efficient frontier, and had the insight on which Sharpe would later build in developing a simplified (single-index) version of the model. Much academic work in finance followed, by Tobin among many others.

The economic significance of Markowitz's contribution is paramount. His is both a rigorous and an operational model that quantifies risk and introduces it on an equal footing with expected return, hence recognizing the essential trade-off involved between them. Also, as a result of the model, the variability of returns from an individual asset is distinguished from its contribution to portfolio risk, and full meaning is given to the concept of diversification: it is important not only to hold many securities, but also to avoid selecting securities with high covariances among themselves.

It has been argued that the practical impact of the Markowitz model on actual portfolio construction does not rank as high as its theoretical significance. The model's main practical shortcomings lie in the difficulty of forecasting return distributions, and in that, often, the model yields unintuitive solutions, which happen to be very sensitive to variations in the inputs. Also both the identification of risk with variance and the hypothesis of investor rationality have been questioned. Nevertheless, the conceptual work initiated by Markowitz is either a foundation or a reference for departure on which to base any practical methods, thus securing its place as a classic in both theory and practice. In 1990, Markowitz was awarded, the first Nobel Prize in the field of financial economics, fittingly shared with Sharpe (and Miller).

GABRIEL F. BOBADILLA

Bibliography

Markowitz, H.M. (1952), 'Portfolio selection', *Journal of Finance*, **7**, 77–91.
Markowitz, H.M. (1959), *Portfolio Selection: Efficient Diversification of Investments,* New York: Wiley.

Marshall's external economies

Alfred Marshall (1842–1924), Professor of Political Economy at the University of Cambridge, was the great link between classical and neoclassical economics. He was the founder of the Cambridge School of Economics and Pigou and Keynes were among his pupils. Marshall's *Principles of Economics* (1890) was for many years the Bible of British economists, introducing many familiar concepts to generations of economists.

His industrial district theory relies on the concept of *external economies*: when firms in the same industry concentrate in a single locality, they are more likely to lower cost of production. External economies encourage the specialized agglomeration of firms by increasing the supply of inputs. The larger the supply, the lower the costs of production to all the firms in the locality. So each firm in the area becomes more competitive than if it operated on its own. This concentration of many small businesses with similar characteristics can be an alternative to a larger size for the individual firm (internal economies).

But Marshall went one step further. He stated that these industrial gatherings create something 'in the air' (Marshall's words) that promotes innovation. This environment of geographic proximity and economic decentralization provides an 'industrial atmosphere' to exchange ideas and develop skills within the district. The interaction of buyers, sellers and producers gives rise to 'constructive cooperation'. Constructive cooperation allows even small businesses to compete with much larger ones.

Marshall's industrial theory has been reinterpreted many times as an explanation of new behaviours after the mass production stage. Rival firms manage to cooperate around activities of mutual benefit such as market research and development, recruitment and training processes or common marketing campaigns.

MANUEL NAVEIRA

Bibliography

Marshall, A. (1890), *Principles of Economics: an Introductory Text*, London; Macmillan and Co., Book IV, chs. X and XI.

Marshall's stability

Alfred Marshall (1842–1924) developed his analysis of market stability in two essays written in 1879, one on the theory of foreign trade and the other on the theory of domestic values. Both were printed for private circulation and partially included later in his *Principles* (Marshall, 1890, bk 5, chs. 11, 12 and app. H).

Marshall's interest in market stability arose as a consequence of his awareness of the difficulties posed by the existence of increasing returns for the existence of a long-run competitive equilibrium solution. He believed that a negatively sloped supply curve was not unusual in many industries. Significantly, he discussed stability in an appendix entitled 'Limitations of the use of statical assumptions in regard to increasing returns.'

The Marshallian stability analysis has three main characteristics. The first is that it is formulated in terms of the equilibrium of a single market, without taking into account the reaction of markets other than the one under consideration. The second is that the excess demand price, defined as the difference between demand and supply prices, governs the response of output and not the other way round. Modern stability analysis follows Hicks (1939) in adopting the view that the price response is governed by excess demand. Finally, the market-clearing process does not take place in the short run. For Marshall it takes place in the long run because of the changes required in the firms' scale of production.

Consider an initial equilibrium position and let output fall. If the new demand price is higher than the supply price, firms selling at the former would earn above-normal profits. In that case incumbent firms would raise their production levels and new capital would accrue to the productive sector. Consequently, total output would rise and the market would go back to the initial (stable) equilibrium.

The stability condition is stated by Marshall as follows: 'The equilibrium of demand and supply [. . .] is stable or unstable according as the demand curve lies above or below the supply curve just to the left of that point or, which is the same thing, according as it lies below or above the supply curve just to the right of that point' (Marshall, 1890, app. H, p. 807, n). If the demand curve is always negatively sloped, this implies that the market equilibrium is stable when the supply curve has a positive slope. However, when the supply curve has a negative slope, the Marshallian stability condition is the opposite of the standard one stated in terms of the slope of the excess demand function. That was the reason why Hicks (1939, p. 62) considered that Marshallian analysis is not consistent with perfect competition. However, it would be quite appropriate under monopoly, since in that case an equilibrium position is stable when a small reduction in output makes marginal revenue greater than marginal cost.

JULIO SEGURA

Bibliography
Hicks, J.R. (1939), *Value and Capital*, Oxford: Oxford University Press (2nd edn 1946).
Marshall, A. (1879), 'The Pure Theory of Foreign Trade' and 'The Pure Theory of Domestic Values', reprinted together in 1930 as no. 1 in *Series of Reprints of Scarce Tracts in Economic and Political Science*, London School of Economics and Political Science.
Marshall, A. (1890), *Principles of Economics: An Introductory Text*, London: Macmillan.

See also: Hicksian perfect stability.

Marshall's symmetallism

This is a bimetallic currency scheme, 'genuine and stable' as it was assessed by Alfred Marshall ([1887] 1925, p. 204), based on the gold standard system proposed by David Ricardo in his *Proposals for an Economical and Secure Currency* (1816) but differing from his 'by being bimetallic instead of monometallic' (Marshall [1887] 1925, pp. 204–6; 1923, pp. 65–7; 1926, pp. 28–30).

Marshall's symmetallism is a system of paper currency, exchangeable on demand at the Mint or the Issue Department of the Bank of England for gold and silver, at the same time, at the rate of one pound for 56½ grains of gold together with 20 times as many grains of silver. This proportion between gold and silver established by Marshall was stable but not precise. In fact, in a manuscript note written in the margin of a page of his copy of Gibbs's *The Double Standard* (1881), Marshall proposed a rate of *n* of gold and 18*n* of silver (Marshall [1887] 1925, p. 204; Eshag 1963, p. 115n). The proportion would be fixed higher or lower depending on whether one wished to regulate the value of currency chiefly by one or other metal. 'But if we wished the two metals to have about equal influence,' we should take account of the existing stocks of the two metals (Marshall [1887] 1925, p. 204n; 1926, p. 29) and the changes in their productions. Anyway, the rate would be fixed once and for all. Marshall, finally, proposed that a bar of 100 grammes of gold and a silver bar 20 times as heavy would be exchangeable for about £28 or £30 (Marshall [1887] 1925, pp. 204–5). He proposed to make up the gold and silver bars in gramme weights 'so as to be useful for international trade' (ibid., p. 204; 1923, pp. 64, 66; 1926, p. 14).

The proposal differs from other bimetallic systems that exchange paper currency for gold or silver at a fixed ratio of mintage (or coinage) closely connected to the relative values of the metals in the market; these are not really bimetallic because, when the value of one metal, usually gold, increases to a high level in relation to the other, because the cost of mining and producing gold is going up relatively to that of silver, assuming that the demand of both metals is the same during the process, then bimetallism works as monometallism, usually of silver. In fact, Marshall did not defend bimetallic plans, including the best (his symmetallism), because he believed that in practice they do not contribute to stabilizing prices much more than monometallism (Marshall [1887] 1925, pp. 188, 196; 1926, pp. 15, 27–8, 30–31).

FERNANDO MÉNDEZ-IBISATE

Bibliography
Eshag, Eprime (1963), *From Marshall to Keynes. An Essay on the Monetary Theory of the Cambridge School*, Oxford: Basil Blackwell.
Marshall, Alfred (1887), 'Remedies for fluctuations of general prices', reprinted in A.C. Pigou (ed.) (1925), *Memorials of Alfred Marshall*, London: Macmillan, and (1966) New York: Augustus M. Kelley.
Marshall, Alfred (1923), *Money Credit and Commerce*, reprinted (1965) New York: Augustus M. Kelley.
Marshall, Alfred (1926), *Official Papers by Alfred Marshall*, London: Macmillan.

Marshallian demand

Alfred Marshall (1842–1924) was an outstanding figure in the development of contemporary economics. He introduced several concepts that became widely used in later analysis. His most famous work, *Principles of Economics*, first published in 1890, went through eight editions in his lifetime. Although incomplete, his treatment of demand had a great influence on later developments of consumer theory. He introduced concepts such as the consumer surplus and demand elasticity, and set the framework for the analysis of consumer behaviour. As a tribute to his pioneering contribution, the ordinary demand functions derived from consumers' preferences taking prices and wealth as given are known as Marshallian demand functions.

In the standard demand theory, it is assumed that consumers have rational, convex, monotone and continuous preferences defined over the set of commodity bundles $x \in R^n_+$. Under these assumptions, there exists a continuous, monotone and strictly quasi-concave utility function $u(x)$ that represents these preferences. The consumer maximizes her utility taking the price vector $p \in R^n_{++}$ and wealth level $w > 0$ as given. Hence the utility maximization problem can be specified as follows:

$$\underset{x \geq 0}{Max}\ u(x)$$

$$s.t.\ px \leq w.$$

If $u(x)$ is continuously differentiable, the first-order conditions for an interior solution are

$$\mu = \frac{U_i(x)}{p_i} = \frac{U_j(x)}{p_j} \qquad (i, j = 1, \ldots, n),$$

where μ is the Lagrange multiplier of the optimization problem. Under the above assumptions, the solution to this problem exists. The optimal consumption vector is denoted by $x(p, w) \in R^n_+$ and is known as the Marshallian (or ordinary) demand function. In equilibrium, the price-adjusted marginal utility of the last unit of wealth spent in each commodity must equal the Lagrange multiplier μ, which is the constant marginal utility of wealth. Hence the equilibrium condition implies that the marginal rate of substitution of two arbitrary goods i and j must equal the relative price of both goods.

The Marshallian demand function is homogeneous of degree zero in (p, w), since the budget set does not change when prices and wealth are multiplied by a positive constant. Moreover, in equilibrium it must hold that $px = w$, because of the assumption of monotone preferences (Walras's law holds). Finally, as it is assumed that $p >> 0$ and $w > 0$ (hence, the budget set is compact) it is possible to show that $x(p, w)$ is a continuous function.

XAVIER TORRES

Bibliography

Marshall, A. (1920), *Principles of Economics*, London: Macmillan.

Mas-Colell, A., M.D. Whinston and J.R. Green (1995), *Microeconomic Theory*, Oxford: Oxford University Press.

See also: Hicksian demand, Slutsky equation.

Marshall–Lerner condition

The condition is so called in honour of Alfred Marshall (1842–1924) and Abba P. Lerner (1903–1982), the condition establishes that, starting from an equilibrium in the current account of the balance of payments, a real exchange rate depreciation produces a current account surplus only if the sum of the price elasticities of the export and import demands of a country, measured in absolute values, is greater than one. If the starting point is a disequilibrium, measured in national currency units, it is required that the ratio of exports to imports multiplied by the price elasticity of the exports demand plus the price elasticity of the imports demand be greater than one.

Usually, a country (A) devalues because its balance of trade shows a deficit. A rise in the real exchange rate, or a devaluation, generally makes foreign products more expensive in relation to home products, and so imports expressed in foreign currency tend to decrease. But a devaluation influences A's export earnings too. For the rest of the world, the decrease in A's export prices increases their purchases, and A's exports. These changes seem to assure an improvement in the current account and stability in the exchange market, but this reasoning has assumed that both A's import and export demands are elastic, so the reactions of total expenditure on exports and imports are more than proportional to the changes of their respective relative prices or of the real exchange rate. If foreign demand is inelastic, the export earnings of A will not increase and they could even diminish in a greater proportion than the fall in A's import expenses. The result will be a larger trade deficit and more instability in the exchange rate market. On the other hand, although the volume imported by A falls in terms of units of foreign products, it could happen that, after the devaluation, imports measured in units of national product increase because the devaluation tends to increase the value of every unit of product imported by A in terms of units of A's national product. In this way its effect on the trade balance will remain uncertain.

FERNANDO MÉNDEZ-IBISATE

Bibliography

Chacholiades, Miltiades (1990), *International Economics*, 2nd edn, New York: McGraw-Hill.

Lerner, Abba P. (1944), *The Economics of Control. Principles of Welfare Economics*, New York: Macmillan, pp. 356–62, 377–80, 382–7.

Marshall, Alfred (1879), 'The pure theory of foreign trade', printed privately; reprinted (1974) with 'The pure theory of domestic values', Clifton, NJ: Augustus M. Kelley, pp. 9 (particularly footnote) – 14, 18–28.

Marshall, Alfred (1923), *Money Credit and Commerce*; reprinted (1965) New York: Augustus M. Kelley.

Maskin mechanism

A social choice rule (SCR) maps preferences into optimal allocations. A SCR is monotonic if whenever chooses allocation *A* it keeps the same choice when *A* is equally or more preferred in the ranking of all agents. An SCR satisfies no veto power if it chooses *A* when *A* is top ranking for, at least, all agents minus one.

A mechanism is a message space and a function mapping messages into allocations. A mechanism implements an SCR in Nash Equilibrium (NE) if for any preference profile optimal allocations coincide with those yielded by NE.

Maskin conjectured that, with more than two agents, any SCR satisfying monotonicity and no veto power was implementable in NE. He constructed a 'universal mechanism' to do the job. This is the Maskin mechanism. Even though the spirit was correct, the original proof was not. Repullo, Saijo, Williams and McKelvey offered correct proofs.

In the Maskin mechanism each agent announces the preferences of all agents, an allocation and an integer. There are three possibilities. The first is complete agreement: all agents announce the same preferences and allocation and this allocation is optimal for the announced preferences. The allocation is the one announced by everybody.

The second possibility is a single dissident: a single agent whose announcement differs from the others. The allocation cannot improve the dissident's payoff if her preferences were announced by others. The third possibility is several dissidents: several agents whose messages differ. The allocation is announced by the agent whose message is the highest integer.

The interpretation of the mechanism is that the dissident must prove that she is not manipulating the mechanism in her favour, but pointing out a plot of the other agents to fool the mechanism. With several dissidents, the 'law of the jungle' holds.

This mechanism has been critized because the strategy space is not bounded (if bounded, there might be NE yielding suboptimal allocations) and because, with several dissidents, allocations are dictatorial (if agents renegotiated these allocations, there might be NE yielding suboptimal allocations).

Experiments run with this mechanism suggest that both criticisms are far from the mark. The true problem is that to become a single dissident might be profitable and never hurts. If this deviation is penalized, the frequency of suboptimal NE is about 18 per cent.

LUÍS CORCHÓN

Bibliography

Maskin, E. (1999), 'Nash equilibrium and welfare optimality', *Review of Economic Studies*, **66**, 23–38; originally published with the same title as an MIT mimeo, in 1977.

Minkowski's theorem

Hermann Minkowski (1864–1909) was born in Russia, but lived and worked mostly in Germany and Switzerland. He received his doctorate in 1884 from Königsberg and taught at universities in Bonn, Königsberg, Zurich and Göttingen. In Zurich, Einstein was a student in several of the courses he gave. Minkowski developed the geometrical theory of numbers and made numerous contributions to number theory, mathematical physics and the theory of relativity. At the young age of 44, he died suddenly from a ruptured appendix. Students of analysis remember Minkowski for the inequality that bears his name, relating the norm of a sum to the sum of the norms.

The standard form of Minkowski's inequality establishes that the L^p spaces are normed vector spaces. Let S be a measure space, let $1 \leq p \leq \infty$ and let f and g be elements of $L^p(S)$. Then $f + g \in L^p(S)$ and

$$\| f + g \|_p \leq \| f \|_p + \| g \|_p$$

with equality if and only if f and g are linearly dependent.

The Minkowski inequality is the triangle inequality in $L^p(S)$. In the proof, it is sufficient to prove the inequality for simple functions and the general result that follows by taking limits.

The theorem known as Minkowski's separation theorem asserts the existence of a hyperplane that separates two disjoint convex sets. This separation theorem is probably the most fundamental result in mathematical theory of optimization which underlies many branches of economic theory. For instance, the modern approach for the proof of the so-called 'second theorem of welfare economics' invokes Minkowski's separation theorem for convex sets. The theorem is as follows.

Let A and B be non-empty convex subsets of R^n such that $A \cap B = \varnothing$. Then there exists a hyperplane separating A and B; that is, there exists a point $p \in R^n$ such that

$$\sup_{x \in A} p \cdot x \leq \inf_{x \in B} p \cdot x$$

If, in addition, A is closed and B is compact, we can strengthen the conclusion of the theorem with strict inequality.

One of the important applications of separation theorems is the Minkowski–Farkas lemma, as follows. Let $a_1, a_2, \ldots, a_m$ and $b \neq 0$ be points in R^n. Suppose that $b \cdot x \geq 0$ for all x such that $a_i \cdot x \geq 0$, $i = 1, 2, \ldots, m$. Then there exist non-negative coefficients $\lambda_1, \lambda_2, \ldots, \lambda_m$, not vanishing simultaneously, such that

$$b = \sum_{i=1}^{m} \lambda_i a_i.$$

The Minkowski–Farkas lemma plays an important role in the theory of linear programming (for example, the duality theorem), game theory (for example, the zero-sum two-person game), and the theory of nonlinear programming (for example, the Kuhn–Tucker theorem).

EMMA MORENO GARCÍA

Bibliography

Hildenbrand, W. (1974), *Core and Equilibria of a Large Economy*, Princeton, NJ: Princeton University Press.
Minkowski, H. (1896), *Geometrie der Zahlen*, vol. 1, Leipzig: Teubner, pp. 115–17.
Takayama, A. (1985), *Mathematical Economics*, 2nd edn, Cambridge: Cambridge University Press.

See also: Kuhn–Tucker theorem.

Modigliani–Miller theorem

This famous theorem is formulated in two interrelated propositions. Proposition I establishes that the total economic value of a firm is independent of the structure of ownership claims, for example between debt and equity. The proposition holds under reasonably general conditions and it had a big impact in the economics and finance literature because it implies that corporate finance, at least as it relates to the structure of corporate liabilities, is irrelevant to determining the economic value of the assets of the firm. One important corollary of the proposition is that firms can make the investment decisions independently of the way such investment will be financed.

A few years after the first paper was published, Franco Modigliani (1918–2003, Nobel Prize 1985) and Merton H. Miller (1923–2000, Nobel Prize 1990) extended proposition I to the claim that the dividend policy of firms is irrelevant in determining their economic value, under the same conditions that make irrelevant the financial structure.

One way to present the argument is to suppose that the firm divides its cash flows arbitrarily into two streams and issues titles to each stream. The market value of each title will be the present discounted value of the corresponding cash flows. Adding the values of the two assets gives the discounted value of the original undivided stream: the total value of the firm is invariant to the way profits are distributed between different claims. The conclusion applies to the division between debt and equity claims, but also to the division between different types of equity (ordinary or preferred) and between different types of debt (short-term or long-term). But in their original paper the authors proved the proposition in a more straightforward way: in perfect capital markets where individual investors can borrow and lend at the same market rates as business firms, no investor will pay a premium for a firm whose financial structure can be replicated by borrowing or lending at the personal level. This basic result has been useful for identifying other decisions of firms that do not create economic value: for example, if firms divest their assets in a pure financial way so that personal investors can replicate the same diversification in their portfolio of investments.

In a perfect capital market the financing decisions do not affect either the profits of the firm or the total market value of the assets. Therefore the expected return on these assets, equal to the profits divided by the market value, will not be affected either. At the same time, the expected return on a portfolio is equal to the weighted average of the expected returns of the individual holdings, where the weights are expressed in market values.

When the portfolio consists of the firm's securities, debt and equity, from the equation defined above one can solve for the expected return on the equity, r_E, of a levered firm as a function of the expected return on the total assets, r_A, the expected return on debt, r_D, and the debt/equity ratio, D/E, both at market values,

$$r_E = r_A + (r_A - r_D)\,\frac{D}{E}.$$

This is Modigliani and Miller proposition II: the expected rate of return on the stock of a leveraged firm increases in proportion to the debt/equity ratio expressed in market values; the increase is proportional to the spread between r_A, the expected return of the productive assets, and r_D, the expected return on debt.

The expected rate of return on equity, r_E, is the cost of capital for this form of financing, that is, the minimum expected rate of return demanded by investors to buy the asset. With no debt, $D = 0$, this expected return is just the expected return demanded to the productive assets, as a function of their stochastic characteristics (economic risk) and of the risk-free interest rate. Leverage increases the risk of the shares of the firm because the interest payment to debt is fixed and independent of the return on the assets. The debt/equity decision amplifies the spread of percentage returns for the shares of the firm, and therefore the variability of such returns, compared with the variability with no debt in the financial structure. The cost of equity capital for the levered firm increases to compensate shareholders for the increase in the risk of their returns due to the issue of corporate debt.

Modigliani and Miller propositions hold when the division of the cash flows generated by the productive assets of the firm does not affect the size of total cash flows. There are at least two reasons why this may not be the case. The first is the fact that interest payments to debt holders are not taxed at the corporate level. A shift from equity to debt finance therefore reduces the tax burden and increases the cash flow. The second is that there may be bankruptcy costs. Bankruptcy is a legal mechanism allowing creditors to take over when a firm defaults. Bankruptcy costs are the costs of using this mechanism. These costs are paid by the stockholders and they will demand compensation in advance in the form of higher pay-offs when the firm does not default. This reduces the possible pay-off to stockholders and in turn reduces the present market value of their shares.

As leverage increases, the market value of the firm increases with the present value of tax savings and decreases with the increasing expected bankruptcy costs. At some point the market value will reach a maximum which will correspond to the optimal leverage ratio. This is the first extension of the Modigliani and Miller world to the case where institutional and regulatory interventions in the market create imperfections that determine the relevance of the financial decisions. Other extensions have to do with the presence of information asymmetries between shareholders, managers and creditors which create incentive problems and new opportunities to link wealth creation with financial decisions.

VICENTE SALAS

Bibliography

Miller, M.H. and F. Modigliani (1961), 'Dividend policy, growth and the valuation of shares', *Journal of Business*, **34** (4), 411–41.

Modigliani, F. and M.H. Miller (1958), 'The cost of capital, corporation finance and the theory of investment', *American Economic Review*, **48** (3), 261–97.

Montaigne dogma

The gain of one man is the damage of another. Ludwig von Mises coined the eponym in *Human Action*, referring to the French writer Michel E. de Montaigne (1533–92), who wrote: 'let every man sound his owne conscience, hee shall finde that our inward desires are for the most part nourished and bred in us by the losse and hurt of others; which when I considered, I began to thinke how Nature doth not gainesay herselfe in this, concerning her generall policie: for Physitians hold that the birth, increase, and augmentation of everything, is the alteration and corruption of another'. Mises restated the classical anti-mercantilist doctrine according to which voluntary market exchanges are not exploitation or zero-sum games, and said: 'When the baker provides the dentist with bread and the dentist relieves the baker's toothache, neither the baker nor the dentist is harmed. It is wrong to consider such an exchange of services and the pillage of the baker's shop by armed gangsters as two manifestations of the same thing.'

GORKA ETXEBARRIA ZUBELDIA

Bibliography

Mises, Ludwig von (1996), *Human Action*, 4th rev. edn, San Francisco: Fox & Wilkes, pp. 664–6.
Montaigne (1580), *Essais*, reprinted F. Strowski (ed.) (1906), Bordeaux, bk I, ch. 22, pp. 135–6. English translation by John Florio (1603), London: Val. Sims for Edward Blount.

Moore's law

The electronic engineer Gordon E. Moore, co-founder of Intel, observed in 1965 that, in integrated circuits, the transistor density or 'the complexity for minimum component costs has increased at a rate of roughly a factor of two per year; certainly over the short term this rate can be expected to continue, if not to increase'. The press called this 'Moore's law', and in fact the doubling every eighteen months was the pace afterwards. Economists studying the Internet, such as MacKie-Mason and Varian, have observed that 'the traffic on the network is currently increasing at a rate of 6 per cent a month, or doubling once a year', and that 'the decline in both communications link and switching costs has been exponential at about 30 per cent per year'.

CARLOS RODRÍGUEZ BRAUN

Bibliography

MacKie-Mason, Jeffrey and Hal R. Varian, (1995), 'Some economics of the Internet', in Werner Sichel and Donald L. Alexander, (eds), *Networks, Infrastructure and the New Task for Regulation*, Ann Arbor: University of Michigan Press.
Moore, Gordon E. (1965), 'Cramming more components onto integrated circuits', *Electronics*, **38** (8), April.

Mundell–Fleming model

This is an extension of the closed economy IS–LM model to deal with open economy macroeconomic policy issues. There are two ways in which the IS–LM model is expanded. First, it includes the term 'net exports' (NX) in the *IS* curve. Second, it adds a balance of payments equilibrium condition in which net exports equal net foreign investment (NFI). The latter is a function of the domestic interest rate (r), the foreign interest rate (r^*) and the exchange rate (e), following the interest rate parity condition. Prices are assumed to be fixed, both domestically and internationally.

The balance of payments equilibrium condition states that any current account unbalance must be matched with a capital account surplus and vice versa. From this equilibrium condition there can be derived a *BP* curve in the (r, Y) space in which the IS–LM model is represented.

Formally, making exports depend on foreign output, imports depend on domestic output and both on the exchange rate, the equilibrium balance of payment condition can be written as

$$NX\,(e, Y, Y^*) = NFI\,(r, r^*)$$

which can be rewritten as $r = BP(Y)$.

The *BP* curve in the figure is an increasing function, with a smaller slope than the *LM*'s (important for stability). The exchange rate is given along the *BP* curve. Any point above the *BP* curve means that the economy is in a balance of payments surplus, the contrary applying below it. When the *IS* and the *LM* curves, representing the domestic equilibrium, intersect above the *BP* curve, the adjustment will come via an appreciation of the exchange rate under a floating exchange rate regime, or via an inflow of capital and foreign reserves and the corresponding monetary expansion, shifting the *LM* to the right, if the economy has a fixed

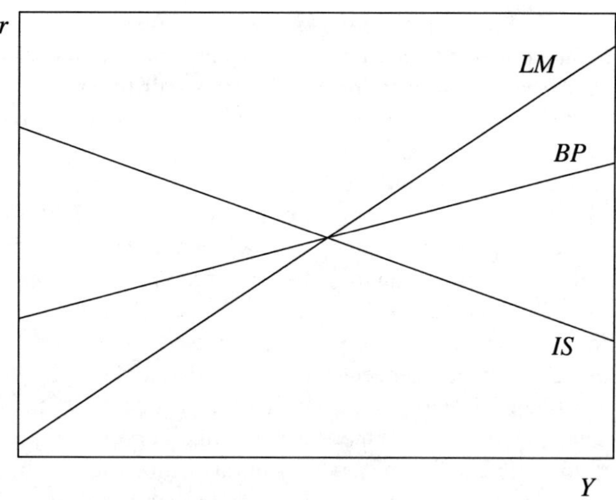

Mundell-Fleming model

exchange rate regime. A small economy version of this model may be written with $r = r^*$ and the *BP* curve being flat.

The main conclusions of the Mundell–Fleming model are the following. An expansionary fiscal policy will raise interest rates and output under a fixed exchange rate regime and, besides these, will appreciate the currency in a floating exchange rate regime. An expansionary monetary policy has no permanent effects under a fixed exchange rate regime (reserves are limited) and will lower interest rates, increase income and depreciate the currency under a floating regime. Further expansions of the Mundell–Fleming model included price variability.

The Mundell–Fleming model was developed in the early 1960s. Interestingly, there was no joint work of the two authors. Both the Robert A. Mundell (b.1932, Nobel Prize 1999) and the J. Marcus Fleming (1911–76) original papers were published in 1962, although Mundell's contributions to the model are collected in four chapters of Mundell (1968), following his 'rule' ('one idea, one paper'). The reason why it is called 'Mundell–Fleming' instead of 'Fleming–Mundell' is that Mundell's work was pioneering and independent of Fleming's, the converse not being true, although both of them worked for the IMF at that time.

MIGUEL SEBASTIÁN

Bibliography

Fleming, J.M. (1962), 'Domestic financial policies under floating exchange rates', *IMF Staff Papers*, **9**, 369–72.

Mundell, R.A. (1968), 'The appropriate use of fiscal and monetary policy under fixed exchange rates', *IMF Staff Papers*, **9**, 70–77.

Mundell, R.A. (1968), *International Economics*, New York: Macmillan.

See also: Hicks–Hansen model.

Musgrave's three branches of the budget

This originated in a methodological artifice of great pedagogical utility, still viable today, devised in 1957 by Richard Musgrave (b.1910). In that contribution a pattern was configured, based on which the process of revenue and public expenditure could be analyzed in mixed market economies. This position attempts to respond to a simple but radical question: why in these economies did an important part of the economic activity have its origin in the public sector's budget?

Musgrave outlines a theory of the optimal budget where, in answer to this query, he affirms that the nature of the diverse functions carried out by the public sector is so heterogeneous that it does not allow a univocal answer. Functions should be distinguished and handled independently, even though they are part of an interdependent system. Musgrave considered it convenient to distinguish three main functions within the public sector budget: to achieve adjustments in the allocation of resources, to make adjustments in the distribution of income and to get economic stabilization. Each of these functions is carried out by a specific branch of the Budget Department. These branches could be denominated respectively the allocation branch, in charge of the provision of public goods from the perspective of economic efficiency, the distribution branch, centered on the modification of income distribution generated by the free interplay of market forces, and the stabilization branch, interested in the infra-utilization of productive resources and global economic stability. This set of functions shows to what extent there is no unique normative rule that guides the budgetary behavior of modern states. On the contrary, there is a multiplicity of objectives identified by the three functions mentioned above that, hypothetically, for wider expositional clarity, we can consider are pursued by the three branches of the budget acting independently.

In this line, one of the basic principles that are derived from the triple classification of budgetary policy is that public expenditure levels and income distribution should be determined independently of the stabilization objective. In the same way, the distinction between allocation and distribution leads us to the principle that (with the purpose of obviating ineffective increments of public expenditure in the name of distributive objectives) redistribution should be carried out fundamentally through the tax system. The difference among functions established by Musgrave is analytical, but this does not exclude the historical perspective. In fact, what Musgrave did was to fuse in a multiple theory the diverse functions assigned to the budget by public finance researchers over time. Indeed, the three functions are precisely the three topics to the study of which public finance researchers have been devoted (the importance given to each varying through time), as can be seen in a brief journey through the history of public finance thought.

Nevertheless, the pedagogical utility of this separation of functions is limited in practice, among other considerations, by the existence of conflicts between the pursued objectives, as the available instruments do not generate effects exclusively on a single branch, but on the set of branches. This division of labor implied by the Musgravian contribution, the author's most significant one, was and still is very attractive. Musgrave's conceptual division of the government's program into allocation, distribution and stabilization branches retains its analytical power. To a great extent this separation of functions has coincided approximately with basic specialization lines in academic economics. The stabilization branch has been developed by macroeconomists, the allocation branch by microeconomists, and the distribution branch by welfare economists, along with contributions from ethical philosophers and political scientists.

José Sánchez Maldonado

Bibliography

Musgrave, R.A. (1957), 'A multiple theory of budget determination', *Finanzarchiv*, New Series **17** (3), 333–43.

Muth's rational expectations

In his pathbreaking paper of 1961, J.F. Muth (b.1930) introduced the simple idea that individuals when making predictions, or forming expectations, use all the information at their disposal in the most efficient way. In spite of being little known for more than a decade, by the end of the 1970s the notion of 'rational expectations' put forward by Muth had had a formidable impact on macroeconomics, on the theory of economic policy, on the use of econometrics models and on finance.

The information available to the individual, his information set, includes the story of both the variable to be forecast and of all other relevant variables, the story of the individual's forecasting errors, and whatever model the individual uses to understand the working of the economy. The efficient use of the information set means forecasting errors are uncorrelated with any element of the information set, including previous forecasting errors. Therefore agents do not make systematic errors when forming their expectations.

Rational expectations were introduced in macroeconomics by Lucas and Sargent and Wallace in order to reinforce the natural rate hypothesis proposed by Friedman. Under rational expectations a systematic monetary policy would not affect the level of income and would affect the price level proportionally (neutrality of money). The result was derived under the assumption that individuals have complete information (they are supposed to know the true model of the economy). But the neutrality result can also be obtained under incomplete information. More crucial happens to be the assumption of market-clearing flexible prices. If for some reason prices do not clear markets, money is not neutral even under rational expectations with complete information.

Rational expectations have had a great impact on the theory of macroeconomic policy. A particular policy would not have the expected effect if it is perceived as transitory or if it is not credible. Policies may not be credible because the Government itself is generally untrustworthy, but economic agents can also react to the inconsistency of particular policies of a Government in which they otherwise trust. There are two types of inconsistencies: (a) contemporaneous inconsistency between two programs (a monetary contraction to reduce inflation contemporaneous to a very expansive fiscal policy) and (b) time inconsistency (individuals' perception that governments will not stick to a policy if it has some cost for them). Moreover, changes in individuals' beliefs (about future policies, or about the equilibrium value of some relevant variable) would alter behavior without a change in policies.

It is usual practice to use econometric models, estimated from a sample period when some policies were implemented, to evaluate how the economy would react if some other program were to be carried out. The Lucas critique claims that this practice is unwarranted. Estimated parameters reflect individuals' behavior, and their decisions are affected by their anticipation of the consequences of policies. Therefore parameters' values depend on the specific policy program adopted. Hence parameters estimated when a different program was in place cannot be used to evaluate new policies. The same applies when an econometric model is used to evaluate a change in the economic environment (a crash in the stock market, for example).

CARLOS SEBASTIÁN

Bibliography

Lucas, R.E. Jr (1976), 'Econometric policy evaluation: a critique', in K. Brunner and A.H. Metzler (eds), *The Phillips Curve and Labor Markets*, Carnegie-Rochester Conference Series on Public Policy, vol. 1, Amsterdam: North-Holland, pp. 19–46.

Muth, J.F. (1961), 'Rational expectations and the theory of price movements', *Econometrica*, **29** (6), 315–35.

Sargent, T.J. (1986), *Rational Expectations and Inflation*, New York: Harper & Row.

Sargent, T.J. and N. Wallace (1976), 'Rational expectations and the theory of economic policy', *Journal of Monetary Economics*, **2**, 169–83.

See also: Lucas critique.

Myerson revelation principle

Under incomplete information, traditional economic theory cannot predict the outcome of an exchange relationship. Game theory, in turn, is able to find the preconditions necessary to reach an agreement, but the predictability of prices is reduced, and therefore the planning capacity of economists (see Mas-Colell *et al.*, 1995, ch. 23). The revelation principle deals with the feasibility of implementation (existence) of a social choice function that is efficient and consistent with individual incentives. Indirectly, it is also related to the design of institutional arrangements that leads to the Pareto-efficient solution in a decentralized economy; so the final aim of this line of work is to improve our collective choice designs.

Economists have a standard definition for the social choice function. However, its classical formulation has an intrinsic limitation: as the utility function parameters are private information of each agent, it is not possible to obtain the composition function. In other words, we cannot know the social preferences without knowledge of the individual ones. Therefore it is required to design a mechanism that induces agents to reveal the true value of their type to make the implementation of the social choice function possible.

An example to illustrate this can be an auction problem with unknown utility functions. Consider a sealed bid auction on a unique and indivisible commodity, with one seller (with zero reservation price) and two bidders (with monetary valuations θ_1; $\theta_2 \geq 0$). Let $\vec{x}$ be the ownership vector. It has three possible configurations, $\vec{x} = (1, 0, 0)$ if no trade happens, $\vec{x} = (0, 1, 0)$ or $\vec{x} = (0, 0, 1)$ if the auction winner is the first or the second person, respectively. On the other side, call $\vec{m}$ the vector of monetary transfers between individuals (as usual a positive number is an inflow). Feasibility implies that the addition of all components of $\vec{m}$ is non-positive: $\Sigma_{i=1}^{3} m_i \leq 0$. Of course, we suppose a strictly positive marginal utility of money. $\hat{\theta}_i$ is the valuation revealed by each bidder.

A simple and (ex post) efficient social choice function is to award the good to the highest bidder, paying the corresponding bid. That is,

$$\begin{cases} \vec{x} = (0, 1, 0), \vec{m} = \hat{\theta}_1(1, -1, 0) & \text{if } \hat{\theta}_1 \geq \hat{\theta}_2 \\ \vec{x} = (0, 0, 1), \vec{m} = \hat{\theta}_2(1, 0, -1) & \text{otherwise.} \end{cases} \tag{1}$$

Nevertheless, as θ_i is private information, each agent has incentives to reveal a valuation inferior to their true preferences (as individuals wish to pay as little as possible for the good), hence $\hat{\theta}_i < \theta_i$. But the bid cannot be too small either, because this reduces the chances of winning the bid, as the other person's valuation is also private information.

Another efficient social choice function is the second-bid auction

$$\begin{cases} \vec{x} = (0, 1, 0), \vec{m} = \hat{\theta}_2(1, -1, 0) & \text{if } \hat{\theta}_1 \geq \hat{\theta}_2 \\ \vec{x} = (0, 0, 1), \vec{m} = \hat{\theta}_1(1, 0, -1) & \text{otherwise.} \end{cases} \tag{2}$$

In this case, the good goes to the highest bidder but the price paid is the second offer (the lowest one). This gives individuals incentives for telling the truth. Individual *i* will not try to reveal a valuation inferior to her own (that is, $\theta_i > \hat{\theta}_i$) as this reduces her chances of winning without a monetary gain, because the payment depends on the other person's bid, but not on her own. Any bet superior to the real value ($\hat{\theta}_i > \theta_i$) is not optimal either because, from that point on, the marginal expected utility becomes negative: the increase in the probability of winning is multiplied by a negative value ($\hat{\theta}_j > \theta_i$). In other words, it does not make any sense to win a bid when your competitor can bet more than your valuation of the good.

Thus the social choice function described in (2) is an efficient implementable function. Even with private information, the incentives scheme compels the individuals to reveal their true preferences. A more detailed example of an implementable social choice function can be found in Myerson (1979, pp. 70–73).

Another perspective from which to study our problem is to investigate the design of an institutional arrangement (in an economic sense) that induces individuals to take the (socially) desired solution. Such an institution is called a 'mechanism'. Of course, the important point is the relationship between a social choice function and a specific mechanism; that is, the mechanism that implements the social choice function f.

The revelation principle offers a frequently applicable solution: if the institution is properly designed so that individuals do not have incentives to lie, it is enough to ask them about their preferences.

JAVIER RODERO-COSANO

Bibliography

Gibbard, A. (1973), 'Manipulation of voting schemes: a general result', *Econometrica*, **41**, 587–601.

Mas-Colell, A., Michael D. Whinston and Jerry R. Green (1995), *Microeconomic Theory*, Oxford: Oxford University Press.

Mirrlees, J. (1971), 'An exploration in the theory of optimum income taxation', *Review of Economic Studies*, **38**, 175–208.

Myerson, R.B. (1979), 'Incentive compatibility and the bargaining problem', *Econometrica*, **47**, 61–73.

See also: Arrow's impossibility theorem, Gibbard–Satterthwaite theorem.

N

Nash bargaining solution

This is a solution, axiomatically founded, proposed by John F. Nash (b.1928, Nobel Prize 1994) in 1950 to the 'bargaining problem'.

A two-person bargaining situation involves two individuals who have the opportunity to collaborate in more than one way, so that both can benefit from the situation if they agree on any of a set of feasible agreements. In this context a 'solution' (in game-theoretic terms) means a determination of the amount of satisfaction each individual should expect to obtain from the situation. In other words: how much should the opportunity to bargain be worth to each of them.

In order to find a solution, the problem is idealized by several assumptions. It is assumed that both individuals are 'highly rational', which means that their preferences over the set of lotteries (that is, probability distributions with finite support) in the set of feasible agreements are consistent with von Neumann–Morgenstern utility theory. In this case the preferences of each individual can be represented by a utility function determined up to the choice of a zero and a scale. It is also assumed that such lotteries are also feasible agreements and that a distinguished alternative representing the case of no agreement enters the specification of the situation.

Then the problem can be graphically summarized by choosing utility functions that represent the individuals' preferences and plotting the utility vectors of all feasible agreements on a plane as well as the disagreement utility vector. It is assumed that the set of feasible utilities $S \subset R^2$ is compact and convex and contains the disagreement point d and some point that strictly dominates d. The bargaining problem is then summarized by the pair (S, d).

A solution is then singled out for every bargaining problem by giving conditions which should hold for the relationship concerning the solution point and the feasible set of each problem. That is, consistently with the interpretation of the solution as a vector of rational expectations of gain by the two bargainers, the following conditions are imposed on *rationality* grounds (denoting by $\Phi(S, d)$ the solution of problem (S, d)).

1. *Efficiency*: if $(s_1, s_2), (s'_1, s'_2) \in S$ and $s_i > s'_i$ (for $i = 1, 2$), then

$$(s'_1, s'_2) \neq \Phi(S, d).$$

A problem (S, d) is symmetric if $d_1 = d_2$ and $(s_2, s_1) \in S$, whenever $(s_1, s_2) \in S$.

2. *Symmetry*: if (S, d) is symmetric, then $\Phi_1(S, d) = \Phi_2(S, d)$.
3. *Independence of irrelevant alternatives*: given two problems with the same disagreement point, (S, d) and (T, d), if $T \subseteq S$ and $\Phi(S, d) \in T$, then $\Phi(T, d) = \Phi(S, d)$.

Given that von Neumann–Morgenstern utility functions are determined up to a positive affine transformation, the solution must be invariant w.r.t. positive affine transformations.

4. For any problem (S, d) and any $a_i, b_i \in R (a_i > 0, i = 1, 2)$, if $T(S, d) = (T(S), T(d))$ is the problem that results from (S, d) by the affine transformation $T(s_1, s_2) = (a_1 s_1 + b_1, a_2 s_2 + b_2)$, then $\Phi(T(S, d)) = T(\Phi(S, d))$.

The first condition shows that rational individuals would not accept an agreement if something better for both is feasible. The second requires that, given that in the model all individuals are ideally assumed equally rational, when the mathematical description of the problem is entirely symmetric the solution should also be symmetric (later, Nash, 1953, replaces this condition with *anonymity*, requiring that the labels, 1 or 2, identifying the players do not influence the solution). The third expresses a condition of rationality (or consistency): if $\Phi(S, d)$ is the utility vector in S associated with the feasible agreement considered the best, and the feasible set shrinks but such point remains feasible, it should continue to be considered optimal when fewer options are feasible.

Under that previous assumption these three conditions determine a unique solution for every bargaining problem, which is given by

$$\Phi(S, d) = \arg \max_{s \in S, s \geq d} (s_1 - d_1)(s_2 - d_2).$$

That is, the point in S for which the product of utility gains (w.r.t. d) is maximized.

In 1953, Nash re-examined the bargaining problem from a non-cooperative point of view, starting what is known now as 'the Nash program'; that is to say, modeling the bargaining situation as a non-cooperative game in which the players' phases of negotiation (proposals and threats) become moves in a non-cooperative model, and obtaining the cooperative solution, an equilibrium. The main achievement in this line of work is Rubinstein's (1982) alternating offers model.

FEDERICO VALENCIANO

Bibliography

Nash, J.F. (1950), 'The bargaining problem', *Econometrica*, **18**, 155–62.

Nash, J.F. (1953), 'Two-person cooperative games', *Econometrica*, **21**, 128–40.

Rubinstein, A. (1982), 'Perfect equilibrium in a bargaining model', *Econometrica*, **50**, 97–109.

See also: Nash equilibrium, von Neumann–Morgenstern expected utility theorem, Rubinstein's model.

Nash equilibrium

The key theoretical concept used in modern game theory is known as 'Nash equilibrium'. Most of the other solution concepts that have been proposed embody a refinement (that is, strengthening) of it. This concept was introduced by John Nash (b.1928, Nobel Prize 1994) in a seminal article published in 1951 as an outgrowth of his PhD dissertation. It embodies two requirements. First, players' strategies must be a best response (that is, should maximize their respective payoffs), given some well-defined beliefs about the strategies adopted by the opponents. Second, the beliefs held by each player must be an accurate ex ante prediction of the strategies actually played by the opponents.

Thus, in essence, Nash equilibrium reflects both rational behaviour (payoff maximization) and rational expectations (accurate anticipation of others' plan of action). Heuristically, it can be viewed as a robust or stable agreement among the players in the following sense: no single player has any incentive to deviate if the others indeed follow suit. It can also be conceived as the limit (stationary) state of an adjustment process where each player in turn adapts optimally to what others are currently doing.

An early manifestation of these ideas can be found in the model of oligopoly proposed by Augustine Cournot (1838). The key contribution of John Nash was to extend this notion of strategic stability to any arbitrary game and address in a rigorous fashion the general issue of equilibrium existence (see below).

To illustrate matters, consider a simple coordination game where two players have to choose *simultaneously* one of two possible actions, A or B, and the payoffs entailed are as follows:

1\2	A	B
A	2, 1	0, 0
B	0, 0	1, 2

In this game, both strategy profiles (*A, A*) and (*B. B*) satisfy (1)–(2), that is, they reflect rational behaviour and rational expectations. The induced equilibrium multiplicity how-ever, poses, a difficult problem. How may players succeed in coordinating their behaviour on one of those two possibilities so that Nash equilibrium is indeed attained? Unfortunately, there are no fully satisfactory answers to this important question. One conceivable alternative might be to argue that, somehow, players should find ways to communicate before actual play and thus coordinate on the same action. But this entails embedding the original game in a larger one with a preliminary communication phase, where equilibrium multiplicity can only become more acute.

Another option is of a dynamic nature. It involves postulating some adjustment (or learning) process that might provide some (non-equilibrium) basis for the selection of a specific equilibrium. This indeed is the route undertaken by a large body of modern literature (cf. Vega-Redondo, 2003, chs 11–12). Its success, however, has been limited to addressing the problem of equilibrium selection only for some rather stylized contexts.

But, of course, polar to the problem of equilibrium multiplicity, there is the issue of equilibrium existence. When can the existence of some Nash equilibrium be guaranteed? As it turns out, even some very simple games can pose insurmountable problems of non-existence if we restrict ourselves to pure strategy profiles. To understand the problem, consider for example the Matching Pennies Game, where two players have to choose simultaneously heads (*H*) or tails (*T*) and the payoffs are as follows:

1\2	H	T
H	1, −1	−1, 1
T	−1, 1	1, −1

In this game, for each of the four possible strategy profiles, there is always a player who benefits from a unilateral deviation. Thus none of them may qualify as Nash equilibrium of the game. Intuitively, the problem is that, given the fully opposite interests of players (that is, if one gains the other loses), accuracy of prediction and individual optimality cannot be reconciled when players' strategies are deterministic or pure. Given this state of affairs, the problem can only be tackled by allowing for the possibility that players can 'hide' their action through a stochastic (mixed) strategy. Indeed, suppose that both players were to choose each of their two pure strategies (heads or tails) with equal probability. Then, even if each player would know that this is the case (that is, beliefs are correct concerning the mixed strategy played by the opponent), neither of them could improve (in expected payoff terms) by deviating from such a mixed strategy. In a natural sense, therefore, this provides accuracy of ex ante beliefs and individual optimality, as required by (1)–(2) above.

Nash (1951) showed that such an extension to mixed strategies is able to tackle the existence issue with wide generality: (Nash) equilibrium – possibly in mixed strategies – exists for all games where the number of players and the set of possible pure strategies are all finite. Building upon this strong existence result, the notion of Nash equilibrium has ever since enjoyed a pre-eminent position in game theory – not only as the main tool used in most specific applications but also as the benchmark concept guiding later theoretical developments.

FERNANDO VEGA-REDONDO

Bibliography

Cournot, A. (1838), *Recherches sur les Principes Mathématiques de la Théoríe des Richesses,* Paris: Hachette.
Nash, J. (1951), 'Non-cooperative games', *Annals of Mathematics*, **54**, 286–95.
Vega-Redondo, F. (2003), *Economics and the Theory of Games,* Cambridge, MA: Cambridge University Press.

See also: Cournot's oligopoly model.

Negishi's stability without recontracting

This is named after Japanese economist Takashi Negishi (b.1933). A fundamental problem beyond the existence of a static competitive general equilibrium consists of establishing a plausible dynamical mechanism whose equilibrium configuration coincides with the static equilibrium solution and enjoys some form of stability. Stability is a crucial dynamical property essentially implying that the whole state space (global stability) or just a neighbourhood of each equilibrium (local stability) asymptotically collapses to equilibria under the action of the dynamics. This property has important economic implications, such as the fact that any set of initial observations of the considered economic variables will converge to market-clearing values under the market dynamics. Furthermore, the equilibrium solution will remain robust under perturbation, in accordance with economic facts.

The modern formulation (after Samuelson) of the Walrasian mechanics for adjustment of the price system in a pure exchange competitive economy with n individual agents and m commodities is typically given by the following system of differential equations

$$\frac{dP_j}{dt} = X_j(P, \bar{X}) - \bar{X}_j \quad j = 1, 2, \ldots, m$$

$$\frac{d\bar{X}_{ij}}{dt} = F_{ij}(P, \bar{X}) \quad i = 1, 2, \ldots, n, j = 1, 2, \ldots, m, \tag{1}$$

where

- $P(t) = (P_1(t), P_2(t), \ldots, P_m(t))$ is the price vector of the economy;
- $\bar{X}(t) = (\bar{X}_{ij}(t))_{1\leq i\leq n, 1\leq j\leq m}$ is a matrix monitoring the distribution of the stock of commodities among agents, so that $\bar{X}_{ij}(t)$ represents the ith agent's holding of the jth good at time t;
- $X_j(P, \bar{X}) = \sum_{i=1}^{n} X_{ij}(P, \bar{X}_i)$ renders the aggregate demand for the jth commodity, the ith agent's demand X_{ij} for the jth good being obtained by maximizing a well-behaved utility function $U_i(X_{i1}, X_{i2}, \ldots, X_{im})$ subject to the budget constraint $\sum_{j=1}^{m} P_j X_{ij} = \sum_{j=1}^{m} P_j \bar{X}_{ij}$;
- F_{ij} are certain prescribed functions, aiming to represent the opportunities for agents to exchange their holdings $\bar{X}_{ij}$ with each other.

Since there is no production, the total amounts of each commodity remain constant, that is, $\bar{X}_j(t) \equiv \sum_{i=1}^{n} \bar{X}_{ij}(t) = \bar{X}_j$ for all t, which in turn requires that $\sum_{i=1}^{n} F_{ij}(P, \bar{X}) = 0$ for $j = 1, 2, \ldots, m$.

The first set of evolution equations in (1) reflects the stylized fact that the marginal variation of a commodity price and the corresponding excess demand have the same sign, whereas the equations of the second set specify how the holdings of agents may evolve in time when exchanged according to the allowed trading rules.

An equilibrium of the system (1) is given by a price vector P^* and a distribution matrix $\bar{X}^*$ such that

$$X_j(P^*, \bar{X}^*) = \bar{X}_j^* \quad \text{for} \quad j = 1, 2, \ldots, m.$$

The dynamical system (1) is globally stable if, for any solution $(P(t), \bar{X}(t))$,

$$(P(t), \bar{X}(t)) \rightarrow (P^*, \bar{X}^*) \quad \text{as} \quad t \rightarrow \infty$$

for some equilibrium $(P^*, \bar{X}^*)$. If the equilibrium points are not isolated, but any solution has equilibrium as limit points, the system is named quasi-stable.

Under the assumption that no actual trade is allowed at disequilibria, it holds that $F_{ij} = 0$, so that not only $\bar{X}_j$ but $\bar{X}$ is a constant matrix, and the model dynamics is steered by the price equations in (1). Although no transaction takes place until equilibrium is reached, recontracting may be permitted. This term refers to a mechanism of fictional trading through which agents renegotiate their demands after learning the prices announced by a market manager, in their turn sequentially computed from a device expressed by (1). This important case corresponds with a so-called *tâtonnement* price adjustment process embodied by the Walrasian auctioneer that manages recontracting.

In the non-recontracting case, holdings among agents vary according to the exchange laws defined in (1) and $\bar{X}$ will not be constant. In order to analyse non-recontracting stability, different specifications of the trading rules defined by the F_{ij} may be considered (Negishi, 1962). Negishi (1961) deals with the general case of a barter exchange process, that is, even though the quantities $\bar{X}_{ij}$ may vary via trading, the total value of the stock of commodities held by each agent is not altered. This amounts to the F_{ij}s satisfying

$$\sum_{j=1}^{m} P_j \frac{d\bar{X}_{ij}}{dt} = \sum_{j=1}^{m} P_j F_{ij} = 0 \quad i = 1, 2, \ldots, n.$$

Negishi showed that any non-*tâtonnement* barter exchange dynamics is quasi-stable in the case that all commodities are (strict) gross substitutes. He also proved that global stability holds under the further assumption that all the agents share the same strictly quasi-concave and homogeneous utility function. Proofs make essential use of Walras's law, that can be derived from the rational behaviour of demanders under standard assumptions.

JOSÉ MANUEL REY

Bibliography

Negishi, T. (1961), 'On the formation of prices', *International Economic Review*, **2**, 122–6.
Negishi, T. (1962), 'The stability of a competitive economy: a survey article', *Econometrica*, **30**, 635–69.

See also: Hicksian perfect stability, Lyapunov stability, Marshall's stability, Walras's auctioneer.

von Neumann's growth model

The John von Neumann (1903–57) model, first published in 1932, is a multisectorial growth model; its crucial characteristics are constant coefficients; alternative technologies, without technical change; joint production; unlimited natural resources and labour force availability.

Joint production makes it feasible to deal with capital goods and depreciation in a special way. A capital good of age t is classified as different from the same good with age $(t + 1)$; this last capital good is the result of a process using the first one in a joint production activity. Model variables are as follows:

- q_{ij} is the stock of input i required to operate process j at unit level;
- s_{ij} is the stock of i produced at the end of period $(t + 1)$ when process j operates at unit level;
- $x_j(t)$ is operational level of activity j, period t;
- $p_i(t)$ is price of product i at the beginning of time period t;

- $r(t)$ is rate of profit corresponding to time period t.

Workers consume a fixed vector. Capitalist are considered as non-consumers. System formalization is as follows. First, total outputs produced at the end of time period t must be greater than or equal to inputs necessary for production at the end of time period $(t + 1)$:

$$\sum_{j=1}^{m} s_{ij}x_j(t) = \sum_{j=1}^{m} q_{ij}x_j(t + 1).$$

Secondly, capitalist competition implies that income processes cannot generate a rate of profit greater than the common rate of profit,

$$[1 + r(t)]\sum_{i=n}^{n} p_i(t)q_{ij} \geq \sum_{i=1}^{n} p_i(t+1)s_{ij}.$$

To close the model we need to add some additional constraints. A group refers to the non-negativity of prices and levels of activity. The rest of the constraints are known as the 'rule of profit' and the 'rule of free goods'. The 'rule of profit' refers to every activity and excludes non-profit activities:

$$[1 + r(t)]\sum_{i=1}^{m} p_i(t)q_{ij} \geq \sum_{i=1}^{m} p_i(t + 1)s_{ij} \Rightarrow x_j(t + 1) \equiv 0.$$

The rule of 'free goods' refers to every good and classifies as free goods those with excess supply,

$$\sum_{j=1}^{m} s_{ij}x_j(t) \geq \sum_{j=1}^{m} q_{ij}x_j(t + 1) \Rightarrow p_i(t) \equiv 0.$$

The von Neumann stationary state verifies

$$p(t + 1) = p(t) = p$$
$$r(t + 1) = r(t) = r$$
$$x(t + 1) = x(t) = (1 + \lambda)\, x(t),$$

where λ is the equilibrated rate of growth, common to all sectors.

Price vectors and activity levels are semipositive; total input and output values are positive and the rate of profit equals the equilibrating rate of growth.

Morishima (1964) has formulated a relevant generalization of the model, considering (a) there is labour force finite growth; (b) workers are consumers, depending on wages and prices; (c) capitalists are also consumers: they consume a constant proportion of their income and are sensitive to prices.

McKenzie (1967), among others, has contributed to exploring the properties of the model.

JOSEP MA. VEGARA-CARRIÓ

Bibliography

McKenzie, L.W. (1967), 'Maximal paths in the von Neumann model', in E. Malinvaud and M. Bacharach (eds), *Activity Analysis in the Theory of Growth and Planning*, London: Macmillan Press, pp. 43–63.

Morishima, M. (1964), *Equilibrium, Stability and Growth*, Oxford: Clarendon Press.

von Neumann, J. (1945–46), 'A model of general economic equilibrium', *Review of Economic Studies*, **13**, 1–9.

von Neumann–Morgenstern expected utility theorem

Modern economic theory relies fundamentally on the theory of choice. The current foundation for the use of utility functions as a way to represent the preferences of so-called rational individuals over alternatives that consist of bundles of goods in various quantities is axiomatic. It is based on the proof that, if individual preferences (understood as binary relations of the type 'bundle $x = a$ is at least as good as bundle x = b' on the set of possible bundles faced by the individual) satisfy some axioms (in particular those of completeness, transitivity and continuity), then one can ensure the existence of a continuous utility function $U(x)$ that represents those preferences. That is, a function that assigns a real number (or utility) to each of the relevant bundles x with the convenient property that, for the represented individual, a bundle a will be at least as good as another bundle b if, and only if, $U(a) > U(b)$. An obvious advantage of having such a function is, for example, that the economic choices of the individual can be mathematically represented as the result of maximizing such utility under the relevant set of constraints imposed by the environment (for example, a budget constraint in the typical static model of consumer theory).

When the alternatives faced by individuals are associated with uncertain outcomes, the theory of choice needs to be extended. The expected utility theorem of John von Neumann (1903–57) and Oskar Morgenstern (1902–77) (1944, pp. 15–31) is the extension that, for more than half a century now, has provided economists (and other interested scientists) with the most powerful tool for the analysis of decisions under uncertainty.

The extension required, in the first place, having a way to represent the risky alternatives. Each risky alternative can be seen as leading to each of n possible outcomes (for example, several bundles of goods, x_1, x_2, . . ., x_n) with some probabilities $p_1, p_2, \ldots p_n$, respectively (for simplicity, the presentation will focus on the choice among alternatives that have a finite number (n) as possible outcomes, but the framework has a natural extension for dealing with infinitely many possible outcomes). A vector of probabilities over the possible outcomes, $L = (p_1, p_2, \ldots p_n)$, is known as a 'lottery'. Individual preferences over risky alternatives can then be thought of as a binary relationship of the type 'lottery $L = a$ is at least as good as lottery $L = b$' over the set of possible lotteries. On such preferences one can impose, perhaps after some technical adaptation, the same rationality and continuity axioms as in the standard theory of choice under certainty.

The important contribution of von Neumann and Morgenstern was, however, to discover that, given the special structure of lotteries (which, contrary to the bundles of goods considered in the theory of choice under certainty, consist of probability distributions on mutually exclusive outcomes), it was reasonable to add an extra axiom to the theory: the 'independence axiom'. In words, this axiom says that, if one makes a probabilistic mix between each of two lotteries and a third one, the preference ordering of the two resulting compound lotteries does not depend on the particular third lottery used. Intuitively, and tracing a parallel with the theory of choice between consumption bundles, the independence axiom rules out the existence of 'complementarity' between the lotteries that form a compound lottery. Imposing the absence of complementarity in this context is natural since each of the lotteries in a probabilistic mix cannot be 'consumed' together but, rather, one instead of the other.

Under the independence axiom, individual preferences over lotteries allow the 'expected utility representation'. In essence, one can prove that there exists an assignment of so-called von Neumann–Morgenstern utilities u_i to each of the $i = 1, 2, \ldots, n$ possible lottery outcomes, such that the utility of any lottery L can be computed as the *expected utility* $U(L) = p_1u_1 + p_2u_2, + \ldots + p_nu_n$ (see Mas-Colell *et al.* (1995, pp. 175–8) for a modern and didactic proof). The reason why $U(L)$ is referred to as the expected utility of lottery L is obvious: it yields an average of the utilities of the various possible outcomes of the lottery weighted by the probabilities with which they occur under the corresponding lottery.

The expected utility theorem has been very useful for the development of the theory of choice under uncertainty and its important applications in modern micro, macro and finance theory. However, the key hypotheses of the theorem, especially the independence axiom, have been criticized from various fronts. Constructed examples of choice between simple lotteries, such as the Allais paradox, show that individuals may frequently behave in a way inconsistent with the hypotheses. Machina (1987) contains a good review of this and related criticisms and the theoretical reaction to them.

JAVIER SUÁREZ

Bibliography

Machina, M. (1987), 'Choice under uncertainty: problems solved and unsolved', *Journal of Economic Perspectives*, **1** (1), 121–54.
Mas-Colell, A., M. Whinston and J. Green (1995), *Microeconomic Theory*, New York: Oxford University Press.
von Neumann, J. and O. Morgenstern (1944), *Theory of Games and Economic Behavior*, Princeton, NJ: Princeton University Press.

See also: Allais paradox, Ellsberg paradox, Friedman–Savage hypothesis.

von Neumann–Morgenstern stable set

A game in characteristic function form is a pair (N, v), where N is the non-empty set of players and v is the characteristic function defined on the family of subsets of N such that $v(\varnothing) = 0$. A non-empty subset of N is called 'coalition' and $v(S)$ is interpreted as the worth of coalition S.

An imputation is any *n*tuple x of real numbers satisfying $x_i \geq v(\{i\})$ for all $i \in N$ and $\Sigma_{i\in N} x_i = v(N)$. An imputation $y = (y_1, \ldots, y_n)$ *dominates* an imputation $x = (x_1, \ldots, x_n)$ with respect to a non-empty coalition S if the following two conditions are satisfied: $\Sigma_{i\in N} y_i \leq v(S)$, and $y_i > x_i$ *for all* $i \in S$.

The first condition admits imputation y as dominating imputation x only if y is feasible in the sense that players in S can guarantee themselves the amount prescribed by y. The second condition implies that every player in S strictly prefers y to x.

A stable set of a game (N, v) is defined to be a set of imputations A such that

- no y contained in A is dominated by an x contained in S (internal stability);
- every y not contained in A is dominated by some x contained in A (external stability).

John von Neumann (1903–57) and Oskar Morgenstern (1902–77) consider a stable set as a characterization of what may be acceptable as a standard of behavior in society. Thus internal stability expresses the fact that the standard of behavior has an inner consistency. It guarantees the absence of inner contradictions. External stability gives a reason to correct deviant behavior that is not conformable to the acceptable standard of behavior.

As an extension of this concept, von Neumann and Morgenstern provide in their book (65.2.1) the basis for a more general theory in the sense that, instead of imputations, they consider an arbitrary set D and an arbitrary relation defined on D.

ELENA IÑARRA

Bibliography

von Neumann, J. and O. Morgenstern, (1944), *Theory of Games and Economic Behavior*, Princeton, NJ: Princeton University Press.

Newton–Raphson method

This method computes zeros of nonlinear functions through an iterative procedure that constructs the best local linear approximation to the function and takes the zero of the approximation as the next estimate for the zero of the function. The method can be easily extended to the computation of solutions for systems of nonlinear equations of the form $F(x) = 0$. In this case, it starts with an initial estimate of the solution x_0, and improves it by computing $x_{k+1} = x_k - \nabla F(x_k)^{-1}F(x_k)$.

The procedure is guaranteed to obtain a solution x^* with arbitrary precision as long as the initial estimate x_0 is close enough to this solution and the Jacobian $\nabla F(x^*)$ is non-singular.

The main application of the method and its variants is the computation of local solutions for unconstrained or constrained optimization problems. These problems arise in multiple contexts in economic theory and business applications. In these cases, the method is applied to the computation of a solution for a system of equations associated with the first-order optimality conditions for such problems.

The method derives its name from Joseph Raphson (1648–1715) and Sir Isaac Newton (1643–1727). Raphson proposed the method for the computation of the zeros of equations that shares his name in a book (*Analysis aequationum universalis*) published in 1690, while Newton described the same method as part of his book *Methodis Serierum et Fluxionem*, written in 1671, but not published until 1736.

F. JAVIER PRIETO

Bibliography

Newton, I. (1736), *Methodis Serierum et Fluxionem.*
Raphson, J. (1690), *Analysis aequationum universalis.*

Neyman–Fisher theorem

Also known as the 'Neyman–Fisher factorization criterion', this provides a relatively simple procedure either to obtain sufficient statistics or to check whether a specific statistic could be sufficient.

Fisher was the first to establish the factorization criterion as a sufficient condition for sufficient statistics in 1922. Years later, in 1935, Neyman demonstrated its necessity under certain restrictive conditions. Finally, Halmos and Savage extended it in 1949 as follows:

> Let $\wp = \{P_\theta, \theta \in \Omega\}$ be a family of probability measures on a measurable space (Θ_X, A) absolutely continuous with respect to a σ-finite measure μ. Let us suppose that its probability densities in the Radon–Nicodym sense $p_\theta = dP_\theta/d\mu$ exist a.s. [μ] (almost sure for μ).
>
> A necessary and sufficient condition for the sufficiency with respect to $\wp$ of a statistic T transforming the probability space (Θ_X, A, P_θ) into (Θ_T, B, P_T) is the existence $\forall \theta \in \Omega$ of a $T^{-1}(B)$-measurable function $g_\theta T(x)$ and an A-measurable function $h(x) \neq 0$ a.s. $[P_\theta]$, both defined $\forall x \in \Theta_x$, non-negatives and μ-integrable, such that $p_\theta(x) = g_\theta T(x) \cdot h(x)$, a.s. [μ].

Densities p_θ can be either probability density functions from absolutely continuous random variables or probability functions from discrete random variables, among other possibilities, depending on the nature and definition of μ.

In common economic practice, this factorization criterion adopts simpler appearances. Thereby, in estimation theory under random sampling, the criterion is usually enounced as follows:

> Let X be a random variable belonging to a regular family of distributions $F(x; \theta)$ which depends on a parameter θ (mixture of absolutely continuous and discrete random variables on values not depending on the parameter) representing some characteristic of certain population. Moreover, let $x = (X_1, X_2, \ldots, X_n)$ represent a random sample size n of X, extracted from such a population.
>
> A necessary and sufficient condition for the sufficiency of a statistic $T = t(x)$ with respect to the family of distributions $F(x; \theta)$ is that the sample likelihood function $L_n(x; \theta)$ could be factorized like $L_n(x; \theta) = g(T; \theta) \cdot h(x)$. Here '$g$' and '$h$' are non-negative real functions, 'g' depending on sample observations through the statistic exclusively and 'h' not depending on the parameter.

When the random variable is absolutely continuous (discrete), function $g(t; \theta)$ is closely related to the probability density function (probability function) of the statistic T. Thus the criterion could be equivalently enounced assuming the function $g(t; \theta)$ to be exactly such probability density function (probability function). In this case, the usually complex work of deducing the distribution $x \mid T$ of the original observations conditioned to the statistic T becomes easier, being specified by $h(x)$. According to this factorization criterion, any invertible function of a sufficient statistic $T^* = k(T)$ is a sufficient statistic too.

Likewise, an exponential family defined by probability density functions such as $f(x; \theta) = k(x) \cdot p(\theta) \cdot \exp[c(\theta)'T(x)]$ always admits a sufficient statistic T.

FRANCISCO J. CALLEALTA

Bibliography

Fisher, R.A. (1922), 'On the mathematical foundation of theoretical statistics', *Philos. Trans. Roy. Soc.*, Series *A*, **222**, 309–68.

Halmos, P.R. and L.J. Savage (1949) 'Application of the Radon–Nikodym theorem to the theory of sufficient statistics', *Ann. Math. Statist.*, **20**, 225–41.

Neyman, J. (1935), 'Sur un teorema concernente le cosidette statistiche sufficienti', *Giorn. Ist. Ital. Att.*, **6**, 320–34.

Neyman–Pearson test

This is a framework for hypothesis testing that differed considerably from Fisher's, giving rise to some controversy. Nowadays, it is the basis of modern hypothesis testing.

Egon S. Pearson (1895–1980), son of Karl Pearson, was born in England. He joined his father's department at University College, London. When his father resigned, he assumed one of the two positions created as replacements, the second position being for R.A. Fisher. Jerzy Neyman (1894–1981) was born in Russia. He went to England to work with Karl Pearson and then started to work with E.S. Pearson, on a general principle for hypothesis testing.

Testing a null hypothesis was introduced by Fisher as a procedure to form an opinion about some parameter. A limitation in Fisher's formulation is that for each null hypothesis one could construct several test statistics, without providing a way to choose the most appropriate. Conversely, Neyman and Pearson (1928) viewed hypothesis testing as a means to decide between two options: the null hypothesis (H_0) and the alternative hypothesis (H_1), while at the same time controlling the chances of errors. The Neyman–Pearson specification of both hypotheses is $H_0{:}\theta\in\Omega_0$, against $H_1{:}\theta\in\Omega_1$, $\Omega_0\cap\Omega_1 = 0$. The two errors here are rejecting H_0 if it is true (type I error), and accepting it when it is false (type II error). Through the design of the test it is possible to control the probability of each error. There is, however, a trade-off between them.

Given a test statistic $\delta(x)$, we reject H_0 when $\mid \delta(x) \mid > c$ (for some constant c). The probability of type I error is, then, $P(\mid \delta(x) \mid > c); H_0 \text{ true}) = \alpha$ and it is often called the size of the test. In the Neyman–Pearson test, H_0 is more important than H_1. Consequently, the analyst should choose a small α. Given α, the analyst chooses the test statistic that minimizes the type II error. Neyman and Pearson (1933) solve the problem of obtaining a statistical test in order to obtain an optimal test (minimizing type II error). The limitation however, is, that they provide optimal tests only in one simple case. Let $f(x; \theta)$ denote the distribution of the sample (density function or mass function). Let us consider testing H_0: $\theta = \theta_0$ against H_1: $\theta = \theta_1$, using a test with rejection region R defined as

$$x\in R \text{ if } f(x; \theta_1) > kf(x; \theta_0), \qquad (1a)$$

$$x\in R^c \text{ if } f(x; \theta_1) \leq kf(x; \theta_0), \qquad (1b)$$

for some $k \geq 0$ and $P(X\in R \mid \theta = \theta_0) = \alpha$. Then, by the Neyman–Pearson lemma, such a test is an optimal test of size α. Also, if there exists a test satisfying (1), then every optimal test of size α coincides with (1). Hence, should an optimal test exist, it is a function of $f(x, \theta_1)/f(x; \theta_0)$. The specific form of such a function can be a complex problem that needs to be solved in each situation. There have been some extensions of this lemma that makes it possible to build nearly optimal tests in more complex problems.

ISMAEL SÁNCHEZ

Bibliography

Neyman, J. and E.S. Pearson (1928), 'On the use and interpretation of certain test criteria for purposes of statistical inference, part I', *Biometrika*, **20**, 175–240.

Neyman, J. and E.S. Pearson (1933), 'On the problem of the most efficient tests of statistical hypothesis', *Philosophical Transactions of the Royal Society, A*, **231**, 289–337.

O

Occam's razor

This is a logical principle named after the medieval Franciscan friar–philosopher William of Occam (1285?–1349?), stating that the number of entities required to explain anything should not be increased unnecessarily. This principle is also called the law of economy, parsimony or simplicity. It is usually interpreted as 'the simpler the explanation, the better'. Sometimes it is quoted in one of its original Latin forms, 'pluralitas non est ponenda sine necessitate', 'frustra fit per plura quod potest fieri per pauciora' or 'entia non sunt multiplicanda praeter necessitatem'. A basic scientific principle, it can heuristically distinguish theories that make the same predictions, and indicate which to test first, but does not guarantee the finding of a correct answer.

VICTORIANO MARTÍN MARTÍN

Bibliography

Occam, W. (1324), *Quodlibetal Questions*, Quodlibeta no. 5, 9,1, art. 2.

Thorburn, W.M. (1918), 'The myth of Occam's razor', *Mind*, **27**, 345–53.

Okun's law and gap

Okun's law is the empirical regularity between unemployment rate and GNP first estimated by Arthur M. Okun (1928–80), Chairman of the Council of Economic Advisers in the 1960s.

According to Okun, 'in the postwar period [and in the US economy], on average, each extra percentage point in the unemployment rate above four per cent has been associated with about a three per cent decrement in real GNP' (Okun, 1983, pp. 146, 148). Almost two decades after the result was first published (in 1962), Okun wrote:

> Nearly twenty years ago, I found in the data of the fifties an approximate rule of thumb that an increase of one percentage point in unemployment was associated with a decrement of about three percentage points in real GNP. The rule of thumb held up so well over the next decade that some of my professional colleagues named it 'Okun's Law'. (Okun, 1981, p. 228).

In J. Tobin's words, it became 'one of the most reliable empirical regularities of macroeconomics' (Tobin, 1987, p. 700). The result was arrived at after implementing three statistical methods, thereby giving rise to three versions of the 'law'.

First differences (growth) version

Using quarterly observations from 1947 to 1960, Okun estimated the following linear regression

$$\Delta U_t = 0.30 - 0.30 g_t,$$

where ΔU_t denotes the change in unemployment rate and g_t the growth rate of real GNP (both U_t and g_t measured in percentage points). Therefore, 'for each extra one per cent of *GNP*, unemployment is 0.3 points lower' (Okun, 1983, p. 148). Assuming (as Okun did) that the previous estimation could be inverted, one would obtain the more usual textbook way in which the growth version of the law is expressed,

$$g_t = 1 - 3.3\Delta U_t,$$

so that 'one percentage more in the unemployment rate means 3.3 per cent less GNP' (ibid.).

Concerning the intercept of the equation, a constant unemployment rate is associated with a positive (full employment) output growth rate because of (a) gains in labour productivity (due to technological progress and to physical and human capital accumulation), and (b) growth in the labour force. As for the slope, several factors explain why reductions in the unemployment rate should induce higher proportional increments in the output growth rate around its trend (or why the estimated coefficient of ΔU_t should be greater than one). Higher participation rates due to less discouraged workers; increased number of hours per worker (not necessarily in the same job); lower on-the-job unemployment (labour hoarding); and more intensive use of plant and equipment.

Trial gaps (level) version

Alternatively, using quarterly observations from 1953 to 1960, Okun estimated also the following regression:

$$U_t = 3.72 + 0.36gap_t,$$

where U_t stands for unemployment rate and gap_t is the (estimated) GNP gap (both in percentage points), where the potential GNP was 'derived from a 3.5 per cent trend line through actual real GNP in mid-1955' (Okun, 1983, p. 149). Assuming once again that the estimation could be inverted, one obtains

$$gap_t = 2.8\ (U_t - 3.72).$$

Therefore 'an increment of unemployment of one per cent is associated with an output loss equal to 2.8 per cent of potential output (. . .). The estimated unemployment rate associated with a zero gap is 3.72 per cent, not too far from the 4.0 per cent ideal' Okun claimed as a principle that 'potential GNP should equal actual GNP when $U = 4$', and textbooks usually refer to this rate as the natural rate of unemployment when explaining Okun's law (ibid. p. 149). This version of Okun's result stresses its economic policy- oriented relevance: 'Focus on the "gap" helps to remind policymakers of the large reward [in terms of increased production] associated with such an improvement [the reduction of the unemployment rate]' (ibid., p. 146). Had other factors been controlled for in the regression, the effect of unemployment would of course have been substantially reduced (Prachowny, 1993, Freeman, 2001).

Fitted trend and elasticity version

Finally, in a less cited version, Okun confirmed his rule of thumb without assuming a trend for the potential output but rather estimating it, claiming that 'each one percentage point reduction in unemployment means slightly less than 3 per cent increment in output (near the potential level)' (Okun, 1983, p. 150).

Is the three-to-one ratio a true 'law', valid at any time and everywhere? Clearly not. As Okun himself admitted, 'During the late seventies, the three-to-one ratio no longer approximated reality' (Okun, 1981, p. 228). Considering, for instance, the growth version of the law for different countries, two patterns for the coefficient (in absolute value) of g_t clearly show up. First, it differs across economies: countries whose firms offer their workers a high level of job stability and where labour market rigidities are stronger usually display lower coefficients. And, second, it has increased over time. Several reasons are pointed out for structural breaks in the dynamics of output and unemployment: augmented international competition among world economies has forced firms to be less committed to job stability, fewer legal restrictions on hiring and firing have reduced turnover costs and labour hoarding by firms, and increased female participation implies higher competition among workers.

CRUZ ANGEL ECHEVARRÍA

Bibliography

Freeman, D.G. (2001), 'Panel tests of Okun's law for ten industrial economies', *Economic Inquiry*, **39** (4), 511–23.

Okun, A.M. (1981), *Prices and Quantities: A Macroeconomic Analysis*, Washington, DC: The Brookings Institution.

Okun, A.M. (1983), 'Potential GNP: its measurement and significance', in Joseph A. Pechman (ed.), *Economics for Policy Making, Selected Essays of Arthur M. Okun*, Cambridge, MA: MIT Press, pp. 145–58; article first published (1962) in *Proceedings of the Business and Economic Statistics Section, American Statistical Association*, Washington: ASA, 98–103.

Prachowny, M.F.J. (1993), 'Okun's law: theoretical foundations and revised estimates', *The Review of Economics and Statistics*, **75** (2), 331–6.

P

Paasche index

The Paasche price index, P_p, is a weighted aggregate index proposed by German economist H. Paasche (1851–1925), defined as

$$Pp = \frac{\sum_{i=1}^{n} p_{it} q_{it}}{\sum_{i=1}^{n} p_{i0} q_{it}}$$

where p_{it} is the price of commodity i ($i = 1, \ldots, n$) in period t, q_{it} is the quantity of such a commodity in that period, and p_{i0} is the price of commodity i in period 0 (the base year). The numerator of P_p shows the cost of a basket of goods purchased in the year t at prices of that year, whereas the denominator displays the cost of the same basket of goods at the base year prices. As in the case of the Laspeyres index, P_p allows computing the rate of variation of the value of a basket of goods, with the difference that the Paasche index uses the current quantities as weights (q_{it}). Therefore, as the weights vary through time, P_p is not an accurate index to use on a continuing basis (it is not used, for example, for the construction of the consumer price index, because it would need to carry out a permanent consumption survey). Moreover, P_p tends to underestimate the effect of a price increase, because it uses the current year quantities as weights, which are likely to be smaller than in the base year when prices increase.

If prices are used as weights instead of quantities, it is possible to compute the Paasche quantity index, P_q, defined as

$$Pq = \frac{\sum_{i=1}^{n} q_{it} p_{it}}{\sum_{i=1}^{n} q_{i0} p_{it}},$$

This index is used in the consumer theory to find out whether the individual welfare increases from period 0 to period t. If P_q is greater than 1, it is possible to state that the consumer welfare is greater at the current year than in the base year.

CÉSAR RODRÍGUEZ-GUTIÉRREZ

Bibliography

Allen, R.G.D. (1975), *Index Numbers in Theory and Practice*, Chicago: Aldine Publishing Company.

See also: Divisia index, Laspeyres index.

Palgrave's dictionaries

The *Dictionary of Political Economy*, edited by Sir R.H. Inglis Palgrave (1827–1919), a one-time banker, author of different writings on aspects of banking practice and theory, and editor of *The Economist*, appeared in three volumes in 1894, 1896 and 1899. These were reprinted, with corrections and additions, during the first two decades of the twentieth century. A new edition by H. Higgs was published between 1923 and 1926 under the title *Palgrave's Dictionary of Political Economy*. The primary object of this was 'to provide the student with such assistance as may enable him to understand the position of economic thought at the present time and to pursue such branches of inquiry as may be necessary for that end'.

These goals were reasonably well

fulfilled. Palgrave was fortunate in being able to enlist the support of important scholars, such as W.J. Ashley, E. Cannan, F.Y. Edgeworth, J.K. Ingram, J.N. Keynes, M. Pantaleoni, H.R. Tedder and H. Sidgwick. Edgeworth's 126 entries were enough to confer distinction on the Dictionary. Six decades later, it was edited as *The New Palgrave: A Dictionary of Economics*. Launched in 1982, with all four volumes available by 1987, it contains approximately 2000 articles, written by more than 900 contributors; 50 entries from the original Palgrave were reprinted here (these were selected to emphasize the continuity between the 'old' Palgrave and the 'new').

Both the great increase in its size and the fact that it required three editors (J. Eatwell, M. Milgate and P. Newman) are evidence of the vitality of economics in the twentieth century. The *New Palgrave* attempts to define the state of the discipline by presenting a comprehensive and critical account of economic thought. Like its predecessor, it strives to place economic theory in historical perspective. It includes over 700 biographical entries – even some on living economists aged 70 or more in 1986. Most articles are followed by a useful bibliography.

Despite its broad scope, some of the editors's choices have been questioned: The *New Palgrave* virtually excludes empirical material; the mathematical aspects of modern economics do not receive sufficient attention and neither do institutional and policy issues; finally, it is strongly oriented to the presentation of Sraffian, Marxian and Post-Keynesian doctrine. Nevertheless, it is an unquestionably authoritative reference work on economic theory and the work of those economists who contributed to its development.

JESÚS ASTIGARRAGA

Bibliography

Milgate, M. (1987), 'Palgrave, Robert Harry Inglis (1827–1919)', 'Palgrave's *Dictionary of Political Economy*', in J. Eatwell, M. Milgate and P. Newman (eds), *The New Palgrave: A Dictionary of Economics*, vol. III, London: Macmillan, pp. 789–92.

Milgate, M. (1992), 'Reviewing the reviews of the New Palgrave', *Revue Européenne des Sciences Sociales*, **30** (92), 279–312.

Stigler, G.J. (1988), 'Palgrave's Dictionary of Economics', *Journal of Economic Literature*, **26** (4), 1729–36.

Palmer's rule

This empirical rule was adopted in 1827 and formulated in 1832 in a memorandum by G.W. Norman, of the Board of Directors of the Bank of England, with margin notes by John Horsley Palmer, governor of the bank. It established that, in normal times, the bank had to keep reserves of currency and precious metals equivalent to a third of its liabilities (total deposits and notes issued), with the other two-thirds in government securities and other interest-yielding assets. Once this portfolio had been established, the bank's active transactions (discounts, loans and investments) had to be kept approximately constant, so that changes in currency circulation would be due to gold entering or leaving the country. In this way, the circulation would behave as if it were metallic. The rule, on some occasions broken, was in line with the theories of the currency school as part of its debate during the first half of the nineteenth century with the banking school, providing the ideal basis for a permanent currency policy for the central bank. According to Schumpeter, it anticipates the principle of Peel's law (1844) and might be adopted pending some regulation of this type.

ANTÓN COSTAS

Bibliography

Horsefield, J.K. (1949), 'The opinions of Horsley Palmer', *Economica*, **16** (62), May, 143–58;

reprinted in T.S. Ashton and R.S. Sayers, (eds) (1953), *Papers in English Monetary History*, Oxford: Clarendon Press, pp. 126–31.
Viner, J. (1937), *Studies in the Theory of International Trade*, New York: Harper & Brothers.

See also: Peel's law.

Pareto distribution

This is a power law distribution coined after the Italian economist Vilfredo Pareto (1848–1923) in 1897. He questioned the proportion of people having an income greater than a given quantity x and discovered that this was proportional to an inverse power of x. If P denotes the probability or theoretical proportion and X the income or any other random variable following a Pareto law, the formal expression for the answer, in terms of the cumulative distribution function is $P(X > x) = (k/x)^{\alpha}$ for $X > k$. The value k is the minimum value allowed for the random variable X, while the (positive) parameter α is the power law slope. If α is less than one, there is no finite mean for the distribution. If it is less than two, there is no finite variance, and so on. In general, the tails in this distribution are fatter than under the normal distribution. An interesting property is that the distribution is 'scale-free', which means that the proportion of small to large events is always the same, no matter what range of x one looks at. This is very useful for modelling the size of claims in reinsurance.

EVA FERREIRA

Bibliography

Pareto, Vilfredo (1897), *Cours d'Economie Politique*, Lausanne: Rouge.

Pareto efficiency

Modern welfare economics is based on the notion of efficiency (or optimality) proposed by Vilfredo Pareto (1909). To give a formal definition, consider an *exchange economy* with m consumers and n goods, where each consumer i is characterized by a consumption set $X_i \subset R^n$, preferences over consumption bundles described by a utility function u_i: $X_i \to R$, and an initial endowment $e_i \in R^n$. An *allocation* is an m-tuple $x = (x_1, \ldots, x_m)$ such that $x_i \in X_i$ for all i, and

$$\sum_{i=1}^{m} x_i = \sum_{i=1}^{m} e_i.$$

In words, an allocation is a distribution of the economy's aggregate endowment among the consumers such that the bundle corresponding to each consumer belongs to her consumption set. An allocation x is said to be Pareto-efficient if there is no allocation $x' = (x'_1, \ldots, x'_m)$ such that $u_i(x'_i) \geq u_i(x_i)$ for all i and $u_i(x'_i) > u_i(x_i)$ for some i, that is, if it is impossible to make any consumer strictly better off without making some other consumer worse off. It is important to realize that, in general, there are infinitely many Pareto-efficient allocations, so it is a weak notion of efficiency. Moreover, it is a notion that ignores distributional issues that require interpersonal comparisons of utilities. Thus extremely unequal allocations may be Pareto-efficient.

The key insight of Pareto (1909, mathematical appendix) was to link his notion of efficiency with the properties of competitive equilibrium allocations. A *competitive equilibrium* is a pair (p, x) where $p \in R^n$ is a price vector and x is an allocation such that, for all i, x_i maximizes $u_i(x_i)$ subject to the budget constraint $p \cdot x_i \leq p \cdot e_i$. The first welfare theorem states that, if (p, x) is a competitive equilibrium, then under very weak assumptions x is Pareto-efficient. This result formalizes the intuition of Adam Smith that a set of individuals pursuing their own interests through competitive markets leads to an efficient allocation of resources. The second welfare theorem states that, if x is a Pareto-efficient allocation, then under somewhat stronger assumptions there exists a price vector p such that (p, x) is a competitive equilibrium for a suitable redistribution of the initial endowments. This result shows how competitive markets may be used to decentralize any Pareto-efficient allocation.

Somewhat surprisingly, the proof of the first welfare theorem is almost trivial. Suppose, on the contrary, that there exists an allocation x' such that $u_i(x'_i) \geq u_i(x_i)$ for all i, and $u_i(x'_i) > u_i(x_i)$ for some i. Then the definition of competitive equilibrium (together with a very weak assumption on preferences like local non-satiation) implies that $p \cdot x'_i \geq p \cdot e_i$ for all i, with strict inequality for some i, so

$$p \cdot \sum_{i=1}^{m} x'_i > p \cdot \sum_{i=1}^{m} e_i,$$

contradicting the assumption that

$$\sum_{i=1}^{m} x'_i = \sum_{i=1}^{m} e_i.$$

The notion of Pareto efficiency as well as the welfare theorems can be easily extended to economies with production. They can also be extended to economies with uncertainty, although this requires the existence of a complete set of contingent markets. With incomplete markets, competitive equilibrium allocations are not in general Pareto-efficient, although in certain special cases they can be shown to be 'constrained Pareto-efficient', that is efficient relative to the set of available markets. For a thorough discussion of these issues, as well as complete proofs of the welfare theorems, see Mas-Colell *et al.* (1995, chs 16, 19).

The notion of Pareto efficiency is also used outside the field of competitive equilibrium analysis. For example, in cooperative game theory it is one of the assumptions that characterize the Shapley value, in cooperative bargaining theory it is one of the axioms used to derive the Nash bargaining solution, and in social choice theory it is one of the assumptions in the proof of Arrow's impossibility theorem.

RAFAEL REPULLO

Bibliography

Mas-Colell, A., M.D. Whinston and J.R. Green (1995), *Microeconomic Theory*, Oxford: Oxford University Press.

Pareto, V. (1909), *Manuel d'Économie Politique*, Paris: Giard et Brière.

See also: Adam Smith's invisible hand, Arrow's impossibility theorem, Arrow–Debreu general equilibrium model, Nash bargaining solution, Shapley value.

Pasinetti's paradox

As is well known, the factor–price curve ($w - r$) has a negative slope. When we consider several $w - r$ curves generated by different techniques, nothing excludes multiple intersections, with the possibility of return of techniques; as a matter of fact, it is easy to build numerical examples. This fact has analytical implications that we will analyse briefly.

We will use the factor–price curve (Figure 1) as the tool for analysis. Formula (1) refers to one specific linear technique and can be focused in terms of k, the intensity of capital; k is ABC tangent:

$$q = rk + w$$
$$k = (q - w)/r \qquad (1)$$

Consider now two techniques, a and b (Figure 2); technique a corresponds to the straight line. Technique a is used when r is small; at the transition point from technique a to b, k decreases. If r increases, the technique used is b and, as can be seen, k increases. If r rises, technique a is again used and at the transition point from technique a to b, k increases: A is a reswitching point.

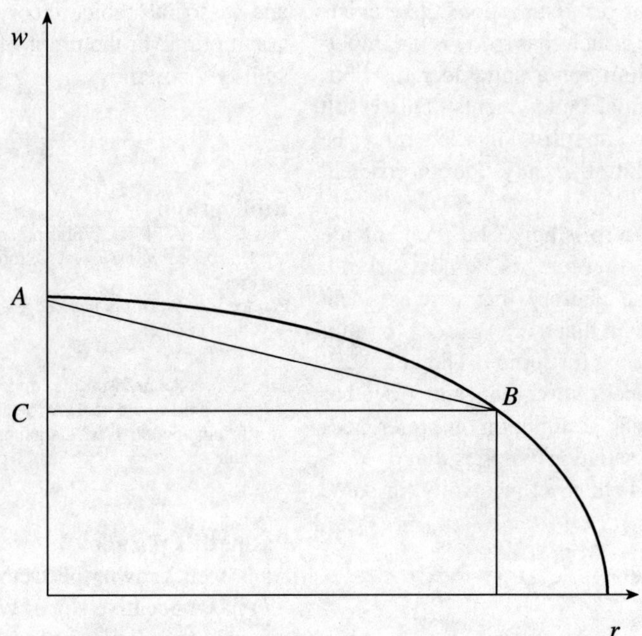

Pasinetti's paradox, technique a

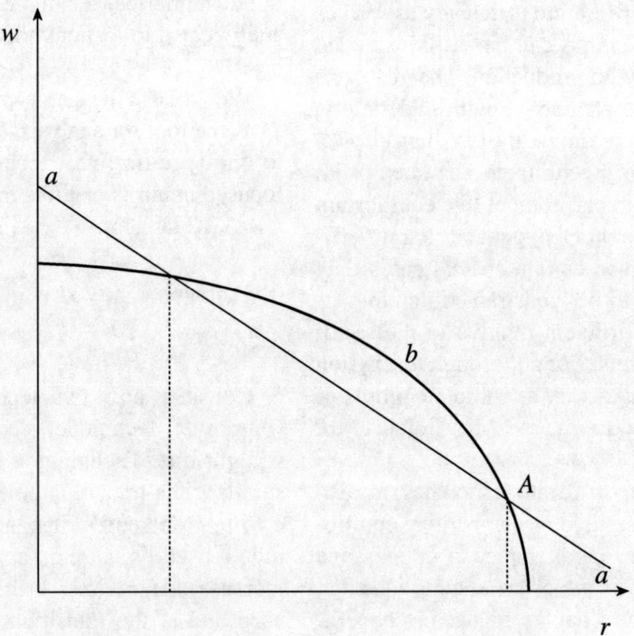

Pasinetti's paradox, technique b

This simple analysis has relevant consequences:

- reswitching destroys the view of a monotonous order of techniques, in terms of *k*;
- reduction of *r* does not necessarily increase capital intensity;
- the rate of profit is not a capital scarcity indicator.

These are the main reasons for the central role reswitching has played in the so-called 'Cambridge controversy on capital' (see L.L. Pasinetti, P.A. Samuelson and R.M. Solow, among others).

JOSEP MA. VEGARA-CARRIÓ

Bibliography

Burmeister, E. (1980), *Capital Theory and Dynamics*, Cambridge: Cambridge University Press.

Samuelson, P.A. and F. Modigliani (1966), 'The Pasinetti paradox in neoclassical and more general models', *Review of Economic Studies*, **33** (4), 269–301.

Patman effect

Increasing interest rates fuel inflation. Named after American lawyer and congressman Wright Patman (1893–1976), a scathing critic of the economic policies of President Herbert Hoover and Secretary of the Treasury Andrew Mellon, the term was coined or at least used by James Tobin (1980, p. 35) in his discussion of stabilization and interest costs. Driskill and Shiffrin (1985) said that under certain circumstances the interest rate effect on price levels may be a matter of macroeconomic concern, although their model 'does not support Patman's view that it is senseless to fight inflation by raising interest rates' (ibid., 160–61). Seelig (1974) concluded that only if interest rates had been double their average values in the period 1959–69 would they have become an important determinant of prices. Driskill and Shiffrin add:

> Monetary economists have always had an uneasy relationship with the populist view, associated with the late Congressman Wright Patman, that high interest rates 'cause' inflation. While interest rates are indeed a cost of doing business and may affect price determination, the traditional position of monetary economists is that restrictive monetary policy will, in the long run, reduce both inflation and interest rates. (1985, 149)

Myatt and Young (1986) pointed out that macroeconomics models focused on aggregate demand of the 1950s or 1960s were unable to assess the Patman effect, and that the theoretical studies of the aggregate supply, after the OPEC oil prices shocks, had come to reveal other ways in which high interest rates may have inflationary effects. They conclude: 'There is no evidence of a Patman effect in the recent era of the US economy. There is evidence, however, of inflation having a strong causal influence on both nominal and real interest rates' (113).

ROGELIO FERNÁNDEZ DELGADO

Bibliography

Driskill, R.A. and S.M. Sheffrin (1985), 'The "Patman effect" and stabilization policy', *Quarterly Journal of Economics*, **100** (1), 149–63.

Myatt A. and G. Young (1986), 'Interest rates and inflation: uncertainty cushions, threshold and "Patman" effects', *Eastern Economic Journal*, **12** (2), 103–14.

Seelig, Steven (1974), 'Rising interest rates and cost push inflation', *Journal of Finance*, **29** (4), 1049–61.

Tobin, James (1980), 'Stabilization policy ten years after', *Brookings Papers on Economic Activity*, **1**, 19–89.

Peacock–Wiseman's displacement effect

These two British authors, Alan Turner Peacock (b.1922) and Jack Wiseman (b.1919), observed that public expenditure increased in the UK between 1890 and 1955. However, it did not rise at a more or less regular rate, but showed a series of plateaux and peaks, which seemed to be associated with periods of war or of preparation for war.

On the basis of these data, they formulated their 'displacement effect' hypothesis:

1. Governments try to increase public expenditure but they cannot go further than the burden of taxation considered tolerable by their citizens.
2. From time to time, there are some major social disturbances, such as warfare. During the periods when citizens accept additional tax increases, their higher tolerance explains the peaks and the so-called 'displacement effect'.

Once the disturbance is over, citizens will probably continue to tolerate a higher tax burden, allowing in this way for public expenditure in new services. Therefore each plateau after a peak will be higher than the previous one. Peacock and Wiseman call this second step the 'inspection effect'. They admit, nevertheless, that this hypothesis does not explain the growth of public expenditure in all countries and at all times, and also that changes in public expenditure can be influenced by a number of different factors.

Many authors have included the 'displacement effect' in a secular rising tendency of the share of the public expenditure with sporadic upward shifts of the trend line.

JUAN A. GIMENO

Bibliography

Henrekson, M. (1993), 'The Peacock–Wiseman hypothesis', in N. Gemmel (ed.), *The Growth of the Public Sector*, Aldershot, UK and Brookfield, US: Edward Elgar, pp. 53–71.

Peacock, A. and J. Wiseman (1961), *The Growth of Public Expenditure in the United Kingdom*, Princeton, NJ: Princeton University Press.

See also: Wagner's law.

Pearson chi-squared statistics

Let $Y_1, Y_2, \ldots, Y_n$ be a random sample of size n with discrete realizations in $\chi = \{1, 2, \ldots, k\}$ and iid. according to a probability distribution $p(\theta)$; $\theta \in \Theta$. This distribution is assumed to be unknown, but belonging to a known family,

$$P = \{p(\theta) \equiv (p_1(\theta), \ldots, p_k(\theta)) \colon \theta \in \Theta\},$$

of distribution on χ with $\Theta \subset R^t (t < k - 1)$. In other words, the true value of the parameter $\theta = (\theta_1, \ldots, \theta_t) \in \Theta$ is assumed to be unknown. We denote $\hat{p} = (\hat{p}_1, \ldots, \hat{p}_k)$ with

$$\hat{p}_j = \frac{Xj}{n},$$

where X_j is the number of data taking the value j; $j = 1, \ldots, k$.

The statistic $(X_1, \ldots, X_k)$ is obviously sufficient for the statistical model under consideration and is multinomial distributed; that is, for $\theta \in \Theta$,

$$Pr(X_1 = x_1, \ldots, X_k = x_k) = \frac{n!}{x_1! \ldots x_k!} p_1(\theta)^{x_1} \times \ldots \times p_k(\theta)^{x_k} \quad (1)$$

for integers $x_1, \ldots, x_k \geq 0$ such that $x_1 + \ldots + x_k = n$.

To test the simple null hypothesis,

$$H_0\colon p = p(\theta_0), \quad (2)$$

where θ_0 is prespecified, the Pearson's statistic, X^2, is given by

$$X^2(\theta_0) \equiv \sum_{j=1}^{k} (X_j - np_j(\theta_0))^2 / np_j(\theta_0). \quad (3)$$

A large observed value of (3) leads to rejection of the null hypothesis H_0, given by (2). Karl Pearson (1857–1936) derived in 1900 the asymptotic (as sample size n increases) distribution of $X^2(\theta_0)$ to be a chi-squared distribution with $k - 1$ degrees of freedom as $n \to \infty$, where k is fixed. Thus, if $X^2(\theta_0) >$

$\chi^2_{k-1,\alpha}$ (the 100α per cent quantile of a chi-squared distribution with $k - 1$ degrees of freedom) then the null hypothesis (2) should be rejected at the 100α per cent level. The assumption that k is fixed is important because, if $k \to \infty$ when $n \to \infty$, then the asymptotic null distribution of (3), under some regularity conditions, is a normal distribution instead of a chi-squared distribution.

If the parameter $\theta \in \Theta$ is unknown, it can be estimated from the data $X_1, \ldots, X_n$. If the expression (1) is almost surely (a.s.) maximized over $\Theta \subset R^t$ at same $\hat{\theta}$, then $\hat{\theta}$, is the maximum likelihood point estimator. Consider now the more realistic goodness-of-fit problem of testing the composite null hypothesis:

$$H_0: p = p(\theta); \quad \theta \in \Theta \subset R^t (t < k - 1). \quad (4)$$

The Pearson's statistic $X^2(\hat{\theta})$, under the null hypothesis (4), converges in distribution to the chi-squared distribution with $k - t - 1$ degrees of freedom as $n \to \infty$, where k is assumed to be fixed.

LEANDRO PARDO

Bibliography

Bishop, Y.M.M., S.E. Fienberg and P.M. Holland (1975), *Discrete Multivariate Analysis: Theory and Practice*, Cambridge, MA: The MIT Press.

Peel's law

Principle established by the Bank Charter Act of 1844 and the British Bank Act of 1845, both promoted under the administration of Sir Robert Peel (1788–1850), so that bank notes would be issued 'on a par', that is note for gold. This measure, like the restoration of the gold standard in 1816, the Resumption Act of 1819, also by Peel, and Palmer's rule, responded to a strong current of public and political opinion in England that attributed the crisis of the first third of the nineteenth century to the irresponsible issuing of notes and certificates on the part of banks. The intention and effect of Peel's law was to compel local banks to stop issuing certificates and limit the issuing of notes. This legislation tried to put into practice the theory that bank transactions must be separated from currency control. It was in line with the theories of the currency school which, in its controversy with the banking school, in order to carry out effective control of the money supply, defended a restrictive conception of payment means limited to Bank of England notes, 100 per cent cover of gold reserves for notes, and the centralization of these reserves in the Bank of England.

ANTÓN COSTAS

Bibliography

Kindleberger, Charles P. (1984), *A Financial History of Western Europe*, London: George Allen & Unwin.
Viner, J. (1937), *Studies in the Theory of International Trade*, New York: Harper & Brothers.
Whale, P.B. (1944), 'A retrospective view of the Bank Charter Act of 1844', *Economica*, **11**, 109–11.

See also: Palmer's rule.

Perron–Frobenius theorem

The names of Oskar Perron (1880–1975) and Ferdinand Georg Frobenius (1849–1917) come together in the so-called Perron–Frobenius theorem, that states the remarkable spectral properties of irreducible non-negative matrices: they have a simple positive dominant eigenvalue (the so-called 'Frobenius root'), with a positive associated eigenvector. Moreover, no other eigenvalue has a non-negative eigenvector associated, and the Frobenius root increases with the entries of the matrix.

In his 1907 paper, Perron proves the result for positive matrices, namely those matrices whose entries are all positive numbers. A similar result was obtained by Frobenius in 1908. Then, in 1912, he introduced the concept of irreducibility and generalized the previous result.

This remarkable result was rediscovered by economists as a consequence of their investigations on the input–output analysis initiated by Wassily Leontief. McKenzie (1960) and Nikaido (1970) provide an interesting unifying view of the main results related to non-negative matrices and input–output analysis. Further applications, in particular in a dynamical setting, have been widely used, and numerous extensions of the Perron–Frobenius theorem have appeared in recent literature.

CÁRMEN HERRERO

Bibliography

Frobenius, G. (1908), 'Uber Matrizen aus Positiven Elementen', *Sitzungberiche der Königlichen Preussien Akademie der Wissenscahften*, pp. 471–3; 1909, pp. 514–18.

Frobenius, G. (1912), 'Uber Matrizen aus Nicht Negativen Elementen', *Sitzungberiche der Königlichen Preussien Akademie der Wissenscahften*, pp. 456–77.

McKenzie, L.W. (1959), 'Matrices with dominant diagonals and economic theory', in K.J. Arrow, S. Karlin and P. Suppes (eds), *Mathematical Methods in the Social Sciences*, Stanford: Stanford University Press, 1960.

Nikaido, H. (1970), *Introduction to Sets and Mappings in Modern Economics*, Amsterdam: North-Holland, (Japanese original Tokyo, 1960).

Perron, O. (1907), 'Zur Theorie der Matrizen', *Mathematischen Annalen*, **64**, 248–63.

See also: Leontief model.

Phillips curve

This has been, and still is, a very important instrument in macroeconomic analysis. The original work is due to the New Zealander A.W. Phillips (1914–75), who, using English data for the period 1861–1957, discovered that the relationship between wage inflation and unemployment was negative. When unemployment was high inflation was low and vice versa.

Later on, P. Samuelson and R. Solow undertook the same kind of exercise using data for the USA and for the period 1900–1960. They also concluded that, with some exceptions, the data showed a negative relation between unemployment and inflation.

The relevance of the Phillips curve for economic policy derives from one clear implication: it seemed that economies could choose between different combinations of unemployment and inflation. 'We can achieve a lower level of unemployment experiencing a higher level of inflation' was the underlying belief on which many macroeconomic policies were designed until the 1970s, when the relation between these two variables was no longer evident. At the end of the 1970s and through the 1980s, economies experienced increases in inflation together with increases in unemployment; that is to say, stagflation.

The theoretical and empirical work that has been undertaken on the Phillips curve has been enormous. It is impossible to do justice to all, but we can concentrate on some results. The case for the stable trade-off was shattered, on the theoretical side, in the form of the natural rate hypothesis of Friedman (1968) and Phelps (1968). These two authors argued that the idea that nominal variables, such as the money supply or inflation, could permanently affect real variables, such as output or unemployment, was not reasonable. In the long run, the behaviour of real variables is determined by real forces.

Besides, the research showed that, if expectations about inflation were included in the theoretical models, instead of only one Phillips curve there was a family of Phillips curves, the position of each one depending on the expectation held at each period of time. The point at which expectations and realizations about prices or wages coincide was the point at which current unemployment and the natural unemployment rate or, better, the rate of structural unemployment, were equal.

When expectations about price or wage inflation are considered there is a need to model the way in which they are formed. The two main hypotheses developed in economic theory, adaptive expectations and rational expectations, have also played an important role in the discussion of the Phillips curve.

When expectations are modelled as adaptive (agents look at the past in order to generate expectations for the future) the distinction between the short and long run is important. Economic agents will probably make mistakes in their predictions about price inflation in the short run, but this will not happen in the long run because it is natural to assume that they can, and will, learn from experience. If expectations are wrong (short–run) the Phillips curve can be negatively sloped, but in the long run (when expectations are correct), the Phillips curve will be a vertical line at the structural unemployment level. In this last case the implication that there was a trade-off between inflation and unemployment is no longer true.

When agents form their expectations about prices or wages in a rational way, results differ. The distinction between the short and the long run ceases to matter. Rational expectations mean that 'on average' agents will not make mistakes in their predictions or that mistakes will not be systematic. Rationality on expectation formation implies that the Phillips curve will not have a negative slope; on the contrary the economy will experience, 'on average', a vertical Phillips curve. The possibility of choosing between inflation and unemployment and the possibility of relying on this trade-off for designing economic policy have practically disappeared.

This is clearly shown in the Lucas (1972) imperfect information model that implies a positive relationship between output and inflation – a Phillips curve. Although the statistical output–inflation relationship exists, there is no way of exploiting the trade-off because the relationship may change if policymakers try to take advantage of it. One more step in the argument allows us to understand why the Phillips curve is the most famous application of the Lucas critique to macroeconomic policy.

The consensus nowadays is that economic policy should not rely on the Phillips curve except exceptionally and in the short run. Only then can monetary or fiscal policy achieve increases in output (decreases in unemployment) paying the price of higher inflation. These increases, though, will only be temporary. The natural unemployment or the structural unemployment rate, the relevant ones in the medium or long term, cannot be permanently affected by aggregate demand policies.

CARMEN GALLASTEGUI

Bibliography

Friedman M. (1968), 'The role of monetary policy', *American Economic Review*, **58**, 1–17.

Lucas, Robert E., Jr (1972), 'Expectations and the neutrality of money', *Journal of Political Economy*, **75**, 321–34.

Phelps, Edmund S. (1968), 'Money–wage dynamics and labour market equilibrium', *Journal of Political Economy*, **76** (2), 678–711.

Phillips, A.W. (1958), 'The relationship between unemployment and the rate of change of money wages in the United Kingdom, 1861–1957', *Economica*, **25**, 283–99.

See also: Friedman's rule for monetary policy, Lucas critique, Muth's rational expectations.

Phillips–Perron test

The traditional Dickey–Fuller (DF) statistics test that a pure AR(1) process (with or without drift) has a unit root. The test is carried out by estimating the following equations:

$$\Delta y_t = (\rho_n - 1)y_{t-1} + \varepsilon_t \qquad (1)$$

$$\Delta y_t = \beta_{0c} + (\rho_c - 1)y_{t-1} + \varepsilon_t \qquad (2)$$

$$\Delta y_t = \beta_{0c\tau} + \beta_{1ct} + (\rho_{c\tau} - 1)y_{t-1} + \varepsilon_t. \qquad (3)$$

For equation (1), if $\rho_n < 1$, then the data generating process (GDP) is a stationary zero-mean AR(1) process and if $\rho_n = 1$, then the DGP is a pure random walk. For equation (2), if $\rho_c < 1$, then the DGP is a stationary AR(1) process with mean $\mu_c/(1 - \rho_c)$ and if $\rho_n = 1$, then the DGP is a random walk with a drift μ_n. Finally, for equation (3), if $\rho_{c\tau} < 1$, then the DGP is a trend-stationary AR(1) process with mean

$$\frac{\mu_{c\tau}}{1 - \rho_{c\tau}} + \gamma_{c\tau}\sum_{j=0}^{t}[\rho_{c\tau}^{j}(t - j)]$$

and if $\rho_{c\tau} = 1$, then the GDP is a random walk with a drift changing over time. The test is implemented through the usual *t*-statistic on the estimated $(\rho - 1)$. They are denoted τ, τ_μ and τ_τ, respectively. Given that, under the null hypothesis, this test statistic does not have the standard *t* distribution, Dickey and Fuller (1979) simulated critical values for selected sample sizes.

If the series is correlated at a higher order lag, the assumption of white noise disturbance is violated. An approach to dealing with autocorrelation has been presented by Phillips (1987) and Phillips and Perron (1988). Rather than including extra lags of Δy_t (as in the augmented Dickey–Fuller test), they suggest amending these statistics to allow for weak dependence and heterogeneity in ε_t. Under such general conditions, a wide class of GDPs for ε_t such as most finite order ARIMA (*p*, 0, *q*) models, can be allowed. The procedure consists in computing the DF statistics and the using of some non-parametric adjustment of τ, τ_μ and τ_τ in order to eliminate the dependence of their limiting distributions on additional nuisance parameters stemming from the ARIMA process followed by the error terms. Their adjusted counterparts are denoted $Z(\tau)$, $Z(\tau_\mu)$ and $Z(\tau_\tau)$, respectively.

For regression model (1), Phillips and Perron (PP) define

$$Z(\tau) = (\hat{S}/\hat{S}_{Tm})\tau - 0.5\,(\hat{S}_{Tm}^2/\hat{S}^2)\left\{\hat{S}_{Tm}^2 T^{-2}\sum_{i=2}^{T}(y_{t-1}^2)\right\}^{-1/2},$$

where T is the sample size and m is the number of estimated autocorrelations; $\hat{S}$ and τ are, respectively, the sample variance of the residuals and the *t*-statistic associated with $(\rho_c - 1)$ from the regression (1); and $\hat{S}_{Tm}^2$ is the long-run variance estimated as

$$\hat{S}_{Tm}^2 = T^{-1}\sum_{t=1}^{T}\varepsilon_t^2 + 2T^{-1}\sum_{s=1}^{l} w_{sm}\sum_{t=s+1}^{T}\hat{\varepsilon}_t\hat{\varepsilon}_{t-s},$$

where $\hat{\varepsilon}$ are the residuals from the regression (1) and where the triangular kernel $w_{sm} = [1 - s(m + 1)]$, $s = 1, \ldots, m$ is used to ensure that the estimate of the variance $\hat{S}_{Tm}^2$ is positive.

For regression model (2), the corresponding statistic is

$$Z(\tau_\mu) = (\hat{S}/\hat{S}_{Tm})\tau_\mu - 0.5\,(\hat{S}_{Tm}^2/\hat{S}^2)T\left\{\hat{S}_{Tm}^2\sum_{2}^{T}(y_t - \bar{y}_{-1})^2\right\}^{-1/2},$$

where $\hat{S}$ and $\hat{S}_{Tm}$ are defined as above, but with residuals from equation (2); $\bar{y}_{-1} = (T - 1)^{-1}\sum_2^T y_{t-1}$, and τ_μ is the *t*-statistic associated with $(\rho_n - 1)$ from the regression (2).

Finally, for regression model (3) we have

$$Z(\tau_\tau) = (\hat{S}/\hat{S}_{Tm})\tau_\tau - (\hat{S}_{Tm}^2 - \hat{S}^2)T^3\{4\hat{S}_{Tm}[D_{xx}]^{1/2}\}^{-1},$$

where $\hat{S}$ and $\hat{S}_{Tm}^2$ are defined as above, but with the residual obtained from the estimation of (3). τ_τ is the *t*-statistic associated with $(\rho_{c\tau} - 1)$ from the regression (3). D_{xx} is the determinant of the regressor cross product matrix, given by

$$\begin{aligned} D_{xx} = {} & [T^2(T^2 - 1)/12]\sum y_{t-1}^2 - T(\sum t y_{t-1})^2 + \\ & T(T + 1)\sum t y_{t-1}\sum y_{t-1} - \\ & [T(T + 1)(2T + 1)/6](\sum y_{t-1})^2. \end{aligned}$$

The PP statistics have the same limiting distributions as the corresponding DF and

ADF statistics, provided that $m \to \infty$ as $T \to \infty$, such that $m/T^{1/4} \to 0$.

SIMÓN SOSVILLA-RIVERO

Bibliography

Dickey, D.A. and W.A. Fuller (1979), 'Distribution of the estimators for autoregressive time series with a unit root', *Journal of the American Statistical Association*, **74**, 427–31.

Phillips, P.C.B. (1987), 'Time series regression with a unit root', *Econometrica*, **55**, 277–301.

Phillips, P.C.B. and P. Perron (1988), 'Testing for a unit root in time series regression', *Biometrika*, **75**, 335–46.

See also: Dickey–Fuller test.

Pigou effect

The Keynesian transmission mechanism of monetary policy relies on the presence of some sort of nominal rigidity in the economy, so that a monetary expansion can have an effect on three crucial relative prices: the real interest rate, the real exchange rate and real wages. Thus a fall in the real interest rate will boost current demand by inducing firms and households to advance their purchases of durable goods. Also, in an open economy, monetary policy may affect the real exchange rate, increasing net exports. Finally, nominal rigidities bring about changes in real wages and mark-ups that induce firms to supply the amount of goods and services that is needed to meet the additional demand.

Arthur C. Pigou (1877–1959) was a professor of Political Economy at Cambridge during the first decades of the twentieth century. Although his work focused mainly on welfare economics, he also made substantial contributions to macroeconomics (Pigou, 1933). In his work, Pigou argued that monetary policy could have a substantial impact on real variables, over and above its effects on relative prices, and in particular even if the interest rate does not change. Real balances may increase after a monetary expansion if some prices adjust slowly. To the extent that real balances are perceived as part of households' financial wealth, this leads to a rise in consumption and output. This channel through which monetary policy affects output and employment is known as the Pigou or 'real balance' effect. It was later generalized by some authors (for example Modigliani, 1963) to consider the effect of total financial wealth on consumption (the wealth effect).

The Pigou effect was seen as a way of overcoming the 'liquidity trap' that an economy can fall into during deep recessions. If the demand for money becomes infinitely elastic at low interest rates, further increases in the money supply will be of little help to set the main channel of the Keynesian transmission mechanism in motion. If the reduction in nominal rates does not take place and expected inflation is low, then real interest rates will hardly react to monetary impulses, failing to bring about the additional demand. This feature of the Pigou effect has contributed to putting it back into the limelight when some economies in severe recessions have faced very low inflation rates and the nominal interest is close to the zero bound.

Some economists have criticized the disproportionate focus on interest rates by many central banks when conducting their monetary policies, with total disregard for the evolution of monetary aggregates (James Tobin, 1969). If money has a direct effect on output and inflation that is not captured by the evolution of the interest rate, the latter cannot be a sufficient instrument to conduct a sound monetary policy. The economic literature has turned its attention to those mechanisms that may explain such a direct effect. The Pigou effect is one of them; others include non-separability between real balances and consumption in households' preferences (so that the marginal utility of consumption is not independent of money), the effect of monetary policy on the spread among the returns of different assets, the presence of liquidity constraints or interest rate premia in external borrowing that may be alleviated by increases in the money supply.

Despite the substantial attention that the direct effect of monetary aggregates on economic activity has stirred recently, a fair appraisal of the real balance effect tends to diminish its importance as a relevant piece of the monetary transmission mechanism. Some authors have found a (small) direct effect of real balances on output, but the Pigou effect is not likely to be the best candidate to account for this. For one thing, the monetary base makes up only a tiny proportion of households' total wealth. Besides, price rigidity is not an immanent feature of the economy; rather, it changes over time and it becomes less severe as economies become more competitive.

JAVIER ANDRÉS

Bibliography

Modigliani, F. (1963), 'The monetary mechanism and its interaction with real phenomena', *Review of Economics and Statistics*, **45** (1), 79–107.

Pigou, Arthur. C. (1933), *The Theory of Employment*, London: Macmillan.

Tobin, J. (1969), 'A general equilibrium approach to monetary theory', *Journal of Money, Credit, and Banking*, **1**, 15–29.

See also: Keynes effect, Keynes's demand for money.

Pigou tax

A Pigou tax is a tax levied on the producer of a negative externality in order to discourage her activity and thus to achieve the social optimum. Similarly, a Pigou subsidy can be advocated to encourage an activity that creates a positive externality.

The idea was introduced by the English economist Arthur C. Pigou in his book *The Economics of Welfare* (1920). Pigou extended Alfred Marshall's concept of externalities. In particular, he first distinguished between marginal social costs and marginal private costs, and between marginal social benefits and marginal private benefits. The Pigou tax aims to 'internalize the externality' by adjusting the private costs to account for the external costs. Thus the externality-generating party will bear the full costs of her activity: that is, her private costs as perceived after introducing the tax are equal to the social costs. Formally, the Pigou tax is a per unit tax equal to the difference between the marginal social costs and marginal private costs at the optimal level of production.

This work provided the first basis for government intervention to correct market failures. Indeed, this approach has an important drawback: the government must have perfect information about costs.

Pigou's analysis was predominant until the 1960s, when Ronald Coase demonstrated its irrelevance if property rights are properly assigned and the people affected by the externality and the people creating it could easily get together and negotiate. Nonetheless, most economists still regard Pigou taxes on pollution as a more feasible and efficient way of dealing with pollution (see Baumol and Oates, 1988).

PEDRO ALBARRÁN

Bibliography

Baumol, W.J. and W.E. Oates (1988), *The Theory of Environmental Policy*, Cambridge University Press.

Pigou, A.C. (1920), *The Economics of Welfare*, London: Macmillan.

See also: Coase theorem, Marshall external economies.

Pigou–Dalton progressive transfers

A universal agreement on the meaning of 'inequality' is obviously out of the question, yet we all would agree that a distribution in which everybody has exactly the same income is less unequal than another one in which the same total income is allocated to one person only, leaving the rest with zero income. Can we go beyond agreeing on the ranking of such extreme distributions?

Dalton (1920) proposed a criterion designed to gain widespread acceptability: 'if we transfer one unit of income from anyone to a person with lower income, the resulting distribution should be considered less unequal than the original one'.

Atkinson (1970) gave new life to this intuitive criterion when he demonstrated that it is equivalent to all risk-averse utilitarian social welfare functions preferring one distribution over the other, and also equivalent to the Lorenz curve of one distribution lying everywhere above the other. This principle has nothing to offer when two distributions differ by a mix of progressive and regressive (towards higher incomes) transfers, or when the two distributions have a different total income.

Nowadays the Pigou–Dalton principle is the cornerstone of inequality measurement and is unquestionably taken as universally acceptable. Yet, in many experiments people often rank distributions violating the Pigou–Dalton principle. Is this principle that 'natural'? Indeed, a continued sequence of such transfers would end up in a perfectly egalitarian distribution. Suppose that we measure the task still ahead by the share of total income which remains to be transferred to achieve perfect equality. Consider now a progressive transfer between two individuals both above the mean income. This would leave the share to be transferred unchanged because, on our way towards full equality, this transfer will eventually have to be undone. To continue on this line, consider now all possible progressive transfers among individuals above the mean, combined with transfers among the ones below the mean (but no transfer across the mean). The end distribution will have the population concentrated on two points: the conditional expected incomes above and below the mean. It is unclear that this bipolar distribution should be considered as less unequal than the original one.

JOAN M. ESTEBAN

Bibliography

Atkinson, A.B. (1970), 'On the measurement of inequality', *Journal of Economic Theory*, **2**, 244–63.
Dalton, H. (1920), 'The measurement of the inequality of incomes', *Economic Journal*, **30**, 348–61.

See also: Atkinson's index, Lorenz curve.

Poisson's distribution

Siméon-Denis Poisson (1781–1840) formulated in 1837 a probability distribution now commonly called the Poisson distribution.

A random variable X taking values over the set 0, 1, 2, 3 . . . (count variable) is said to have a Poisson distribution with parameter μ ($\mu > 0$) if its probability function is $P(X = k) = e^{-\mu}\mu^k/k!$, for $k = 0, 1, 2, \ldots$. The parameter μ is the expectation of X, that is, representing its population mean. Poisson derived this distribution as a limit to the binomial distribution when the chance of a success is very small and the number of trials is large. If $\mu > 10$, Poisson distribution can be approximated by means of the Gaussian distribution.

Many phenomena can be studied by using the Poisson distribution. It can be used to describe the number of events that occur during a given time interval if the following conditions are assumed:

1. The number of events occurring in non-overlapping time intervals are independent.
2. The probability of a single event occurring in a very short time interval is proportional to the length of the interval.
3. The probability of more than one event occurring in a very short time interval is negligible.

Hence a Poisson distribution might describe the number of telephone calls arriving at a telephone switchboard per unit time, the number of people in a supermarket checkout line or the number of claims incoming to an insurance firm during a period of time.

From a practical point of view, an important tool related to the Poisson distribution is the Poisson regression. This is a method for the analysis of the relationship between an observed count with a Poisson distribution and a set of explanatory variables.

PEDRO PUIG

Bibliography

Poisson, S.D. (1837), *Recherches sur la probabilité des jugements en matière criminelle et en matière civile, précédés des règles générales du Calcul des Probabilités*, Paris: Bachelier.

See also: Gaussian distribution.

Poisson process

Siméon-Denis Poisson (1781–1840) published the fundamentals of his probability ideas in 1837.

Let $\{N(t),t = 0, 1, 2, \ldots\}$ be a counting process in discrete time, where $N(t)$ is the total number of events occurred up to time t. $N(t)$ is a 'Poisson process' if its probability function $p_n(t) = P(N(t) = n)$, $n = 0, 1, 2, \ldots$, is the solution of the following system of differential equations

$$\left.\begin{array}{l} p'_n(t) = -\lambda \cdot p_n(t) + \lambda \cdot p_{n-1}(t) \\ p'_0(t) = -\lambda \cdot p_0(t) \end{array}\right\} n \geq 1$$

with $\lambda > 0$. Thus it can be interpreted as a pure birth process, with instantaneous birth rate λ. The previous system leads to

$$p_n(t) = \frac{(\lambda t)^n}{n!} \cdot e^{-\lambda t}, n = 0, 1, 2, \ldots,$$

corresponding to a Poisson distribution with parameter λt, $\wp(\lambda t)$. An important property is that the time elapsed between two successive occurrences is exponentially distributed with mean $1/\lambda$

This stochastic process can also be defined assuming only independent increments, $N(0) = 0$ and a Poisson probability function $\wp(\lambda t)$. Alternatively, the Poisson process can be obtained as a renovation process. Because of these mild conditions, the Poisson process is a powerful tool with applications in economics, finance, insurance and other fields.

This homogeneous version (λ does not depend on t), is the simplest. However, it can be generalized in several ways, obtaining spatial, non-homogeneous or compound processes, among others.

JOSE J. NÚÑEZ

Bibliography

Poisson, S.D. (1837), *Recherches sur la probabilité des jugements en matière criminelle et en matière civile, précédées des règles générales du Calcul des Probabilités*, Paris: Bachelier.

See also: Poisson's distribution.

Pontryagin's maximum principle

Many classes of decision problems in economics can be modelled as optimization programmes, where for example the agents maximize their utility under constraints on their decisions. In some particular cases the goal is to find the best values for some variables that control the evolution of a system, continuously through time. The Pontryagin maximum principle provides a set of necessary conditions that the solution of such a control problem must satisfy, and a procedure to compute this solution, if it exists.

Let $x(t)$ denote a piecewise-differentiable n-dimensional state vector and $u(t)$ a piecewise-continuous m-dimensional control vector, defined on the fixed time interval $[0, T]$. The associated control problem is to find the values of x and u that solve the following:

$$\max. \int_0^T f(t, x(t), u(t))dt$$

subject to

$$x'(t) = g(t, x(t), u(t)), \quad x(0) = x_0$$
$$u(t) \in U,$$

where the functions f and g are continuously differentiable. The maximum principle states that necessary conditions for $x^*(t)$ and $u^*(t)$ to be optimal for the preceding problem are that there exist a constant λ_0 and continuous functions $\lambda(t)$, not all of them identical to zero, such that (1) at all $t \in [0, T]$, except perhaps at discontinuity points of $u^*(t)$, it holds that

$$\lambda'(t) = -\nabla_x H(t, x^*(t), u^*(t), \lambda(t)), \quad \lambda(T) = 0$$

where the Hamiltonian function H is defined as

$$H(t, x, u, \lambda) = \lambda_0 f(t, x, u) + \sum_{i=1}^{n} \lambda_i g_i(t, x, u);$$

and (2) for each $t \in [0, T]$, for all $u \in U$ it holds that

$$H(t, x^*(t), u, \lambda(t)) \leq H(t, x^*(t), u^*(t), \lambda(t)).$$

These conditions also provide a procedure to compute a solution for the control problem: given values for the control variables $u(t)$, optimal values can be obtained for the adjoint variables $\lambda(t)$ from (1), and for the state variables $x^*(t)$ from $x'(t) = g(t, x(t), u^*(t))$; these values can then be used to compute optimal values for the control variables $u^*(t)$ from (2).

This result is due to the Russian mathematician Lev Semenovich Pontryagin (1908–88). Pontryagin graduated from the University of Moscow in 1929; despite being blind as a result of an accident at age 14, he carried out significant work in the fields of algebra and topology, receiving the Stalin prize in 1941, before changing his research interests to the fields of differential equations and control theory, around 1950. In 1961, he published, jointly with three of his students, a book where he proposed and proved the maximum principle described above; Pontryagin received the Lenin prize for this book.

FRANCISCO JAVIER PRIETO

Bibliography

Pontryagin, L.S., V.G. Boltyanskii, R.V. Gamkrelidze and E.F. Mishchenko (1962), *The Mathematical Theory of Optimal Processes* (trans. K.N. Trirogoff, ed. L.W. Neustadt), Interscience, New York: John Wiley.

Ponzi schemes

These are economic strategies in which borrowers link continuous debt contracts as a method of financing outstanding debts. Minsky was probably the first economist to use the concept 'Ponzi financing unit' to characterize some economic agents whose behaviour generate financial instability (1975, p. 7). A Ponzi agent is an entrepreneur who invests in the long term using credit to finance that expenditure. This agent knows that there is no possibility of being able to pay even the interest commitments with his net income cash receipts. Therefore he must continuously demand new credits to pay off old debts. The rationale of this high-risk strategy is based on the hope that, in the long term, the level of the 'Ponzi agent' earnings will be high enough to pay off the debt. These economics agents are very vulnerable to any change in money market conditions. Any unexpected increase in interest rates affects their debt commitments, and as their earnings will be obtained in the long period, the possibility of succeeding in this strategy will be really low. The larger the number of these Ponzi agents the most fragile the financial system will be. The 'Ponzi concept', coined by Minsky, has been used by some economists to explain experiences of financial markets instability and some of the financial problems in transition market economies.

Recently, the expression 'Ponzi scheme' has been used in a more general sense, extending the concept to a pure financial context. In this new ground a Ponzi agent will be a borrower who continuously incurs debts knowing that, to return capital and interest debts, he will have to incur new debts perpetually. In this modern view, a Ponzi scheme or game is not necessarily a destabilizing system; a Ponzi finance unit could follow a fully rational strategy, as long as decisions form a sequence of loan market transactions with positive present value (O'Connell and Zeldes, 1988, p. 434). Most present works based on the Ponzi approach focus on the experiences of public debt policies, social security systems and public pension funds. Although he did not use explicitly the term 'Ponzi game', this idea was first presented by Diamond in 1965, using an overlapping generations model. He underlined the existence of a perpetual flow of new lenders (new generations) who enable governments to issue new public debt as a strategy for financing old debt. These new researchers are trying to ascertain the conditions under which governments following a Ponzi scheme can be considered sound (Blanchard and Weil, 1992; Bergman, 2001).

Although his eponym is not necessarily used in a pejorative way in economic theory, Charles Ponzi was in fact a swindler. He was an Italian immigrant who settled in Boston at the beginning of the twentieth century. In December 1919, he founded The Securities Exchange Company, with the apparent objective of obtaining arbitrage earnings from operations of postal reply coupons in signatory countries of the Universal Postal Convention. To finance these operations he issued notes payable in 90 days, with a 50 per cent reward. But his real business was to pay off the profits of old investors with the deposits of new ones. Finally, in August 1920, he was charged with fraud and jailed for three and half years. His adventure had lasted eight months.

ANA ESTHER CASTRO

Bibliography

Bergman, M. (2001), 'Testing goverment solvency and the no ponzi game condition', *Applied Economics Letters*, **8** (1), 27–9.

Blanchard, O. and P. Weil (1992), 'Dynamic efficiency, the riskless rate, and debt Ponzi games and the uncertainty', NBER Working Paper 3992.

Minsky, H.P. (1975), 'Financial resources in a fragile financial environment', *Challenge*, **18**, 6–13.

O'Connell, S.A. and S.P. Zeldes (1988), 'Rational Ponzi games', *International Economic Review*, **29** (3), 431–50.

Prebisch–Singer hypothesis

Argentinian economist Raúl Prebisch (1901–86) was the first Secretary General of the United Nations Commission for Latin America (UNCLA) and, between 1964 and 1969, Secretary General of the United Nations Conference on Trade and Development (UNCTAD). Hans Singer was born in Germany in 1910 and studied at Bonn and Cambridge; his early publications were surveys on the problem of unemployment under the supervision of J.M. Keynes; in 1947, he began to work for the United Nations.

Like Prebisch, Singer exerted a huge influence upon the neo-Kaldorian and neo-Marxist theorists of development. What is known as the 'Prebisch–Singer hypothesis' was argued independently in 1950 by their authors against classical economists who claimed that the terms of trade between primary commodities and manufactures have to improve over time because the supply of land and natural resources was inelastic. Prebisch's data showed that the terms of trade of Third World countries specializing in producing and exporting primary products would tend to deteriorate. Singer assessed the 'costs' of international trade for developing countries and joined Prebisch in blaming colonialism for them. Third World countries were being driven into a state of 'dependency' on the First World and were reduced to the condition of producers of raw materials demanded by the industrial First World within a 'center–periphery' relationship. Consequently, they argued that protectionism and import-substitution industrialization were necessary if developing countries were to enter a self-sustaining development path. The Prebisch–Singer hypothesis was very popular in the 1950s and the 1960s, but as time moved on policies based on it failed and a neoclassical reaction began to gain supporters.

In 1980, J. Spraos opened the statistical debate with some major criticisms of the core of Prebisch's data, concluding that the United Kingdom's net barter terms of trade used by Prebisch should not be taken as typical of the industrial world. Recently, Y.S. Hadass and J.G. Williamson (2001) have constructed a new data set for the 'center' and the 'periphery' in the 1870–1940 period and have calculated new terms of trade between them. Their estimates suggest that 'the net impact of these terms of trade was very small' (p. 22) and that the fundamentals inside developing countries mattered most to growth. Moreover, the terms of trade did not deteriorate in the periphery. On the contrary, they improved, but with bad consequences: 'the long run impact of these relative price shocks reinforced industrial comparative advantage in the center, favoring the sector which carried growth [that is, industry], while it reinforced primary product comparative advantage in the periphery, penalizing the sector which carried growth' (ibid.).

JOSÉ L. GARCÍA-RUIZ

Bibliography

Hadass, Y.S. and J.G. Williamson (2001), 'Terms of trade shocks and economic performance 1870–1940: Prebisch and Singer revisited', NBER Working Paper 8188.

Prebisch, R. (1962),'The economic development of Latin America and its principal problems', *Economic Bulletin for Latin America*, **1**, 1–22.

Singer, H.W. (1950), 'The distribution of gains between investing and borrowing countries', *American Economic Review*, **40**, 478–85.

Spraos, J. (1980), 'The statistical debate on the net barter terms of trade between primary commodities and manufactures', *Economic Journal*, **90**, 107–28.

R

Radner's turnpike property

Among other assumptions, Solow's model for economic growth incorporated a constant savings rate (Solow, 1956). The model was able to explain a variety of empirical regularities of actual economies, but it had undesirable features, such as a zero correlation between savings and any other variable. The same implication would apply to investment in a closed economy with no government. An additional important limitation of Solow's approach was the impossibility of addressing the discussion on optimal policy design due to the constant savings rate assumption. Optimality was then brought into the model by assuming a benevolent central planner that cares about consumers' welfare, and imposes consumption and savings choices so as to maximize the lifetime aggregate utility of the representative consumer (Cass, 1965; Koopmans, 1965).

The benevolent planner's economy is characterized by two differential equations: one, common to Solow's model, describing the time evolution of the per-capita stock of physical capital, the other describing the time evolution of the optimal level of consumption. Solow's economy is globally stable, converging from any initial position to the single steady-state or long-run equilibrium in the economy, at which per capita variables would remain constant forever. Unfortunately, the same result does not arise in the benevolent planner's economy, with endogenous consumption and savings (or investment) decisions. That model has a saddle-point structure: there is a single one-dimensional trajectory in the (consumption, physical capital) space which is stable. If the economy is at some point on that stable manifold, it will converge to the single steady state, eventually achieving constant levels of per capita consumption and productive capital. On the other hand, if it ever falls outside the stable manifold, the economy will diverge to either unfeasible or suboptimal regions.

Consequently, the role for the planner is to announce a level of initial consumption so that, given the initial capital stock, the economy falls on the stable manifold. The subsequent trajectory, taking the economy to steady state is optimal, achieving the highest possible time-aggregate utility level for the representative consumer, given the initial level of capital. Different economies will differ on their steady state levels of physical capital and consumption, as well as on the optimal level of initial consumption, for the same initial stock of physical capital. When the steady state is reached, per capita physical capital and consumption no longer change, implying that the neighbour levels of both variables grow at the same rate as the population. Technically speaking, however, this 'balanced growth' situation is never reached in finite time, since the growth rates of per capita variables fall to zero as the economy approaches the steady state. With a finite time horizon, the saddle-point property implies that the optimal path consists of moving quickly from the initial stock of physical capital to the neighbourhood of the steady state, diverging away from it only when necessary to guarantee that the terminal condition on the stock of capital is reached at the very end of the time horizon. This is known as the 'turnpike property' (Radner, 1961).

ALFONSO NOVALES

Bibliography
Cass, D. (1965), 'Optimum growth in an aggregative model of capital accumulation', *Review of Economic Studies*, **32**, 233–40.
Koopmans, T.C. (1965), 'On the concept of optimal economics growth', *The Econometric Approach to Development Planning*, Amsterdam: North-Holland.
Radner, R. (1961), 'Paths of economic growth that are optimal with regard only to final states', *Review of Economic Studies*, **28**, 98–104.
Solow, R. (1956), 'A contribution to the theory of economic growth', *Quarterly Journal of Economics*, **70**, 65–94.

See also: Cass–Koopmans criterion, Solow's growth model and residual.

Ramsey model and rule
Frank Plumpton Ramsey (1903–30) was a mathematician who wrote three classical papers on economics. The first paper was on subjective probability and utility; the second one derives the well-known 'Ramsey rule' about optimal taxation for productive efficiency; the third paper (1928) contains the basis of modern macroeconomic dynamics, known as the 'Ramsey model'.

The Ramsey model addresses optimal growth. The starting point is a simple, direct question: 'How much of its income should a nation save?' The main intuition to answer this question, which Ramsey himself attributed to John Maynard Keynes, is the trade-off between present consumption and future consumption. In Ramsey's words: 'Enough must therefore be saved to reach or approach bliss some time, but this does not mean that our whole income should be saved. The more we saved the sooner we would reach bliss, but the less enjoyment we shall have now, and we have to set the one against the other.'

Ramsey developed this intuition by means of a model that became the basic tool of modern macroeconomic dynamics some 35 years later, when Tjalling Koopmans (1963) and David Cass (1965) reformulated the Ramsey model using optimal control theory.

To deal with the intertemporal optimization problem sketched above, Ramsey postulated a one-good world in which capital and labour produce output which can be used either for consumption or for capital accumulation. The objective function he used to evaluate the alternative time paths of consumption was the infinite sum of the utility of consumption minus the disutility of working. Population growth and technological progress, which would have made the problem intractable given the available mathematical tools at the time, were assumed away. Two more simplifying assumptions were the absence of time discounting, which Ramsey considered 'ethically indefensible and arises mainly from the weakness of the imagination', and the existence of a bliss point, defined as the 'maximum conceivable rate of enjoyment'. These assumptions lead to the following optimization problem:

$$\min \int_0^\infty [B - U(C) + V(L)]dt$$

$$\text{subject to } \frac{dK}{dt} + C = F(K, L),$$

where B is the 'maximum conceivable rate of enjoyment', $U(C)$ is the utility of consumption, C, $V(L)$ is the disutility of working, L the quantity of labour and K is capital. Thus Ramsey put forward two main elements of intertemporal optimization: an intertemporal objective function and a dynamic budget constraint. Since then, many macroeconomic and microeconomic issues have been framed within the spirit of the Ramsey model.

Ramsey derived the solution to the optimal savings problem in three different ways. Building first on economic intuition, he realized that the marginal disutility of labour should equal at any time the marginal product of labour times the marginal utility of consumption at that time. Also the marginal utility of consumption at time t should equal the marginal utility of consumption at time t

+ 1 that could be achieved by accumulating a unit of capital at t. These two conditions can also be obtained by applying calculus of variation or by solving the integral in the optimization problem through a change of variable (t replaced by K). Either way, the final result is the so-called 'Keynes–Ramsey rule':

$$F(K, L) - C = \frac{B - [U(C) - V(L)]}{U'(C)};$$

that is, 'the rate of saving multiplied by the marginal utility of consumption should always be equal to the amount by which the total net rate of enjoyment falls short of the maximum possible rate'.

Although not recognized at the time, this analysis constitutes the foundations of optimal growth theory. Nowadays, the canonical model that macroeconomists use to teach and start discussion of optimal accumulation and optimal savings clearly resembles Ramsey's formulation. In this model infinite-horizon households own firms and capital and have an intertemporal utility function which takes into account both the fact that the 'size' of the household may grow in time (population growth) and time discounting. Firms have access to a constant returns to scale production function with Harrod's neutral technological progress and produce output, hiring labour and renting capital in competitive factor markets. Thus firms employ factors paying for their marginal products and earn zero profits. The optimal household consumption path is given by the solution to the maximization of the intertemporal utility function subject to the budget constraint, which establishes that, at the optimal path of consumption, the rate of return of savings must equal the rate of time preference plus the decrease of the marginal utility of consumption. This implies that consumption increases, remains constant or decreases depending on whether the rate of return on savings is higher, equal or lower than the rate of time preference.

JUAN F. JIMENO

Bibliography

Cass, D. (1965), 'Optimal growth in an aggregative model of capital accumulation', *Review of Economic Studies*, **32**, 233–40.

Koopmans, T.C. (1963), 'On the concept of optimal economic growth', Cowles Foundation discussion paper 163, reprinted in T.C. Koopmans (1965), *The Econometric Approach to Development Planning*, Amsterdam: North-Holland.

Ramsey, F.P. (1928), 'A mathematical theory of savings', *Economic Journal*, **38**, 543–9.

See also: Harrod's technical progress.

Ramsey's inverse elasticity rule

Ramsey (1927) formulated the inverse elasticity rule as a criterion to allocate indirect taxes. According to such a rule, without externalities, taxes on goods and services always have efficiency costs, but these costs can be minimal if the tax burden is distributed among taxpayers in an inverse proportion to the elasticity of their demand. The efficiency costs of a tax can be measured by the reduction in the amount of the good consumed when taxes are added to the price. Since the reduction in quantities consumed is larger the lower the price elasticity of the demand, the efficiency costs will be minimal when the tax burden is heavier in goods and services with lower elasticity.

To sustain the Ramsey rule it is necessary to ignore cross elasticity and the income effect of price variation. In the presence of cross elasticity, taxing a good will displace demand to other goods and the efficiency costs of the tax will depend on the value not only of their own elasticity but also of the crossed one. With respect to the income effect, raising prices could affect demand by means of reallocating goods and services in the consumption bundle of the taxpayer. Sometimes the income effect compensates the price effect, as happens with certain basic goods. Taxing these goods would reduce the real income of the taxpayers and the quantity consumed of the good would increase. Considering the income effect invalidates the elasticity of demand as an index of consumer reaction to prices and eliminates the significance of the inverse elasticity rule.

The Ramsey rule was extended and applied to the optimal regulation of monopoly prices by Boiteux (1956). The reformulation of the idea says that the optimal way to allocate fixed costs among different products, in the case of a multi-product monopoly industry, is to distribute them, moving a higher proportion of the fixed costs to those products with lower elasticity of demand.

Assuming that regulators approve prices as a mark-up over marginal costs, the share of fixed costs to allocate to each different product (i) will be exactly:

$$\frac{p_i - cm_i}{p_i} = \frac{\delta}{\varepsilon_i},$$

where p is the price of each product (i), cm the marginal costs of i, ε_i the price elasticity of each product demand and δ is a constant that defines the level of prices and is related to the Lagrange multiplier of the optimization process.

The main problems when using the Ramsey rule as a regulatory criterion to guide the setting of tariffs or prices are that obtaining acute and precise information about elasticity of the demand of every product or segment of the market can be extremely difficult for regulators, and that applying the inverse elasticity rule could mean that the burden on the less wealthy consumers is much higher than the burden on the wealthier. The distributive consequences of the rule can make it socially unacceptable.

MIGUEL A. LASHERAS

Bibliography

Boiteux, M. (1956), 'Sur la gestion des monopoles publics astreints à l'equilibre budgetaire', *Econometrica*, **24**, 22–40.

Ramsey, F. (1927), 'A contribution to the theory of taxation', *Economic Journal*, **27** (1), 47–61.

Rao–Blackwell's theorem

Let $\{P_\theta\}_{\theta\in\Theta}$ be a family of distribution on a sample space χ, and T be an unbiased estimator of $d(\theta)$ with $E_\theta(T^2) < \infty$. Let S be a sufficient statistic for the family $\{P_\theta\}_{\theta\in\Theta}$. Then the conditional expectation $T' = E_\theta(T/S)$ is independent of θ and is an unbiased estimator of $d(\theta)$. Moreover, $Var_\theta(T') \leq Var_\theta(T)$ for every θ, and $Var_\theta(T') < Var_\theta(T)$ for some θ unless T is equal to T' with probability 1.

LEANDRO PARDO

Bibliography

Rohatgi, V.K. (1976), *An Introduction to Probability Theory and Mathematical Statistics*, New York: John Wiley and Sons.

Rawls's justice criterion

John Rawls (1921–2002) develops a theory of justice with the aim of generalizing and formalizing the traditional theory of social contract proposed by Locke, Rousseau and Kant. In his theory, Rawls introduces a characterization of the principles of justice, and as a result he presents a criterion of justice based on considerations of fairness.

Rawls's justice criterion is founded on the combination of two principles: the principle of fair equality of opportunity and the difference principle. The difference principle as stated by Rawls implies that social and economic inequalities are to be arranged so that they are to the greatest benefit of the least advantaged. These principles are to be applied in a lexicographic order, with a priority of justice over efficiency: fair opportunity is prior to the difference principle, and both of them are prior to the principle of efficiency and to that of maximizing welfare.

According to Rawls's justice criterion,

egalitarianism would be a just consideration as long as there is no unequal alternative that improves the position of the worst off, and inequalities are morally acceptable if and only if they improve the position of the most unfavored. With this justice criterion based on fairness, Rawls attempts to overcome the weaknesses and inconsistencies of utilitarianism.

Rawls claims that a principle of justice that aims to define the fundamental structure of a society must be the result of a social agreement made by free and rational persons concerned with their own interests. According to Rawls, a justice criterion can only be considered reasonable if it is chosen in a set-up where all individuals are equal. Rawls describes the original position as the set-up where individuals can choose just rules and principles. He characterizes the original position as an initial hypothetical position where individuals are assumed to be situated behind a veil of ignorance: they do not know their particular characteristics as individuals (their beliefs, their interests, their relations with respect to one another, the alternatives they are to choose and so on) and they are forced to evaluate the principles based only on general considerations, without any reference to bargaining strengths and weaknesses. He argues that, behind the veil of ignorance, individuals' best interests coincide with the principles of liberty and moral freedom and they are satisfied by selecting his justice criterion.

ENRIQUETA ARAGONÉS

Bibliography

Rawls, J. (1971), *A Theory of Justice*, Cambridge, MA: Belknap Press of Harvard University Press.

Reynolds–Smolensky index

Reynolds and Smolensky (1977) suggested an index that allows us to summarize the redistributive effect of an income tax by the reduction in the Gini coefficient (a relative inequality index) of the distribution of income achieved by the tax:

$$\Pi^{RS} = G_X - G_{X-T} = 2\int [L_{X-T}(p) - L_X(p)]dp.$$

This index, which was also proposed by Kakwani (1977), measures twice the area between the Lorenz curves for pre-tax ($L_X(p)$) and post-tax income ($L_{X-T}(p)$), under the assumption that the tax involves no reranking in the transition from pre- to post-tax income. The Reynolds and Smolensky (1977) proposal was to measure the reduction in the Gini coefficient for income arising from the application of both taxes and government expenditure benefits. They obtained a redistributive effect measure for all taxes by (arbitrarily) attributing government expenditure benefits proportionately. These authors made a first application of the index to the United States tax system.

Kakwani (1977) proposed to decompose the Reynolds–Smolensky measure into two terms: the average rate of tax on net income (t) and the Kakwani progressivity index (Π^K). This latter index summarizes 'disproportionality' in tax liabilities of payments in terms of the area between the pre-tax income Lorenz Curve ($L_{X-T}(p)$) and the concentration curve for taxes with respect to the pre-tax ranking ($L_T(p)$):

$$\Pi^{RS} = t/(1 - t)\,\Pi^K$$
$$\Pi^K = 2\int [L_{X-T}(p) - L_T(p)]dp.$$

This decomposition of the Reynolds–Smolensky index has been found valuable in empirical work where the trends in tax level and in 'disproportionality' in tax liabilities across time or between countries can help us to understand trends in the redistributive effect. The relationship between redistributive effect and progressivity has motivated a large body of theoretical as well as empirical literature. The influences of tax design and of the pre-tax income distribution upon redistributive effect and progressivity has been determined and assessed; both indices have been decomposed across taxes and extended to benefits and to evaluating the net fiscal system.

However, the former decomposition no longer holds when re-ranking in the transition from pre- to post-tax income is present. In that case, the decomposition must be corrected by a term capturing the contribution of re-ranking to the redistributive effect of the tax. This term is given by the difference between the Gini coefficient and the concentration index for post-tax income (Kakwani, 1984).

MERCEDES SASTRE

Bibliography

Reynolds, M. and E. Smolensky (1977), *Public Expenditure, Taxes and the Distribution of Income: The United States, 1950, 1961, 1970*, New York: Academic Press.

Kakwani, N.C. (1977), 'Measurement of tax progressivity: an international comparison', *Economic Journal*, **87**, 71–80.

Kakwani, N.C. (1984), 'On the measurement of tax progressivity and redistributive effect of taxes with applications to horizontal and vertical equity', *Advances in Econometrics*, **3**, 149–68.

See also: Gini's coefficient, Kakwani index.

Ricardian equivalence

This is a proposition according to which fiscal effects involving changes in the relative amounts of tax and debt finance for a given amount of public expenditure would have no effect on aggregate demand, interest rates and capital formation. The proposition, as stated above, was not directly introduced by David Ricardo but by Robert Barro, in 1974. Although the formal assumptions under which this equivalence result holds are quite stringent, the intuition behind it is fairly straightforward. We need note only two ideas. First, any debt issuance by the government implies a stream of interest charges and principal repayments that should be financed in the future by taxation, the current value of debt being equal to the present discounted value of future required taxation. Second, if agents behave on the basis of their perceived permanent income (wealth), they will always act as if there were no public debt in the economy, and the way the government finances their expenditure will have no effect on economic activity.

Interestingly, Barro did not acknowledge in his 1974 paper any intellectual debt to Ricardo or to any other classical economist. It was only two years later that James Buchanan documented the close connection between Barro's proposition and some public finance analysis contained in Ricardo's *Principles of Political Economy and Taxation* and, especially, in the essay 'Funding System', both published two and a half centuries earlier than Barro's paper. Buchanan therefore suggested naming the proposition the 'Ricardian equivalence theorem', a term immediately accepted by Barro and consistently used by the whole profession since.

Some, however, have argued that much of what Ricardo wrote in 1820 was already present, albeit with less clarity, in Adam Smith's *Wealth of Nations*, published some decades earlier. Indeed, Smith dwelt on the economic effects of both taxation and debt issuance as alternative sources of government finance, although the equivalence result does not emerge in a clear manner. Ricardo's analysis is much sharper, particularly with respect to the first idea expressed above: in financial terms the government can equally service a debt, issued today for an amount X, if households make a downpayment of X today, to afford to pay taxes in the future. Much less obvious is whether Ricardo would actually subscribe to the second idea behind Barro's proposition: namely, that the former financial equivalence result necessarily implies that public deficits do not have any meaningful economic effect. Actually, he suggests in 'Funding System' that people are somewhat myopic as they would react much more to current than to future expected taxation. At a minimum, it could be contended that Ricardo himself would have been somewhat sceptical about the empirical relevance of the 'Ricardian equivalence theorem'.

In fact, there is no need to resort to agents' irrationality to question the practical applicability of Ricardian equivalence. Indeed, as mentioned above, this proposition requires a number of strong assumptions. In particular, agents must behave as if they were going to live forever; that is, they must care a lot about their children (intergenerational altruism) or have strong bequest motives. Otherwise, as they would always be able to assign a positive probability of future taxes required to service debt being paid by other people after they die, they would feel wealthier if government expenditure were financed by debt issuance rather than taxation, thereby making Ricardian equivalence fail. Similarly, the proposition requires that agents should not be liquidity-constrained, as they should be able to borrow against future income in order for the permanent income hypothesis to hold. If they were subject to borrowing limits, they would always prefer to pay taxes in the future. Actually, the issuance of public debt would help them to make use now of income that would otherwise only be available for consumption in the future. This implies that they would spend more if government policy favoured debt financing over taxation. Finally, Ricardian equivalence relies on the assumption that taxes are lump-sum. To the extent that taxes were distortionary, the intertemporal sequencing of taxation implied by the government financial strategy would actually matter.

It is not difficult to find compelling evidence against each of those important assumptions required for Ricardian equivalence to hold. It is much more difficult, however, to prove that such a failure undermines the overall empirical plausibility of the proposition. Indeed, the available econometric analyses of the issue find it difficult to reject Ricardian hypotheses such as the irrelevance of public debt or deficits on consumption and interest rate equations. This suggests that, while it is difficult to refute the idea that the world is not Ricardian, the relationship between government financial policy and the real economy does not seem to be absolutely at odds with the implications of Ricardian equivalence.

FERNANDO RESTOY

Bibliography

Barro, R.J. (1974), 'Are government bonds net wealth?', *Journal of Political Economy*, **82**, 1095–118.

Ricardo, D. (1820), *Funding System*, reprinted in P. Sraffa (ed.) (1951), *The Works and Correspondence of David Ricardo*, vol. IV, Cambridge: Cambridge University Press. The original was published as a supplement of the *British Encyclopaedia*.

Seater, J.J. (1993), 'Ricardian equivalence', *Journal of Economic Literature*, **31**, 142–90.

Ricardian vice

This is the name given by Schumpeter to the method used by David Ricardo whereby an already simplified economic model is cut down by freezing one variable after another, establishing ad hoc assumptions until the desired result emerges almost as a tautology, trivially true (Schumpeter, 1954, p. 473). The idea that some economists have used, and abused, this path has led to fruitful debates questioning the excessive abstraction and reductionism in deductive economics.

ESTRELLA TRINCADO

Bibliography

Schumpeter, Joseph A. (1954), *History of Economic Analysis*, New York: Oxford University Press.

Ricardo effect

This is one of the main microeconomic explanations for additional savings tending to be invested in more roundabout and capital-intensive production processes. Increases in voluntary savings exert a particularly important, immediate effect on the level of real wages. The monetary demand for consumer goods tends to fall whenever savings rise. Hence it is easy to understand why increases in savings *ceteris paribus* are followed by decreases in the relative prices of final consumer goods. If, as generally occurs, the wages or rents of the original factor labor are initially held constant in nominal terms, a decline in the prices of final consumer goods will be followed by a rise in the real wages of workers employed in all stages of the productive structure. With the same money income in nominal terms, workers will be able to acquire a greater quantity and quality of final consumer goods and services at consumer goods' new, more reduced prices. This increase in real wages, which arises from the growth in voluntary saving, means that, in relative terms, it is in the interest of entrepreneurs of all stages in the production process to replace labor with capital goods. Via an increase in real wages, the rise in voluntary saving sets a trend throughout the economic system toward longer and more capital-intensive productive stages. In other words, entrepreneurs now find it more attractive to use more capital goods than labor. This constitutes a powerful effect tending toward the lengthening of the stages in the productive structure.

According to Friedrich A. Hayek, David Ricardo was the first person to analyze explicitly this effect. Ricardo concludes in his *Principles* (1817) that

> every rise of wages, therefore, or, which is the same thing, every fall of profits, would lower the relative value of those commodities which were produced with a capital of a durable nature, and would proportionally elevate those which were produced with capital more perishable. A fall of wages would have precisely the contrary effect.

And in the well-known chapter 'On Machinery', which was added in the third edition, published in 1821, Ricardo adds that 'machinery and labour are in constant competition, and the former can frequently not be employed until labour rises'.

This idea was later recovered by Hayek, who, beginning in 1939, applied it extensively in his writings on business cycles. Hayek explains the consequences that an upsurge in voluntary saving has on the productive structure to detract from theories on the so-called 'paradox of thrift' and the supposedly negative influence of saving on effective demand. According to Hayek,

> with high real wages and a low rate of profit investment will take highly capitalistic forms: entrepreneurs will try to meet the high costs of labour by introducing very labour-saving machinery – the kind of machinery which it will be profitable to use only at a very low rate of profit and interest.

Hence the Ricardo effect is a pure microeconomic explanation for the behavior of entrepreneurs, who react to an upsurge in voluntary saving by boosting their demand for capital goods and by investing in new stages further from final consumption. It is important to remember that all increases in voluntary saving and investment initially bring about a decline in the production of new consumer goods and services with respect to the short-term maximum which could be achieved if inputs were not diverted from the stages closest to final consumption. This decline performs the function of freeing productive factors necessary to lengthen the stages of capital goods furthest from consumption. In a modern economy, consumer goods and services which remain unsold when saving increases fulfill the important function of making it possible for the different economic agents (workers, owners of natural resources and capitalists) to sustain themselves during the time periods that follow. During these periods the recently initiated lengthening of the productive structure causes an inevitable slowdown in the arrival of new consumer goods and services at the market. This slowdown lasts until the completion of all the new, more capital-intensive processes that have been started. If it were not for the consumer goods and services that remain unsold as a result of saving, the temporary drop in the supply of new consumer goods would trigger a substantial rise in the relative price of these goods and considerable difficulties in their provision.

JESÚS HUERTA DE SOTO

Bibliography

Hayek, F.A. (1939), *'Profits, Interest and Investment' and Other Essays on the Theory of Industrial Fluctuations*, reprinted in (1975) London: Routledge, and Clifton: Augustus M. Kelley, p. 39.

Hayek, F.A. (1942), 'The Ricardo Effect', *Economica*, **9** (34), 127–52; republished (1948) as chapter 11 of *Individualism and Economic Order*, Chicago: University of Chicago Press, pp. 220–54.

Hayek, F.A. (1969), 'Three elucidations of the Ricardo effect', *Journal of Political Economy*, **77** (2), March/April; reprinted (1978) as chapter 11 of *New Studies in Philosophy, Politics, Economics and the History of Ideas*, London: Routledge & Kegan Paul, pp. 165–78.

Ricardo, David (1817), *On the Principles of Political Economy and Taxation*, reprinted in Piero Sraffa and M.H. Dobb (eds) (1982), *The Works and Correspondence of David Ricardo*, vol. 1, Cambridge: Cambridge University Press, pp. 39–40, 395.

Ricardo's comparative costs

In 1817, David Ricardo (1772–1823) established the first theoretical and convincing explanation of the benefits of international free trade and labour specialization, afterwards called the 'comparative advantage principle'. It can be enunciated as follows: even if a country has an absolute cost disadvantage in all the goods it produces, there will be one or more goods in which it has a comparative cost advantage with respect to another country, and it will be beneficial for both to specialize in the products in which each has a comparative advantage, and to import the rest from the other country. A country has absolute advantage in one product when it produces it at a lower cost than the other country. The comparative advantage refers to the relative production cost of two different goods inside each nation: a country has comparative advantage in one good when its production is less costly in terms of the other good than it is in the other country.

Ricardo used an example of two countries, England and Portugal, producing two goods, cloth and wine, that has become one of the most famous in the history of economic thought:

> England may be so circumstanced, that to produce the cloth may require the labour of 100 men for one year; and if she attempted to make the wine, it might require the labour of 120 men for the same time. England would therefore find it her interest to import wine, and to purchase it by the exportation of cloth. To produce the wine in Portugal, might require only the labour of 80 men for one year, and to produce the cloth in the same country, might require the labour of 90 men for the same time. It would therefore be advantageous for her to export wine in exchange for cloth. This exchange might even take place, notwithstanding that the commodity imported by Portugal could be produced there with less labour than in England. Though she could make the cloth with the labour of 90 men, she would import it from a country where it required the labour of 100 men to produce it, because it would be advantageous to her rather to employ her capital in the production of wine, for which she would obtain more cloth from England, than she could produce by diverting a portion of her capital from the cultivation of vines to the manufacture of cloth. (Ricardo, 1817, ch. 7)

This text contains the essence of the principle of comparative advantage. Even though

Ricardo did not quantify the gains obtained by both countries after the specialization, a simple exercise will show that he was right. Suppose that, in England, the cost of producing a piece of cloth is 10 hours of labour, and 12 for a litre of wine. In Portugal these costs are, respectively, nine and eight hours. Portugal has absolute cost advantage in the production both of wine and of clothes. But in England wine is comparatively more costly than cloth, as it requires two more hours; and in Portugal the less expensive product is wine. This means that England has a comparative cost advantage in the production of cloth, while Portugal has it in the production of wine, as follows.

If we measure the market value of products in terms of hours of work, as Ricardo does, we can deduce, for instance, that in England with one piece of cloth (value = 10 hours) it is possible to buy less than a litre of wine (10/12 litres), as a litre of wine requires in England 12 hours of labour to be produced. But in Portugal with the same piece of cloth it is possible to buy more than a litre of wine (9/8 litres). So to exchange a piece of cloth for wine it is better to go to Portugal – if we assume, as Ricardo does, free trade between both countries. It seems clear, then, that England benefits from specializing in the production of cloth and importing wine from Portugal. The same reasoning leads to the conclusion that, for Portugal, the best option is to specialize in the production of wine, in which she has comparative advantage, and import cloth from England.

Ricardo proved that specialization and trade can increase the living standards of countries, independently of their absolute costs. His theory was presented during the debates about the growing level of corn prices in England, and Ricardo, as many others, argued that protectionism was one of its main causes. His argument served as a firm basis for the promoters of free trade, and was decisive in abolishing the protectionist Corn Laws in 1846.

JOSÉ M. ORTIZ-VILLAJOS

Bibliography

Blaug, Mark (ed.) (1991), *David Ricardo (1772–1823)*, Pioneers in Economics 14, Aldershot, UK and Brookfield, US: Edward Elgar.

De Vivo, G. (1987), 'Ricardo, David (1772–1823)', in J. Eatwell, M. Milgate and P. Newman (eds), *The New Palgrave. A Dictionary of Economics*, vol. 4, London: Macmillan, pp. 183–98.

Ricardo, David (1817), *On the Principles of Political Economy and Taxation*, reprinted in P. Sraffa (ed.) (1951), *The Works and Correspondence of David Ricardo*, vol. I, Cambridge: Cambridge University Press.

Ricardo–Viner model

Jacob Viner (1892–1970) extended the Ricardian model by including factors other than labor, and by allowing the marginal product of labor to fall with output. The Ricardo–Viner model was later developed and formalized by Ronald Jones (1971). Michael Mussa (1974) provided a simple graphical approach to illustrate the main results. It constitutes a model in its own right, but it can also be viewed as a short-term variant of the Heckscher–Ohlin model, with capital immobile across sectors. Capital and land inputs are fixed but labor is assumed to be a variable input, freely and costlessly mobile between two sectors. Each of the other factors is assumed to be specific to a particular industry. Each sector's production displays diminishing returns to labor. The model is used to explain the effects of economic changes on labor allocation, output levels and factor returns, and is particularly useful in exploring the changes in the distribution of income that will arise as a country moves from autarky to free trade.

YANNA G. FRANCO

Bibliography

Jones, Ronald W. (1971), 'A three-factor model in theory, trade and history', in J.N. Bhagwati, R.A.

Mundell, R.W. Jones and J. Vanek (eds), *Trade, Balance of Payments, and Growth: Essays in Honor of C.P. Kindleberger*, Amsterdam: North-Holland, pp. 3–21.
Mussa, Michael (1974), 'Tariffs and the distribution of income: the importance of factor specificity, substitutability and intensity in the short and long run', *Journal of Political Economy*, **82** (6), 1191–203.

See also: Heckscher–Ohlin theorem, Ricardo's comparative costs.

Robinson–Metzler condition

Named after Joan Robinson and Lloyd A. Metzler, although C.F. Bickerdike, J.E. Meade and others contributed to the idea and are sometimes linked to the eponym, the condition refers to a post-devaluation trade balance adjustment under a comparative static approach in the context of international equilibrium and under a system of fluctuating exchange rates. The adjustment analysis is applied through elasticity both in exports and in imports. The Robinson–Metzler condition focuses on the four elasticities in play, in order to predict the global result of all the adjustments that determine the new balance of trade: the foreign elasticity of demand for exports, the home elasticity of supply for exports, the foreign elasticity of supply for imports, and the home elasticity of demand for imports. The final balance of trade will depend on the intersection of all of them.

ELENA GALLEGO

Bibliography

Bickerdike, Charles F. (1920), 'The instability of foreign exchange', *Economic Journal*, **30**, 118–22.
Robinson, Joan (1950), 'The foreign exchanges', in Lloyd A. Metzler and Howard S. Ellis (eds), *Readings in the Theory of International Trade*, London: George Allen and Unwin, pp. 83–103.

See also: Marshall–Lerner condition.

Rostow's model

Walt Whitman Rostow's (1916–2003) model is a stages theory of economic development. Rostow divided 'the process of economic growth' (that was the title of one of his books) into five 'stages of economic growth' (the title of his most famous book). These stages are traditional society, the setting of the preconditions for growth, the 'take-off' into self-sustained growth, the drive towards economic maturity, and the age of high mass consumption.

Little explanation is required about the meaning and nature of these stages. Traditional society is characterized by 'limited production functions based on pre-Newtonian science'. This early stage is not unlike Joseph Schumpeter's 'circular flow', which occupies a similar place in Schumpeter's theory of economic development. The preconditions for growth entail a series of social changes which are previous to industrialization: improvement of political organization ('the building of an effective centralized national state'), new social attitudes, a drop in the birth rate, an increase in the investment rate, a jump in agricultural productivity. The third stage, the take-off, is central to the model in more than one way. It brings about the most radical and swift social change: an approximate doubling in the rate of investment and saving, fast political and institutional modernization, and rapid industrialization. Two distinctive features of Rostow's take-off are that it is spearheaded by a limited number of 'leading sectors', whose rate of growth is higher than those of other, following sectors, which in turn are divided into 'supplementary growth' and 'derived growth' sectors; and that it is relatively brief, spanning a generation.

The other two stages are less interesting from a theoretical point of view. There is, however, a key phrase in *The Stages of Economic Growth* (p. 58) which summarizes the basic idea behind the model: 'By and large, the maintenance of momentum for a generation persuades the society to persist, to concentrate its efforts on extending the tricks of modern technology beyond the sectors modernized during the take-off.' It is this persistence which leads the modernized economy into the drive to maturity, which is characterized as 'the period when a society has effectively applied the range of [. . .] modern technology to the bulk of its resources'. Once society has successfully performed its take-off, its own self-propelled inertia drives it into maturity and mass consumption or 'post-maturity', when, problems of supply being solved, attention shifts to 'problems of consumption, and of welfare in the widest sense'.

This model, which had a tremendous echo in the 1960s and 1970s among academics, politicians and even a wide lay audience, elicits a few comments. First of all, Rostow's model belongs to a wide group of stages theories of historical development, especially those relating to economic history, from Roscher and Hildebrand to Colin Clark and Gerschenkron, through Marx and Schmoller. Second, it combines a stylized description and periodization of western economic history with some economic theories much in vogue in the 1950s and 1960s, such as the Harrod–Domar conditions for balanced growth. Rostow was a student of the British Industrial Revolution and his model is a good fit with British modern economic history. He also allowed for a variant of the model, that of the 'born-free' countries, those ex-colonies without a medieval past, such as the United States and Canada, which were born to nationhood already in the preconditions stage.

Third, its key idea and most original feature is expressed by his statements about 'persistence' and 'self-sustained growth': according to Rostow's model, when an economy has crossed a certain threshold of development, there is an inertia that keeps it growing. Hence its attractive aeronautical metaphor: once an airplane has overcome gravity in take-off, it (normally) stays airborne. Fourth, Rostow's model had clear and intended political implications, which were expressed in the subtitle of *The Stages: A Non-Communist Manifesto*. He explicitly tried to offer an alternative interpretation of modern history to Karl Marx's vision. In so doing, Rostow drew an optimistic picture of the Soviet Union's economic development, viewing it as parallel to the growth of the United States and gave support to the theory of convergence of capitalism and communism, much in vogue at the time.

Naturally, Rostow's model provoked heated debate, all the more so since its author was a close adviser to Presidents Kennedy and Johnson, and an ardent supporter of the Vietnam War. Henry Rosovsky spoke about 'the take-off into self-sustained controversy'; Phyllis Deane, for instance, denied that British investment rates were as high during take-off as Rostow stated, and Robert Fogel studied the development of American railways to deny that they played the role of leading sector that Rostow attributed to them. Gerschenkron pointed out that there is no definite set of preconditions or 'prerequisites', and that the different growth paths followed by diverse countries were largely results of varying arrays of development assets. It has also been remarked that, contrary to Rostow's specific predictions, some countries, such as Argentina, Russia or China, had very long take-offs, which in fact were partial failures, something the model did not account for. Many other criticisms could be cited, but Rostow's model and terminology have endured, if not for their explanatory power, at least for their descriptive value.

GABRIEL TORTELLA

Bibliography

Gerschenkron, Alexander (1962): 'Reflections on the concept of "prerequisites" of modern industrialization', *Economic Backwardness in Historical Perspective*, Cambridge, MA: Harvard University Press, pp. 31–51.

Rostow, W.W. (1953), *The Process of Economic Growth*, Oxford: Clarendon Press.
Rostow, W.W. (1960), *The Stages of Economic Growth. A Non-Communist Manifesto*, Cambridge: Cambridge University Press.

See also: Gerschenkron's growth hypothesis, Harrod–Domar model.

Roy's identity

Roy's identity is a consequence of the duality of utility maximization and expenditure minimization in consumer theory, and relates the Walrasian demand to the price derivative of the indirect utility function. It can be proved as a straightforward application of the envelope theorem. The importance of Roy's identity is that it establishes that the indirect utility function can legitimately serve as a basis for the theory of demand. Formally, Roy's identity states the following.

Suppose that $u(x)$ is a continuous utility function representing a locally non-satiated and strictly convex preference relation defined on the consumption set R^L_+, where $x \in R^L_+$. Suppose that the indirect utility function $v(p, m)$ is differentiable at $(\bar{p}, \bar{m}) >> 0$, where $\bar{p} = (\bar{p}_1, \bar{p}_2, \ldots, \bar{p}_L)$ is a given vector of prices of goods 1, 2, . . ., L, and $\bar{m}$ is a given level of income. Let $x(p, m)$ be the Walrasian demand function. Then, for every l = 1, 2, . . ., L, the Walrasian demand for good 1, $x_l(p, m)$, is given by

$$x_l(\bar{p}, \bar{m}) = -\frac{\partial v(\bar{p}, \bar{m})/\partial p_l}{\partial v(\bar{p}, \bar{m})/\partial m}.$$

As an example, let $L = 2$ and let the utility function be Cobb–Douglas, given by $u(x) = x_1x_2$. Maximizing the utility function subject to the budget constraint $\bar{p}_1x_1 + \bar{p}_2x_2 = \bar{m}$ yields the two Walrasian demand functions $x_1(\bar{p}, \bar{m}) = \bar{m}/2\bar{p}_l$, l = 1, 2. The indirect utility function is obtained by substituting the demand functions back into the utility function, $v(\bar{p}, \bar{m}) = \bar{m}^2/4\bar{p}_1\bar{p}_2$. Applying Roy's identity, we recover the Walrasian demand functions

$$-\frac{\partial v(\bar{p}, \bar{m})/\partial p_l}{\partial v(\bar{p}, \bar{m})/\partial m} = \frac{\bar{m}}{2\bar{p}_l} = x_l(\bar{p}, \bar{m}), \text{ for l} = 1, 2.$$

CRISTINA MAZÓN

Bibliography

Roy, René (1942), *De l'utilité, Contribution à la théorie des choix*, Paris: Hermann & Cie

Rubinstein's model

Two players bargain over the partition of a surplus of fixed size normalized to one. They take turns to make offers to each other until agreement is secured. Player 1 makes the first offer. If the players perpetually disagree then each player's pay-off is zero. They are assumed to be impatient with the passage of time and share a common discount factor of $\delta \in (0, 1)$ so that a euro received in period t is worth δ^{t-1}, where $t \in \{1, 2, 3 \ldots\}$. This infinite-horizon bargaining game with perfect information, due to Rubinstein (1982), has many Nash equilibria: any partition of the surplus can be obtained in an equilibrium. Nevertheless, this game has a unique subgame-perfect equilibrium. In this equilibrium, the players reach an inmediate agreement in period 1, with player 1 earning $1/(1 + \delta)$ and player 2 earning $\delta/(1 + \delta)$. Let M and m denote respectively the supremum and the infimum of the continuation pay-offs of a player in any subgame-perfect equilibrium of any subgame that begins in period t with this player making an offer. As the responder will be the proposer in period $t + 1$ his reservation values in t are δM and δm. Therefore, by subgame perfection, the following inequalities should hold: $M \leq 1 - \delta m$, and $m \geq 1 - \delta M$. It follows that $M = m = 1/(1 + \delta)$. So a player's subgame-perfect equilibrium pay-off is uniquely determined.

The subgame-perfect equilibrium strategies are as follows: a player who receives an offer accepts it if and only if he is offered at least $\delta/(1 + \delta)$, while, when he has to make a proposal, offers exactly $\delta/(1 + \delta)$ to the other player. To see that the equilibrium strategies are unique, notice that, after every history, the proposer's offer must be accepted in equilibrium. If players have different discount factors δ_1 and δ_2, a similar reasoning, using the stationarity of the game, proves that the equilibrium partition is $(v, 1 - v)$ where $v = (1 - \delta_2)/(1 - \delta_1\delta_2)$. This is one of the main insights of Rubinstein's model. A player's bargaining power depends on the relative magnitude of the players' respective costs of making offers and counter-offers, with the absolute magnitudes of these costs being irrelevant to the bargaining outcome.

Define $\delta_i = \exp(-r_i\Delta)$, $i = 1, 2$, where $\Delta > 0$ is the time interval between consecutive offers and $r_i > 0$ is player i's discount factor. It is straightforward to verify that the limiting, as $\Delta \to 0$, subgame-perfect equilibrium pay-offs pair $(v, 1 - v)$ is identical to the asymmetric Nash bargaining solution of this bargaining problem.

This basic alternating offers game is a stylized representation of two features that lie at the heart of most real-life negotiations. On the one hand, players attempt to reach an agreement by making offers and counter-offers. On the other hand, bargaining imposes costs on both players. Such a game is useful because it provides a basic framework upon which richer models of bargaining and applications can be built.

GONZALO OLCINA

Bibliography

Rubinstein, A. (1982), 'Perfect equilibrium in a bargaining model', *Econometrica*, **50**, 97–109.

Shaked, A. and J. Sutton (1984), 'Involuntary unemployment as a perfect equilibrium in a bargaining model', *Econometrica*, **52**, 1351–64.

See also: Nash bargaining solution, Nash equilibrium.

Rybczynski theorem

One of the building blocks of the Heckscher–Ohlin model, the Rybczynski theorem, named after the Polish economist Tadeusz Mieczyslaw Rybczynski (b.1923), is the symmetric counterpart to the Stolper–Samuelson theorem. Just as the latter demonstrates the close link connecting commodity prices to factor prices, the former proves, under suitable conditions, the existence of a well-defined relationship between changes in factor endowments and changes in the production of goods in the economy.

The following assumptions, standard in the Heckscher–Ohlin model, are set: the economy is made up of two sectors, each producing a homogeneous good (X and Y) by employing two factors, named labor (L) and capital (K), under constant returns to scale; the total endowment of each factor is fixed to the economy and both factors are perfectly mobile across sectors; there are no transaction costs or taxes and competition prevails throughout. It is further assumed that one industry (say X) is more capital-intensive than the other (Y). Then the theorem states that, if relative prices are held constant, an increase in the quantity of one factor 'must lead to an absolute expansion in production of the commodity using relatively much of that factor and to an absolute curtailment of production of the commodity using relatively little of the same factor' (Rybczynski, 1955, (p. 338).

This result, easily proved using the Edgeworth box or elementary algebra, agrees with economic intuition. First, notice that, for good prices to be constant, factor prices have to be constant too, and this entails, given constant returns to scale, that factor intensities have to remain unchanged in both industries as well. Let us now supose an increase in the total endowment of one factor, say labor. To keep factor intensities constant, the extra labour has to be allocated to the labor-intensive industry (*Y*) where it will be combined with capital released from *X* (made available by the contraction of production in *X*). But *X*, being capital-intensive, releases more capital per unit of labor as its production goes down. Hence production goes up in *Y* by more than the increase in the labor endowment, the excess production being afforded by the contraction of the production of the capital-intensive sector.

TERESA HERRERO

Bibliography

Rybczynski, T.M. (1955), 'Factor endowments and relative commodity prices', *Economica*, **22**, 336–41.

See also: Heckscher–Ohlin theorem, Jones's magnification effect, Stolper–Samuelson theorem.

S

Samuelson condition

Paul A. Samuelson (b.1915, Nobel Prize 1970) is one of the most influential economists of the twentieth century. Trained in Harvard University by Hansen, Schumpeter and Leontief, he developed most of his prolific work in the MIT. His wide range of studies covers nearly all branches of economic theory. An outstanding contribution to macroeconomics is the overlapping generations model of general equilibrium (1958). Its application to public finance results in the condition presented here which refers to the sustainability of a pay-as-you-go pension system. According to Samuelson, a pension system will remain balanced if and only if its average internal rate of return does not exceed the growth rate of the fiscal base, which, under the assumption of a constant tax rate, is equal to the growth rate of employment plus the growth rate of the average wage.

The simplest version of the model, where individuals live only two periods (during the first one they work and pay contributions and in the second they receive a pension) allows us to obtain easily the Samuelson condition. If N_t represents the population born in period t, n is the growth rate of population and ρ its survival rate, the financial surplus of a pay-as-you-go pension system, B_t, can be expressed as

$$B_t = \tau(w_t e_t N_t) - \alpha\rho(w_{t-1} e_{t-1} N_{t-1}), \quad (1)$$

where τ is the contribution rate, w_t the real wage, e_t the employment rate and α the percentage of the fiscal base received as a pension. As stated by equation (1), the system has a surplus in period t if

$$\frac{e_t}{e_{t-1}}(1 + n)(1 + \gamma) \geq \frac{\alpha\rho}{\tau}, \quad (2)$$

where γ is the growth rate of wages. The left side of (2) is the growth rate of the system's income, which, when the employment rate, e, remains constant, is almost equal to $1 + n + \gamma$. The right side of (2) is equal to $1 + r$, where r is the internal rate of return of the pension system, since individuals pay τw_{t-1} and receive αw_{t-1} with probability ρ. Then, substituting in (2) we get the classical Samuelson proposition of financial equilibrium in a pay-as-you-go pension system: $n + \gamma \geq r$.

JORDI FLORES PARRA

Bibliography

Samuelson, P.A. (1958), 'An exact consumption–loan model of interest with or without the social contrivance of money', *Journal of Political Economy*, **66** (6), 467–82.

Sard's theorem

The American mathematician Arthur Sard (1909–80), Professor at Queens College, New York, made important contributions in fields of mathematics such as linear approximation and differential topology. Sard's theorem is a deep result in differential topology that is a key mathematical tool to show the generic local uniqueness of the Walrasian equilibria.

Let U be an open set of R^n and let F be a continuously differentiable function from U to R^m. A point $x \in U$ is a critical point of F if the Jacobian matrix of F at x has a rank smaller than m. A point $y \in R^m$ is a critical value of F if there is a critical point $x \in U$ with $y = F(x)$. A point of R^m is a regular value of F if it is not a critical value.

Sard's theorem states as follows. Let $p > \max(0, n - m)$. If F is a function of class C^p (that is, all the partial derivatives of F to the pth order included, exist and are continuous), then the set of critical values of F has Lebesgue measure zero in R^m.

A model of exchange economy with a unique equilibrium requires very strong assumptions and, thus, economies with multiple equilibria must be allowed for. Such economies provide a satisfactory explanation of equilibrium and allow the study of stability provided that all the equilibria of the economy are locally unique. In the common situation in which the set of equilibria is compact, local uniqueness is equivalent to finiteness.

In Debreu (1970) an exchange economy with n consumers is defined by an n-tuple of demand functions and an n-tuple of initial endowments $e = (e_1, \ldots, e_n)$. If the demands remain fixed an economy is actually defined by the initial endowments e. Let $W(e)$ denote the set of all equilibrium prices of the economy defined by e. Under middle assumptions and using Sard's theorem, it is shown that the set of initial endowments for which the closure of $W(e)$ is infinite has zero measure.

On the other hand, in Smale (1981), Sard's theorem and market-clearing equations have been used, rather than fixed point methods, to show equilibrium existence and, in a constructive way, to find the equilibrium points.

CARLOS HERVÉS-BELOSO

Bibliography

Debreu, G. (1970), 'Economies with a finite set of equilibria', *Econometrica*, **38** (3), 387–92.

Sard, A. (1942), 'The measure of the critical points of differentiable maps', *Bull. Amer. Math. Soc.*, **48**, 883–90.

Smale, S. (1981), 'Global analysis and economics', in K. Arrow and M. Intriligator (eds), *Handbook of Mathematical Economics*, Amsterdam: North-Holland, ch. 8.

Sargan test

Sargan tests, named after John Denis Sargan (b.1924), are specification tests for a class of linear and non-linear econometric models. The hypothesis under test is the set of overidentifying restrictions arising from the orthogonality conditions required for instrumental variable (IV) estimation. The test statistics have become a standard complement when reporting IV estimates. In Sargan's own words (1958), they provide 'a significance test for the hypothesis that there is a relationship between the suggested variables with a residual independent of all the instrumental variables'. In order to illustrate the form of the test statistic, consider the model $y_t = x'_t\beta_0 + u_t$ where x_t and β_0 are $q \times 1$ vectors of predetermined variables and parameters, respectively. Let z_t denote an $r \times 1$ vector of predetermined instrumental variables, so $E(z_t u_t) = 0$ with $r > q$. (If x's and z's contain (independent) measurement errors, the disturbance u_t includes both the structural shock and a linear combination of measurement errors). In standard matrix notation, consider the residuals $\hat{u} = y - X\hat{\beta}$ where

$$\hat{\beta} = [X'Z(Z'Z)^{-1}Z'X]^{-1} X'Z(Z'Z)^{-1}Z'y$$

is the optimally weighted IV estimator. Sargan's test statistic is

$$J = T\frac{\hat{u}'Z(Z'Z)^{-1}Z'\hat{u}}{\hat{u}'\hat{u}}.$$

Under the null and under suitable regularity conditions, its limiting distribution is chi-square with $r - q$ degrees of freedom. A large value will lead to rejection. If the orthogonality conditions are satisfied the vector

$$\frac{1}{T}Z'u$$

of sample covariances should be small, allowing for sampling variation. The test statistic is a quadratic form of

$$\frac{1}{T} Z'\hat{u}$$

where the weighting matrix corrects for sampling variation and the use of residuals to replace unobservable disturbances.

Sargan (1958) proposed the test and derived its asymptotic distribution under the null in the framework of a linear model which explicitly allowed for both simultaneity and measurement errors. His original motivation was the estimation of macroeconomic models using time series data. In Sargan (1959) he considered a generalization to nonlinear-in-parameters IV models. Hansen (1982) extended this type of specification test to a more general non-linear generalized method of moments (GMM) framework with dependent observations; this is the well known 'J-test' of overidentifying restrictions. For a discussion of the connection between Sargan's work and the GMM, see Arellano (2002).

PEDRO MIRA

Bibliography

Arellano, M. (2002), 'Sargan's instrumental variable estimation and GMM', *Journal of Business and Economic Statistics*, **20**, 450–59.

Hansen, L.P. (1982) 'Large sample properties of generalized method of moments estimation', *Econometrica*, **50**, 1029–54.

Sargan, J.D. (1958), 'The estimation of economic relationships using instrumental variables', *Econometrica*, **26**, 393–415.

Sargan, J.D. (1959), 'The estimation of relationships with autocorrelated residuals by the use of instrumental variables', *Journal of the Royal Statistical Society*, Series B, **21**, 91–105.

Sargant effect

This refers to an increase in the supply of savings in the economy caused by a fall in the rate of interest. Philip Sargant Florence (1890–1982) pointed out that a continuous decrease in the interest rate in a period of recession could be accompanied by an increase in annual additions to the capital stock, as individuals who save in order to obtain a periodical revenue from their capital will have to save more. Alfred Marshall considered the Sargant effect as an exception to the theory that states that the short-run savings supply curve is positively sloped. He said that, as a consequence of human nature, a decrease in the interest rate will generally tend to limit wealth accumulation, because every fall in that rate will probably drive people to save less than they otherwise would have done (Marshall, 1890, p. 195). Gustav Cassel criticized Sargant's theory by assuming that, as people can save only a certain amount of their present income, a fall in the rate of interest does not increase the supply of savings, but it lengthens the period during which they will have to save (Blaug, 1996, pp. 386, 501).

JAVIER SAN JULIÁN

Bibliography

Blaug, Mark (1996), *Economic Theory in Retrospect*, 5th edn, Cambridge: Cambridge University Press.

Marshall, Alfred (1890), *Principles of Economics*, 8th edn 1920; reprinted 1977, London: Macmillan.

Say's law

Jean-Baptiste Say (1767–1832) was born in Lyons to a protestant family of textile manufacturers. After a political career marked by his opposition to Napoleonic autocracy, he came to manage a textile firm himself. His intellectual efforts were directed at establishing the foundations of a spontaneously ordered free society, after the disorders of the French Revolution had led public opinion to believe that harmony and progress demanded direction from the centre. After the fall of Napoleon, he taught the first public course of political economy in France and in 1830 took over the chair in Political Economy of the

Collège de France. He debated with the classical economists in England, and spread the teachings of Adam Smith on the continent of Europe.

According to Say's law, 'products always exchange for products'. This as yet incomplete formulation is to be found in the *Traité d'économie politique* (1st edn, 1803). The more complete version, called 'la loi des débouchés' according to which 'production generates its own demand' and therefore every output will in the end find an outlet, was formulated by Say after reading James Mill. For Say, as for the majority of classical economists, exchanges in the market are to be seen as barter trades: a general glut was impossible since taking a good to market implies effectively demanding another good in exchange.

The first critics of this theory, such as Lauderdale, Malthus or Sismondi, pointed out that cyclical crises are an observable fact. They variously underlined the danger that the present level of output could not be sustained unless people were ready to exert themselves sufficiently to acquire power to consume, or unless the 'value' of the output was maintained by high prices. Malthus in particular proposed an artificial boost to unproductive consumption and increases in the level of agricultural protection to create a vent for surplus output. Later in the century, Marx added that crises would increase in frequency and harshness, leading to the collapse of the capitalist system.

The elements of Say's law are as follows:

1. Money only facilitates barter and changes nothing in the real world.
2. Savings are always invested and spent. This idea is also to be found in Turgot and Smith.
3. Saving rather than consumption is the source of economic growth.

James Mill independently discovered this principle when criticising Lauderdale's excess investment theory in 1804 and then developed it in *Commerce Defended* (1808), where he did not forget to mention Say. His improvement of the principle that output generates its own demand adds the following:

4. The necessary and spontaneous equality of production and demand in the economy as a whole springs from the fact that total output is necessarily equivalent to total purchasing power since the rewards of labour, capital and land reaped in production become the demand for goods and services.
5. Though total demand and supply must be equivalent, disproportionalities can arise within the economy because of individual miscalculations. These disproportionalities explain crises, which must be partial and temporary in a properly functioning economy.

Thus, for the earlier classical economists, an insufficiency of aggregate demand is impossible; indeed there is no such thing as 'aggregate demand'. What appears to be a general crisis is really a temporary lack of harmony in the supply and demand of some particular goods and services. Even in the deepest of crises there is demand for many goods and the redundant stock of output can be placed when prices fall sufficiently. This is also applicable to unemployment.

John Stuart Mill, in his essay, 'Of the Influence of Consumption upon Production' (MS 1829–30, 1844), introduced money and credit into the model:

6. Crises are always partial and are preceded by investment mistakes owing to which there is excess supply of the output of such investment, for whose products people do not want to pay a price covering costs.
7. As money is not only a means of payment but also a store of value, in a

monetary economy it is possible to sell without buying. Such hoarding increases when confidence starts to fail because of investment errors becoming apparent. In a credit economy, the effect of hoarding is magnified by a flight to liquidity and bankruptcy spreads through the economy.
8. All this takes on the appearance of a general slump that will, however, quickly and spontaneously correct if prices, wages and interest rates adjust.

Léon Walras, in his *Éléments d'économie politique pure* (1874), gave a more complete formulation of Say's law, known today as Walras's law: as a consequence of basic interrelations among individuals in a general equilibrium system, the sum of the value of excess demands must be zero.

A new wave of criticism rose against Say's law with Keynes (1936): an excessive propensity to save could lead to aggregate consumption being too weak for aggregate production to take off. The result could be attempted overinvestment, a fall in national income and an increase in involuntary unemployment.

Once facts refuted early Keynesianism, economists returned to Say's law under the guise of rational expectations theory: all available information is discounted into current decisions by speculators and therefore markets clear. Hence, as Turgot–Smith, Say, and J. and J.S. Mill say, there can be no general gluts and whatever cyclical phenomena may recur will be due to real disproportions caused by technological shocks displacing inferior investments. Those co-movements will correct, the more flexible demand and supply prices are.

PEDRO SCHWARTZ

Bibliography

Keynes, J.M. (1936), *The General Theory of Employment Interest and Money*, London: Macmillan.

Mill, James (1808), *Commerce Defended*, London: C. and R. Baldwin.

Mill, John Stuart (MS 1829–30, 1844), 'Of the influence of consumption upon production', *Essays on Some Unsettled Questions of Political Economy*, reprinted 1967, *Collected Works*, vol. IV, University of Toronto Press.

Say, Jean Baptiste (1803), *Traité d'économie politique*, 2nd edn, 1814; reprinted 1971, 'Des Débouchés', Livre Premier, Chapitre XV, Paris: Calmann-Lévy, 137–47.

Sowell, Thomas (1972), *Say's Law. An Historical Analysis*, Princeton: Princeton University Press.

See also: Turgot–Smith theorem, Walras's law.

Schmeidler's lemma

Consider an economy with a continuum of agents where endowments and preferences of all agents are common knowledge. Assume also that agents can form groups (coalitions) binding themselves to any mutually advantageous agreement. In this economy we define the core as the set of allocations that cannot be improved upon by any coalition. The concept of the core allows an extension of the first welfare theorem stating that a Walrasian equilibrium cannot be blocked by the coalition of the whole. This is an important result that relies on a very demanding informational assumption. It is often the case that agents have knowledge of the characteristics of a limited number of other agents. Alternatively, we can think of transaction costs of forming coalitions, or of institutional constraints putting an upper limit on the size of coalitions. Under any of these interpretations, the lack of communication between the agents restricts the set of coalitions that can be formed. Schmeidler's lemma says that, given an economy with S agents and a coalition E blocking an allocation by means of an allocation f, we can find an arbitrarily smaller sub-coalition of positive measure, $v(F) \leqq \varepsilon$ that also blocks the same allocation using f.

Formally, let (S, Σ, λ) be an atomless measure space, $f, g: S \to R^n$ be λ-integrable functions, and v be a finite measure on Σ, absolutely continuous with respect to λ. Given a set $E \in \Sigma$ such that $\lambda(E) > 0$ and $\int_E f d\lambda = \int_E g d\lambda$, then for every positive number ε there is a Σ-measurable subset of E, say F, such that: $\lambda(F) > 0$, $v(F) \leqq \varepsilon$ and $\int_F f d\lambda = \int_F g d\lambda$.

Mas-Colell provides an interesting interpretation of this result by considering that the economy only needs a few well-informed agents to reach a Walrasian equilibrium. These few agents would be the arbitrageurs. That is, with most of the agents in the economy being passive, it would be enough for a small profit-maximizing group of agents performing optimally to place the economy in equilibrium.

XAVIER MARTINEZ-GIRALT

Bibliography

Schmeidler, D. (1972), 'A remark on the core of an atomless economy', *Econometrica*, **40** (3), 579–80.

Schumpeter's vision

In his 1954 *History of Economic Analysis*, J.A. Schumpeter (1883–1950) stated that 'analytic effort is of necessity preceded by a preanalytic cognitive act that supplies the raw material for the analytic effort. In this book, this preanalytic cognitive act will be called Vision' (p. 41). We '*see* things in a light of' our vision (Schumpeter's emphasis). This is sometimes called 'ideology', 'world view', 'cosmovision' or, after Kuhn (1962), 'paradigm'.

Schumpeter is talking about 'the dangers of ideological bias' and how to detect and eliminate ideological elements through standard scientific procedure. Despite any original inevitable contamination, the scientific process, through 'factual work and theoretical work' (called poetically by Schumpeter 'the cold steel of analysis') refines and completes the original vision and will 'eventually produce *scientific models*', that is, value-free positive economics. So Schumpeter's position is similar to Friedman's (1953): ideology is one of the possible legitimate motivations of a research, but not relevant for the correctness of its result; 'explanation, however correct, of the reasons why a man says what he says tells us nothing about whether it is true or false' (Schumpeter, 1954, p. 36).

But throughout the *History* runs the idea that vision is something not only legitimate, as Friedman states, but also good, necessary to grasp the data – and sentiments – about the world in one comprehensible hypothesis. Scientific procedures not only take away the bad elements of the original vision, but build a better one: 'In an endless sequence both activities [conceptualizing the content of the vision and hunting for further empirical data] improve, deepen and correct the original vision' (ibid., p. 45). And so the idea of 'Schumpeter's preanalytic vision' is usually quoted in support of non-canonical approaches.

MANUEL SANTOS-REDONDO

Bibliography

Backhouse, R.E. (1996), 'Vision and progress in economic thought: Schumpeter after Kuhn', in Laurence S. Moss (ed.), *Joseph A. Schumpeter, Historian of Economics. Perspectives on the History of Economic Thought*, London: Routledge, pp. 21–32.

Friedman, Milton (1953), 'The methodology of positive economics', *Essays in Positive Economics*, Chicago: University of Chicago Press, pp. 3–43.

Kuhn, Thomas S. (1962, 1970), *The Structure of Scientific Revolutions*, 2nd edn, Chicago and London: University of Chicago Press, pp. 10–22, 43–51.

Schumpeter, J.A. (1954), *History of Economic Analysis*, New York: Oxford University Press, pt I, pp. 6–11, 33–47); pt IV, p. 893.

Schumpeterian entrepreneur

According to Joseph A. Schumpeter (1883–1950), economic development is the consequence of changes caused by exceptional 'innovating entrepreneurs' that introduce in the economic system new products or new ways of organizing production. They are not inventors, they put the inventions into the production process and the market, following intuition and a desire to create, rather than economic calculus; and this innovation is the key factor of economic development. Then the rest of the firms, led by managers that simply organize companies in the way they were organized in the past, imitate the successful entrepreneur and so change the 'production function' of the system.

This 'creative destruction', caused by the entrepreneur in an economy that formerly rested in equilibrium without development, leads to a change in the parameters of economic activity, those in which the rational calculus of utility (rationalistic and unheroic) works. This entrepreneurial function was a theoretical construction necessary to understand how the economic system works, no matter who was performing that role: a capitalist, a manager, a pure entrepreneur, or even the state itself. But when it came to reality and history, Schumpeter described the importance of the entrepreneur as something belonging to a romantic past. In *Capitalism, Socialism and Democracy* (1942), his most successful book, in an epigraph entitled 'The obsolescence of the entrepreneur', Schumpeter wrote: 'The romance of earlier commercial adventure is rapidly wearing away, because so many things can be strictly calculated that had of old to be visualised in a flash of genius.' It has been suggested that he was impressed by the performances of 'big business' and their R&D effort, after moving to America. But, with some difference in emphasis, the same view was apparent in the 1934 English edition of his *Theory of Economic Development*, and even in the original 1911 German edition.

The political element of the theory of the entrepreneur was important from the beginning (Schumpeter himself thought it was entrepreneurship that made capitalism a meritocracy): instead of state planning, developing countries need more entrepreneurial spirit. The main obstacle remains, however, for an economic theory of the entrepreneur: the difficulty of integrating the concepts into the formal apparatus of static economics. The theory of the entrepreneur, with significant sociological content, was placed within the economics of development more than microeconomics. Schumpeter's ideas on innovation are alive today in the economics of innovation and technological change, even without his original hero, the individual entrepreneur.

MANUEL SANTOS-REDONDO

Bibliography

Santarelli, E. and E. Pesciarelli (1990), 'The emergence of a vision: the development of Schumpeter's theory of entrepreneurship', *History of Political Economy*, **22**, 677–96.

Schumpeter, Joseph A. (1911), *The Theory of Economic Development,* trans. R. Opie from the 2nd German edition, Cambridge: Harvard University Press, 1934; reprinted 1961, New York: Oxford University Press, pp. 57–94.

Schumpeter, Joseph A. (1942, 1975) *Capitalism, Socialism and Democracy,* New York: Harper and Row, pp. 131–42.

Schumpeter, Joseph A. (1947), 'The creative response in economic history', *The Journal of Economic History,* November, 149–59; reprinted in Ulrich Witt (ed.) (1993), *Evolutionary Economics*, Aldershot, UK and Brookfield, US: Edward Elgar, pp. 3–13.

Schwarz criterion

The Schwarz information criterion (SIC), also known as the Bayesian information criterion (BIC), is a statistical decision criterion that provides a reference method for choosing or selecting a model (or the right dimension of the model) among competing alternatives for a given set of observations. A desirable property of the SIC is that it leads to the choice of the correct model with unit probability asymptotically (it is asymptotically optimal).

The criterion is defined as to choose that model for which

$$SIC = \ln(L_{ML}) - \frac{k}{2}\ln(N)$$

is the highest (largest) among alternatives; where L_{ML} is the likelihood function of the model evaluated in the maximum likelihood estimate, N is the number of observations, and k is the number of parameters (dimension) of the model. The second term in SIC is a penalty for the number of parameters included in the model; the criterion always looks for the more parsimonious model in large samples.

This criterion originates from the Bayesian odds ratio between models. Under some conditions (models of iid data – independent and identical distributed data – or stationary time series data), the dependence on the prior can be avoided on the odds ratio asymptotically. Its popularity stems from the fact that it can be computed without any consideration of what a reasonable prior might be.

This criterion is not valid when the models under consideration contain non-stationary components, and it is a poor approximation of the original Bayes odds ratio in finite samples.

J. GUILLERMO LLORENTE-ALVAREZ

Bibliography

Schwarz, G. (1978), 'Estimating the dimension of a model', *Annals of Statistics*, **6** (2), 461–4.

Scitovsky's community indifference curve

This analytical device was introduced by the Hungarian economist Tibor Scitovsky (1910–2002) to compare the national welfare under different trade policies. The CIC, also called Scitovsky's contour, is defined as the geometrical locus of the points that represent the different combinations of goods that correspond to the same distribution of welfare among all the members of the community. It is shown that Scitovsky contours are minimum social requirements of total goods needed to achieve a certain prescribed level of ordinal well-being for all. The community indifference curve has the same geometric properties as individuals' indifference curve; that is, negative slope and convexity towards the origin. Other important properties of this curve are as follows: movements along a CIC do not imply that individual utilities are being held constant; aggregate utility is increasing as community indifference curves move away from the origin; movements to higher indifference curves do not mean that the utility of all consumers has increased; and the slope of community indifference curves is constant along a ray through the origin.

Scitovsky employed Marshallian offer curves superimposed on a community indifference map to demonstrate that to impose tariffs on international trade is generally in the rational interest of single countries. Nations acting independently to advance their own welfare could lead the world into a downward spiral of protectionism and impoverishment. Therefore there is nothing natural about free trade and, if we want it to obtain, it must be imposed and enforced.

ANA MARTÍN MARCOS

Bibliography

Scitovsky, T. (1942), 'A reconsideration of the theory of tariffs', *Review of Economic Studies*, **9** (2), 89–110.

Scitovsky's compensation criterion

One of the main contributions of Tibor Scitovsky (1910–2002) was to find a cycling problem in the well accepted Kaldor and Hicks compensation criteria to solve eligibility problems in welfare economics. The first criterion recommends a move from situation 1 to situation 2 if the gainers from the move can compensate the losers and still be better off, whereas the Hicks one presents situation 2 as preferred to situation 1 if the losers from the move cannot profitably bribe the gainers to oppose the change. A problem with these criteria is that they can lead to cycles, where a change from situation 1 to situation 2 is recommended, but, afterwards, a change back from situation 2 to situation 1 is recommended, too. This cycling phenomenon is known as the 'Scitovsky paradox' because he found this inconsistency problem in such criteria applied until the moment to look for changes resulting in economic improvements.

To solve the 'reversal' paradox, Scitovsky (1941) proposed a 'double' criterion: situation 1 is preferable to situation 2 if and only if both the Kaldor and the Hicks criteria are simultaneously satisfied. In terms of normal and inferior goods, and using the typical measure of welfare in this type of problem, the compensating variation, the Hicks–Kaldor criterion recommends a move from situation 1 to situation 2 if the sum of both compensating variations, of losers and of winners, is positive. However, if the sum of both compensating variations but also of the alternative move from situation 2 to situation 1 is positive we will have a cycling problem. A necessary condition for the Scitovsky paradox to hold is the good providing utility to be an inferior one for at least one party in the society. Hence, if such good is a normal one for both parties, the Scitovsky compensation criterion will be able to be applied in order to find one situation clearly superior to the other.

JOSÉ IGNACIO GARCÍA PÉREZ

Bibliography

Scitovsky, T. (1941), 'A note on welfare propositions in economics', *Review of Economic Studies*, **IX**, 77–88.

See also: Chipman–Moore–Samuelson compensation criterion, Hicks compensation criterion, Kaldor compensation criterion.

Selten paradox

This refers to the discrepancy between game-theoretical reasoning and plausible human behaviour in the 'chain-store game' devised by Reinhard Selten (b.1930, Nobel Prize 1994) in 1978. In this simple extensive-form game, a monopolist faces a set of *n* potential competitors in *n* different towns who successively decide whether or not to enter the market. The game is played over a sequence of *n* consecutive periods. In every period *k*, potential entrant *k* must make a decision. If the decision is to stay out, then this potential entrant and the monopolist receive pay-offs *e* and *m*, respectively, with $m > e$. If the decision is to enter, the monopolist can react cooperatively, in which case both receive pay-off *c*, with $m > c > e$, or aggressively, in which case both receive pay-off *a*, with $e > a$. After each period, the potential entrant's decision and the monopolist's reaction are made known to all the players.

Using an inductive argument, it is easy to prove that the unique subgame perfect equilibrium of this game prescribes that, in every period, the potential entrant enters and the monopolist reacts cooperatively. In spite of this clear recommendation of game theory, it seems plausible that, in practice, the monopolist will react aggressively in the first periods of the game, in order to build a reputation and so deter potential entrants. Selten writes that 'the fact that the logical inescapability of the induction theory fails to destroy the plausibility of the deterrence theory is a serious phenomenon which merits the name of a paradox'.

To explain this paradox, Selten constructed a limited rationality theory of human decision making. Since then, several authors have suggested that a real-life game is slightly different, and have shown that, by including a small amount of incomplete information in Selten's game, the game-theoretical solution is much more in accordance with plausible behaviour.

IGNACIO GARCÍA-JURADO

Bibliography
Selten, R. (1978), 'The chain store paradox', *Theory and Decision*, **9**, 127–59.

Senior's last hour
This expression was coined by Karl Marx in volume I, chapter 9 of *Capital* to refer to the idea that the whole net profit is derived from the last hour of the workday, used by Nassau Senior in his opposition to the proposal for the Ten Hours Act.

Nassau William Senior (1790–1864), professor of Political Economy at Oxford and at King's College London, was actively involved in the setting of economic policy. He advised the Whig Party and served on the Poor Laws (1832–4) and Irish Poor Law (1836) commissions; in 1841, he drew up the report of the Unemployed Hand-loom Weavers Commission, in which the conclusions reached expressed a radical opposition to government assistance for the unemployed weavers and were in fact contrary to the very existence of trade unions.

In 1837, Senior tried to prove his point on the 'last hour' by means of a hypothetical arithmetic example, which for Mark Blaug was unrealistic, that assumed a one-year turnover period, with capital being 80 per cent fixed and 20 per cent working, a gross profit margin of 15 per cent and an approximate 5 per cent depreciation; if the workday is eleven and a half hours (23 half hours, to quote Senior), the first ten hours only produce enough of the final product to replace the raw materials and wages advanced: 'Of these 23-23ds . . . twenty . . . replace the capital – one twenty-third . . . makes up for the deterioration on the mill and machinery . . . The remaining 2-23ds, that is, the last two of the twenty-three half hours every day produce the net profit of ten per cent' (Senior, 1837, pp. 12–13).

With these premises, Senior's conclusion could only be that 'if the number of working hours were reduced by one hour per day (price remaining the same), the net profit would be destroyed – if they were reduced by an hour and a half, even gross profit would be destroyed' (p. 13). Therefore the Ten Hours Act should not be enacted, given the serious risk involved for British cotton manufacture.

Senior's blunder, as Marx demonstrated and J.B. DeLong later confirmed in 1986, stems from considering that the turnover period is invariable with regard to changes in the length of the work day, without taking into account that, with a reduction in the working hours, 'other things being equal, the daily consumption of cotton, machinery, etc. will decrease in proportion . . . workpeople will in the future spend one hour and a half less time in reproducing or replacing the capital advanced' (Marx, 1867, p. 224). Another analytical error, that according to Schumpeter revealed Senior's lack of technical expertise, was to presume that the productivity per man-hour was constant. In fact, the Ten Hours Act was passed a decade later, and the British cotton textile industry did not experience the disasters predicted by Senior.

Both Bowley, in his *Nassau Senior and Classical Economics* of 1937, and Johnson (1969) tried to defend Senior's competence, mentioning the use of faulty empirical data, the presumption of constant returns and certain errors which for Johnson consisted basically in confusing stocks and flows in the calculation of returns. DeLong (see Pullen 1989), together with a general criticism of Senior's postulates, highlighted a mathematical error given that, using the same data, he concluded that, even if the work day were reduced to ten hours, only a 20 per cent reduction in net profit would result – a conclusion already drawn by Blaug. Marx made no indication of this. The subsequent correction formulated by Pullen (1989) regarding DeLong's criticism was based on a note introduced by Senior in the third edition of the *Letters on the Factory Act*. This correction was perhaps irrelevant since, even if the arithmetical accuracy of Senior's calculations were accepted, his errors remain.

SEGUNDO BRU

Bibliography

Johnson, O. (1969), 'The "last hour" of Senior and Marx', *History of Political Economy*, **1** (2), 359–69.

Marx, K. ([1867] 1967), *Capital*, New York: International Publishers.

Pullen, J.M. (1989), 'In defence of Senior's last hour-and-twenty-five minutes, with a reply by J. Bradford DeLong, and a rejoinder by Pullen', *History of Political Economy*, **21** (2), 299–312.

Senior, N.W. (1837), *Two Letters on the Factory Act, as it affects the cotton manufacture, addressed to the Right Honourable the President of the Board of Trade*; reprinted 1965, in *Selected Writings on Economics: A Volume of Pamphlets 1827–1852*, New York: Kelley.

Shapley value

This is due to Lloyd S. Shapley (b.1923). The Shapley value can be considered together with the *core* (also conceived by Shapley) as the most prominent solution concept in cooperative game theory. It assigns to each game in characteristic function form v a unique vector $\phi\, v$ that can be interpreted as the prospects of the players in the game. Alternatively, the Shapley value can be thought of as a reasonable agreement attained via consensus or arbitrated compromise, or even a measure of the players' utility for playing the game.

To define the value Shapley used an axiomatic approach; that is, he imposed three transparent and reasonable conditions that characterize uniquely the value. The 'symmetry' axiom prescribes that the names of the players should not affect the value. The 'carrier' axiom requires that players in any carrier of the game distribute precisely the total worth among themselves (a *carrier* of v is a coalition N such that $v(S \cap N) = v(S)$ for any coalition S). The third axiom, called 'additivity', requires that, for any two games, v and w, it holds $\phi v + \phi w = \phi(v + w)$.

Symmetry and carrier axioms fully determine the value of the unanimity games (a game u_S is called upon to be the unanimity game on coalition S if $u_S(T) = 1$ if $S \subseteq T$ and 0 otherwise). Since these games form a basis of the space of games, the additivity axiom yields the Shapley characterization.

The formula to calculate the Shapley value of a player i in the game v is given by

$$\phi_i v = \sum_{S \subseteq N \backslash \{i\}} \frac{s! \cdot (n - s - 1)!}{n!} v(S \cup \{i\} - v(S))$$

when N is the set of all the players, and $s = | S |$, and $n = | N |$.

This formula has a probabilistic interpretation. Assume that the grand coalition N is going to be assembled in a room, so the players randomly form a queue outside this room, and only one player enters at a time. When player i enters, all the members in the room form a coalition, say $S \cup \{i\}$, and his marginal contribution to the worth of this coalition is $v(S \cup \{i\} - v\,(S))$. There are $n!$ ways in which the players can be ordered in the queue, and $s! \cdot (n - s - 1)!$ ways in which the coalition $S \cup \{i\}$ is formed when i enters. Thus the Shapley value of any player is precisely his expected marginal contribution, when all the orders in the queue have the same probability.

The first applications of the Shapley value were to measure the distribution of the power among the voters of a political system. It has been also extensively applied to cost allocation problems to determine the distribution of the cost of carrying out a joint project among several agents. Other significant application is to the study of market games, where it is shown that the Shapley value coincides with the core, and hence with the competitive equilibrium of non-atomic economies.

JOSÉ MANUEL ZARZUELO

Bibliography

Roth, A.E. (1988), *The Shapley Value*, New York: Cambridge University Press.
Shapley, L.S. (1953), 'A value for n-person games', in H.W. Kuhn and A.W. Tucker (eds), *Contributions to the Theory of Games II* in *Annals of Mathematic Studies 28*, Princeton: Princeton University Press, pp. 307–17.

Shapley–Folkman theorem

This originated in the private correspondence of Lloyd S. Shapley and I.H. Folkman and was published in Ross M. Starr (1969). The theorem is as follows. Let F be a family of compact sets S in E^n such that, for all $S \in F$, the ratio of S is no greater than L. Then, for any subfamily $F' \subset F$ and any $x \in$ convex hull of $\sum_{S \in F'} S$, there is a $y \in \sum_{S \in F'} S$ such that $| x - y | \leq L\sqrt{n}$.

In words, the theorem determines an upper bound to the size of non-convexities in a sum of non-convex sets and was extended by Starr by measuring the non-convexity of the sets $S \in F$. It was originally used to demonstrate that, in a pure exchange economy with non-convex preferences, the divergence from equilibrium is bounded and that, for a large enough number of agents, there are allocations arbitrarily close to equilibrium (Starr, 1969), a result later on extended to the case of exchange and production economies with increasing returns to scale. Another standard use of the Shapley–Folkman theorem is to demonstrate the convergence of the core of a competitive economy to the set of Walrasian equilibria (Arrow and Hahn, 1971).

JULIO SEGURA

Bibliography

Arrow, K.J. and F.H. Hahn (1971), *General Competitive Analysis*, San Francisco: Holden Day.
Starr, R.M. (1969), 'Quasi-equilibria in markets with non-convex preferences', *Econometrica*, **37** (1), 25–38.

Sharpe's ratio

Sharpe's ratio is one of many statistics used to analyse the risk and return of a financial investment at a single glance. The modern portfolio theory assumes that the mean and the standard deviation of returns are sufficient statistics for evaluating the performance of an investment portfolio. In particular, higher returns are desirable but higher risks are not. Thus, in order to choose between alternative investments with different levels of returns and risk, a measure capable of summarizing both in one is needed. In this sense Sharpe's ratio is understood as a measure of the risk-adjusted performance of an investment.

Named after its developer, William Sharpe (b.1934, Nobel Prize 1990), it quantifies the amount of excess return earned by any portfolio or financial asset per unit of risk. As a matter of fact, it was originally called the 'reward-to-variability ratio'. The ratio is calculated by taking the portfolio's mean return, minus the risk-free return, divided by the standard deviation of these returns. The excess return in the numerator can be understood as the difference between the return of the acquired portfolio and the short position taken to finance it. The standard deviation measures only the risk of a portfolio's returns, without reference to a market index and in the same way for any type of asset or portfolio. Taking into account both the excess return and the risk of the portfolio, the ratio can be useful for choosing between alternative risky portfolio investments. The higher its Sharpe's ratio the better a portfolio's returns have been relative to the amount of investment risk it has taken. According to this, investors should choose the alternative with the higher Sharpe's ratio. Thus it somehow reveals the desirability of a portfolio.

However, as a raw number, the ratio is meaningless except for comparisons between alternative investments. Without additional information, a given ratio does not mean very much; investors are not able to infer from it whether the investment is appropriate or not. Only comparing the Sharpe's ratio for one portfolio with that of another do investors get a useful idea of its risk-adjusted return relative to alternative investments. Although applicable to several types of financial investments, it is typically used to rank the risk-adjusted performance of mutual funds with similar objectives.

As Sharpe (1994) himself points out, in using the ratio in the financial decision process an ex ante version of the ratio should be obtained. Consequently, the expected excess return and the predicted standard deviation of a given portfolio must be estimated in order to compute the ratio. When it is calculated from historical returns and used to choose between alternative investments, an implicit assumption about the predictive capability of past returns is being imposed.

One final point regarding the practical implementation of Sharpe's ratio in choosing the best alternative investment should be highlighted. While the ratio takes into account both expected returns and risk, it does not consider the correlation of these alternative investments with the existing portfolio. Thus the investment portfolio with the highest Sharpe's ratio may not be the best alternative if its correlation with the rest of the portfolio is sufficiently high to increase dramatically the final portfolio's risk. Therefore, only if the alternative investments show similar correlations with the investor's portfolio, should Sharpe's ratio be used to select between them.

EVA FERREIRA

Bibliography

Sharpe, William F. (1966), 'Mutual fund performance', *Journal of Business*, **39**, 119–38.

Sharpe, William F. (1994), 'The Sharpe Ratio', *Journal of Portfolio Management*, Fall, 49–58.

Shephard's lemma

The lemma, named after Ronald W. Shephard (1912–82), is a consequence of the duality of profit maximization and cost minimization in producer theory, and it relates a cost function to the cost-minimizing input demands that underlie it. It can be proved as a straightforward application of the envelope theorem.

Shephard's lemma has had a far-reaching influence on applied econometrics; since the cost function may be easier to estimate than the production function, it is used to derive the cost-minimizing input demands from the cost function. It is sometimes applied to consumer theory, relating the expenditure function to the Hicksian demand functions.

Formally, Shephard's lemma states the following. Suppose that $c(w, y)$ is the cost function of a single output technology, where $w >> 0$ is the vector of the n input prices, and y is the output level. Let $x_i(w, y)$ be the cost-minimizing input demand for input i, $i = 1, \ldots n$. If the cost function is differentiable with respect to w at $(\bar{w}, y)$, for a given vector of input prices $\bar{w}$, then

$$\frac{\partial c(\bar{w}, y)}{\partial w_i} = x_i(\bar{w}, y), \text{ for } i = 1, \ldots, n.$$

As an example, let $n = 2$ and let the production function be Cobb–Douglas, given by $y = \sqrt{x_1 x_2}$. Minimizing cost $\bar{w}_1 x_1 + \bar{w}_2 x_2$ subject to producing a given level of output y yields the cost-minimizing input demands $x_i(\bar{w}, y) = y\sqrt{\bar{w}_j/\bar{w}_i}$, $i, j = 1, 2, j \neq i$. The cost function is obtained by substituting the cost-minimizing input demands back to $\bar{w}_1 x_1 + \bar{w}_2 x_2$, $c(\bar{w}, y) = 2y\sqrt{\bar{w}_1 \bar{w}_2}$. Applying Shephard's lemma, we recover the cost-minimizing input demands from the cost function:

$$\frac{\partial c(\bar{w}, y)}{\partial w_i} = y\sqrt{(\bar{w}_j/\bar{w}_i)} \quad i, j = 1, 2, j \neq i.$$

CRISTINA MAZÓN

Bibliography

Shephard, R. (1953), *Cost and Production Functions*, Princeton University Press.

Simons's income tax base

Henry Simons (1899–1946) provided in 1938 a good conceptual framework for the problem of defining income for tax purposes. According to Simons, personal income is the algebraic sum of (a) the market value of rights exercised in consumption, and (b) the change in the value of the store of property rights between the beginning and end of the period in question.

In other words, it is merely the result obtained by adding consumption during the period to 'wealth' at the end of the period and then subtracting 'wealth' at the beginning.

This definition of personal income for tax purposes contains equity and efficiency considerations and is a useful enough frame of reference for the difficulties encountered in establishing legal definitions. According to this normative criterion, all accretions to the tax unit during the period are, ideally, included in the tax base, allowance being made for the cost of obtaining income. Personal income equals variations in net worth plus consumption during a given period. Therefore distinctions between sources or forms of use of income, or whether the latter is regular or irregular, realized or accrued, expected or unexpected, become irrelevant. All reductions of net worth also have to be taken into account, whatever their form. All that matters is the amount the tax unit could consume while maintaining the value of its net worth, or alternatively the amount by which a unit's net worth would have increased if nothing had been consumed, these definitions being applied to a given period of time.

Of course, this was all presented at a high level of abstraction. Problems arise when attempting to define net personal consumption or adequately to measure changes in net worth, and when giving these concepts a legal and practical form. There is an extensive literature on the subject. The most outstanding aspect of Simons's contribution is that it demands a comprehensive income tax base. The choice of income as an appropriate measure of the ability to pay taxes is ultimately a question of social philosophy, but, once the choice is made, and income is the yardstick selected to measure individuals' relative circumstances, it should include all accretions to wealth and all the factors affecting the prosperity or economic position of the individuals concerned.

Simons's definition of income was more complete than Haig's previous 'the net accretion to one's economic power between two points in time'. Personal prosperity is, in short, a good measure of the ability to pay taxes. This provides the rationale for comprehensive tax bases, or at least broad ones, and also for global income taxes, since an essential feature of Simons's approach is that all types of income are treated in the same way. Broad income tax bases are still predominant in tax systems. Global income taxes, however, for administrative and economic reasons, have lost the battle.

EMILIO ALBI

Bibliography

Haig, R.M. (1921), 'The concept of income', in R.M. Haig (ed.), *The Federal Income Tax*, New York: Columbia University Press.

Simons, H.C. (1938), *Personal Income Taxation*, University of Chicago Press.

Slutsky equation

Evgeny Evgenievich Slutsky (1880–1948) published widely in mathematics, statistics and economics. He approached value theory by firmly adopting Pareto's definition of a (cardinal) utility function. After obtaining the first- and second-order conditions for a constrained optimum he used the bordered

Hessian approach to provide a fundamental relation in consumer theory, generally known as the 'Slutsky equation' (1915).

This equation shows that the response of consumer demand to a change in market prices can be expressed as a sum of two independent elements, the substitution and the income effects. The first one gives the change in demand due to a variation in relative prices keeping utility constant. The income effect measures the alteration in demand due to a proportionate change in all prices, or of a compensating variation in money income, following which the consumer attains a new utility level. Nowadays this equation is easily proved with the aid of duality theory. Think of a consumer with money income y facing a vector p of market prices. Call her Marshallian and income-compensated demands for commodity j, $x_j^D = X_j^D(y, p)$ and $x_j^c = X_j^c(U, p)$, respectively. Let $y = m(U, p)$ be her expenditure function and assume full differentiability. Taking derivatives with respect to the price p_j of commodity j, we know by the envelope theorem that

$$X_j^c(U, p) = \partial m(U, p)/\partial p_j$$

and, by duality,

$$X_j^c(U, p) = X_j^D(m(U, p), p).$$

Again take derivatives, this time with respect to p_i, rearrange terms and Slutsky's equation follows:

$$\frac{\partial X_j^D(y, p)}{\partial p_i} = \frac{\partial X_j^c(U, p)}{\partial p_i} - x_i^C \frac{\partial X_j^D(y, p)}{\partial y},$$
$$(\forall i, \forall j, i, j = 1, 2, \ldots, n),$$

where the first and second terms on the right-hand side are the substitution effect S_{ji}, and income effect, respectively. When $S_{ji} > 0$ (< 0) commodities i and j are said to be net substitutes (net complements). Slutsky proved that $S_{jj} \leq 0$ and $S_{ji} = S_{ij}$, $\forall i$, $\forall j$. Both properties can be tested using ordinary demand data.

Hicks and Allen (1934) improved upon Slutsky's result by showing that the matrix of substitution effects is negative semidefinite when preferences are convex independently of the particular function representing those preferences, thus liberating utility theory from the last cardinality strings attached to it. Their work settled for good the controversy about how to define the degree of substitutability between any pair of commodities and effectively completed standard consumer theory. The symmetry and negative semidefiniteness of the substitution matrix, together with Walras's law and the homogeneity of degree zero of demands, remain the only general predictions of demand theory to date. They can be used as constraints in the estimation of individual demand parameters (albeit not, except under exceptional circumstances, in the estimation of *aggregate* demand functions). And most importantly, when the four predictions hold, Hurwicz and Uzawa showed (1971) that preferences become integrable and individual demand data can be fed into an algorithm to compute the indifference curves, and thus a utility function, generating the data. Individual welfare analysis becomes possible.

In suboptimal worlds the desirability of implementing a particular policy is measured against the cost of leaving things as they are or of adopting alternative courses of action. The never-ending controversies on income tax reform rely on the estimation of income effects on the hours of work where the Slutsky condition is imposed as a constraint on the data. The deadweight loss of taxing the consumption of particular commodities, establishing quotas or determining the effects of rationing depend on the degree of net complementarity with other goods. So do the criteria ruling the optimality of proportional commodity taxation. Policies that do not affect marginal incentives are generally less costly from a welfare point of view since their degree of inefficiency depends crucially on the induced substitution effect on the choice of a consumer.

The welfare cost of any public policy affecting the budget set of a consumer is often valued by the Hicksian compensating variation of the income required for maintaining the consumer at a benchmark welfare level after the induced change in prices and income. This cardinal standard can then be compared with the value obtained for alternative plans of action. However, the attempt to extend its use in cost–benefit analysis to derive aggregate money measures of welfare gains following the adoption of a particular project has proved to be at best problematic, since it ignores distributional issues. It may also be nonsensical because a positive sum of compensating variations, although a necessary condition for a potential Pareto improvement is not sufficient.

CARMEN CARRERA

Bibliography

Slutsky, E. (1915), 'Sulla teoria del bilancio del consumatore', *Giornale degli Economisti,* **51**, 1–26; translated as 'On the theory of the budget of the consumer', in G.J. Stigler and K.E. Boulding (eds) (1953), *Readings in Price Theory*, London: George Allen and Unwin, pp. 27–56.

Hicks, J.R. and R.G.D. Allen (1934), 'A reconsideration of the theory of value', Parts I and II, *Economica*, N.S.; Feb. (1), 52–76; May (2), 196–219.

Hurwicz, L. and H. Uzawa (1971), 'On the integrability of demand functions' in J.S. Chipman *et al.* (eds), *Preferences, Utility and Demand Theory*, New York: Harcourt Brace Jovanovich.

See also: Hicksian demand, Marshallian demand.

Slutsky–Yule effect

This refers to a distorting outcome that may arise from the application of certain common filtering operations on a time series resulting in the appearance of spurious cyclical behaviour, that is, fictitious cycle components not actually present in the original data but mere artefacts of the filtering operation. We may note in passing that such a 'distorting' phenomenon is but a particular case of general Slutsky–Yule models (ARMA), whose system dynamics can convert random inputs into serially correlated outputs; this notwithstanding, the term is usually reserved for the spurious outcome just described.

In practice, the spurious cycle usually appears when both averaging and differencing filters are applied concurrently to the same data set; that is, when differences are taken (possibly with the idea of removing the trend) after some sort of averaging has already taken place (possibly in order to smooth the data). More generally, differencing operations tend to attenuate long-term movements, while averaging is used to attenuate the more irregular components. The combined effect is meant to emphasize certain of the intermediate medium-range movements, as is usually the case, for example, in underlying growth estimation or business cycle extraction, although, as the present topic illustrates, sometimes with undesired side-effects.

Mechanical detrending by use of the so-called HP filter (Hodrick and Prescott, 1980) may also lead to reporting spurious cyclical behaviour. For instance, as Harvey and Jaeger (1993) point out, applying the standard HP filter (noise-variance ratio set to 1600) to a simple random walk produces detrended observations with the appearance of a business cycle (7.5 years) for quarterly data.

A simple historical example of the consequences of the Slutsky–Yule effect, as described by Fishman (1969, pp. 45–9), will serve as illustration. In the Kuznets (1961) analysis of long swings in the economy, the data were first smoothed by applying a five-year moving average that would attenuate short-range cyclical and irregular components.

The second filter involved a differencing operation of the form $y_t = x_{t+5} - x_{t-5}$. Kuznets concluded that the average period of the cycle he was observing in the data was about 20 years, but these movements could well correspond to a spurious cycle induced by the two filtering operations.

The manner in which the Slutsky–Yule effect may appear is easier to appreciate in the frequency domain by way of the gain functions associated with a particular filter: these functions measure the amount by which cyclical movements of different periods are enhanced or diminished by the filter. Consider the gain function associated with the difference operator, $\Delta_s = 1 - L^s$. This is given by $G(\omega) = 2\sin(s\omega/2)$, which is zero at the origin and at multiples of $2\pi/s$. Thus, in effect, it eliminates the long-term movements or trend, together with certain periodic movements. In contrast, the gain of the averaging operator $M_m = (1 + \ldots + L^{m-1})/m$ is given by

$$G(\omega) = \frac{\sin(m\omega/2)}{m\sin(\omega/2)},$$

which is equal to one at the origin but relatively small at high frequencies. Therefore it eliminates highly irregular movements but leaves the trend untouched. The overall effect of the averaging operator M_m followed by the differencing operator Δ_s has a gain function that shows a large peak corresponding to movements of a certain period which are therefore much enhanced with respect to the rest, the striking point being that, by a suitable choice of m and s, such peak may be made to correspond closely to movements of any desired period. In the Kuznets case above, we find that $m = 5$ and $s = 10$ give us a gain function with a large peak corresponding to movements around a period of 21.65 years.

Another interesting example of the Slutsky–Yule effect is that which occurs when estimating the underlying annual growth rates of certain economic indicators such as industrial production or price indices. This is again commonly done by way of the $M_m \times \Delta_s$ filter described above, in spite of the fact that some choices of the m, s values are potentially dangerous. For example, if, say, $m = s = 3$ or $m = s = 12$, it can be shown that the resulting gain function has a large peak corresponding to a period roughly around eight or 32 observations, respectively. It is not then surprising that such indicators may appear to show strong cycles that are in fact unwarranted by the actual data.

F. JAVIER FERNÁNDEZ-MACHO

Bibliography

Fishman, G.S. (1969), *Spectral Methods in Econometrics*, Cambridge, MA: Harvard University Press,.

Harvey, A. and A. Jaeger (1993), 'Detrending, stylised facts and the business cycle', *Journal of Applied Econometrics*, **8**, 231–47.

Hodrick, R.J. and E.C. Prescott (1980), 'Post war U.S. business cycles: an empirical investigation', *Discussion Paper 451*, Carnegie-Mellon University.

Kuznets, S.S. (1961), *Capital and the American Economy: Its Formation and Financing*, New York: NBER.

Snedecor F-distribution

The American mathematician and physicist George Waddel Snedecor (1881–1974) worked as statistical consultor in the fields of biology and agriculture and was the first director of the Statistical Laboratory organized in 1933 under the Iowa State University President's Office. His major influence came from his *Statistical Methods* (first published in 1937 under the title *Statistical Methods Applied to Experiments in Biology and Agriculture*). In Cochran's words, 'this book [. . .] has probably been more widely used as reference or text than any other in our field' (1974, p. 456).

The F-probability distribution is the ratio

of two chi-square distributions, each one divided by its degree of freedom. The probability density function of an $F_{m,n}$ is

$$f(x) = \frac{\Gamma\left(\frac{m+n}{2}\right)\left(\frac{m}{n}\right)^{m/2} x^{\frac{m}{2}-1}}{\Gamma\left(\frac{m}{2}\right)\Gamma\left(\frac{n}{2}\right)\left(1+\frac{mx}{n}\right)^{\frac{m+n}{2}}},$$

where Γ is the gamma function and m and n are the degrees of freedom of each chi-square.

The F-distribution is J-shaped if $m \leq 2$, and if $n > 2$ it is unimodal. If $m, n > 2$, the modal value

$$\frac{m-2}{m} \frac{n}{n+2}$$

is below 1 and the mean value $(= n(n-2))$ above 1, therefore the distribution is always positively skewed. As m and n increase, the F-distribution tends to normality and the t^2 distribution is a particular case of F-distribution where $m = n = 1$.

The F-distribution is mainly used to develop critical regions for hypothesis testing and for constructing confidence intervals. Examples of F-tests arising from normal random variables are tests for random-effects models, for the ratio of two normal variances and for the multiple correlation coefficient. F-tests also arise in other distributional situations such as the inverse Gaussian distribution, the Pareto distribution and Hotelling's T^2 distribution.

JULIO SEGURA

Bibliography

Cochran, W.G. (1974), 'Obituary. George W. Snedecor', *Journal of the Royal Statistical Society*, Serie A, **137**, 456–7.

Kendall, M. and A. Stuart (1977), *The Advanced Theory of Statistics*, 4th edn, London and High Wycombe: Charles Griffin & Company.

See also: Gaussian distribution, Hotelling's T^2 statistic, Pareto distribution, Student t-distribution.

Solow's growth model and residual

The Solow (1956) growth model solved the instability problem which characterized the Harrod and Domar models, under which a balanced growth path was an unstable knife-edge particular solution. Robert M. Solow (b.1924, Nobel Prize 1987) formulated a long-run growth model which accepted all the Harrod–Domar assumptions except that of the fixed coefficients production function. As Solow showed in his model, the assumption of fixed proportions was crucial to the Harrod–Domar analysis since the possibility of the substitution between labour and capital in the standard neoclassical production function allows any economy to converge to a stable growth path independently of its initial conditions.

In his basic specification, Solow assumed a one-sector production technology represented by

$$Y_t = A_t F[K_t, L_t],$$

where output (Y) is assumed to be net of the depreciation of capital (K), and the population (L) grows at the constant rate n:

$$L_t = L_0 e^{nt}.$$

By identifying labour supply and demand, Solow assumed full employment, as the real wage equals the marginal productivity of labour.

Production function $F(.)$ is said to be neoclassical since it satisfies the following conditions: (i) $F(.)$ is continuously differentiable with positive and diminishing marginal products with respect to K and L; (ii) marginal productivities for each input which tend to infinity when K and L approach zero, and equivalently tend to zero as each input tends to infinity (that is, Inada conditions are satisfied); and (iii) constant returns to scale. The first condition ensures that the substitution between K and L is well defined. The second property guarantees that a unique steady state exists. Finally, the third condition allows the production function to be written in per capita units, that is,

$$y_t = \frac{Y_t}{L_t} = f(k_t),$$

where $k_t = K_t/L_t$.

Each period, a constant fraction s of output is invested to create new units of capital, and the remaining fraction $(1 - s)$ is consumed. Taking this assumption into account, net capital investment is given by

$$\dot{K}_t = I_t = sY_t.$$

Since $\dot{K}_t/K_t = \dot{k}_t/k_t - n$, capital accumulation can be written as

$$\dot{k}_t = sf(k_t) - nk_t.$$

As the Inada conditions imply that $\lim_{k\to\infty} f'(k_t) = 0$ and $\lim_{k\to 0} f'(k_t) = 0$, the differential equation above for k_t has a unique and stable steady state k^* such that

$$sf(k^*) = nk^*.$$

Thus the equilibrium value k^* is stable and the system will converge towards the balanced growth path whatever the initial value of the capital to output ratio. This stationary state for k^* implies that the capital stock and output grow in steady state at the same rate of growth n, maintaining the capital to output ratio constant.

As Solow showed, this basic model can be easily extended to an economy which exhibits exogenous neutral technological change. If technical change is Harrod-neutral the production function can be written as

$$Y_t = F[K_t, A_tL_t],$$

where the productivity parameter grows at the constant exogenous rate of technical progress g: $A_t = e^{gt}$. In this case the economy has again a unique stable steady state in which K_t/Y_t is constant, since both aggregates grow at the rate $n + g$, whereas the real wage grows forever at the rate of growth g.

The Solow model was generalized by Cass (1965) and Koopmans (1965) to allow the saving rate s to be determined endogenously by optimizing agents who maximize their intertemporal utility. In the mid-1980s the assumption of an exogenous rate of technical progress was replaced by formal analysis of the determinants of the long-run rate of growth of productivity in what have been called 'endogenous growth models'. More recently, Mankiw *et al.* (1992) generalized the Solow model including human capital in the production function. These authors showed that the basic Solow model was qualitatively right in explaining the empirical evidence on postwar productivity differences in large samples of countries, but the estimated effects of saving and population growth of income were too large. Since human capital accumulation was correlated with the investment rate and population growth, its inclusion allowed these authors to match the data much better with the predictions of the augmented Solow model.

RAFAEL DOMENECH

Bibliography

Cass, D. (1965), 'Optimum growth in an aggregative model of capital accumulation', *Review of Economic Studies*, **32**, 233–40.

Koopmans, T. (1965), 'On the concept of optimal economic growth', *The Econometric Approach to Development Planning*, Amsterdam, North-Holland.

Mankiw, N., D. Romer and D. Weil (1992), 'A contribution to the empirics of economic growth', *Quarterly Journal of Economics*, **107** (2), 407–37.

Solow, R. (1956), 'A contribution to the theory of economic growth', *Quarterly Journal of Economics*, **70**, 65–94.

See also: Cass–Koopmans criterion, Harrod's technical progress, Harrod–Domar model, Radner's turnpike property.

Sonnenschein–Mantel–Debreu theorem

Consider an exchange economy with m consumers and n goods, where each consumer i is characterized by an excess demand function $z_i(p) = x_i(p) - e_i$, defined for all nonnegative prices $p \in R^n_+$, where $x_i(p)$ and e_i are, respectively, the demand function and the initial endowment of consumer i. Under standard conditions, $z_i(p)$ is continuous, homogeneous of degree one, and satisfies $p \cdot z_i(p) = 0$. Clearly, the aggregate excess demand function $z(p) = \Sigma^m_{i=1} z_i(p)$ also has these properties.

The question posed by Sonnenschein (1973), Mantel (1974) and Debreu (1974) is whether $z(p)$ satisfies any other restrictions. The answer is negative. Specifically, their theorem states (with different degrees of generality) that, given an arbitrary function $z(p)$ satisfying continuity, homogeneity of degree one, and Walras's law ($p \cdot z(p) = 0$), there is an economy with $m \geq n$ consumers whose aggregate excess demand function coincides with $z(p)$. This result implies that further (and in fact strong) assumptions are needed to guarantee that market demands have the characteristics of individual consumer demands.

RAFAEL REPULLO

Bibliography

Debreu, G. (1974), 'Excess demand functions', *Journal of Mathematical Economics*, **1**, 15–21.
Mantel, R. (1974), 'On the characterization of aggregate excess demand', *Journal of Economic Theory*, **7**, 348–53.
Sonnenschein, H. (1973), 'Do Walras' identity and continuity characterize the class of community excess demand functions?', *Journal of Economic Theory*, **6**, 345–54.

Spencer's law

'The more things improve the louder become the exclamations about their badness' (Spencer, 1891, p. 487). S. Davies (2001) coined the eponym after the Victorian sociologist Herbert Spencer (1820–1903), who mentioned examples such as poverty, drink, education and the status of women and children. Davies, adding pollution and the quality of environment, explains Spencer's law as prompted by the lack of historical perspective, the perception problem whereby a phenomenon like poverty is not noticed when it is widespread, and the psychological appeal of pessimism. He also emphasizes the need to exaggerate a problem in order to attract more attention to it, and that the pretended solutions always carry specific agenda and demand more government intervention.

Spencer, who did not speak of a law but of a 'paradox', remarked that, 'while elevation, mental and physical, of the masses is going on far more rapidly than ever before . . . there swells louder and louder the cry that the evils are so great that nothing short of a social revolution can cure them'. He distrusted those who believe 'that things are so bad that society must be pulled to pieces and reorganized on another plan', but he was an anti-socialist not ultra-conservative, and opposed militarism, imperialism and economic inequalities (there are references to another Spencer's law meaning equality of freedom). He denies 'that the evils to be remedied are small' and deplores the lack of 'a sentiment of justice', but says that the question is 'whether efforts for mitigation along the lines thus far followed are not more likely to succeed than efforts along utterly different lines' (1891, pp. 490–93, 516–17). He rightly predicted that 'when a general socialistic organization has been established, the vast, ramified and consolidated body of those who direct its activities . . . will have no hesitation in imposing their rigorous rule over the entire lives of the actual workers; until, eventually, there is developed an official oligarchy, with its various grades, exercising a tyranny more gigantic and more terrible than any which the world has seen'.

Spencer advocated 'the slow modification of human nature by the discipline of social life', and also highlighted the risks of democratic or parliamentary economic and social interventions: 'a fundamental error pervading the thinking of nearly all parties, political and social, is that evils admit of immediate and radical remedies' (ibid., pp. 514–15).

CARLOS RODRÍGUEZ BRAUN

Bibliography

Davies, Stephen (2001), 'Spencer's law: another reason not to worry', *Ideas on Liberty*, August.

Spencer, Herbert (1891), 'From freedom to bondage', reprinted 1982, in *The Man versus the State. With Six Essays on Government, Society and Freedom*, Indianapolis: Liberty Classics.

Sperner's lemma

Consider a triangle T and assign to each vertex a different label. Divide T into smaller (elementary) triangles and denote the vertices of these triangles according to the following two criteria (Sperner's labeling): (i) the label of a vertex along the side of T matches the label of one of the vertices spanning that side; (ii) labels in the interior of T are arbitrary.

The lemma is as follows: Any Sperner-labeled triangulation of T must contain an odd number of elementary triangles possessing all labels. In particular (since zero is not an odd number) there is at least one.

The lemma generalizes to the n-dimensional simplex. To illustrate, consider the following example, due to Schmeidler. Let the n-dimensional simplex be a house. Triangulate it into rooms that are the elementary subsimplices. A side of the room is called a door if its edges are labeled with the first n of the $n + 1$ label. A room is fully labeled if it has one and only one door. The lemma says that, starting at any door on the boundary of the simplex and going from room to room through doors whenever possible, we either end up in a room with only one door or back at the boundary. In the former case, we have found a fully labeled room. In the latter case there are still an odd number of doors to the outside that we have not used. Thus an odd number of them must lead to a room inside with only one door.

The importance of Sperner's lemma is that it is an existence result. Finding fully labeled subsimplices allows us to approximate fixed points of functions, maximal elements of binary relations and intersections of sets. This is particularly important in general equilibrium analysis as this lemma can be used to prove Brouwer's fixed point theorem. Also, solving the fair-division problem is a relevant application of the lemma.

XAVIER MARTÍNEZ-GIRALT

Bibliography

Sperner, E. (1928), 'Neuer Beweis für die Invarianz der Dimensionszahl und des Gebietes', *Abhandlungen aus dem Mathematischen Seminar der Hamburgischen Universität*, **6**, 265–72.

See also: Brouwer fixed point theorem.

Sraffa's model

Piero Sraffa (1898–1983), in his book, *Production of Commodities by Means of Commodities*, presented various forms of his disaggregated model: single-product industries, multi-product industries, fixed capital and non-reproducible inputs. In this book the mathematics are reduced to a minimum; fortunately, his followers have made good use of them, in such a way that his claims have been clarified and completed.

The best-known version is that of single-product industries with circulating capital and positive physical surplus, which appears in part I of the book. Its productive processes are

$$\{A_a, B_a, \ldots, K_a, L_a\} \rightarrow A$$
$$\{A_b, B_b, \ldots, K_b, L_b\} \rightarrow B$$
$$\ldots$$
$$\{A_k, B_k, \ldots, K_k, L_k\} \rightarrow K;$$

and its price equations take the form

$$(A_a p_a + B_a p_b + \ldots + K_a p_k)(1 + r) + L_a w = Ap_a$$
$$(A_b p_a + B_b p_b + \ldots + K_b p_k)(1 + r) + L_b w = Bp_b$$
$$\ldots$$
$$(A_k p_a + B_k p_b + \ldots + K_k p_k)(1 + r) + L_k w = Kp_k,$$

where $a, b \ldots$ 'k' are the goods, $A, B, \ldots$ and K are the quantities of each commodity produced, $A_a, B_a, \ldots, K_k$ are the inputs, p_a, $p_b, \ldots, p_k$ the prices, r the rate of profit and w the wage rate.

On the basis of successive models, Sraffa showed that, using the production methods and the social criteria for the distribution of the surplus, which are observable and technically measurable data, as a starting point, it is possible to obtain the prices, the rate of profit and the relationship between wages and profits. In this way, he demonstrated the internal coherence of the classical approach, in particular that of Ricardo and Marx, and placed production and surplus at the very centre of the theoretical development. Moreover, by proving the inevitable joint determination of the rate of profit and of prices, he illustrated the theoretical weakness of any technical measurement of capital and, therefore, the similar weakness of the aggregates based on the marginal productivity of capital, which had been widely used by neoclassical theory.

Using the standard commodity as *numéraire*, Sraffa obtained the well-known relationship $r = R(1 - w)$, where R is the maximum rate of profit, showing that r is determined by the magnitude of the surplus. Furthermore, R is a constant of the system and is a good global measurement of the technical level and the reproductive capacity of the economic system.

Similarly, by introducing the concepts of basic and non-basic goods and considering the requirements to obtain a single commodity as net product, he made clear the productive interdependencies and defined what he described as 'subsystems'. In doing so, he opened the way for the analysis of vertical integration, subsequently developed by Pasinetti (1973).

At the end of his work he broached the problem of the re-switching of techniques, demonstrating that one technique may be the cheapest for two rates of profit and yet not be so for intermediate rates. This represented a break with the inverse evolution between rate of profit and intensity of capital, which is typical of many differentiable functions of aggregate production. As such, it was a decisive element in the 'Cambridge Controversies in the Theory of Capital' and, as Samuelson has recognised, represents Sraffa's undeniable contribution to economic theory.

JULIO SÁNCHEZ CHÓLIZ

Bibliography

Sraffa, P. (1960), *Production of Commodities by Means of Commodities*, Cambridge: Cambridge University Press.

Pasinetti, L.L. (1973), 'The notion of vertical integration in economic analysis', *Metroeconomica*, **25**, 1–29.

Stackelberg's oligopoly model

Also known as a 'model of leadership in quantity', this was initially proposed by the German economist Heinrich von Stackelberg (1905–46) in 1934, and depicts a situation where some firms in a market have the capacity to anticipate the reaction of rivals to changes in their own output, which allows them to maintain a certain strategic leadership. It is formally presented as a duopoly model where firms, which are profit maximizers, take their decisions about the quantity to produce in a sequential way. Firstly, the firm that acts as the leader chooses its output. Secondly, the other firm, that will be the follower, after observing the output of the leader, chooses its own level of production. The peculiarity of the model lies in the capacity of the leader to increase its profits using the knowledge about the potential reaction of its competitor.

In terms of game theory, this model is a kind of consecutive game whose solution is obtained by backward induction. In the second stage, the follower chooses the output, q_F, that maximizes its profits:

$$\underset{q_F}{Max}\, B_F = p(Q)q_F - c(q_F) = p(q_L + q_F)q_F - c(q_F),$$

where $p(Q)$ stands for the inverse market demand function and $c(q_F)$ is the follower's cost function. The first-order condition of this problem (given that the output produced by the leader, q_L, in the first stage is known) is

$$\frac{\partial B_F}{\partial q_F} = p(Q) + p'(Q)q_F - c'(q_F) = 0.$$

This equation defines the follower's reaction function, $q^*_F = R_F(q_L)$, that is equivalent to the reaction curve in the duopoly of Cournot, providing the best response in terms of the follower's output to the leader's decision.

In the first stage of the game, the leader chooses the level of output that maximizes its profits, taking into account the knowledge about the follower's reaction,

$$\begin{aligned}\underset{q_L}{Max}\, B_L &= p(Q)q_L - c(q_L)\\ &= p(q_L + q_F)q_L - c(q_L)\\ &= p(q_L + R_F(q_L))q_L - c(q_L).\end{aligned}$$

The first-order condition requires that

$$\frac{\partial B_L}{\partial q_L} = p(Q) + p'(Q)\left[1 + \frac{dR_F(q_L)}{dq_L}\right]q_L - c_L'(q_L) = 0.$$

The equilibrium in this market is obtained by solving this equation together with the follower's reaction function. In equilibrium the quantity produced by the leader is lower than in the Cournot model (where the decisions are simultaneous) and the profits are higher, reflecting its 'first moving advantage'. In contrast, the output and profits of the follower are smaller.

The Stackelberg solution only has sense as equilibrium when the leader is forced to produce the announced quantity. Obviously, if both firms behave as followers, the equilibrium reverts to the Cournot solution. Alternatively, if both firms behave as leaders, the price and the individual and joint profits will be lower than those of the Cournot and the Stackelberg models.

ELENA HUERGO

Bibliography

Cournot, A. (1897), *Researches into the Mathematical Principles of the Theory of Wealth*, trans. N.T. Bacon, New York: Macmillan; originally published in 1838.

Stackelberg, H. von (1952), *The Theory of the Market Economy*, trans. A.T. Peacock, New York: Oxford University Press.

See also: Cournot's oligopoly model.

Stigler's law of eponymy

Arguably a disquieting entry for the present dictionary, the law is stated thus by American statistician Stephen M. Stigler: 'No scientific discovery is named after its original discoverer.' Drawing on the well-known Mertonian work on the role of eponymy in the sociology of science, Stigler (who stresses: 'the Law is not intended to apply to usages that do not survive the academic generation in which the discovery is made') argues that the practice is a necessary consequence of the reward system that seeks not only originality but impartial merit sanctioned at great distance in time and place by the scientific community; that is, not by historians but by active scientists 'with more interest in recognizing general merit than an isolated achievement'. According to Mark Blaug, the law in economics has both examples (Say's law, Giffen's paradox, Edgeworth box, Engel's curve, Walras's law, Bowley's law, Pigou effect) and counter-examples (Pareto optimality, Wicksell effect).

CARLOS RODRÍGUEZ BRAUN

Bibliography

Blaug, Mark (1996), *Economic Theory in Retrospect*, Cambridge: Cambridge University Press.

Stigler, Stephen M. (1980), 'Stigler's law of eponymy', *Transactions of the New York Academy of Sciences*, **11** (39), 147–57.

Stolper–Samuelson theorem

The theorem predicts a strong link between changing world trade prices and the distribution of income. Wolfgang Friedrich Stolper (1911–2002) and Paul Anthony Samuelson (b.1915, Nobel Prize 1970) used the Heckscher–Ohlin model in 1941 to state that an increase in the relative price of a domestic good as a result of an import tariff raises the return of the factor used intensively in the production of the good relative to all other prices. Thus the imposition of a tariff raises the real return to the country's scarce factor of production. The reason for this is that, as the tariff increases the price of the importable good, the production in the import-competing sector expands and the demand for the factor used intensively in this sector increases.

The relation between factor prices and commodity prices became one of the pillars over which the Heckscher–Ohlin model was reconsidered in the second half of the twentieth century. The theorem explains the effects on factor prices of any change in the price of a good. For example, when growth or investment affects a country's endowments, the change in the Heckscher–Ohlin model causes a change in the price of one of the goods.

The theorem has relevant implications for advanced countries. While the Heckscher–Ohlin theory predicts that free trade would benefit GNP in both advanced and developing countries, the Stolper–Samuelson theorem predicts that 'certain sub-groups of the labouring class, e.g. highly skilled labourers, may benefit while others are harmed' (1941, p. 60). If a country has lots of skilled labour, its exports will tend to be intensive in skilled labour, but if unskilled labour is more abundant, its exports will be intensive in unskilled labour. Rich countries have relatively more skilled labour, so free trade should raise the wages of skilled workers and lower the wages of the unskilled. From this process arises the controversial notion that the standard of living of the workers must be protected from the competition of cheap foreign labour.

JOAN CALZADA

Bibliography

Salvatore, Dominick (1995), *International Economics*, 5th edn, Englewood Cliffs, NJ: Prentice-Hall, pp. 235–6.

Stolper, W.F. and P.A. Samuelson (1941), 'Protection and real wages', *Review of Economic Studies*, **9** (1), 58–73.

See also: Heckscher-Ohlin theorem, Jones's magnification effect, Rybczynski theorem.

Student t-distribution

From a mathematical point of view, the t-distribution is that of the ratio of two independent random variables,

$$t_v = \frac{Z}{U},$$

where Z has a standard normal distribution $N(0, 1)$ and

$$U = \sqrt{\frac{x_v}{v}},$$

where X_v is a variable with a chi-squared distribution with v degrees of freedom.

The origin of the t-distribution was the work of W.S. Gosset, a chemist turned statistician by the necessities of his work at Guiness's Brewery in Dublin. In fact this distribution is a nice example of interaction between theory and practice, and represented the beginning of investigations of sampling statistics in real samples. The distribution appeared in Student (1907). The pseudonym 'Student' had been adopted by Gosset who was not allowed to publish the paper using his real name owing to a very conservative attitude of the Guiness's Brewery towards scientific publication by its employees.

Student's paper was unusual preeminently because it attempted to deal with small samples at a time when all the emphasis was laid on the asymptotic behavior of sample statistics. Gosset investigated the distribution of

$$t = \frac{\bar{x} - \mu}{S/\sqrt{n}}$$

where $\bar{x}$ and S^2 are the sample mean and sample variance of a random sample of size n from a normal population $X \sim N(\mu; \sigma)$.

With large samples, the estimated standard deviation S could be assumed to be very close to the exact value of σ and therefore the asymptotic distribution of t would be $N(0; 1)$. With small samples, allowance had to be made for the error in the estimation of σ. The fewer the observations, the greater the allowance that must be made for error in the estimate S. For that reason, the distribution of t depends on the sample size through the degrees of freedom $v = n - 1$, although it lacks the unknown scale parameter σ.

The probability density of t with v degrees of freedom is

$$\int f(t_v) = \frac{1}{\sqrt{\pi v}} \frac{\Gamma\left(\frac{v+1}{2}\right)}{\Gamma\left(\frac{v}{2}\right)} \frac{1}{\left(1 + \frac{t^2}{v}\right)^{\frac{v+1}{2}}} \text{ for } |t| < \infty,$$

where $\Gamma(x) = \int_0^\infty y^{x-1} e^{-y} dy$.

The expected value and the variance of t_v are

$$E(t_v) = 0 \qquad \text{for } v > 1,$$

$$V(t_v) = \frac{v}{v-2} \qquad \text{for } v > 2.$$

Like the normal density, $f(t_v)$ is symmetric around its expected value and for values of $v > 30$ the approximation of $f(t_v)$ by $N(0; 1)$ gives very reasonable results.

In the figure the densities of $f(t_v)$ for $v = 1$ and $v = 10$ have been plotted together with the density of $N(0; 1)$. It is important to observe that $f(t_v)$ has longer tails than the standard normal *p.d.* This fact can be used to model data with some mild outliers.

Gosset was involved in agricultural experiments as well as with laboratory tests for growing barley for beer. When he visited the School of Agriculture in Cambridge he met F.J.M. Stratton, who was the tutor of Fisher, and made the introduction between Fisher and Gosset. After exchanging several letters, one of which contained the mathematical proof of the distribution of t_v made by Fisher, it is now evident that it was Fisher who realized that a unified treatment of the test of significance of a mean, of the difference between two means, and of simple and partial coefficients of correlation and regressions in random normal samples, could be done using the t distribution that was appropriate for testing hypotheses in an abundance of practical situations.

The general idea is that, if $\hat{\theta}$ is a random sample estimate of some population parameter θ, such that $\hat{\theta} \sim N(\theta; \sigma_{\hat{\theta}})$ and $S_{\hat{\theta}}$ is an

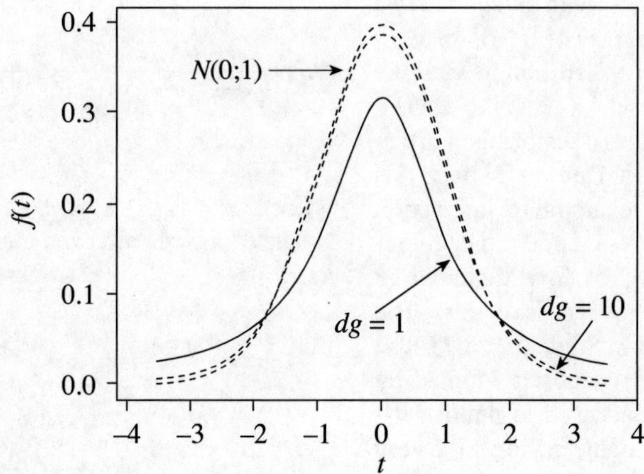

Student t-distribution

estimation of $\sigma_{\hat{\theta}}$ made with v degrees of freedom, then the statistics

$$t = \frac{\hat{\theta} - \theta}{S_{\hat{\theta}}}$$

will have a *t*-distribution with v degrees of freedom.

In time series analysis, the t-distribution is used for testing the significance of the estimated model's parameters, and for outlier detection.

ALBERT PRAT

Bibliography

Student (1907), 'On the probable error of the mean', *Biometrika*, **5**, 315.

Suits index

This index of tax progressivity was introduced by Daniel Suits (1977). It is a measure of tax progressivity. It varies from +1 at extreme progressivity to –1 for extreme regressivity. A value 0 of the index implies a proportional tax. The index is related to the Lorenz curve and the Gini concentraton ratio in the following way. In a diagram where the accumulated percentage of families is in the *X* axis and the accumulated percentage of total income is in the *Y* axis, the Gini coefficient is calculated as the proportion of the area above the curve that relates these two variables and the 45 degree line over the area of the triangle below the 45 degree line.

The Suits index is calculated in the same way, but in a space formed by the accumulated percentage of total income and the accumulated percentage of total tax burden. One of the most useful properties of the index is that, even though it is defined to identify the degree of progressivity of individual taxes, the indexes associated with each tax have the property of additivity, allowing the index to identify the progressivity of systems of taxes. In particular, if S_i is the index for tax *i*, the index of a system formed by *N* taxes will be

$$S = \frac{1}{\sum_{i=1}^{N} r_i} \sum_{i=1}^{n} r_i S_i,$$

where r_i is the average tax rate of tax *i*.

GABRIEL PÉREZ QUIRÓS

Bibliography

Suits, D.B. (1977), 'Measurement of tax progressivity', *American Economic Review*, **67** (4), 747–52.

See also: Gini's coefficient, Kakwani index, Lorenz's curve, Reynolds–Smolensky index.

Swan's model

Working independently, Australian economist Trevor Swan (b.1918) developed in 1956 what turned out to be a special case of Solow's (1956) model. Like Solow, Swan assumes that (net) investment is a constant fraction of output, but he restricts his analysis to the case of a Cobb–Douglas production function.

Using a simple diagram, Swan shows that, given constant returns to scale in capital and labour and a constant and exogenous rate of population growth, the economy converges to a long-run equilibrium in which output per capita increases if and only if the rate of technical progress is positive, and that increases in the investment ratio raise equilibrium output but have only transitory effects on the growth rate. He also explores the implications of decreasing returns to scale (caused by the introduction of a fixed factor of production) and of endogenizing the rate of population growth along Ricardian lines (so as to keep output per head constant over time or rising at some desired rate).

ANGEL DE LA FUENTE

Bibliography

Solow, R. (1956), 'A contribution to the theory of economic growth', *Quarterly Journal of Economics*, **70**, 65–94.

Swan, T. (1956), 'Economic growth and capital accumulation', *Economic Record*, Nov., 334–61.

See also: Solow's growth model and residual.

T

Tanzi–Olivera Effect

This refers to the negative effect on tax revenues of the combination of inflation and tax collection lags. In the absence of indexation, these lags will erode the real value of government revenue and deteriorate the budget situation. The corrosive impact of this effect on public revenue is particularly important in countries suffering hyperinflation. It may create a vicious circle, in which the reduction in the real value of tax revenues increases the public deficit, thereby provoking new inflationary tensions which, in turn, may reduce further tax revenues.

This effect can originally be traced back to studies by Argentinean Julio Olivera (1967), from Buenos Aires University, on the negative consequences of inflation on the budget. He noticed that, while public spending was linked to current inflation, public revenues were linked to past inflation, the disparity having a negative bearing on the deficit.

Years later, Italian Vito Tanzi (1977), from the IMF, arrived at the same result, which was thus labelled the 'Olivera–Tanzi' or 'Tanzi–Olivera' effect. According to research by Tanzi, in 1976, losses in real tax revenue due to deferred tax collection in Argentina were as high as 75 per cent of total tax income. Later research showed that real tax revenue losses in the 1980s in Argentina exceeded 2 per cent of GDP during periods of inflation acceleration.

While both Olivera and Tanzi focused on Latin America, the Tanzi–Olivera effect has also been at work recently in transition economies in Eastern Europe.

EMILIO ONTIVEROS

Bibliography

Olivera, J.H.G. (1967), 'Money, prices and fiscal lags: a note on the dynamics of inflation', *Quarterly Review Banca Nazionale del Lavoro*, **20**, 258–67.

Tanzi, V. (1977), 'Inflation, lags in collection, and the real value of tax revenue', *IMF Staff Papers*, **24** (1), March, 154–67.

Taylor rule

This rule arose in the context of the long academic debate about whether monetary policy (or even public policy in general) is better conducted by following predetermined rules or by the exercise of discretion. J.B. Taylor was concerned in 1993 with the fact that, despite the emphasis on policy rules in macroeconomic research in recent years, the notion of a policy rule had not yet become a common way to think about policy in practice. Modern macroeconomics, after the development of the Lucas critique, the rational expectations theory and the time-consistency literature, made clear that policy rules have major advantages over discretion in improving economic performance.

In this context, Taylor considered that it was important to preserve the concept of a policy rule even in an environment where it is impossible to follow rules mechanically. Taylor applied this idea to monetary policy and used some results of his own and others' research that pointed out that (implicit) monetary policy rules in which the short-term interest rate instrument is raised by the monetary authorities if the price level and real income are above target seemed to work better than other rules focused on exchange rate policies or monetary aggregates (measured in terms of ouput and price volatility). Therefore a 'rule' for monetary policy should place some weight on real output, as well as on inflation.

One policy rule that captures this settlement proposed by Taylor and that has become known as the Taylor rule is as follows:

$$r = 2 + p + B_1 y + B_2 (p - 2), \qquad (1)$$
$$B_1 = B_2 = 0.5,$$

where r is the short-term interest rate instrument, p is the (annual) rate of current inflation, y is the percentage deviation of (annual) real GDP from target (trend or potential).

The rule states that, with 2 per cent inflation ($p = 2$, considered close to the definition of price stability), and with no output deviation from trend or potential, nominal interest rate should be 4 per cent. The first argument in (1) relates to the equilibrium real interest rate, that Taylor assumes close to the steady-state growth rate (something that can be deduced, for example, from Solow's growth model).

The rationale behind (1) is that the monetary authority takes into account inflation and growth when setting the official interest rate. More (less) inflation or positive deviation of real GDP from target should lead to higher (lower) interest rates.

Taylor applied (1) for the case of the USA (using r as the federal funds rate) and found that it fitted policy performance during the 1987–92 period remarkably well. Implicit in Taylor's (1993) paper is that if such a rule is used by the monetary authority then it is giving equal weight to inflation and (deviation of) growth ($B_1 = B_2 = 0.5$). Other applications of the rule try to assess whether B_1 is greater or smaller than B_2 and therefore whether monetary authorities are inflation-biased ($B_2 > B_1$) or growth-biased ($B_1 > B_2$).

Taylor did not propose to conduct monetary policy by following (1) mechanically, but as part of a set of information used by the authorities when operating monetary policy.

DAVID VEGARA

Bibliography

Taylor, J.B. (1993), 'Discretion versus policy rules in practice', *Carnegie-Rochester Conferences on Public Policy*, Amsterdam: North Holland, **39**, 195–214.

See also: Lucas critique, Solow's growth model and residual.

Taylor's theorem

The English mathematician Brook Taylor (1685–1731) established that every smooth real-valued function can be approximated by polynomials, whenever the value of the function and their derivatives are known in a fixed point. The following theorems are known as Taylor's theorem for one and several variables, respectively (we note that Johann Bernoulli published in 1694 a result equivalent to Taylor's expansion).

Theorem 1 Let $f: D \to R$ be a real-valued function of one variable $q + 1$ times differentiable, with $D \subseteq R$ open, and let $x^0 \in D$. If $x \in D$ is such that $t \cdot x + (1 - t) \cdot x^0 \in D$ for all $t \in [0, 1]$, then $f(x) = P_q(x, x^0) + R_q(x, x^0)$, where

$$P_q(x, x^0) = f(x^0) + \frac{1}{1!} \cdot f'(x^0) \cdot (x - x^0) + \frac{1}{2!} \cdot f''(x^0) \cdot (x - x^0)^2 + \ldots + \frac{1}{q!} \cdot f^{(q)}(x^0) \cdot (x - x^0)^q$$

is the Taylor polynomial of degree q of f in x^0, and

$$R_q(x, x^0) = \frac{1}{(q + 1)!} \cdot f^{(q+1)}(t_0 \cdot x + (1 - t_0) \cdot x^0) \cdot (x - x^0)^{q+1}$$

for some $t_0 \in (0, 1)$, is the Lagrange form of the remainder term of f in x^0.

This result has been extended to real-valued functions of several variables.

Theorem 2 Let $f: D \to R$ be a real-valued function of n variable $q + 1$ times differentiable, with $D \subseteq R^n$ open, and let x^0

$\in D$. If $x \in D$ is such that $t \cdot x + (1 - t) \cdot x^0 \in D$ for all $t \in [0, 1]$, then $f(x) = P_q(x, x^0) + R_q(x, x^0)$.

$$P_q(x, x^0) = f(x^0) + \frac{1}{1!} \cdot \sum_{i=1}^{n} \frac{\partial f}{\partial x_i}(x^0) \cdot (x_i - x_i^0)$$

$$+ \frac{1}{2!} \cdot \sum_{i,j=1}^{n} \frac{\partial^2 f}{\partial x_i \partial x_j}(x^0) \cdot (x_i - x_i^0)$$

$$\cdot (x_j - x_j^0) + \ldots + \frac{1}{q!}$$

$$\cdot \sum_{i_1,\ldots,i_q=1}^{n} \frac{\partial^q f}{\partial x_{i_1} \ldots \partial x_{i_q}}(x^0)$$

$$\cdot (x_{i_1} - x_{i_1}^0) \ldots (x_{i_q} - x_{i_q}^0)$$

is the Taylor polynomial of degree q of f in x^0, and

$$R_q(x, x^0) = \frac{1}{(q+1)!} \cdot \sum_{i_1,\ldots,i_{q+1}=1}^{n} \frac{\partial^{q+1} f}{\partial x_{i_1} \ldots \partial x_{i_{q+1}}}(t_0 \cdot x$$

$$+ (1 - t_0) \cdot x^0) \cdot (x_{i_1} - x_{i_1}^0)$$

$$\ldots (x_{i_{q+1}} - x_{i_{q+1}}^0)$$

for some $t_0 \in (0, 1)$, is the Lagrange form of the remainder term of f in x^0.

JOSÉ LUIS GARCÍA LAPRESTA

Bibliography

Taylor, B. (1715), *Methodus Incrementorum Directa e Inversa*, London.

Tchébichef's inequality

A simple version of the Tchébichef inequality, also known as Bienaymé–Tchébichef inequality, after I.J. Bienaymé (1796–1878) and Pafnuty L. Tchébichef (1821–94), states that, for any distribution of a non-negative random variable X with expected value μ, the probability that the variable is bigger that t is of size t^{-1}. Formally,

$$Pr\{X > t\} \leq \frac{\mu}{t}.$$

For any random variable X with finite kth moment, the last inequality gives the more precise bound

$$Pr\{|X - \mu| > t\} \leq \frac{v_k}{t^k}.$$

where v_k is the kth central absolute moment. For $k = 2$, $v_2 = \sigma^2$ is the variance of the distribution and Tchébichef inequality provides an interpretation for this variance. The inequality also shows that the tails of the distribution decrease as t^{-k} increases when v_k is finite, and it proves that convergence in mean square, or more general k-norms, implies the convergence in probability.

Historically the Tchébichef inequality is related to the proof of the weak law of large numbers.

JOAN CASTILLO FRANQUET

Bibliography

Tchébichef, P.L. (1867), *Liouville's J. Math. Pures. Appl.*, **12** (2), 177–84.

Theil index

Consider an economy with n individuals. Let y_i be the income of the ith individual, y the income distribution,

$$\mu = (\sum_{1}^{n} y_i)/n$$

the mean income and $s_i = y_i/n\mu$ the share of the ith individual in total income. The Theil index, introduced in Theil (1967), is

$$T(y) = \frac{1}{n} \sum_{i=1}^{n} \frac{y_i}{\mu} \, ln \, \frac{y_i}{\mu} = \sum_{i=1}^{n} s_i \left[ln(s_i) - ln(\frac{1}{n}) \right].$$

$T(y)$ is simply the measure of entropy (disorder) in the theory of information applied to the measurement of income inequality. Analytically, the Theil index is just a weighted geometric average of the relative (to the mean) incomes. Economically, it can be interpreted as a measure of the distance between the income shares (s_i) and the population shares ($1/n$).

The use of the Theil index is justified by its properties: $T(y)$ is a relative index (homogeneous of degree zero) that, besides satisfying all the properties any inequality measure is required to meet, is also decomposable. That is, if the population is divided into $k(= 1, 2, \ldots, p)$ groups (for instance, regions of a country, gender or education) total inequality can be written as:

$$I(y) = \sum_{k=1}^{p} w(n_k, \mu_k) I(y^k) + I(\mu_1 e^1, \mu_2 e^2, \ldots, \mu_p e^p)$$

where the first term of the right side is the inequality within groups and the second term of the right side is the inequality between groups, n_k and y^k are the number of individuals and the income distribution in group k, $w^k = w(n_k, \mu_k)$ is a weight (which depends on the mean and the number of individuals in the kth group) and $\mu_k e^k$ is a vector with n_k coordinates, all of them equal to the mean income of the kth group (the income distribution of the kth group if there was no inequality within the group). Therefore an index is also decomposable if, for any income distribution and any partition of the population into p groups, total inequality can be written as the sum of inequality within groups (equal to a weighted sum of the inequality within each group) and inequality between groups (due to the differences of mean income between the groups). In the case of $T(y)$ the weights w^k are equal to the share of each group in total income ($w(n_k, \mu_k) = n_k \mu_k / n\mu$).

$T(y)$ is not, however, the only additively decomposable measure. Shorrocks (1980) showed that a relative index is additively decomposable if and only if it is a member of the generalized entropy family, $GE(\alpha)$:

$$GE(\alpha) = \frac{1}{\alpha^2 - \alpha}\left[\frac{1}{n}\sum_{i=1}^{n}\left(\frac{y_i}{\mu}\right)^{\alpha} - 1\right].$$

For the measure of parameter α, the weights of the decomposition are $w(n_k, \mu_k) = (n_k n)/(\mu_k/\mu)^{\alpha}$. When $\alpha \to 1$, $GE(\alpha) \to T$.

IGNACIO ZUBIRI

Bibliography

Shorrocks, A.F. (1980), 'The class of additively decomposable inequality measures', *Econometrica*, **48**, 613–25.

Theil, H. (1967), *Economics and Information Theory*, Amsterdam: North-Holland.

Thünen's formula

Also known as 'model' or 'problem', this was named after Johann Heinrich von Thünen (1783–1850), a North German landowner from the Mecklenberg area, who in his book *Der isolirte Staat* (1826) designed a novel view of land uses and laid down the first serious treatment of spatial economics, connecting it with the theory of rent. He established a famous natural wage formula $w = \sqrt{ap}$, w being the total pay-roll, p the value of the natural net product, and a the fixed amount of a subsistence minimum spent by the receivers. Thanks to the quality of his purely theoretical work, Schumpeter places him above any economist of the period.

Educated at Göttingen, Thünen spent most of his life managing his rural estate and was able to combine the practical farming with a sound understanding of the theory. The model assumed that the land was a homogenous space in which the distances to the market place determine the location of rural activities. It is a uniform flat plain, equally traversable in all directions, where an isolated market town is surrounded by rural land that can be used for different purposes; the costs of transporting the crops from these uses differ. Farmers at greater distances can pay only a lower rent because of the higher transportation costs for taking their products to the city. Each crop can be produced with different cultivation intensities.

The essence of Thünen's argument is that land use is a function of the distance to the market and that differential rents will arise as a consequence of transport costs. Several rings of agricultural land-use practices surround the central market place. The land within the closest ring around the market will produce products that are profitable in the market, yet are perishable or difficult to transport. As the distance from the market increases, land use shifts to producing products that are less profitable in the market yet are much easier to transport. In Thünen's schematic model the essential question was the most efficient ordering of the different zones. This approach has been picked up in modern applications of urban land-use patterns and other spatial studies where transportation costs influence decisions on land use.

The general approach of Thünen illustrated the use of distance-based gradient analysis (for example, the change in value for a variable such as land rent with increasing distance from the city center). His work also foreshadowed research on optimization in land allocation to maximize the net return associated with land-use activities. Shortly before his death, he asked that his formula be carved into his tombstone.

JESÚS M. ZARATIEGUI

Bibliography

Hoover, M. and F. Giarratani, (1971), *An Introduction to Regional Economics*, Pittsburg: Knopf.

Schumpeter, J.A. (1961), *History of Economic Analysis*, New York: Oxford University Press, pp. 465–8.

Thünen, J.H. von (1826), *Der isolirte Staat in Beziehung auf Landwirthschaft und Nationalökonomie*, reprinted 1990, Aalen: Scientia Verlag, pp. 542–69. The first volume was published in 1826, and part one of volume two in 1850; the rest of volume two and volume three appeared in 1863.

Tiebout's voting with the feet process

Charles Tiebout explained in 1956 the link between satisfaction of citizens and diversity of local jurisdictions. He asserts that the best way to measure voters' preferences for the combination of taxes and expenditures is to observe their migration from community to community, what is known as 'voting with the feet'. Tiebout's theory is based on several assumptions, some of them realistic, others less so.

First, it is assumed that the voters are completely mobile; in the real world such mobility exists for only a certain few. Another assumption is that voters know the differences in taxes and expenditures from one community to the next. In the real world this is mostly true, but the problem is that these patterns change from year to year. Tiebout's third assumption is that there is a number of communities large enough to satisfy all possible preferences of voters. A fourth claim is that employment restrictions are not a factor; this is not always true in the real world. Fifth, Tiebout asserts that public services of one jurisdiction have no effect on any other jurisdiction; that is, there are no externalities. Although this is not realistic, Tiebout notes that these externalities are not as important for the functionality of his model. Tiebout's sixth assumption seems somewhat to contradict the first. He states that there is an optimal community size, along with a seventh assumption, that communities strive to attain the optimal level. This would imply that, when the community has reached its optimal size, it is no longer on the market for voters to choose.

If people do vote with their feet, then most

taxes and expenditures should come at the local level, not at the national level.

NURIA BADENES PLÁ

Bibliography

Tiebout, C. (1956), 'A pure theory of local expenditure', *Journal of Political Economy*, **64**, 416–24.

See also: Buchanan's clubs theory.

Tinbergen's rule

Named after Jan Tinbergen (1903–1994, Nobel Prize 1969), the rule sets out that policy makers need exactly the same number of instruments as the targets in economic policy they wish to attain. Tinbergen (1952) wrote: 'z_1-policy is necessary and sufficient for target y_1, whereas z_2 and z_3 policy is necessary and sufficient for targets y_2 and y_3. The most extreme case is a corresponding partition into groups of one variable each. In that case each target t_k can only be reached by z_k-policy.' And he added a note: 'economists or economic politicians holding the opinion that there is such a one-by-one correspondence between targets and instruments evidently assume a very special structure' (ibid., p. 31). Tinbergen tried to help reach a mathematical solution for the first formal models in economic policy, reducing internal contradictions and making targets compatible with the available instruments. Mundell (1968, p. 201) referred thus to the rule: 'Just as a mathematical system will be "overdetermined" or "underdetermined" if the number of variables differs from the number of equations, so a policy system will not generally have a unique attainable solution if the number of targets differs from the number of instruments.'

ANA ROSADO

Bibliography

Mundell, R.A. (1968), *International Economics*, New York: Macmillan.
Tinbergen, J. (1952), *On the Theory of Economic Policy*, Amsterdam: North-Holland.
Tinbergen, J. (1956), *Economic Policy: Principles and Design*, Amsterdam: North-Holland.

Tobin's *q*

The ratio *q* defines the relationship between the economic value of an asset and the cost of replacing the services it produces with the best available technology. James Tobin (1918–2002, Nobel Prize 1981) wrote in 1969, 'the rate of investment, the speed at which investors wish to increase the capital stock, should be related, if to anything, to *q*, the value of capital relative to its replacement costs' (p. 23). The sentence provides a definition of the variable *q*, introduced by Tobin in the paper to make a distinction between the market value of an existing capital good (present value of the future expected income stream that can be generated by the asset) and the price of the new capital goods, equal to the cost of producing them. Second, the definition establishes a relationship between the value of *q* and the decision to invest: when *q* is greater than one the economic value of the asset is higher than the cost of producing the same flow of services (replacement cost) and therefore the demand of new capital goods, investment, will increase. On the other hand, when *q* is less than one it is cheaper to buy an existing asset than to produce a new one and we should observe more trade of existing assets than production of new ones. The value of *q* equal to one gives an equilibrium condition.

Tobin's conjecture that investment should be a function of the ratio *q* was formally shown by Fumio Hayashi 13 years later, introducing adjustment costs in a neoclassical model of the value-maximizing firm. The adjustment costs imply that it is costly for the firm to install or remove capital with the marginal cost being an increasing function of the rate at which investment takes place. The value-maximizing firm will satisfy the optimality condition of equality between the marginal cost and marginal value of a given investment flow in period *t*. The cost includes the purchase price of the asset and the marginal adjustment cost. The value is equal to the present discounted value of expected future marginal profits. In Hayashi's model the rate of investment is a function of marginal *q*, that is, the ratio between the market value and the replacement cost of the last unit of investment. The marginal *q* is more difficult to observe than the average one, which, if the firm is listed in the stock market, will be equal to the ratio between the market value of debt and equity, and the replacement cost of the productive assets. Hayashi provides conditions under which marginal *q* can be properly replaced by average *q* in investment models (constant returns to scale and competitive product markets, among others) and subsequently numerous '*q* models of investment' have been estimated in different countries, many of them using firm-level data.

In this framework, the ratio *q* is a sufficient statistic to explain the investment rate. However, many empirical papers find that variables such as cash flow of the firm also explain investment when the ratio *q* is included in the investment equation. This result is interpreted either as evidence that firms have to accommodate investment to financial constraints as well as to adjustment costs, and/or as evidence that average *q* is not a good approximation to marginal *q*, either because there are measurement errors (the replacement cost of the assets is difficult to calculate) or because the conditions of constant returns to scale or competitive product markets are not satisfied in the data. In the end, cash flow may be a better approximation to marginal *q* than average *q*.

A *q* ratio of one also implies that the rate of return of invested capital valued at replacement cost is equal to the rate of return of market-valued capital. In other words, the rate of return on invested capital is equal to the (opportunity) financial cost of that capital. A *q* equal to one is consistent with economic profits equal to zero. On the other hand, if *q* is greater than one, the firm earns extraordinary profits and may continue to do so in the future. Therefore its market value includes not only the present discounted value of the future profits earned with the already invested assets, but also the future growth prospects of the firm, and in particular the economic profits of the new projects not yet in place. A *q* value lower than one should predict that the firm will divest nonprofitable projects in the near future or that the firm itself may disappear since the assets it owns are worth more in alternative uses than in the present ones. It should not be a surprise, then, that average *q* has become a popular ratio to evaluate the economic profits of firms and to discover possible sources of market power and rents, for example through the endowment of intangible assets.

VICENTE SALAS

Bibliography

Hayashi, F. (1982), 'Tobin's marginal *q* and average *q*: a neo-classical interpretation', *Econometrica*, **50** (1), 213–24.

Tobin, J. (1969), 'A general equilibrium approach to monetary theory', *Journal of Money, Credit and Banking*, **1** (1), 15–29.

Tobin's tax

James Tobin (1918–2002), a follower of Keynes and a Nobel Prize winner in 1981, proposed first in 1972 and again in 1978 the creation of a tax on all transactions denominated in foreign currencies. For more than 25 years the proposal was ignored by most economists, but the dramatic increase in the number of transactions in world foreign exchange markets during the past two decades (nowadays, approximately 1 billion dollars are negotiated in these markets in a single day), along with the string of recent currency crises (from Europe in 1992 and

1993 to Argentina in 2001), made economists and politicians consider the suitability of establishing capital control mechanisms, among which Tobin's tax is one of the most popular.

In his 1978 paper, James Tobin expressed his concern about the disappointing functioning of floating exchange rate systems (set up after the collapse of the fixed rates system of Bretton Woods) in a world of international capital mobility. In particular, Tobin denounced two major problems: on the one hand, the deleterious effects of huge exchange rate fluctuations on national economies; on the other, the inability of flexible exchange rates, in Tobin's belief and contrary to what textbooks established, to assure autonomy of macroeconomic policies. In order, in his words, to 'throw some sand in the well-greased wheels' (of international capital markets) and solve these problems, Tobin thought that some kind of capital control mechanism was needed. Hence he proposed the creation of a small international proportional tax on all transactions denominated in foreign currencies, that would have to be paid twice: when foreign currencies are bought and again when they are sold. As a by-product, the tax would provide an important amount of resources that could help developing countries. The fact that the size of the tax would be independent of the length of time between buy and sell operations would achieve the end of disproportionately penalizing short-term trades versus longer-term ones.

The discussion around all features related to Tobin's tax over the past decade has been fruitful. The justifications for implementing the tax can be summed as follows. First, even a small tax (say 0.1 per cent) would virtually eliminate all short-run movements of capital (except in the context of virulent speculative attacks against fixed currencies); in this regard, the only reservation is that, until today, economists have not been able to prove that short-run movements of capital are destabilizing. A second reason, and the most important one in Tobin's opinion, is that the tax would restore the autonomy of monetary and fiscal national policies, albeit modestly, given its proposed size. Finally, the significant financial resources collected could be used to aid the developing world, the main justification in favour of the tax in the view of members of so-called 'anti-globalization' groups; paradoxically, Tobin considered the potential collected resources to be only a by-product of his proposal, never the principal goal.

It seems unlikely that Tobin's tax will become a reality, at least in the near future, owing to two main obstacles. First, there is a political problem: the geographical coverage of the tax must be complete because otherwise the exchange markets business would migrate to countries that have not implemented the tax. The second and most important objection concerns the definition of the tax base. At least, the tax should apply on spot, future, forward and swap currency transactions; but some economists fear that financial engineering would manage to create new exempt instruments that would, in the end, eliminate the effects of the tax.

In short, Tobin's tax is a well-intentioned idea that, however, faces great feasibility problems. Therefore economists should perhaps look for alternative capital control instruments.

MAURICI LUCENA

Bibliography

Grunberg, I., I. Kaul and M. Ul Haq (eds) (1996), *The Tobin Tax. Coping with Financial Volatility*, New York: Oxford University Press.

Tobin, J. (1978), 'A proposal for international monetary reform', *Eastern Economic Journal*, **4** (3–4), 153–9.

Tocqueville's cross

This is the name given by Alan Peacock to his formalization of Alexis de Tocqueville's idea that people would not support a tax increase on social groups of an income bracket immediately above theirs, because this is the status they expect to attain, and people take decisions, not on the basis of their current situation but rather on their expectations about the future. Tocqueville approaches the question from an historical point of view, develops the classical economist's argument that linked universal suffrage and redistribution demands, and reflects on different situations in which the percentage of the politically enfranchised population increases from a to a'. As this percentage goes up (or income redistribution becomes more unequal), relative income (y) falls (from c to c') and preferences for direct taxes soar to b', because newly enfranchised people come from a lower class, and support redistribution in the hope that a higher tax level will be paid by the highest social class.

JESÚS DE LA IGLESIA

Bibliography

Peacock, Alan (1992), *Public Choice Analysis in Historical Perspective*, New York: Cambridge University Press, pp. 46–53.

Tocqueville, Alexis de (1835–40), *Democracy in America*, reprinted 1965, Oxford: Oxford University Press, pp. 150–55, 598–600.

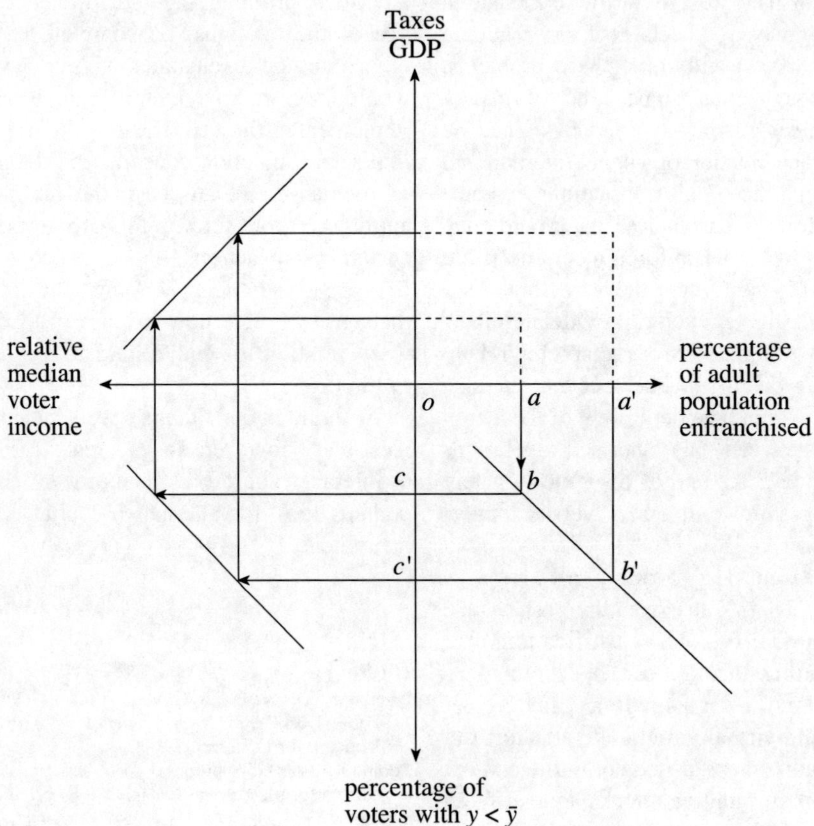

Tocqueville's cross

Tullock's trapezoid

During the 1960s monopoly power was severely criticized on the grounds of the generation of a deadweight loss, an excess of marginal value over marginal opportunity costs which is not collected by anyone or any institution. In the figure *ecf* represents the demand curve, *ed* is the marginal revenue curve and the *adf* the marginal cost curve, therefore *c* is the monopoly equilibrium and *f* the competitive one. This welfare cost from monopoly was labelled a 'Harberger triangle' (*A* or *cdf* in the figure).

When the broader use of statistics allowed economists to measure the magnitude of the welfare cost, it seemed to be really small compared with the general belief that monopolies were really distorting. Arnold Harberger was himself amazed by the results; Leibenstein attempted to reconcile the small estimates with the serious problem of monopoly and he coined the term 'X-efficiency', which refers to a hypothetical loss in efficiency due to the failure of a monopolist to maximize profit. But Gordon Tullock disagreed with Leibenstein and offered an alternative explanation for the apparently small cost generated by monopoly. The social cost should not be restricted to the triangle *A* or (*cdf*), because there is an additional social cost captured by the rectangle *C* (or *abcd*) which was viewed merely as a transfer.

In public choice, the 'Tullock rectangle' sets the boundaries for rent-seeking costs. When there is a pure transfer or surplus, economic agents will compete for its capture. If that competition is open in the sense that there are few barriers to entry, economic agents will enter and dissipate the resources to capture the transfer up to (or beyond) the point of complete dissipation. Tullock argues that a firm that has monopoly power due to an entry barrier may have had to invest in order to achieve that barrier and keep it high. So, following the Tullock example, a firm that currently faces severe competition will get an economic profit that is near zero. If all of the other firms were to drop out of the industry, the firm would earn a monopoly

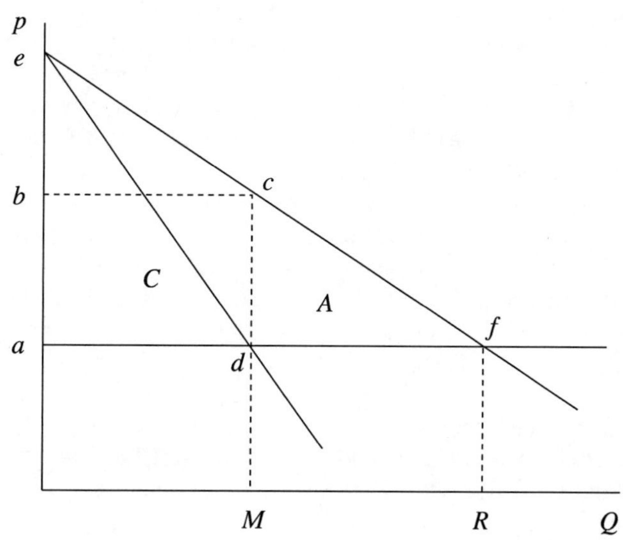

Tullock's trapezoid

power of, say, 100 monetary units. Assuming that the firm could force the other firms out of the industry by investing 99 monetary units, it would maximize profit by making the investment. In the figure, its monopoly profit (*C* area) would be 100, but proper accountancy would record a profit of only 1. So the greater monopoly power would be associated with only a small accounting profit, and it would explain the low social cost due to monopoly. Thus, a 'public finance view' would consider a social cost measured by a triangle (*A*), as the 'public choice view' would consider a trapezoid (*A* + *C*).

NURIA BADENES PLÁ

Bibliography

Tullock, G. (1967), 'The welfare costs of tariffs, monopolies and theft', *Western Economic Journal*, **5**, 224–32.
Tullock, G. (1998), 'Which rectangle?', *Public Choice*, **96**, 405–10.
Tullock, G. (2003) 'The origin of the rent-seeking concept', *International Journal of Business and Economics,* **2** (1), 1–18.

See also: Harberger's triangle.

Turgot–Smith theorem

Saving decisions derived from frugality are the source of investment and therefore of economic growth. J.A. Schumpeter identified the idea and its authors: French minister and economist Anne Robert Jacques Turgot (1727–81) and Adam Smith. He attributed to the former the analytic paternity and to the latter the role of mere diffuser. After Smith, 'the theory was not only swallowed by the large majority of economists: it was swallowed hook, line, and sinker' (Schumpeter, 1954, pp. 323–6).

Turgot formulated the theory in his *Reflections on the Production and Distribution of Wealth* (1766, LXXXI, LXXXII, CI, included in Groenewegen, 1977) and in the final part of the *Observations on a Paper by Saint-Pèravy* (1767, also included in Groenewegen, 1977). His notions on saving and investment are part of a new capital theory that generalized François Quesnay's analysis of agricultural advances to all branches of economic activity. In opposition to the predominant view according to which money not spent on consumption would leak out of the circular flow, Turgot argues that savings, accumulated in the form of money, would be invested in various kinds of capital goods, and so would return to circulation immediately. He analyses five uses of the saved funds: investing in agriculture, manufacturing or commercial enterprises, lending at interest, and purchasing land. Each of these provides a different but interrelated profitability, and an equilibrium position is achieved through the competitive process and the mobility of capital. Turgot excludes hoarding for its irrationality (lack of profitability) and because money was mainly a medium of exchange.

Adam Smith picked up Turgot's theses and in the *Wealth of Nations* (1776, bk II, ch. 3) he developed his own doctrine on the determinant role of frugality and saving in capital accumulation. Smith's most celebrated and influential formulation of the theorem is: 'What is annually saved is as regularly consumed as what is annually spent, and nearly in the same time too; but it is consumed by a different set of people' (1776, p. 337). This was not accurate because it blurred the difference between consumption and investment. But what Smith meant was that investment results in income payments, which in turn are spent on consumption. Also excluding the hoarding possibility, the Smithian dictum of 'saving is spending' was dominant among classical and neoclassical economists, but met with the criticisms of Malthus, Sismondi, Marx, Keynes and their followers.

VICENT LLOMBART

Bibliography

Groenewegen, Peter D. (1977), *The Economics of A.R.J. Turgot*, The Hague: Martinus Nijhoff.
Schumpeter, Joseph A. (1954), *History of Economic Analysis*, London: George Allen & Unwin.
Smith, Adam (1776), *An Inquiry into the Nature and Causes of the Wealth of Nations*, 2 vols, reprinted 1976, ed. R.H. Campbell and A.S. Skinner, Oxford: Clarendon Press.

See also: Say's law.

V

Veblen effect good

In his *Theory of the Leisure Class* (1899), Thorstein Veblen (1857–1929) developed the theory of 'conspicuous consumption'. The wealthy 'leisure class' made a lot of conspicuous expenditure as a way to show its status. In American culture, with class distinctions blurred, this pattern is imitated by the middle and lower classes. Then 'pecuniary emulation' becomes the explanation of consumer behaviour, and not neoclassical demand theory, which Veblen thought unrealistic.

Neoclassical economics has abstracted this sociological and cultural explanation for consumption – the very formation of tastes and consumption patterns – and developed it as a particular case in which the utility we get from a commodity is derived not only from its intrinsic or instrumental qualities, but from the price we pay for it. This is called the 'Veblen effect' and was formally presented by Leibenstein in 1950. In order to know the effects that conspicuous consumption has on the demand function, we separate the effect of a change in price into two effects: the price effect and the 'Veblen effect'. Previously we divided the price of the good into two categories: the real price, the money we pay for the good in the market, and the 'conspicuous price', the price other people think we have paid for the commodity. Traditionally it is thought that fashion clothing, fashion products, fancy cars or even diamonds are in demand as a means of signalling consumer wealth. If there is a difference between the two prices, the resulting possible equilibria may yield an upward-sloping Veblenian demand curve, an exception similar to Giffen goods but with a very different explanation. In this way we use the Veblen explanation for consumption within the neoclassical framework of microeconomics, but only for some particular kind of goods.

MANUEL SANTOS-REDONDO

Bibliography

Leibenstein, H. (1950), 'Bandwagon, snob and Veblen effects in the theory of consumers' demand', *Quarterly Journal of Economics*, **64**, 183–207; reprinted in W. Breit and H.M. Hochman (eds) (1971), *Readings in Microeconomics*, 2nd edn, New York: Holt, Rinehart and Winston, pp. 115–16.

Veblen, Thorstein ([1899] 1965), *The Theory of the Leisure Class*, New York: Augustus M. Kelley, pp. 68–101.

Verdoorn's law

Dutch economist Petrus Johannes Verdoorn (1911–82) wrote in 1949 an article (published in Italian) that acquired fame only after 20 years. He studied the relationship between labour productivity and output during the inter-war period, using data of 15 countries and different industrial sectors, and found a close connection between the growth of productivity and the growth of industrial output. This empirical observation is the basis of Verdoorn's law, which says that production growth causes productivity growth. Verdoorn explained his results as follows: 'Given that a further division of labour only comes about through increases in the volume of production; therefore the expansion of production creates the possibility of further rationalisation which has the same effect as mechanisation' (1949, 1993, p. 59).

Increasing returns to scale and technical progress, then, are the bases of Verdoorn's law: the expansion of production leads to the invention of new manufacturing methods, increasing productivity. Nicholas Kaldor (1966) was the first to point out the importance of Verdoorn's work, and began to use it in his research. This is why this law is also known as the Kaldor–Verdoorn law.

JOSÉ M. ORTIZ-VILLAJOS

Bibliography

Boulier, B.L. (1984), 'What lies behind Verdoorn's law?', *Oxford Economic Papers*, **36** (2), 259–67.

Kaldor, N. (1966), *Causes of the Slow Rate of Economic Growth of the United Kingdom*, Cambridge: Cambridge University Press.

Verdoorn, P.J. (1949), 'Fattori che regolano lo sviluppo della produttività del lavoro', *L'industria*, **I**, 45–53; English version: 'On the factors determining the growth of labour productivity', in L. Pasinetti (ed.) (1993), *Italian Economic Papers*, **II**, Bologna: Il Mulino and Oxford University Press, pp. 59–68.

Verdoorn, P.J. (1980), 'Verdoorn's law in retrospect: a comment', *Economic Journal*, **90**, 382–5.

See also: Kaldor's growth laws.

Vickrey auction

William Vickrey (1914–96) was awarded the Nobel Prize in 1996 (jointly with James A. Mirrlees) for his fundamental contribution to the economic theory of incentives under asymmetric information. His main research focus was on the fields of auction theory and optimal income taxation.

Two questions are central in the auction literature. Which type of auction is better from the seller's point of view, and do auctions introduce distortions in the allocation of objects so that they are not always sold to the person with the highest valuation?

Vickrey attached particular importance to the second price auction (often referred to as the Vickrey auction). In this kind of auction, the object is sold to the highest bidder who only pays the next highest price offered (the 'second price'). This mechanism leads individuals to state bids equal to their true valuation of the object. Hence the object goes to the person that values it the most (the bid is efficient even with private information), and this person pays the social opportunity cost which is the second price. Vickrey made another crucial contribution to the formalization of auctions: the revenue equivalent theorem. Comparing second price and first price (where the winner pays his/her bid) auctions when the participants are risk-neutral and the individual valuations are independent drawings from the same distribution, Vickrey proved that the two types of auction are equivalent: the person with the highest valuation obtains the object, and the expected revenue is the same in both auctions.

The game-theoretical approach proposed by Vickrey still has a central role in auction theory and in the design of resource allocation mechanisms aimed at providing socially desirable incentives.

DAVID PÉREZ-CASTRILLO

Bibliography

Vickrey, W. (1961), 'Counterspeculation, auctions and competitive sealed tenders', *Journal of Finance*, **16**, 8–37.

W

Wagner's law

The 'law of increasing expansion of public and particularly state activities', known as 'Wagner's law', was formulated by German economist Adolf Wagner (1835–1917) in 1883 and developed in other writings until 1911. This law was just the result of empirical observation in progressive countries, at least in Western Europe: the expansion of state expenditure in absolute terms and as a percentage of national income. Wagner included in this rule not only central and local governments but public enterprises as well.

'Its explanation, justification and cause is the pressure for social progress and the resulting changes in the relative spheres of private and public economy, especially compulsory public economy' (Wagner, 1883, 1958, pp. 9–10). Although many authors think that Wagner was only discussing the nineteenth century and not future events, much of the literature applied and tested his law, with controversial results, during the twentieth century.

Linking increased public expenditure to ideas such as progressive countries, social pressure and 'new' public services (not only to the traditional services of defence, law and order), Wagner seems to be conceiving the future in similar terms to what he had observed. But he recognized that there must be a limit to the expansion of the public sector due to financial difficulties, since fiscal requirements imply expenditure in household budgets.

JUAN A. GIMENO

Bibliography

Gemmel, N. (1993), 'Wagner's law and Musgrave's hypotheses', in N. Gemmel (ed.), *The Growth of the Public Sector*, Aldershot, UK and Brookfield, US: Edward Elgar, pp. 103–20.

Peacock, A. and A. Scott (2000), 'The curious attraction of Wagner's law', *Public Choice*, **102**, 1–17.

Wagner, A. (1883, 1890), *Finanzwissenschaft* (2nd and 3rd edns), partly reprinted in R.A. Musgrave and A.T. Peacock (eds) (1958), *Classics in the Theory of Public Finance*, London: Macmillan, pp. 1–15.

Wald test

The Wald test, or Wald method, is used to test a set of (linear or non-linear) restrictions on a parameter vector θ $(q \times 1)$, say, for which we have available an asymptotically normal estimator. Wald (1943) developed the method in the context of maximum likelihood (ML) estimation, but nowadays it is used in general estimation settings.

Let $\hat{\theta}$ be an estimator of θ based on sample size n, such that

$$\sqrt{n}(\hat{\theta} - \theta) \xrightarrow{d} N(0, \Sigma), \qquad (1)$$

where $\xrightarrow{d}$ denotes convergence in distribution as $n \to \infty$, and $N(0, \Sigma)$ is a (multivariate) normal distribution of mean zero and variance–covariance matrix Σ (which may depend on θ). Assume we have a consistent estimator $\hat{\Sigma}$ of Σ.

Consider the null hypothesis H_0: $h(\theta) = 0$, where $h(.)$ is a continuously differentiable $r \times 1$ $(r \leq q)$ vector-valued function of θ, and the alternative hypothesis H_1: $h(\theta) \neq 0$. The Wald test statistic for H_0 is

$$W = n\hat{h}'\{\hat{H}\hat{\Sigma}\hat{H}'\}^{-1}\hat{h} \qquad (2)$$

where $\hat{h} = h(\theta)$ and $\hat{H}$ is the $(r \times q)$ matrix of partial derivatives $H = \partial h(\theta)/\partial\theta$ evaluated at $\hat{\theta}$. In the classical set-up, H is a regular matrix (as a function of θ) and of full column rank, and Σ is non-singular (thus, $\hat{H}\hat{\Sigma}\hat{H}'$ has regular inverse). Under H_0, W is asymptotically chi-square distributed with r degrees of freedom; that is, $W \xrightarrow{d} \chi^2_r$; hence the (asymptotic α-level (Wald) test of H_0 rejects H_0 when $W > c_{\alpha,r}$, where $c_{\alpha,r}$ is the (1 – α)100th per centile of the χ^2_r (i.e., $P[\chi^2_r > c_{\alpha,r}] = \alpha$). The value $c_{\alpha,r}$ is called the 'critical value' of the test.

A very simple example of a Wald test arises when θ is scalar (that is, $q = 1$) and H_0: $\theta = \theta_0$ (that is, $h(\theta) = \theta - \theta_0$). In this simple setting,

$$W = n(\hat{\theta} - \theta_0)^2/\hat{\sigma}^2 = \left(\frac{(\hat{\theta} - \theta_0)}{\hat{\sigma}/\sqrt{n}}\right)^2,$$

where $\hat{\sigma}/\sqrt{n}$ is (asymptotically) the standard deviation of $\hat{\theta}$; in this case, W is the square of a 'standardized difference' or, simply, the square of a 'z-test'.

A popular example of the Wald test arises in the regression setting $y = X\beta + \in$, where $y(n \times 1)$ and X $(n \times K)$ correspond to the values of the dependent and independent variables, respectively, $\beta(K \times 1)$ is the vector of regression coefficients, and $\in$ $(n \times 1)$ is the vector of disturbances. Let H_0: $A\beta = \alpha$, where A $(r \times K)$ and a $(r \times 1)$ are a matrix and vector, respectively, of known coefficients. Assume, for simplicity of exposition, $\text{var}(\in) = \sigma\ ^2 I_n$ and A of full rank. It is well known that $b = (X'X)^1 X'y$, the OLS estimator of β, satisfies $\sqrt{b}(b - \beta) \xrightarrow{d} N(0, \Sigma)$, where $\Sigma = \sigma^2\{n^{-1}X'X\}^{-1}$; thus, W of (2) is $W = (Ab - a)'\{\hat{\sigma}^2 A(X'X)^{-1} A'\}^{-1}(Ab - a)$, where $\hat{\sigma}^2$ is a consistent estimate of $\hat{\sigma}^2$.

When $\hat{\sigma}^2$ is the usual unbiased estimate of σ^2, $\hat{\sigma}^2 = s^2 = \Sigma_i^n e_i^2/(n - K)$, it can be seen that $F = W/r$ is the classical F-test for H_0. Under normality of $\in$, F is distributed exactly (for all sample sizes!) as an F-distribution with r and $n - K$ degrees of freedom. In fact when $q = 1$ and H_0: $\theta = \theta_0$, the equality $W = rF$ expresses then W (= F) is the square of the familiar t-test statistic (that is, the square of the 't-value'). Under normality and small samples, the F-test may give a more accurate test than the (asymptotic) Wald test; for large samples, however, both the F and Wald test are asymptotically equivalent (note that, owing to this equivalence, the F-test is asymptotically robust to non-normality).

In the non-standard case where H and Σ; Σ are not of full rank, the Wald test still applies provided that (a) in (2) we replace the regular inverse with the Moore-Penrose inverse; (b) we use as degrees of freedom of the test $r = r\ (H\ \Sigma\ H')$; and (c) we assume $r = r\ \{\hat{H}\hat{\Sigma}\hat{H}'\} = r\{H\Sigma H'\}$ with probability 1, as $n \to \infty$. (Here, $r(.)$ denotes rank of the matrix).

For a fixed alternative that does not belong to H_0, the asymptotic distribution of W is degenerate. However, under a sequence of local alternatives (see Stroud, 1972) of the form $H1$: $\sqrt{n}h(\theta) = \ell$ where $\ell(\boldsymbol{r} \times \mathbf{1})$ is a fix vector, it holds $W \xrightarrow{d} \chi^2(r, \lambda)$ where $\chi^2(r, \lambda)$ is a non-central chi-square distribution of r degrees of freedom and non-centrality parameter $\lambda = \ell'\{H\,\Sigma\,H'\}^{-1}\ell$. Such a non-degenerate asymptotic distribution of W has been proved useful for approximating the power of the test (that is, the probability of rejecting H_0 when in fact H_0 does not hold) when the alternatives of interest are not too deviant from H_0. (In the non-standard set-up of Σ singular, ℓ need is assumed to be in the column space of $H\,\Sigma\,H'$).

The Wald test is asymptotically equivalent to the other two classical large-sample tests, the log-likelihood ratio (LR) test and the Lagrange multiplier (LM) (also called Score) test.

For non-linear restrictions, the Wald test has the disadvantage of not being invariant to re-parameterization of the null hypothesis H_0. Consider, for example, $\theta = (\theta_1, \theta_2)'$ and the restriction H_0: θ_1,θ_2 = 1; an alternative expression for this restriction is H_0: $\theta_1 = 1/\theta_2$. In fact, these two alternative parameterizations of H_0 can be seen to yield different values for W, hence possibly different conclusions of the test.

A consistent estimate $\hat{\Sigma}$ of Σ is needed to construct the Wald test. When alternative estimates for Σ are available, the issue can be posed of which of them is more adequate. For example, in the context of ML estimation $\hat{\Sigma}$ can be based either on the observed information (the Hessian) or on the expected information matrices, with this choice having been reported to affect substantially the size of the Wald test.

ALBERT SATORRA

Bibliography

Stroud, T.W.F. (1972), 'Fixed alternatives and Wald formulation of the non-central asymptotic behavior of the likelihood ratio statistic', *Annals of Mathematical Statistics*, **43**, 447–54.

Wald, A. (1943), 'Tests of statistical hypotheses concerning several parameters when the number of observations is large', *Transactions of the American Mathematical Society*, **54** (3), 426–82.

Walras's auctioneer and tâtonnement

The most striking thing about Walras's auctioneer is not that, as with many other characters that have shaped our world or our minds, nobody has ever seen him but the fact that Walras himself never knew of his existence. Walras's auctioneer was an invention that saw the light some decades after the death of his alleged inventor.

In his *Élements* (1874), Walras established the foundations of general equilibrium theory, including the definition of equilibrium prices as the solution to a system of equations, each representing the balance of supply and demand in one market. But how were these prices implemented? Walras was adamant in seeking an answer to what even today is perhaps the most important of the open questions in economics. He argued that, in real markets, a tâtonnement (groping) process would lead to them: prices below the equilibrium levels would render supply insufficient to meet demands, and vice versa. The markets would then grope until they found a resting place at equilibrium prices.

One shortcoming of this description of the workings of real markets is that consistency requires that trade materialize only after the right prices are found. In well-organized markets, like some financial markets, this is guaranteed. However, in more decentralized markets, individual trades cannot wait for all markets to clear. Faced with this difficulty, Walras's tâtonnement became more and more either a way to prove the existence of equilibrium prices or an ideal way to conceive gravitation towards them. It became more a convenient parable to explain how prices *could* be found than a description of how prices were found. And it is in this context of diminished ambition that the Walrasian auctioneer was brought into the history of economic thought, to the scarcely heroic destiny of leading this groping process, quoting and adjusting imaginary prices in the search for the equilibrium finale.

ROBERTO BURGUET

Bibliography

Walras, L.M.E. (1874–7), *Eléments d'économie politique pure*, Lausanne: Rouge; definitive edn (1926), Paris: F. Pichon.

Walras's law

The idea that markets are not isolated but that there is an interrelationship among the markets for different commodities is the central contribution of Léon Walras (1834–1910) to economic science. As an outcome of this idea, Walras's law emerges.

In a Walrasian economic model, any trader must have a feasible and viable net consumption plan; that is, the trader's demand for any commodity implies the offer of commodities in exchange for it. For each trader the total value (in all markets) of their planned supply must exactly equal the total value (in all markets) of their planned demand. That relation shows that the individual budget equation (constraint) is met.

Considering this fact, the relationship between the aggregation of those individual budget equations for all traders can be observed. By aggregating, the value of the total demand of all traders, summed over all markets, has to be equal to the sum of the value of the total supply by all traders in all markets. If we now look at this aggregated relationship, it can be said that the aggregated value of the net demanded quantities (total demand minus total supply, called 'demand excess' in the literature) has to be equal to zero. In other words, this reflects the fact that, at whatever level the prices an economy are, the sum of the individual positive and negative quantities in all markets is identically zero, and this is true whether all markets are in (general) equilibrium or not. This relationship is known as Walras's law.

To be more precise, Walras's law can be defined as an expression of the interdependence among the excess demand equations of a general equilibrium system that arises from the budget constraint (see Patinkin, 1987).

Walras's law has several fundamental implications: (i) if there is positive excess of demand in one market then there must be, corresponding to this, negative excess demand in another market; (ii) it is possible to have equilibrium without clearance of all markets explicitly taking into account all the simultaneous interactions and interdependences that exist among markets in the economy. As a main conclusion of (i) and (ii), it can be said, first, that the equilibrium conditions in N markets are not independent, that is, there is an interrelationship among markets. Suppose we have N markets in the economy. If each trader's budget constraint holds with equality and $N - 1$ markets clear, then the Nth market clears as well. So it is possible to neglect one of the market-clearing conditions since it will be automatically satisfied. Second, given that the markets are interrelated, either all markets are in equilibrium, or more than one is in disequilibrium, but it is not possible to find the situation where only one market is in disequilibrium.

ANA LOZANO VIVAS

Bibliography

Patinkin, D. (1987), 'Walras law', *The New Palgrave, A Dictionary of Economics*, London: Macmillan, vol. 4, pp. 864–8.

Walras, L.M.E. (1874–7), *Élements d'économie politique pure*, Lausanne: Rouge; definitive edn (1926), Paris: F. Pichon.

See also: Say's law.

Weber–Fechner law

The works of German physiologist Ernst Heinrich Weber (1795–1878) and of German psychologist Gustav Theodor Fechner (1801–87) may be considered as landmarks in experimental psychology. They both tried to relate the degree of response or sensation of a sense organ to the intensity of the stimulus. The psychophysiological law bearing their names asserts that equal increments of sensation are associated with equal increments of the logarithm of the stimulus, or that the just noticeable difference in any sensation results from a change in the stimulus with a constant ratio to the value of the stimulus (Blaug, 1996, p. 318).

By the time Weber (1851) and Fechner (1860) published their findings, political economy was to some extent becoming ready to welcome every bit of evidence relating to human perception and response to several economic situations. As a consequence, this law was likely to be coupled with the analysis of the consequences of a change in the available quantities of a commodity (the idea that equal increments of a good yield diminishing increments of utility, the analysis of consumers' responses to changes in prices, the tendency of individuals to evaluate price differences relative to the level of the initial price, or to the analysis of the different attitudes towards risk), the increment in gratification diminishing with the increase of a man's total wealth.

William Stanley Jevons first linked the Weber–Fechner law to economic analysis, by giving a supposedly sound psychophysiological foundation to the idea that commodities are valued and exchanged according to their perceived marginal utility.

ANTÓNIO ALMODOVAR

Bibliography

Blaug, Mark (1996), *Economic Theory in Retrospect*, 5th edn, Cambridge: Cambridge University Press.
Schumpeter, J.A. (1954), *History of Economic Analysis*, New York: Oxford University Press, p. 1058.

Weibull distribution

This is a popular probability distribution for duration data. It was developed by Wallodi Weibull (1939), a Swedish engineer, in a seminal paper on the strength of materials. The use of this distribution to adjust data did not attract much attention until the 1950s, when the success of the method with very small samples in reliability analysis could not be ignored.

Nowadays the Weibull distribution is widely used in many areas to model processes duration, especially in engineering, biomedical sciences and economics. Applications in economics include the estimation of the duration of unemployment, firms' lifetime, investment decision making and durable products.

Let T be a nonnegative random variable representing the duration of a process. The Weibull probability density function is $f(t) = \lambda\beta(\lambda t)^{\beta-1}\exp\{-(\lambda t)^{\beta}\}$, $t > 0$ where $\lambda > 0$ and $\beta > 0$ are parameters. The exponential distribution is a special case of the Weibull distribution with $\beta = 1$.

The success of Weibull distribution to adjust data is due to its versatility. Depending on the value of the parameters, the Weibull distribution can model a variety of life behaviours. This property can be easily shown using the hazard function, $h(t)$. The hazard function specifies the instantaneous rate of death, failure or end of a process, at time t, given that the individual survives up to time t:

$$h(t) = \lim_{\Delta t \to 0} \frac{\Pr(t \leq T \leq t + \Delta t \mid T \geq t)}{\Delta t}.$$

The Weibull distribution's hazard function is $h(t) = \lambda\beta(\lambda t)^{\beta-1}$. This function is increasing if $\beta > 1$, decreasing if $\beta < 1$ and constant if $\beta = 1$. Thus the model is very flexible and provides a good description of many types of duration data. This versatility is the reason for the wide use of Weibull distribution in many areas.

TERESA VILLAGARCÍA

Bibliography

Weibull, W. (1939), 'A statistical theory of the strength of materials', *Ing. Vetenskaps Akad. Handl.*, **151**, 1–45.

Weierstrass extreme value theorem

In its simplest version, this theorem states that every continuous real valued function f defined on a closed interval of the real line (that is: f: $[a, b] \to R$) attains its extreme values on that set. In other words: there exist $x_1, x_2 \in [a, b]$ such that $f(x_1) \leq f(x) \leq f(x_2)$ for every $x \in [a, b]$.

Such a theorem was proved in the 1860s by the German mathematician Karl Theodor Wilhelm Weierstrass (1815–97), whose standards of rigour strongly affected the future of mathematics. A remarkable example of his achievements is the discovering in 1861 of a real function that, although continuous, had no derivative at any point. Analysts who depended heavily upon intuition were astounded by this counterintuitive function.

Karl Weierstrass is known as the Father of Modern Analysis. His theorem has many generalizations of an analytical, topological or ordinal nature. For instance, it is true that

1. Every continuous real valued function f defined on a non-empty closed and bounded subset of the n-dimensional space R^n attains its extreme values on that set.
2. Every continuous real valued function f defined on a non-empty compact topological space X attains its extreme values on that set.
3. For every continuous total preorder $\preccurlyeq$ defined on a non-empty compact set X there exist elements $x_1, x_2 \in X$ such that $x_1 \preccurlyeq x \preccurlyeq x_2$ for an y $x \in X$.

Weierstrass's extreme value theorem has many applications in mathematical economics. For instance, it is often used in situations in which it is important to guarantee the existence of optimal points related to preference relations or utility functions of an economic agent.

ESTEBAN INDURÁIN

Bibliography

Poincaré, Henry (1899), 'L'œuvre mathématique de Weierstrass', *Acta Mathematica*, **22**, 1–18.

White test

This is a general test for heteroskedasticity that, in contrast to other tests, does not require the specification of the nature of the heteroskedasticity. This test can only be applied to large samples.

The null hypothesis is that the sample variance of least squares residuals (Var $u = \sigma^2 I$) is homoskedastical H_0: $\sigma_i^2 = \sigma^2 I$ for all i, and the alternative, that variance is heteroskedastical (Var $u = \sigma^2\Omega''\Omega \neq$ I) H_1: $\sigma_i^2 \neq \sigma^2$.

The test is based on the comparison of the variance–covariance matrix of the ordinary least squares (OLS) estimators of the model ($\hat{\beta}$) under the null hypothesis,

$$\text{Var } \hat{\beta} = \sigma^2(X'X)^{-1},$$

and under heteroskedasticity,

$$\text{Var } \hat{\beta} = \sigma^2(X'X)^{-1}\,(X'\Omega X)\,(X'X)^{-1},$$

When the null hypothesis is true, the two estimated variance–covariance matrices should, in large samples, differ only because of sampling fluctuations. White has devised a statistical test based on this observation. Heteroskedasticity, if it exists, can be caused by the regressors from the equation being estimated (X_i), their squares (X_i^2) and the cross-products of every pair of regressors.

White's test can be computed as T^*R^2, where T is the sample size and R^2 comes from an auxiliary regression of the square of OLS residuals ($\hat{u}_t^2$), on a constant, the regressors from the original equation being estimated (X_i), their squares (X_i^2) and the cross-products of every pair of regressors.

In general, under the null of homoskedasticity, the statistic of White is asymptotically distributed as chi-squared $T^* R^2 \xrightarrow{d} \chi^2(q)$ with q degrees of freedom, where q is the number of independent variables in the auxiliary regression excluding the constant. If this statistic is not significant, then $\hat{u}_t^2$ is not related to X_i and X_i^2 and cross-products and we cannot reject the hypothesis that variance is constant.

NICOLÁS CARRASCO

Bibliography

White, H. (1980), 'A heteroskedastic-consistent covariance matrix estimator and a direct test for heteroskedasticity', *Econometrica*, **48**, 817–38.

Wicksell effect

This notion refers to the change in the value of capital associated with a change in the rate of interest or rate of profit. Two effects are distinguished: a price and a real effect. While the latter involves a change of technique, the former refers to a given technique (to a given set of capital goods). A negative price effect results when, for some range of the rate of profit, a higher value of capital (per person) is associated with a higher rate of profit. A positive price effect results when a higher value of capital is associated with a lower rate of profit. A neutral price effect results when the value of capital is invariant to changes in the rate of profit. As the real effect involves a choice of technique, the analysis focuses on switch points. A negative real effect results when the technique adopted at lower rates of profit has a value of capital per person lower than the technique adopted at higher rates of profit. A positive real effect results when the technique adopted at lower rates of profit has a value of capital per person higher than the technique adopted at a higher rate of profit.

Although the term was introduced by Uhr (1951), the notion was fully developed, following Robinson, during the 'Cambridge controversy in the theory of capital'. In this context, three main issues should be singled out: the specification of the endowment of capital as a value magnitude, the determination of the rate of profit by the marginal product of capital, and the inverse monotonic relationship between the rate of profit and the 'quantity' of capital per person.

Knut Wicksell (1851–1926) himself casts doubt on the specification of the value of capital, along with the physical quantities of labour and land, as part of the data of the system. 'Capital' is but a set of heterogeneous capital goods. Therefore, unlike labour and land, which 'are measured each in terms of its own *technical* unit ... capital ... is reckoned ... as a sum of *exchange value*' (Wicksell, 1901, 1934, p. 49). But capital goods are themselves produced commodities and, as such, their 'costs of production include *capital* and interest'; thus, 'to derive the value of capital-goods from their own cost of production or reproduction' would imply 'arguing in a circle' (ibid., p. 149). Wicksell further argued that the marginal product of social capital is always less than the rate of interest (profit) (cf. ibid. p. 180). This is due to the revaluation of capital brought about by the fall in the rate of profit and the rise of the wage rate consequent upon an addition to existing capital.

The central issue at stake is the dependence of prices on the rate of profit, which was already well known to Ricardo and Marx. Sraffa (1960) provides a definitive analysis of that dependence: prices are invariant to changes in the rate of profit only in the special case in which the proportions of labour to means of production are uniform in all industries. From the standpoint of the value of capital, it is only in this case that a neutral-price Wicksell effect is obtained. In the general case of non-uniform 'proportions', variations in the rate of profit 'give rise to complicated patterns of price-movements with several ups and downs' (ibid., p. 37). Indeed, these price variations apply to capital goods as to any produced commodity. Thus, as the rate of profit rises, the value of capital, of given capital goods, 'may rise or it may fall, or it may even alternate in rising and falling' (ibid., p. 15). So both negative and positive-price Wicksell effects are obtained and they may even alternate. It follows that neither the value of capital nor the capital intensity of production can be ascertained but for a previously specified rate of profit. As Sraffa argues, 'the reversals in the direction of the movement of relative prices, in the face of unchanged methods of production, cannot be reconciled with any notion of capital as a measurable quantity independent of distribution and prices'. Indeed, this being so, it seems difficult to sustain the argument that the marginal product of capital determines the rate of profit.

Sraffa's analysis of prices in terms of their 'reduction to dated quantities of labour' can be taken as applying to the variations in the relative cost of two alternative techniques. The analysis then shows the possibility of multiple switches between techniques. This implies that techniques cannot be ordered transitively in terms of their capital intensities (or of the rate of profit). While the reswitching of techniques involves negative real Wicksell effects ('reverse capital deepening'), its non-existence does not preclude them. And negative real effects do indeed rule out the inverse monotonic relationship between the rate of profit and capital per person.

CARLOS J. RICOY

Bibliography

Ferguson, C.E. and D.L. Hooks (1971), 'The Wicksell effect in Wicksell and in modern capital theory', *History of Political Economy*, **3**, 353–72.
Sraffa, P. (1960), *Production of Commodities by Means of Commodities*, Cambridge: Cambridge University Press.
Uhr, C.G. (1951), 'Knut Wicksell, a centennial evaluation', *American Economic Review*, **41**, 829–60.
Wicksell, K. (1893), *Über Wert, Kapital and Rente*, English edn (1954), *Value, Capital and Rent*, London: Allen & Unwin.
Wicksell, K. (1901), *Föreläsningar i nationalekonomi. Häft I*, English edn (1934), *Lectures on Political Economy. Volume I: General Theory*, London: Routledge & Kegan Paul.

See also: Pasinetti's paradox, Sraffa's model.

Wicksell's benefit principle for the distribution of tax burden

According to this principle, the taxpayer's contributions should have a fiscal burden equivalent to the benefits received from the public expenditure, which implies a quid pro quo relation between expenditure and taxes.

The benefit principle solves at the same time the problem of tax distribution and the establishment of public expenditure. Within a society respectful of individual freedom, the benefit principle guarantees that no one will pay taxes on services or public activities he or she does not want.

A problem related to the benefit principle is that it does not contemplate the joint consumption of public goods, which allows the taxpayer to hide his real preferences for the public goods and to consume them without paying.

In this context, Knut Wicksell's (1851–1926) contribution has two main aspects. On the one hand, it stresses the political essence of the taxation problem. A true revelation of preferences is unlikely, as it is that individuals will voluntarily make the sacrifice of taxation equal to the marginal benefit of the expenditure.

Wicksell defends the principle of (approximate) unanimity and voluntary consent in taxation. State activity can be of general usefulness, the next step being to weigh the expected utility against the sacrifice of taxation.

This decision should not neglect the interest of any group and unanimity is the rule that ensures this. Moreover, unanimity is equivalent to the veto power, and for this reason Wicksell proposes approximate unanimity as the decision rule. On the other hand, Wicksell points out an important aspect of public activity which is different from the first one, such as achieving a just income distribution, because 'it is clear that justice in taxation presupposes justice in the existing distribution of property and income' (Wicksell, 1896, p. 108).

This distinction between the problem of achieving a just distribution of income and the different problem of assignment of the costs of public services is surely Wicksell's main contribution to public economics.

CARLOS MONASTERIO

Bibliography

Musgrave, R. (1959), *The Theory of Public Finance*, New York: McGraw-Hill.
Wicksell, K. (1896), 'Ein neues Prinzip der gerechten Besteuerng', *Finanztheoretische Untersuchungen*, Jena. English trans. J.M. Buchanan,'A new principle

of just taxation', in R. Musgrave and A. Peacock (eds) (1967), *Classics in the Theory of Public Finance*, New York: St. Martin's Press, pp. 72–118.

Wicksell's cumulative process

Swedish economist Johan Gustav Knut Wicksell (1851–1926) first developed his analysis of the cumulative process in *Geldzins und Güterpreise* (*Interest and Prices*), published in 1898. After presenting his capital and monetary theory, he analysed the relation between interest rates and prices movements. Money (or bank) and natural (or real) rates of interest are two different variables in his theory. The first is determined in the long period by the second, but the current level of both variables need not be the same. If there is a divergence between money and natural rate of interest, prices move in a cumulative process (Wicksell, 1898, pp. 87–102, pp. 134–56 in the English version).

Wicksell's proposal must be understood in the context of the monetary discussions linked to the secular increase of prices in the second half of the nineteenth century. While in his opinion classical quantitative theory was basically correct, he believed it was unable to explain price movements in a credit economy. Nevertheless, the practical use of Wicksell's theory is finally limited because of the nature of the key variable: the natural rate that refers to an expected profit and not to a current value (Jonung, 1979, pp. 168–70).

Wicksell thus presented a brief description of his theory: 'If, other things remaining the same, the leading banks of the world were to lower their rate of interest, say 1 per cent below its originary level, and keep it so for some years, then the prices of all commodities would rise and rise without any limit whatever; on the contrary, if the leading banks were to *raise* their rate of interest, say 1 per cent above its normal level, and keep it so for some years, then all prices would *fall* and fall and fall without limit except zero' (Wicksell, 1907, p. 213).

This process takes place as follows. Let us assume a pure credit economy; the money supply is thus endogenous, in full equilibrium, that is, in a situation of full employment and monetary equilibrium. Then suppose that, as a consequence of technical progress, a change in productivity takes place. Then a divergence between the natural rate and the bank rate of interest ($i_n > i_m$) develops as the latter remains at its original level. As a consequence, entrepreneurs have a surplus profit and their first intention will be to increase the level of production. The entrepreneur's attempt to expand production will result in increased prices. In a situation of full employment, this individual strategy to expand production is ruled out in aggregate terms. The increase of the demand for inputs leads to a higher level of prices. Input owners have a higher income because of the new price level and they increase their demand of consumer goods. Consequently, this action leads to a higher level of prices of consumer goods. At this point, entrepreneurs again find a surplus profit as at the beginning of this process.

As long as the banking system does not change the rate of interest policy, the divergence between market and natural rate of interest will remain, and the process will continue indefinitely. Conversely, if, at the beginning of the process, the natural rate of interest happens to be below the money rate ($i_n < i_m$) a downward cumulative process would ensue; the process develops because wages are flexible enough to maintain full employment.

Of course, as the cumulative process, upward or downward, develops as a consequence of a divergence between natural and money rates of interest, any economic fact which affects both rates can be the cause of the beginning of the process. Particularly relevant in this regard is the role of monetary policy in price stabilization. Insofar as monetary policy is the first determinant of the money rate of interest, this should be adjusted to any change in the natural rate.

The later theoretical influence of the Wicksellian cumulative process was especially important in Sweden. In the 1930s, it became the theoretical background of the dynamic theory of Wicksell's followers in the Stockholm School, mainly Myrdal and Lindahl. Later it also became a reference in the research on the relation between monetary theory and Walrasian value theory (Patinkin, 1952).

JOSÉ FRANCISCO TEIXEIRA

Bibliography

Jonung, Lars (1979), 'Knut Wicksell and Gustav Cassel on secular movements in prices', *Journal of Money, Credit and Banking*, **11** (2), 165–81.

Patinkin, Don (1952), 'Wicksell's "Cumulative Process" ', *Economic Journal*, **62**, 835–47.

Uhr, C. (1960), *Economic Doctrines of Knut Wicksell*, Berkeley: University of California Press, pp. 235–41.

Wicksell, J.G.K. (1898), *Geldzins und Güterpreise: Eine Studie über den Tauschwert des Geldes bestimmenden Ursachen*, Jena; English version (1936) *Interest and Prices*, London: Macmillan.

Wicksell, J.G.K. (1907), 'The influence of the rate of interest on prices', *Economic Journal*, **17**, 213–20.

Wiener process

Suppose that a particle moves along an axis. The particle suffers a displacement constant in magnitude but random in direction. The Wiener process can be viewed as the limit of a sequence of such simple random walks. Assume that between times t and $t + n - 1$, the particle makes a small increment of size $n^{-1/2}$ forwards or backwards with the same probability, so that there are very many but very small steps as time goes by. The characteristic function of this increment is $\cos(tn^{-1/2})$. Then, in the time interval of $[0, h]$, the characteristic function of the particle position (a sum of nh independent increments) is $\cos(tn^{-1/2})^{nh}$. When the number n goes to infinity, the limit distribution of the position has the characteristic distribution $\exp(-t^2h/2)$ which corresponds to the characteristic function of the centered Gaussian distribution with variance h. This continuous time process is the Wiener process, which is also known as the standard Brownian motion. The discovery of this process, in 1828, is credited to Robert Brown, a botanist who observed the random movement of pollen grains under a microscope. Albert Einstein in 1905 gave the first mathematical demonstration of the underlying normal distribution by working with a collection of partial differential equations. However, it was Norbert Wiener (1923) and later Paul Levy (1937–48) who described many of the mathematical properties of this process, which has the following definition.

A Wiener process $\{W(t): t \geq 0\}$ is a stochastic process having: (i) continuous paths, (ii) stationary, independent increments, and (iii) $W(t)$ normally distributed with mean 0 and variance t. Each realization of this process is a real continuous function on $\{t \geq 0\}$ which can be viewed as a 'path'. However, it is impossible to graph these sample paths because, with probability one, $W(t)$ is nowhere differentiable (path with infinite length between any two points). The independent increments requirement means that, for each choice of times $0 \leq t_0 < t_1 < \ldots < t_k < \infty$, the random variables $W(t_1) - W(t_0), W(t_2) - W(t_1), \ldots, W(t_k) - W(t_{k-1})$ are independent. The term 'stationary increments' means that the distribution of the increment $W(t) - W(s)$ depends only on $t - s$. Finally, from (ii) and (iii), it follows that, for every $t > s$, the increment $W(t) - W(s)$ has the same distribution as $W(t - s) - W(0)$ which is normally distributed with mean 0 and variance $t - s$.

The behavior of the Wiener process between two time points can be described by its conditional distribution. From the previous definition, it follows that, for any $t > s > 0$, the conditional distribution of $W(s)$ given

$W(t)$ is normal with mean $(s/t)W(t)$ and variance $s(t - s)/t$. Note that $W(t)$ is also Markov: given the current state $W(s)$, the behavior of the process $\{W(t): t \geq s\}$ does not depend on the past $\{W(u): u \leq s\}$.

The Wiener process is a standardized version of a general Brownian motion and can be generalized in various ways. For instance, the general Brownian motion on $\{t \geq 0\}$ need not have $W(0) = 0$, but may have a non-zero 'drift' μ, and has a 'variance parameter' σ^2 that is not necessarily 1.

The Wiener process is valuable in many fields, especially in finance because of its highly irregular path sample and its assumption which is the same as assuming a unit root in time-series analysis.

OLIVER NUÑEZ

Bibliography

Brown, R. (1828), 'A brief account of microscopical observations made in the months of June, July, and August, 1827, on the particles contained in the pollen of plants; and on the general existence of active molecules in organic and inorganic bodies', *Philosophical Magazine*, N.S. **4**, 161–73.

Doob, J.L. (1953), *Stochastic Processes*, New York: John Wiley & Sons.

See also: Gaussian distribution.

Wiener–Khintchine theorem

This theorem is a classical result in spectral or Fourier analysis of time series. The central feature of this analysis is the existence of a spectrum by which the time series is decomposed into a linear combination of sines and cosines. The spectrum, from statistical physics, is a display of the series at different frequencies, relating how many wave patterns pass by over a period of time. The power spectrum function of a time series is a real valued, non-negative function evaluating the power of the time series at each frequency. The *W–K* theorem states that the power spectrum of a random process is the Fourier transform of its autocorrelation function. The *W–K* relations assert the complete equivalence of the autocovariance function of the stochastic process and its spectral distribution function. The spectral distribution function of a set of frequencies gives the amount of power in the harmonic components of the time series with frequencies in the set considered. The *W–K* theorem is used practically to extract hidden periodicities in seemingly random phenomena. From the mathematical point of view, this is a particular case of the convolution theorem, which states that the Fourier transform of the convolution of two functions equals the product of the Fourier transforms.

ROSARIO ROMERA

Bibliography

Wiener, N. (1949), *Extrapolation, Interpolation and Smoothing of Stationary Time Series with Engineering Applications*, Cambridge, MA.: The MIT Press; New York: Wiley and Sons; London: Chapman & Hall.

See also: Fourier transform.

Wieser's law

Coined by Italian economist Maffeo Pantaeloni, this refers to what was to be called the opportunity cost, also known as alternative cost, presented in 1876 by Austrian economist Friedrich von Wieser (1851–1926) and developed in his later works. Wieser was an early member of the Austrian School of Economics, and succeeded the founder, Carl Menger, at the University of Vienna, but did not share the classical liberal stance upheld by virtually all of its members.

Although the idea of explaining values and costs in terms of forgone opportunities, one of the most widely used in economics ever since, had several antecedents – Cantillon, Thünen, Mill, Menger, Walras and others, not to speak of the medieval *lucrum cessans* of Scholastic lawyers – Wieser formulated the equimarginal principle in production, and defined cost explicitly as sacrifice. In *Social Economics* he says:

> In what does this sacrifice consist? What, for example, is the cost to the producer of devoting certain quantities of iron from his supply to the manufacture of some specifict product? The sacrifice consists in the exclusion or limitation of possibilities by which other products might have been turned out, had the material not been devoted to one particular product . . . It is this sacrifice that is predicated in the concept of costs: the costs of production or the quantities of cost-productive-means required for a given product and thus withheld from other uses.

CARLOS RODRÍGUEZ BRAUN

Bibliography

Wieser, Friedrich von (1876), 'On the relationship of costs to value', in I.M. Kirzner (ed.) (1994), *Classics in Austrian Economics*, vol. 1, London: Pickering & Chatto, pp. 207–34.

Wieser, Friedrich von (1927), *Social Economics* first published in German, (1914), London: George Allen & Unwin, pp. 99–100.

Williams's fair innings argument

First defined by John Harris in 1985, this argument of intergenerational equity in health was developed in 1997 by Alan Williams, professor of Economics at the University of York, and reflects the feeling that there is a number of years broadly accepted as a reasonable life span. According to this notion, those who do not attain the fair share of life suffer the injustice of being deprived of a fair innings, and those who get more than the appropriate threshold enjoy a sort of bonus beyond that which could be hoped for. The fair innings argument implies that health care expenditure, in a context of finite resources, should be directed at the young in preference to elderly people. Discrimination against the elderly dictated by efficiency objectives should, therefore, be reinforced in order to achieve intergenerational equity.

Williams claims that 'age at death should be no more than a first approximation' in order to inform priority setting in health care, 'because the quality of a person's life is important as well as its length' (Williams, 1997, p. 117). According to his view, the number of quality-adjusted life-years an individual has experienced is relevant to allocating health care resources, and future gains should be distributed so as to reduce inequalities in lifetime expectations of health. Williams highlights four characteristics of the fair innings notion: 'firstly, it is outcome-based, not process-based or resource-based; secondly, it is about a person's whole life-time experience, not about their state at any particular point in time; thirdly, it reflects an aversion to inequality; and fourthly, it is quantifiable' (ibid.). The quantification of the fair innings notion requires the computation of specific numerical weights reflecting the marginal social value of health gains to different people.

ROSA MARÍA URBANOS GARRIDO

Bibliography

Harris, J. (1985), *The Value of Life, an Introduction to Medical Ethics*, London: Routledge & Kegan Paul.

Williams, A. (1997), 'Intergenerational equity: an exploration of the "fair innings" argument', *Health Economics*, **6**, 117–32.

Wold's decomposition

Herman Ole Andreas Wold (1908–1992) proved in his doctoral dissertation a decomposition theorem that became a fundamental result in probability theory. It states that any regular stationary process can be decomposed as the sum of two uncorrelated processes. One of these processes is deterministic in the sense that it can be predicted exactly, while the other one is a (possibly infinite) moving average process.

Formally, any zero-mean covariance-stationary process Y_t can be represented as the sum of two uncorrelated processes:

$$Y_t = \kappa_t + \sum_{j=0}^{\infty} \psi_j \varepsilon_{t-j},$$

where κ_t is a deterministic process that can be forecast perfectly from its own past $\kappa_t \equiv \hat{E}(\kappa_t \mid Y_{t-1}, Y_{t-2}, \ldots)$, ε_t is a white noise process, the first coefficient $\psi_0 = 1$ and

$$\sum_{j=0}^{\infty} \psi_j^2 < \infty.$$

As both processes are uncorrelated, the term κ_t is uncorrelated to ε_{t-j} for any j.

The theorem also applies to multiple time series analysis. It only describes optimal linear forecasts of Y, as it relies on stable second moments of Y and makes no use of higher moments.

Finding the Wold representation may require fitting an infinite number of parameters to the data. The approximations by means of a finite set of parameters are the basis of ARMA modelling in Box–Jenkins methodology, with applications in many fields, including economics, medicine and engineering.

EVA SENRA

Bibliography

Wold, H. (1938), *A Study in the Analysis of Stationary Time Series*. Uppsala: Almqvist and Wiksell, 2nd edn 1954.

See also: Box–Jenkins Analysis.

Z

Zellner estimator

When trying to define this topic, we face a preliminary issue, namely, which particular Zellner estimator to discuss? He has been associated with a myriad of alternative estimators such as SUR, iterative SUR, 3SLS, MELO and BMOM, among others, that have appeared in the literature over the last four decades (see, Zellner, 1971, 1997).

However, most researchers probably associate the term 'Zellner estimator' with his seemingly unrelated regressions (SUR) estimator, originally published in Zellner (1962), that is usually more precise than the ordinary least squares (OLS) single equation estimator and has been and is being used in econometrics and many other fields and featured in almost all econometrics textbooks.

The basic principles behind the SUR model, originally derived by analysing the Grundfeld (1958) investment data, focused on the nature of the error terms of a set of equations when m economic agents are operating in similar environments. Consider the following m equations:

$$y_1 = x_1\beta_1 + u_1$$
$$y_2 = x_2\beta_2 + u_2$$
$$\dots$$
$$y_m = x_m\beta_m + u_m,$$

where each y_i ($i = 1, 2, \dots m$) is ($T \times 1$), X_i is ($T \times K_i$), β_i is ($K_i \times 1$) and u_i is ($T \times 1$). These m equations may be written equivalently as $y = x\beta + u$.

Given the block diagonal form of X, applying OLS would be equivalent to the application of OLS to each one of the m equations separately. However, this procedure would not be optimal, for two reasons: (i) the u vector is not homoscedastic, since now $E(u_i u'_i) = \sigma_{ii}I$, and (ii) the off-diagonal terms in var(u) will not be zero, since $E(u'_i u'_j) = \sigma_{ij}I$. Therefore the correct error covariance matrix is $\Omega = \Sigma \otimes I$.

The reason for the label 'SUR' should now be clear. Though initially it may appear that the equation for firm i is unrelated to that for firm j, in fact there may be random effects which are pertinent to both. Under the standard conditions, Zellner (1962) showed that a best linear unbiased, consistent and normally (asymptotically) estimator of β is

$$\hat{\beta}_z = (X'\Omega^{-1}X)^{-1}X'\Omega^{-1}y,$$

with

$$Var(\hat{\beta}_z) = (X'\Omega^{-1}X)^{-1}$$

$$Asy - Var(\hat{\beta}_z) = \frac{1}{T}\lim_{t\to\infty}\left(\frac{X'\Omega^{-1}X}{T}\right)^{-1}.$$

Since Σ is unknown, Zellner proposed the construction of a feasible estimator, as follows:

1. Apply OLS to each equation, obtaining the vector of residuals $\hat{u}_1, \hat{u}_2, \dots \hat{u}_m$ where $\hat{u}_i = [I - X_i(X'_i X'_j)^{-1}X'_i]y_i$ ($i = 1, \dots m$).
2. The diagonal and off-diagonal elements of Σ are estimated by

$$\hat{\sigma}_{ii} = \frac{\hat{u}'_i\hat{u}_i}{n-k_i};\ \hat{\sigma}_{ij} = \frac{\hat{u}'_i\hat{u}_j}{(n-k_i)^{1/2}(n-k_j)^{1/2}}.$$

Also, if u is normally distributed, $\hat{\beta}_z$ is minimum variance unbiased and asymptotically efficient. In general $\hat{\beta}_z$, is more efficient than $\hat{\beta}_{OLS}$, except in two cases in which these estimators are identical: (1) the $\sigma_{ij} = 0$, for $i \neq j$ or (2) the $\mathbf{x_i}$ matrices are identical.

ANTONIO GARCÍA FERRER

Bibliography

Grunfeld, Y. (1958), 'The determinants of corporate investment', unpublished PhD thesis, University of Chicago.

Zellner, A. (1962), 'An efficient method of estimating seemingly unrelated equations and tests for aggregation bias', *Journal of the American Statistical Association*, **57**, 348–68.

Zellner, A. (1971), *An Introduction to Bayesian Inference in Econometrics*, New York: Wiley.

Zellner, A. (1997), *Bayesian Analysis in Econometrics and Statistics: the Zellner View and Papers*, Cheltenham, UK and Lyme, USA: Edward Elgar.